Archibald Pitcairne

THE PHANATICKS

SCOTTISH TEXT SOCIETY

The Scottish Text Society
Fifth Series
no. 10

Archibald Pitcairne

THE PHANATICKS

Edited by
John MacQueen

The Scottish Text Society

2012

First published 2012 by The Scottish Text Society

ISBN 978-1-89797-635-7

A Scottish Text Society publication
Published by The Boydell Press
an imprint of Boydell & Brewer Ltd
PO Box 9, Woodbridge, Suffolk IP12 3DF, UK
and of Boydell & Brewer Inc.
668 Mt Hope Avenue, Rochester, NY 14620-2731, USA
website: www.boydellandbrewer.com

The publisher has no responsibility for
the continued existence or accuracy of URLs for external or
third-party internet websites referred to in this book, and
does not guarantee that any content on such websites
is, or will remain, accurate or appropriate.

A CIP catalogue record for this book is available
from the British Library

Papers used by Boydell & Brewer Ltd are natural, recyclable products
made from wood grown in sustainable forests

Printed and bound in Great Britain by
CPI Group (UK) Ltd, Croydon, CR0 4YY

Contents

Foreword

The Phanaticks is a Scottish comedy, written with stage production in mind, and offering a mainly satiric portrait of Scottish society during the period which saw the overthrow of James VII and the accession of William II and Mary II. The sympathies expressed are mainly Jacobite and Episcopalian, deploring the disastrous effects of the 'Glorious' Revolution on Parliament, the Church, the Universities, and society in general. Underlying the implied sympathy for Episcopalianism, however, is a fairly obvious scepticism, with implications that the authors were not so much churchmen as, at best, Deists – Deists, nevertheless, who found the Episcopalians considerably more attractive than any other section of the populace. There is some emphasis on mathematics as offering a better approach to knowledge than the scholastic logic favoured by Presbyterians. The play prefigures many features of the later Scottish Enlightenment.

Formally, the play is a late Restoration comedy in the tradition of such English pieces as *The Committee* (1662) by Sir Robert Howard (on Cavaliers in relation to Roundheads under the rule of Oliver Cromwell), together with John Crown's *City Politiques* (1683) and *Sir Courtly Nice* (1685), both aimed at Titus Oates and the so-called Popish Plot. Thomas Otway's *Venice Preserved* (1682) presents the latter theme in tragic terms. *The Phanaticks* is unique in its transference of the form to Scotland and a very definite Edinburgh setting, as also in targeting a number of specific individuals and institutions. As the number of manuscripts and printed editions shows, it retained some popularity, or notoriety, throughout the eighteenth and into the nineteenth century. Even by the mid-twentieth century it was deemed too shocking for production in the Edinburgh Festival.

The editor has been so fortunate as to locate three manuscript versions of the play appreciably earlier than any printed text. These demonstrate that such versions were already in circulation soon after the play's first appearance. The different versions make it fairly clear that the work had more than one author; one of them enables us to make a plausible guess at their identity – the physician Archibald Pitcairne, the mathematician and astronomer David Gregory, and the Englishman Bertram Stott. Another manuscript shows that the original language of the play, however modified in later transmission, was consistently Scots, although it is difficult to decide whether it is a very late Middle, or a very early Modern, form of the language. The text was more than once revised, in all probability by the authors. The language confirms that performances took place in Edinburgh, or possibly in some local great house. In view of the difficulties which Allan Ramsay later found in establishing an Edinburgh theatre company, such performances may seem unlikely, but one should recall the remark (Chambers 1847, 321) reported to have been made much later in the century by Pitcairne's elderly daughter, 'me, that hasna been at a theatre since I gaed wi' papa to the Canongate in the year *ten*' – 1710, that is to say. Chambers adduces other evidence that plays continued to be performed, at least occasionally, at the Tennis Court in the Canongate.

I am much indebted to the Council of the Scottish Text Society for their continued help and support; to the Librarians and staff of the National Library of Scotland, Edinburgh; Glasgow University Library; the Wellcome Library, London; Edinburgh University Library, and the Bodleian Library, Oxford; to Dr Nicola Royan of Nottingham University; Dr Sally Mapstone of St Hilda's College, Oxford; Dr Anita Guerrini of the University of California, Santa Barbara, and Oregon State University; Dr David Money of Cambridge University; Professor J. J. McGavin of Southampton University, and Professor Hector MacQueen of the Scottish Law Commission. Mr Alexander Scroggie of Glasgow University has skilfully compiled the Bibliography and Index. As always, my wife, Winifred MacQueen, has made valuable comments as the work progressed. To all, my grateful thanks.

John MacQueen

Introduction

Manuscripts and Printed Editions

The Phanaticks was begun in April 1691 and completed in August or September of that year – that is, according to the **Preface** (below, p. 231). The actual process may have been more complex, as the course of this discussion of the manuscripts and early printed editions will show.

The play is extant in three manuscripts and two significant printed editions.

Manuscripts
A. Edinburgh, National Library of Scotland, Adv.35.4.14, fos. 162r–178r; folio, late 17c. or very early 18c., part of an anonymous common-place book. Distinctively Scots spelling and syntax. No title-page. **Prologue**, **Drammatis** (*sic*) **Personæ**, **Text** (5 Acts, 16 Scenes), **Epilogue**. Holograph corrections and additions, probably in the hand of Archibald Pitcairne. Obscure jottings on fo. 162r. On fo. 178r, in a different hand, unrelated verse, circled: 'Death at the Coblers door coms nere to stand/ He found him always on the mending hand/ Quhil death stood there he caused still foul weather/ He rent the soul quit from the upper lether/ The fute groand & gribed & wes agast/ he sought his aul but death brought him his last/ [?] mors Christi fraus mundi gloria celi/ et furor inferni sint modulanda tibi.'

B. London, Wellcome Library, MS 3916; 4to, early 18c. Calf binding, worn; 130 pp. numbered in gatherings of 8, with layout like that of a printed book. On front inside cover signature of the noted obstetric surgeon and early advocate of the use of chloroform, Sir James Y. Simpson (1811–70); on verso of title-page 'Thomas A. Hill 1854' (not identified). On second leaf recto, a note, presumably by Hill: 'This is a low scurilous (*sic*) production without wit or humour, and quite unworthy of the reputation of Dr. Pitcairn, who is said to have written it. h.' The manuscript is less distinctively Scots in spelling and usage than **A**.

Title-page, 'The/ Assembly/ Or/ Scotch Reformation./ A/ Comedie./ The Third Edition Corrected & enlarged by the authors who is Roges/ Glomerantur in Unum/ Innumeros pestes Erebi quoscunque sinister/ Nox Genuit fœtu – Claudian/ 1691'; **Prologue**; **Dramatis Personæ**; **Text** (5 Acts, 16 Scenes); **Epilogue**.

For 'Roges' see p. xii below. The Latin verses quoted are also to be found in the 1722 and later printed editions. They are taken from a passage (lines 28–30) of the violent satire *In Rufinum* by the late Latin classical poet Claudius Claudianus (c. 370–c. 404), translated 'Hell's numberless monsters are gathered together, Night's children of ill-omened birth' (Platnauer 1976: 29). The satire deals with an unsuccessful attempt by the powers of Hell to overthrow the Roman Empire, re-established by Theodosius (c. 346–95) through the machinations of the praetorian prefect Rufinus (killed 395). The quotation implicitly equates Theodosius with James VII, Rufinus with William of Orange, and the powers of Hell with the ultra-Presbyterians.

The manuscript itself is certainly later than 1691. It is a copy, possibly of a lost manuscript or printed edition dated in that year.

C. Glasgow University Library, MS General 807; 4to, early 18c. Worn calf binding. The pages seem originally to have been ruled. Title-page and opening lines of **Prologue** missing; **Prologue**; **Dramatis Personæ**; **Preface**, in 20 pages, the odd pages numbered in pencil in a later hand; **Text** (5 Acts, 16 Scenes, with pages numbered 1–134) + **Epilogue**. Inserted note: 'MS. Ecclesiastical Play of the Reign of Charles II (!). Donor: – R.D. Murdoch Esq., Fairfield Lodge.' It was donated to the Carnegie Public Library, Ayr; purchased by GUL in June 1982.

Printed editions

1722. *The/ Assembly,/ A Comedy/ By a Scots Gentleman./* Claudian quotation, without attribution/ *London,/ Printed in the Year, MDCCXXII.*; 107 pp.; two editions, 8vo and 12mo, the latter with some correction of misprints in the former. **Drammatis** (*sic*) **Personæ** (without identification of characters); **Prologue** (garbled version with misprints); **Text** (5 Acts, 15 Scenes); **Epilogue**.

1752. *The Assembly:/ or, Scotch Reformation./ A/ Comedy./ As it was acted by the persons in the drama./ Done from the original manuscript written in the year 1692./* Claudian quotation with attribution/ *Printed in the year 1752.* [?Edinburgh], 12mo. **Preface** and **Prologue**, 21 pp., numbered in Roman; **Dramatis Personæ**, 1 unnumbered page with identifications; **Text** (5 Acts, 16 Scenes, pages numbered 1–8; **Epilogue** (unnumbered page).

1752 is the basis for the later 12mo editions of **1766** and **1817**.

In 1972 *The Assembly, by Archibald Pitcairne. A Critical Edition with*

Introduction and Notes by Terence Tobin (Tobin 1972) was published in Purdue University Studies (Lafayette, Indiana). Tobin based his text on **1722**. He was unaware of the manuscripts, all of which may be earlier than **1722**, as **A** certainly is. He therefore regarded **1752** as containing spurious material inserted after the publication of **1722**.

Textual History and Editorial Conventions

The shortest version of the play is **1722**, which lacks the last part of 3.1, 4.3 entire, and part of 5.2 – all passages involving Lord Huffie. Longest are **C** and **1752**, the latter of which claims to be 'done from the original manuscript written in the year 1692' and, like **C**, includes the **Preface**, together with a long passage inserted in 4.4, not present in the other manuscripts. In **C**, as noted above, the title-page and opening lines of the **Prologue** are missing; otherwise the overall similarity to **1752** suggests that **C** may be the 1692 manuscript there mentioned. **C** itself is fairly certainly later than 1692, but may have been copied from an earlier manuscript or print bearing that date. **B** claims to be 'The Third Edition Corrected & enlarged by the authors ... 1691'. For the most part the text resembles that in **A**, but there are many differences, for the most part of a linguistic rather than textual significance.

One may suspect that the texts preserve a series of auctorial revisions, with **1722** representing a rather corrupt form of the *Ur*-text, **A** and **B** versions amended rather later, **C** and **1752** a still later amended version with the **Preface** added. The amendments and additions, I suggest, are all auctorial.

In terms of 'editions', it should be noted that Pitcairne had good relations with several Edinburgh printers and that many of his Latin poems first appeared as printed broadsheets (Macqueen and Macqueen 2009: 42–5). The same may be true of at least one version of *The Phanaticks*. If the chosen version was **B**, the phrase 'The Third Edition' may have been a half-humorous reference to earlier manuscript versions. **1722** might then represent the first, **A** the second, **B**, as it claims, the third, **C** and **1752** a hypothetical fourth.

Despite the fact that **A** sometimes appears to be carelessly copied, its early date and more distinctively Scots spellings and syntax make it the textual choice for this edition. I have attempted to keep its character as far as possible, silently expanding only such abbreviations as might offer difficulties. Manuscript stage directions are italicized and introduced by a single square bracket. Editorial ones are similarly introduced, but are in Roman. I have not attempted to list all variants from other sources, only indicating where something appears to have special significance or interest. The manuscript lacks punctuation. I have added my own.

Authorship

In **B** the play is attributed to a mysterious 'Roges', also described (in plural form!) as 'the authors'. Other manuscripts and early prints present a text which is anonymous. Archibald Pitcairne, M.D., is first named as author in the 1817 print but, in the context of his other works, it is virtually certain that he had at least a major hand in the composition. Nonetheless, it seems likely that he had collaborators. The opening couplet of the **Epilogue** reads 'Our play is done. The Circumstance, the plott,/ Our authors [pl.] out of meer design forgott.' In apparent contradiction of this are lines 33–4 of the **Prologue**, 'Our author [sg.] gentlie doth beseech and pray/ the Criticks favor for his first essay' (a reading which also appears in **1722**). For 'author', however, **B** and **C**, together with the later prints, read 'authors', for 'doth', 'do', and for 'his', 'our'.

Multiple authorship is also suggested by a passage from the end of the **Preface** (Appendix I below):

> This play was begune Just after the king of ffrance took Monse, as is clearly intimated in the first scene. But, by Reasone of some Gentlemans goeing to the Country who was Concerned in itt, it lay Dormant four Moneths, then it was sett about again, and was very soon Compleatted. We Confess it was hastily hudled together, ffor we were not fourthnight about the haill work by Reasone of a Multitude of bussiness the Authors were Intangled in.

In part, this is a modesty *topos*, not to be taken too seriously. Nevertheless it indicates plurality of authors and fits with David Gregorie's personal circumstances in the summer of 1691 (see below, pp. xlv–xlvi).

There remains 'Roges'. Dr Mapstone has suggested to me that this is simply a Scots variant spelling of the word 'Rogues', a spelling on evidence as late as 1684, but not apparently thereafter (see *DOST* and *SND*). If this is so, it is an additional piece of evidence for multiple authorship. The syntax, however, remains peculiar, and it may seem unlikely that the authors would refer to themselves as rogues when the true rogues were the politicians and ministers portrayed in the play, the *pestes* of the quotation from Claudian which follows. *Roges*, I suggest, is a cryptogram. Pitcairne at least was interested in such things (Macqueen and Macqueen 2009: 43). The elaborate initial *R* closely resembles the monogram, *A* intertwined with (not ligatured to) *P*, frequently used elsewhere of himself by *A*rchibald *P*itcairne. If the monogram appeared on the title-page of the manuscript or print of which **B** is a copy, and was misread by the copyist, it seems reasonable to assume that the remaining letters of Roges contain the initials of the co-authors. I cannot suggest an identity for *og* or *es*. Two of Pitcairne's closest friends, however, were David *G*regorie (1661–1708), who in 1692 left the chair of mathematics in Edinburgh University to become Savilian professor of astronomy at Oxford, and the Englishman, Sir Bertram *S*tott (d. c. 1707), about whom very little is known, but whom Pitcairne, recalling Horace, called *Dimidiumque animæ, Deliciasque suæ*, 'the darling half of his soul' (Macqueen and Macqueen 2009: 194; see also below, Appendix II). If one assumes that *og* and *es* are misreading or deliberate distortions of *dg* and *bs*, Gregorie and Stott are likely to have been Pitcairne's collaborators. In the remainder of this introduction, I shall assume that they are.

Title

The usual title, *The Assembly*, is something of a puzzle. The General Assembly, as such, makes no appearance in the play, a point noted in the **Preface**: 'Nor could we bring on the stage all the members of the generall Assemblie, for that would have spoyled the decorum of the play' (below, p. 224). In 1.3, 2.3, 3.3, 4.2 and 5.3, the ministers and elders who appear are called, not the Assembly, but the Committee, a reference, as demonstrated below (pp. xx–xxi) to an ultra-Presbyterian judicial body set up by the 1690 General Assembly, the Commission for the Visitation of Presbyteries on the North and South Sides of Tay. The actions of this Committee are thematically linked to the remainder of the play, which shows the life of an ultra-Presbyterian family, from which two young girls successfully plan their escape. **A**, the earliest text, lacks a title, or any sign that it ever had one. **C** too lacks a title, but a leaf, which probably contained one, is missing. **1722** has the title *The Assembly, a Comedy*, but in **B** and **1752** it is *The Assembly, or Scotch Reformation. A Comedie*.

As a title, *The Assembly* lacks authority. It is possible that there was confusion with Pitcairne's mock-epic on the 1692 General Assembly, *Babell; or The Assembly, a Poem ... By A.P.* (Kinloch 1830), or it may result from the intrusion of a copyist or printer. Line 3 from the **Epilogue**, 'For the phanaticks [the ultra-Presbyterians] whom we represent', suggests as an alternative title *The Phanaticks*, which fits the play under all aspects and which has been adopted for this edition.

Historical Context

The Phanaticks is set in a precise historical context, the latter stages of the Glorious Revolution as it affected Scotland. The times were troubled. The Revolution settlement benefited Whigs and Presbyterians, but left Tories (Jacobites) and Episcopalians in a state of perpetual discontent and open to persecution. This situation the play exploits.

The action turns on a series of contrasting concepts, each important for the political, religious or intellectual history of the times. In Britain, the doctrine of the Divine Right of Kings was associated with the Stewart (latterly usually spelled in the French fashion 'Stuart') royal line and episcopalian church government; Louis XIV of France and the majority of his subjects held to the same belief. The opposing doctrine was that of the Two Kingdoms, the secular monarchy ruling in worldly affairs, in spiritual, however, totally subordinate to what the believer saw as the monarchy of Christ. The latter doctrine was predominant among Presbyterians and Calvinists, and the conflict was a factor, not only in Scottish affairs, but also in the long-lasting European struggle between Louis XIV and William of Orange.

Between the two, no compromise was possible. Early in the eighteenth century Pitcairne wrote a short play, *Tollerators and Con-Tollerators*, the message of which was that in Scottish political and religious life toleration of any kind was an impossible dream. *The Phanaticks* is less explicit, but the implications are identical.

In terms of intellectual history, scholastic logic still dominated universities and was the chosen instrument, in particular, of presbyterian thought. In opposition stood the new Mathematics of change and motion, the instrument of inductive reasoning and of the new science. In the play, at least, it is Episcopalians who favour the latter; see particularly 3.3, 5–24 and 5.1 throughout.

The dogma of Divine Right, that kings in patrilineal succession were appointed by God to supremacy in church and state, together with its corollary, passive obedience to royal authority, began as a hostile response to papal claims of supremacy (Figgis 1922: 14–16, thereafter *passim*). It came to form one aspect of Reformation political thought and was particularly strongly held in certain circles of Scottish society. Adherence to it usually also involved belief in the great antiquity of the

Scottish royal line, both expounded by Sir George Mackenzie of Rose-haugh (1636–91) in his *Jus Regium* (1684) and *Defence of the Antiquity of the Royal Line of Scotland* (1685).

In stark contrast, the doctrine of the Two Kingdoms held that in the spiritual realm the earthly king had no greater status than the least of his subjects, and that, if the king offended, the duty of his pious subjects might be to depose or even execute him. The doctrine was put into words by Andrew Melville (1545–1622) and is implicit in much Covenanting literature, for instance the influential *Lex, Rex* (Rutherford 1644) by the 'sometime professor of divinity in the University of St. Andrews', Samuel Rutherford (c. 1600–61). The book appeared during the English Civil War and there is something ominous in the biblical quotation on the title-page, 'But if ye shall still do wickedly, ye shall be consumed, both ye and your king' (1 Samuel 12. 25) and in the reference, to give only one instance, to the Dutch jurist Hugo Grotius (1583–1645) and his 'seven cases in which the people may have real action against the king to accuse and punish' (Rutherford 1982: 200, column 2).

Episcopalians in general accepted Divine Right, with a spiritual hierarchy under the king – archbishops, bishops, priests and deacons – corresponding to the temporal hierarchy of dukes, marquesses, earls, viscounts and barons. They also acknowledged the corollary, the duty of passive obedience to the king's ordinances. They accepted the royal prerogative. The opposite view was held by Presbyterians who believed in the parity, and ultimate supreme authority, of their ministers assembled in presbyteries, synods and General Assembly.

Episcopalianism and loyalty to the royal house of Stewart were more or less synonymous. A presbyterian Scottish church had been established in 1590, thirty years after the 1560 Reformation, but the then reigning monarch, James VI (1566–1625; from 1603 also James I of England) had a passionate belief in Divine Right, expressed, for instance, in his *True Lawe of Free Monarchies: or, The Reciprock and Mvtvall Dvtie Betwixt a free King, and his Naturall Subiectes* (James VI 1598). By 1610 he had restored the Scottish ecclesiastical hierarchy. Gordon Donaldson notes that he avoided the extreme of the 'proud papal bishops', against which he warned his son, the future Charles I (Donaldson 1965: 207). Some years later, under royal pressure, the 1618 General Assembly, meeting at Perth, passed Five Articles, which required the observance of the main festivals of the Christian Year, private administration of Baptism and Communion, kneeling at Communion, and Confirmation by the bishop – all Episcopalian ceremonials. Although this roused much hostility among convinced Presbyterians, the Articles were ratified by parliament in 1621. A revised Liturgy was licensed for printing, but never appeared. Throughout this period the two Scottish archbishops and thirteen diocesan bishops continued to exercise their functions in relative quiet.

On the whole, James acted with prudence and sensitivity. Not so his son and successor, Charles I (reigned 1625–49). In particular, his attempt to introduce a new liturgy, the *Scottish Prayer Book* of 1637, met widespread opposition culminating in the signing of the National Covenant in 1638. Adherents to this became known as Covenanters. Support, however, was not universal; the Covenant was denounced as destructive of all moral and social order by such poets as William Drummond of Hawthornden (1585–1649) and the Latin poet, Arthur Johnston (1587–1641), and, in terms more directly theological, by the group known as the Aberdeen Doctors, who produced *Generall Demands, Concerning the Late Covenant; Propounded by the Ministers and Professors of Divinitie in Aberdene* (Forbes 1638). Nonetheless, the General Assembly, which met in Glasgow later in the same year, annulled the *Prayer Book*, the Five Articles, and the office of bishop.

The two Bishops' Wars against English royalist forces followed in quick succession (1639, 1640–41). In 1643 came the Solemn League and Covenant, by which Scottish adherents to the Covenant agreed to help the English Parliamentarian forces, on condition that England should accept a Presbyterian church system. Scots forces thereafter fought successfully on the parliamentary side, notably at Marston Moor (1644), but the English parliament did not hold to the bargain.

A moderate Presbyterian, James Graham, 1st Marquess of Montrose (1612–50), was sufficiently a royalist as to wage a brilliant, but brutal and finally unsuccessful, campaign against the Covenanters (1644–45). In 1646 an assembly of mainly presbyterian divines, which met at Westminster 1643–53, produced a Confession of Faith in 33 articles, adopted by the Edinburgh General Assembly of 1647. Episcopalians, on the other hand, continued to use the three traditional Creeds.

From May 1646 until he was sold to the English parliament in February 1647, Charles I was the prisoner of the Scottish army at Newcastle. By the Engagement of 26/27 December, signed when he was imprisoned at Carisbrooke Castle on the Isle of Wight, he came to an agreement with a delegation of moderate Scots Presbyterians, including acceptance of the Solemn League and Covenant . This was rendered null by the Whiggamore Raid on Edinburgh by extreme Covenanters from Ayrshire, leading to Cromwell's being welcomed into the capital on 4 October 1648. Charles was beheaded at Whitehall on 30 January 1649.

Only the most extreme Covenanters endorsed the execution. In Edinburgh Charles II was immediately proclaimed king and on 1 January 1651 he was crowned at Scone. Cromwell, however, had already defeated the Scots army at Dunbar (3 September 1650) and, exactly a year later, routed another, commanded by Charles himself, at Worcester. The king fled to the Continent. Armed resistance, mainly in the Highlands, continued for several years, but, under the Commonwealth, Scotland became part of England and was occupied by English troops. Episcopalian worship was banned; Presbyterianism was tolerated, but allowed no special position.

The 1660 Restoration meant also the restoration of Episcopalianism. Some 250 ministers who adhered strictly to the Covenants were expelled from their parishes. With members of their congregations they took to field-conventicles, which the government attempted to stamp out, only to meet with armed resistance, sometimes leading to actual risings. The main encounters were at Rullion Green in the Pentland Hills, not far from Edinburgh (1666), at Drumclog (1 June 1679) and Bothwell Brig (22 June 1679), both in Lanarkshire, and at Airds Moss in Ayrshire (1680). The Covenanters were victorious only in the minor skirmish at Drumclog.

Under the Test Act of 1681 'all office-bearers in church and state and all electors and members of parliament were obliged to take an oath acknowledging the Confession of Faith of 1560 [not that of 1647, nor yet a statement of Divine Right; a stumbling-block therefore to both sides] accepting the royal supremacy, renouncing the Covenants and all leagues and meetings to treat of any matter of church or state, and forswearing all endeavours to make any alteration in civil or ecclesiastical government' (Donaldson 1965: 379). Some Episcopalians could not stomach the 1560 Confession and joined the Church of England; the Cameronians, followers of the fanatical Covenanter, Richard Cameron (1648–80), killed at Airds Moss, continued a campaign which they had already lost. Persecution of the Cameronians gave to the closing years of Charles II's reign a somewhat exaggerated name, the Killing Times.

James VII (II of England), a converted Roman Catholic, succeeded his brother in 1685. During the Commonwealth he had achieved military distinction in the French service under the great Marshal Turenne (1611–75). He retained a cordial relationship with the king of France, his cousin Louis XIV (1643–1715). In 1678 he fell under suspicion as a result of the Popish Plot, fabricated by Titus Oates (1648–1705). As a consequence, from October 1679 to March 1682 he was removed from London to become King's High Commissioner in Scotland. During his tenure of office there, he oversaw the establishment of the Edinburgh Royal College of Physicians (1681) and the Advocates' Library, now the National Library of Scotland (1682; Sir George Mackenzie of Rose-haugh originated the project). He vindicated the honour of Scotland in a famous golf match against two English noblemen (Macqueen and Macqueen 2009: 176–7 and n.). He favoured tolerance and clemency, even to the defeated at Bothwell Brig. Later, when king, he proposed tolerance for all Christians, including Roman Catholics and Quakers, a measure found acceptable by most Presbyterians. Many, however, retained fears, probably justified, that he planned to restore Catholicism to the position which it had held before the Reformation. The Rye House Plot (1683) was an attempt to exclude him from the succession. After his accession, the rebellions of Argyll and Monmouth (1685) were aimed at his overthrow. The birth of a son and heir, James Francis (1688–1766: 'The Old Pretender'), on 10 June 1688, provoked a crisis.

In 1685 Louis XIV had revoked the Edict of Nantes, promulgated in 1598 by his grandfather, Henri IV, which had given rights to French Protestants, the Huguenots. In 1686 an alliance of European powers, the League of Augsburg, was founded to resist French aggression. The United Provinces, the Netherlands, where many Huguenots had taken refuge, did not originally take part, but when in 1688 Louis declared war on them and devastated the Rhineland, the stadtholder, William of Orange (1650–1702), brought them into the League. William's mother was James VII's sister, Mary, and he had married James's eldest daughter, also Mary. If James had died with no heir-male, William would have stood a fair chance of the succession. One can only speculate how far his disappointment influenced later events.

In England, as in Europe, the friendship of James with Louis became matter for concern. On 5 November William landed with a strong force at Brixham in Devon and found much English support. James with his wife and son left Whitehall on 11 December and after some misadventures arrived in France on Christmas Day.

In February 1689 the English parliament set out a Declaration of Rights in terms of which they accepted William and Mary as joint king and queen; on 11 April the Scottish Convention of Estates (not parliament) issued the strongly presbyterian Claim of Right which led later in the month to the same recognition. Supporters of James became known as Jacobites (Latin *Jacobus*, 'James'). During May England began the Nine Years War against France, becoming, in effect, a member of the League of Augsburg. Scotland made no declaration of war.

For James, the Catholic George Gordon, 1st duke of Gordon (1649–1716), continued to hold Edinburgh Castle, effectively the headquarters of the Scottish army. To gather further military support, John Graham of Claverhouse, 1st viscount Dundee (1648–89), had already in March left Edinburgh. He gathered a force of Highlanders. Edinburgh Castle capitulated on 14 July and, although on 27 July Claverhouse routed the Williamite troops at Killiecrankie on the Perth/Inverness border, he was himself killed in the action. Incompetent attempts to exploit the victory were foiled (21 August) at Dunkeld, Perthshire, by the desperate resistance of the earl of Angus's regiment, the Cameronians, made up of extreme Covenanters, who were prepared to fight, not so much for William as against James. The ultra-presbyterian David Melville (1660–1728), 3rd earl of Leven and (from 1707) 2nd earl of Melville, succeeded Gordon as Governor of Edinburgh Castle (in the play he is Lord Huffie).

Resistance lasted longer in Ireland. James landed at Kinsale, Co. Cork, on 12 March 1689. His forces failed to capture the presbyterian strongholds of Derry and Enniskillen in Ulster and, after his defeat at the Boyne (1 July 1690) he left the country. The war continued under the command of Richard Talbot (1630–91), whom James had created marquess and duke of Tyrconnel in 1689. Tyrconnel successfully held the strategically important towns of Limerick, Athlone and Galway, but in July 1691 the Williamite army forced the crossing of the Shannon. The closely fought battle of Aughrim followed (12 July), where the Irish forces were commanded by the French Marshal St Ruth. They came close to winning the day, but were finally routed after St Ruth had been killed by a cannon-ball. On 3 October 1691 the war ended with the signing of the Treaty of Limerick. Most of the Jacobite army left Ireland for France.

Because three Edinburgh ministers, Dr Strauchan, Mr Andrew Cant and Mr John Macqueene, had refused to pray publicly for King William and Queen Mary, the 1689 Edinburgh parliament passed sentence of deprivation against them and declared their parishes vacant (*RPS* 1689/3/185). The clergymen were Episcopalians who persisted in regarding James as the legitimate monarch. The 1690 parliament, with the earl of Melville (1636–1707) as King's Commissioner and Secretary and the earl of Crawford (1644–98; Lord Whigriddne) as President, passed an 'Act for restoreing the presbyterian ministers who were thrust from their churches since the 1st of January 1661' (*RPS* 1690/4/13). The Westminster Confession of Faith was voted and approved (*RPS* 1690/4/33), as was an Order (*RPS* 1690/4/36) 'directing letters of horning upon the act restoreing presbyterian ministers' – i.e. for proclaiming as outlaws the episcopalian ministers at present holding churches. It was also ruled that a General Assembly was to meet 'on the third Thursday of October next' (*RPS* 1690/4/42).

The climax of these rulings came with an Act (*RPS* 1690/4/43) 'ratifieing the *Confession of Faith* and settleing presbeterian church government'. This declared 'that the church government be established in the hands of and exercised by these presbyterian ministers who were outed since the first of January 1661 for nonconformitie to prelacie, or not complying with the courses of the tyme, and are now restored by the late act of parliament, and such ministers and elders only as they have received or shall hereafter admitt or receave'. These ministers and elders were given the right 'to try and purge out all insufficient, negligent, scandalous and erroneous ministers'. Any 'who prove contumacious in not compearing or be found guilty ... they shall *ipso facto* be suspended from or depryved of their stipends and benefices'.

Also passed was 'An Act for Visitation of universities, colledges and schoolls' (*RPS* 1690/4/79) which included the proviso that professors and other teachers must 'subscryve to the *Confession of Faith* ... and alsoe sweare and subscryve the oath of allegiance to their majesties [William and Mary]'. They must also submit to 'the government of the church now settled by law'. Visitors were appointed 'with full power and commission to them, or majority of them hereby declared, to be their quorum, to meet and visite all universities, colledges and schoolls within this kingdom, and to take tryall of the present professors, principalls, regents, masters and others beareing office therein ... and such as shall be found erroneous, scandalous, negligent, insufficient or disaffected to their majesties' government, or who shall not subscryve to the *Confession of Faith*, swear and subscribe the oath of allegiance and submitt to the government of the church now settled by law to purge out and remove'. Prominent among the Visitors appointed were the earl of Crawford, Mr Gilbert Rule (Mr Salathiel Littlesense), Mr Hugh Kennedy (Moderator) and Mr James Kirktoun (Mr Covenant Planedealer).

A drastic purge of universities and colleges followed in which one of the most notorious events was the replacement of Alexander Monro (d. c. 1715) by Gilbert Rule as Principal of Edinburgh University.

When the General Assembly met, with Mr Hugh Kennedy as Moderator, it was less general than usual. 'Few ventured to Edinburgh from the episcopalian strongholds of the north-east, and the core ... was made up of the sixty "antediluvians" who survived from those ejected at the Restoration' (Ferguson 1968: 14). The Assembly set up two Commissions (*AGA* 1690/15, 16, 17), one for Visitation of Presbyteries on the South Side of Tay, one for those on the North, the main function of both being to carry out the instructions already given by parliament. Among the Commissioners appointed for the South were Mr Hugh Kennedy, Mr Gilbert Rule, Mr James Kir(k)toun, Mr James Frazer (Mr Timothie Turbulent), Mr John Spalding (Cleark), and the earl of Crawford – all antediluvians. Moderation in their activities, although urged on both Commissions, was not observed. James Frazer in particular made shameless use of the 'universall lybell' and its provisions (4.2, 75–82) in his purging of the Church in Fife. In all, more than five hundred ministers were ejected, many on little or no ground, and often suffering great hardship as a consequence. Parishes were left vacant, sometimes for years.

So much for the political and religious context of the play. As for the intellectual, the seventeenth century might be described as the century of mathematics, in particular as applied to motions of all kinds. The crowning achievement was the publication in 1687, four years before *The Phanaticks*, of Isaac Newton's *Philosophiae Naturalis Principia Mathematica* ('Mathematical Principles of Natural Philosophy'; Newton 1687), which offered a compelling explanation of physical phenomena, an explanation, as it appeared to many, which left no room for God, save as a remote First Cause. One consequence was atheism or Deism. The methods used by Newton and his immediate predecessors were wholly opposed to those of the theologians, still making use of the Aristotelian logic of the schoolmen – Presbyterians in particular made use of it – while among Episcopalians there was a tendency to accept mathematics. Induction, using mathematics as its instrument, led from the known to the hitherto unknown and was thus the basis of science, while scholastic deduction, as was claimed by its opponents, remained incapable of establishing anything new.

Samuel Rutherford, an influential Calvinist divine, built his *Lex, Rex* (Rutherford 1644) upon a series of forty-four Questions, with arguments for or against, and a final decision – precisely the method adopted by Aquinas in his *Summa contra Gentiles* and *Summa Theologica*. In the play, Salathiel, as University Principal, goes out of his way to praise such methods and put them in a particular context:

> Our Colledge is doing its duity to send out excellent men to the vine-yeard. Thanks to Mr M–sie, who teaches them to dispatch Cattigo-rietuaclie and Sincategormatice, and Dispise vane philosophie and Mathematicks & Instruct them in many things quhich the Malignants, who want grace, say are contraire to reasone – Indeed, Moderator, they ar above Reasone, and what they are contrarie to it? Quhat hath Carnal reasone or humane learneing to doe with Christ's Spouse?
>
> (3.3, 7–14)

As against this, Francis Bacon was the chief advocate of induction. 'Rejicimus igitur Syllogismus ... tamen ad Naturam Rerum Inductione per omnia ... utimur' (We reject the Syllogism ... for scientific investigation we use only Induction; Bacon 1620, 18). All his followers, those, for example, who were later to form the Royal Society, used, or at least made gestures towards, induction. There had also been anticipations – examples are the heliocentric astronomy of Copernicus (1473–1543) and, more particularly, the elucidation by Kepler (1571–1630) in his *Astronomia Nova* (1609) of the apparently anomalous behaviour of the planet Mars in terms of the laws of planetary motion (Koestler 1959: 317–41; Linton 2004: 177–93).

Induction generally depended on careful observation, for which the newly invented telescope became a suitable instrument, exploited by Galileo (1564–1642). Kepler depended heavily on the earlier naked-eye work of his master, Tycho Brahe (1546–1601).

The Scot John Napier of Merchiston (1550–1617) invented logarithms, an aid to calculation, which also, by its use of the base e, had deep implications for later mathematicians. Other developments in the early part of the century were mainly French. 'Three great Frenchmen, Descartes, Desargues, Pascal, initiated the modern period in geometry. Another Frenchman, Fermat, laid the foundations of modern analysis, and all but perfected the methods of the differential calculus.' Later, 'Newton and Leibniz, between them, actually did create the differential calculus as a practical method of mathematical reasoning. When the century ended, mathematics as an instrument for application to physical problems was well established in something of its modern proficiency' (Whitehead 1938: 69–70).

For the purposes of this volume, the most important of the French mathematicians is René Descartes (1596–1650). 'He abus'd the Great Des Cartes in print' Pitcairne wrote indignantly of a fellow-mathematician and Scot, John Keil (1671–1721), 'Who first invented The true Method of Tangents from which and of which, Dr Barrows method, and Sir Isaac Neuton's fluxions, and Leibnitz's calcul are only Corollaries or abridgements, as shall be seen if I live a little longer, but without reflection on these great men' (Johnston 1979: 56). The reference is to the graphical analysis of curves and tangents in terms of the Cartesian coordinates, x and y – something crucial for calculus as perfected by Pierre de Fermat (1601–65), Isaac Newton (1642–1727) and Gottfried Wilhelm Leibniz (1646–1716).

Descartes himself was an *a priori* or deductive mathematician, who strove unsuccessfully to remain on good terms with the (Catholic)

Church. The systems put forward by Copernicus and Galileo had already been condemned. Kepler had been excommunicated by the Lutherans. Later physicists and astronomers, who made inductive use of mathematics to discover other truths unknown to Scripture, were anathema to many. The climax to the process was the publication, already mentioned, of Newton's *Principia*. This, however, is not directly mentioned in the play, perhaps to indicate the ignorance of the Presbyterians, who refer only to earlier mathematicians. Salathiel makes the (much exaggerated) complaint that, before the purgation, the universities 'wer all o'rgrowne with Cart's [Descartes'] Mathematicks & humane Reasoneings' (3.3, 21–2).

For the theologians and logicians, it was also worrying that the use of mathematics was not limited to physics and astronomy. The Amsterdam Jew Baruch Spinoza (1632–77), for instance, began as a follower of Descartes. His first published book was *Renati des Cartesii principiorum philosophiæ, Mori geometrico demonstratæ* (The philosophic principles of René Descartes demonstrated geometrically; Spinoza 1663). Later he constructed his own geometrical system of ethics, *Ethica ordine geometrico demonstrata* (Ethics demonstrated geometrically: published posthumously in the year of Spinoza's death), which begins with Definitions and Axioms, then proceeds to Propositions, proved in Euclidean fashion and often involving diagrams, Lemmas (subsidiary propositions, assumed to be valid, used in the proof of other propositions) and Corollaries. The basic concept is God; the first Definition reads 'I understand that to be CAUSE OF ITSELF whose essence involves existence and whose nature cannot be conceived unless existing'; the sixth 'God I understand to be a being absolutely infinite, that is, a substance consisting of infinite attributes, each of which expresses eternal and infinite essence'. However, because he developed his philosophy in mathematical rather than biblical terms, did not allow for a Creation, and regarded God as immanent rather than transcendent, the most common charge against him was atheism. Long before his ideas had reached full expression in print, he was excommunicated from the Amsterdam synagogue (July 1656). He was also denounced by the Dutch Calvinist clergy. More than half-a-century after his death, even David Hume (1711–76) described him as an atheist and talked of his 'hideous hypothesis' (Hume 1960: 241). Hume was himself speaking ironically, but his words indicate how most of his contemporaries continued to think.

Spinoza, incidentally, also held that 'The human mind has an adequate knowledge of the eternal and infinite essence of God' and that 'The more we understand individual things, the more we understand God' (Spinoza 1979: 73, 214). Contrast Salathiel's speech quoted above.

Spinoza was not alone. In a the next section of this Introduction I note as part of Pitcairne's undergraduate reading, *The Immortality of the Soul, so farre forth as it is demonstrable from the Knowledge of Nature and the Light of Reason* (More 1659), by the Cambridge Platonist Henry More (1614–87). This too is set out like an extended geometrical demonstration, beginning from Axioms and making use of diagrams. Although later More, like Spinoza, rejected aspects of Cartesianism, at this point he was still a disciple, talking of 'The incomparable Philosophy of Renatus Des-Cartes, whose dexterous wit and through insight into the nature and lawes of Matter, has so perfected the reasons of those Phænomena, that Democritus, Epicurus, Lucretius and others have puzzled themselves about, that there seems nothing now wanting as concerning the way of Philosophizing, but patience and an unprejudiced judgment to peruse what he has writ' (More 1659: 346–7).

In his title More lays emphasis on the value of reason as applied to religious belief. He was also the author of *Enthusiasmus Triumphatus, or, A Discourse of the Nature, Causes, Kinds and Cure, of Enthusiasme* (More 1656). Enthusiasm, in the sense 'a vain confidence of divine favour or communication, ill-directed or misdirected religious emotion' (*OED*), is opposed to reason, and in *The Phanaticks* is presented as peculiarly characteristic of Presbyterians. More's discussion may be summarised by a paragraph from his earlier *Conjectura Cabbalistica*:

> To exclude the use of Reason in the search of divine truth, is no dictate of the Spirit, but of headstrong Melancholy and blinde Enthusiasme, that religious frensie men run into, by lying passive for the reception of such impresses as have no proportion with their faculties. Which mistakes and irregularity, if they can once away with it, they put themselves in a posture of promiscuously admitting anything, and so in due time of growing either moped [melancholy, clinically depressed] or mad, and under pretence of being highly Christians (the right mystery whereof they understand not) of working themselves lower than the lowest of men ... But now seeing the Logos or steady comprehensive wisdom of God, in which all Ideas and their respects are contained, is but universal stable reason, how can there be any pretence of being so highly inspired as to be blown above reason itself? (More 1653: Preface, unnumbered fourth page)

A later mathematician of distinction, John Craig (c. 1663–1731), a pupil of David Gregorie, published his first work, *Methodus figurarum lineis rectis & curvis comprehensarum quadraturas determinandi* (A Method for Establishing the Squares of Figures bounded by straight and curved lines; London, 1685) while he was still an Edinburgh undergraduate (he

matriculated in 1684 and graduated in 1687). His father had been episcopalian minister of Hoddam in Dumfriesshire and he himself became
a Church of England clergyman in the diocese of Salisbury.

In 1699 he published in London his *Theologiæ Christianæ Principia
Mathematica* (Mathematical Principles of Christian Theology; Craig
1699). The title obviously refers to Newton's great work, a point rein-
forced by these words in the 'Preface', addressed to his bishop and
fellow-Scot, Gilbert Burnet (1643–1715): 'When I reflected seriously
on the remarkable advance in the natural sciences ancient and more
modern mathematicians had deduced and demonstrated by Geometry, it
made me hope that it [Geometry] could have a use in Theology' ('Cum
vero serio mecum perponderem quam egregia Scientiarum Naturalium
incrementa ex Geometria deduxerint & demonstraverint tum veteres
tum recentiores Mathematici; fecerunt illa, ut eandem in rebus Theo-
logicis usum aliquem habere posse sperarem'; Præfatio. V). He clarified
his aims in terms more than a little startling for a clergyman: 'As probability generates Faith, so it overturns science, and on the other hand
Certitude generates science and destroys Faith. Thus Science removes
all occasion for doubt, while Faith always leaves some uncertainty in
the mind' ('Sicut enim probabilitas Fidem generat, ita etiam scientiam
evertit; & e contra Certitudo scientiam simul generat & Fidem destruit.
Unde Scientia omnem dubitandi ansam aufert; dum Fides aliquem
semper hæsitationem in mente relinquit'; *ibid.* VII). The primacy of
Faith over Reason is basic to Calvinistic as well as Lutheran theology.
Craig's monograph, however, is directed, not so much against Calvin
and Luther as against the philosopher who created, with Pierre Fermat
(1601–65), the mathematical theory of probability, Blaise Pascal (1623–
62) in whose *Pensées* (Pascal 1670, published posthumously) Faith is
granted the primacy. The first part of Craig's *Principia* is a calculus of
the probability of the biblical narrative, so important to Pascal, which
Craig shows to diminish to vanishing point with the passage of time.
Against this, the final part demonstrates that when Pascal made his
famous bet (*le pari de Pascal*), he was, in fact, betting on a certainty.
Craig defines and emphasises various forms of *voluptas* (pleasure,
delight, happiness) and his final paragraph reads: 'It follows from
Corollaries 1 and 2 and Axioms 2 and 3 that the true Christian [who
bets on an infinity of future delight] is the wisest of all the wise, and
Atheists and Deists [who rely on this life and a few years of chequered
pleasure] are the stupidest of all the stupid' ('Verus Christianus est
omnium sapientum sapientissimus, & Athei ac Deistæ sunt omnium
stultorum stultissimi, sequitur ex Corol. 1 & 2 hujus, & Axiom. 2 & 3';

p. 36). In other words, he has proved the truth of Christianity, not by the Bible but by mathematics.

His monograph received no general approval. Like the rest of the Cambridge Platonists he became an object of hostility to many of his Christian brethren (Patrides 1969: 8–16).

I have mentioned Craig because in some sense he belonged to the circle of Pitcairne and Gregory. Pitcairne refers to him in his *Solutio problematis de historicis* (Pitcairne 1688) and thrice mentions him favourably in letters which survive (Johnston 1979: 38, 39, 54). The interests of the two men overlapped. Pitcairne's *Epistola Archimedis ad Regem Gelonem* (Pitcairne 1688), for example, discusses the possible application of geometry to matters of religion. On 23 September 1694 Pitcairne wrote to his London friend Dr Gray:

> I have a vast propensitie to writ the Relligio mathematici, or Euclidis &c. [The Religion of a mathematician, or, of Euclid etc.] but it cannot be so printed me vivo [during my lifetime]. If I write it, I'l certainlie laugh in my grave if I can understand then what a work there shall be to answer it by those who'l not understand it. The paper (if ever I write it) shall be ane immortal confutation of poperie & of every thing that smells of poperie. (Johnston 1979: 18)

Very possibly Pitcairne had in mind a work by another, earlier physician, the *Religio Medici* (Browne 1643) of Sir Thomas Browne (1605–82). 'The generall scandall of my profession' is Browne's starting point, the general belief that physicians had no religion at all. The change in Pitcairne from *Medici* (physician; a title to which he also had a claim) to the even more disreputable *mathematici* (mathematician) thus has an obvious significance. Hostility to Roman Catholicism, almost wholly lacking in Browne's work, has already been evidenced by Pitcairne's attack on Sir Robert Sibbald.

Pitcairne probably thought that mathematical arguments could establish the existence and attributes of God. Contrast his declaration in a letter to Dr Gregorie (25 February 1706; Johnston 1979: 42–3): 'I am clear that metaphysics [i.e. scholastic arguments] can never prove a Deity, and therfor think our churchmen here have no ground not to be Atheists.' This may also serve as commentary on the startling claim by Novell that 'all are Atheists Except Mathematicians' (5.1, 121).

As Pitcairne noted in a postscript to a letter dated 1 October 1703, Craig eventually distanced himself from Gregorie, probably on political grounds (Craig was a Whig): 'Also take notice that Mr Craig is very far from being a friend to Dr Gregory. This for the politics. I am great with all' (Johnston 1979: 39).

'The scientific philosophy of this age [the seventeenth century] was dominated by physics ... [the] *concepts* ... [of which are] *very unsuited to biology; and set for it an insoluble problem of matter and life and organism, with which biologists are now wrestling*' (Whitehead 1938: 51). Gregorie and, more particularly, Pitcairne were iatromathematicians, physicians, that is to say, who attempted to deploy mathematical methods for the solution of biological problems. Pitcairne's medical writings were famous and often reprinted during the eighteenth century, but in the longer run his methods proved inadequate and became more or less forgotten.

A final seventeenth-century intellectual characteristic, held by most, execrated by a few, is the belief in witches and the need to suppress them, hinted at in the play by the number of references to witch-burning (e.g. 5.1, 168). The Old Ladie is more explicit, referring directly and approvingly (5.2, 45) to an influential work on the subject, *Satans Invisible world Discovered; or, A Choice Collection of Modern Relations, proving evidently against the* Saducees *and* Atheists *of this present Age, that there are* Devils, Spirits, Witches, *and* Apparitions, *from Authentick Records, Attestations of Famous Witnesses, and undoubted Verity ... by Mr George Sinclair, late Professor of Philosophy in the Colledge of* Glasgow (Sinclair 1685).

Sinclair sets himself two main targets, first 'a monstruous rable of men ... following the Hobbesian and Spinosian Principles ... Hobbs the Inglishman is too well known by his Atheisticall writtings. Benedictus Spinosa, or rather Maledictus; a stranger abroad, a profain abuser of the Scripture; will have all those Devils, which CHRIST and his Disciples cast out, to be but Diseases in mens Bodies', second 'the absurd Principles of the Cartesian Philosophy, eagerly maintained by Cartes his Followers' (Preface, unnumbered pp. 8–9). He follows this with a list of fifty-six erroneous Cartesian tenets: 'the Cartesian Novelties far exceed the number of heads, which the Hydra or Lernean Serpent had' (Preface, unnumbered pp. 8–10). Sinclair is consciously following in the footsteps of Henry More in *An Antidote Against Atheism* (More 1653), and of Joseph Glanvill (1636–80) in the posthumously published *Saducismus Triumphatus* (Glanvill 1681). Pitcairne and his co-authors regarded witchcraft as a superstition, cultivated by Presbyterians and bigots. They themselves were, in that sense, Sadducees.

Specific references to logic, mathematics and witchcraft are scattered through the play. Fairly obviously, moreover, the speech of the

Committee members tends to be syllogistic in form, making much use of metaphor and analogy. In 4.2, 93–95, for instance, Mr Covenant Planedealer remarks: in the very style of a scholastic dispute: 'To what our brother hes said, I have two queries, two difficulties, on fear, and a proposall. Or rather two proposalls, two queries, on difficultie, and a fear.' Mr Solomon uses only the imagery of the Song of Solomon. By contrast, the language of Will and Frank, Laura and Violetta, answers to the mode recommended by that early body of Scientists, the Royal Society of London, 'a close, naked, natural way of speaking; positive expressions; clear senses; a native easiness: bringing all things as near the Mathematical plainness, as they can' (Sprat 1959: 113). Among much else, all this is to say the play is a document in the struggle of Moderns with Ancients, a struggle which figured prominently in the literary and scientific worlds of the late seventeenth and early eighteenth centuries.

The Authors

Archibald Pitcairne

Parallels between the text and Pitcairne's other writings, whether Scots or Latin, suggest that his was the main hand in the composition of the play. His life therefore is treated at greater length than that of either of his co-authors.

He was the son of Alexander Pitcairne, merchant and magistrate in Edinburgh, and of Janet Sydserff, born on Christmas Day 1652. Pitcairne, from which the family took its name, is a hamlet near Leslie in Fife. Pitcairnegreen, a small estate near Perth, was the property of Alexander Pitcairne. They were long-established Episcopalians and royalists. One ancestor had fought at Flodden (1513).

Pitcairne's mother was a Sydserff of Ruchlaw in East Lothian. Her family was even more intimately involved with loyalty and Episcopalianism than the Pitcairnes. She was related, for instance, to Thomas Sydserff (1587–1683), bishop of Brechin (1634), translated to Galloway (1635), but excommunicated by the 1638 General Assembly. In 1661, after the Restoration, he returned as bishop of Orkney, but lived in Edinburgh for the rest of his life.

His son, also named Thomas, shared the family political and religious beliefs, but also had literary ambitions. In 1651, after the execution of Charles I and the subsequent coronation of Charles II at Scone, he brought out the Edinburgh news-sheet, *Mercurius Criticus*, and in

1660, after the Restoration, the more influential, although short-lived, *Mercurius Caledonius*. He also published a translation of the posthumously published scientific and political fantasy by Cyrano de Bergerac (1619–55), *L'Histoire comique contenant les états et empires de la Lune* (1656), a translation which he entitled *SELHNARXIA, or, the government of the world in the moon, a comical history/ written by that famous wit and cavaleer of France, Monsieur Cyrano de Bergerac: and done into English by Tho. St Serf, Gent.* (London, 1659).

Selēnarchia appeared during the last throes of the republican Commonwealth and was dedicated, not to any home dignitary but to 'the Right Honourable, the Lord George Douglas, and Lieutenant General Andrew Rutherford, and to all the Noble officers in these two Renowned Regiments of Scots, in service of the Most Christian King of France' – Louis XIV, that is to say. The dedication is intended to 'testifie to the world how happy the name of Scotland is (even now when the waves seem almost to cover her)' ('Epistle Dedicatory', unnumbered third page).

Sydserff's next production, a play, *Tarugo's Wiles: or, The Coffee-House. A Comedy* (London, 1668), was performed, first in London 'at his Highness's the Duke of York's Theater' (the duke of York was the future James VII and II), afterwards at the Tennis Court of the palace of Holyroodhouse in Edinburgh. It was a free adaptation of the Spanish comedy *No puede ser el guardar una mujer* (It's impossible to be a woman's guardian) by Agustin Moreto y Cabaña (1618–69). Act III, interpolated by Sydserff, is set in a coffee-house and offers a satirical portrait of London society under many aspects, including proceedings at the newly founded Royal Society.

Sydserff dedicated the play 'To the Right Honourable, and most Noble Lord, George Marquesse of Huntly, Earl of Egney and Lord Strathbogy', the young 4th marquess, that is to say born c. 1649, who is urged to remember 'the actions and sufferings of your Noble Grandfather, Father and Uncles in our late Fanatick Commotions' (the period of the Commonwealth and the civil wars which preceded it). Huntly's grandfather, the episcopalian 2nd marquess, had been executed on 23 March 1649, two months after Charles I. The 3rd marquess and his brother, Lord Charles Gordon, had been active in the resistance to Cromwell which continued in the Highlands for some time after the defeat of Charles II at Worcester. Sydserff claims that he himself played a part in it.

A connection between Pitcairne and *Tarugo's Wiles* seems to have been long remembered in Edinburgh. In 1694 he delivered his *Dispu-*

tatio de curatione Febrium (Discussion of the cure for fevers) to the Edinburgh Royal College of Physicians. This was printed early in 1695. An anonymous critic, probably Edward Eizat, produced a pamphlet entitled *Apollo Mathematicus, or, the Art of Curing Diseases by the Mathematicks* (Edinburgh, 1695), in which, among much else, the claim was advanced that Pitcairne's emphasis on mathematics as the only source of scientific certainty implied a denial of biblical truth. Pitcairne was thus declared an atheist – a charge that stuck. Another physician, George Hepburn (c. 1669–1759), defended Pitcairne in a rival pamphlet, *Tarrugo unmasked: or, an Answer to a late pamphlet intituled Apollo mathematicus* (Edinburgh, 1695). Among other charges, Hepburn suggested that the hand behind Eizat's pamphlet was that of Sir Robert Sibbald (1641–1722), the Tarrugo, the cunning schemer, of the title. The reference to Sydserff's play is unmistakeable, as is the suggestion that the playwright had some particular relationship with Archibald Pitcairne.

'From 1668 until his death in the following year, St Serfe [*sic*] managed a theatrical company in the Canongate [of Edinburgh]' (Tobin 1972: 13). Pitcairne's own dramatic and literary ambitions may have owed something to the example of his cousin.

During the Commonwealth a Dr John Saintserf (Sydserff) took part in abortive attempts to establish a College of Physicians in Edinburgh (Craig 1976: 47, 50, 52, 355).

Pitcairne's earliest years were passed under the republican Commonwealth, with Scotland officially part of England and episcopalian forms of worship suppressed. These developments cannot have pleased his family and their friends. Their opinions helped to settle the boy's mind in the pattern maintained for the rest of his life.

Archibald attended the High School of Dalkeith, in Midlothian near Edinburgh, where he acquired the knowledge of Latin necessary for the four-year course, leading to the degree of MA, in the Tounis College, the University of Edinburgh, which he entered in 1668. The course was general, 'including both the classics and exact sciences, and culminating in compulsory philosophy' (Davie 1964: 4). The teaching of philosophy might sometimes be arid, as Pitcairne indicates in the play (3.3), but fortunately he was guided through the curriculum by an enlightened regent, Sir William Paterson of Granton (d. 1709), son of a bishop and younger brother of John Paterson (1632–1708), later archbishop of Glasgow. Sir William brought him into contact with the the best of ancient Greek and Renaissance thought. As the anecdote quoted below (pp. xxxii–xxxiii) shows, this included Plato (the *Phaedrus*, probably, and the *Republic*), together with the Platonic commentaries of the Florentine, Marsilio Ficino (1439–99), and such later works as *The Immortality of the Soul* (More 1659) by the Cambridge Platonist Henry More (1614–87). Pitcairne talks of reading 'some bits' of this last – probably the result of its prolixity with more than 600 pages.

In college his closest friend was Robert Lindsay (d. 1675/6), a collateral descendant of the poet and dramatist Sir David Lindsay of the Mount (?1486–1555), author of *Ane Satyre of the Thrie Estaitis*. The young Lindsay shared his passion for philosophy. Another fellow-student was Walter Dennistoun (d. 1700), who became schoolmaster (i.e. headmaster) of the grammar school at Musselburgh, East Lothian. Dennistoun, like Pitcairne, aspired to compose Latin verse, several specimens of which survive. In his own lifetime, as well as posthumously, he became the butt of much of Pitcairne's satirical verse.

Pitcairne graduated on 20 May 1671. His first intention was to qualify as an advocate, a lawyer entitled to plead in the highest Scottish courts. The intensity of his studies, however, made him ill. To recuperate he was sent to France. In Paris he met some Scots medical students and began to develop an interest in the subject. A few months later his father summoned him home. There he turned to mathematics, a subject in which he soon gained considerable expertise and which he continued to practise for the rest of his life. As the title *Apollo mathematicus* has already indicated, it came to form the basis of his medical theory and practice – he became what was called a iatromathematician – but he was also a mathematician in a more orthodox fashion. His contribution to the method of infinite series, essential to the new discipline of calculus, was recognized in the third volume of the *Opera Mathematica* (1693–99) of the English mathematician and cryptographer, John Wallis (1616–1703). He had good relations with Sir Isaac Newton (1642–1727). The mathematician David Gregorie was the closest friend of his maturity and he corresponded with others, such as the brilliant Colin Campbell (1644–1726), Gaelic-speaking minister of the isolated parishes of Ardchattan and Muckairn in Argyle, whom his letters helped to stay abreast of the latest developments in the subject (Johnston 1979: 38–41, 54, 59–64).

In 1675 he returned to Paris to pursue medical studies. Little is known of his time there. A reference in the **Preface** (below, p. 228) suggests that during his stay he may have seen a performance of Molière's *Tartuffe* (1667). The notoriety of the play is perhaps enough, however, to explain the reference. An English translation by the actor and playwright, Matthew Medbourne (?1637–80), had been put on the English stage and published as *Tartuffe: or The French Puritan* (London, 1670).

One anecdote is worth giving, probably in Pitcairne's own words, written some considerable time after the event:

> Robert Lindsay, grandchild [*sic*] to Sir David Lindsay of the Mount, Lyon King at Arms etc. and whose sister was married to David Lyndsay, Melfort's Davie, was most intimat condisciple with AP. These two, reading in the summer 1671, when both graduated by Sir Wm. Paterson, Plato and some bits of Dr. Henrie More, Ficinus, made a bargain that whoever died first should give an account of his condition. Robert Lyndsay succeeded his father as a Clerk to the exchequer, Mount or Month (a mile north-west from Coupar in Fife) being on his 800 merks a year, still in his possession, but really belonging to his father's creditors. He dy'd of an iliac passion in the winter 1675 and 1676, when AP was at Paris. That very night in which Lyndsay died, as AP's letter and Boghall's letter given at Paris agreed, AP dreamt (as a man at Eise) That Lindsay came to him thus, 'Archie, perhaps you heard I'm dead?' 'No, Robin.' 'Ay, but they have buried my body in the Gray-Friars, I am, tho', alive and in a place the pleasures of which cannot be exprest in Scots, Greek or Latin. I have come with a well-sayling small ship in Leith Road to carry you thither.' 'Robin, J'll go with You, but wait till I go to Fife and take leave of my father and mother (who dwelle at Pitcairne Gren) and next to East Lothian to take leave of my aunt Rothlan.' 'Archie, I have but the allowance of one tide and you shall not make your visit in so short a tyme. Forsooth, Archie, J'll come for you at another tyme.'
>
> AP never sleeps a night Since that tyme without dreaming that Robin Lindsay told him that [he] was alive, and in the year '94, when AP had a sickness that every body thought insuperable, as he could not walk without being supported, had never any fear of himself. Robin told him he was delay'd for a time, but he was order'd, and was properlie put to his task, to carry off AP at a tyme, nor was discharged to tell. (BL MS Sloane 3198; punctuation editorial)

The anecdote appears to depend on two sources other than Pitcairne's memory, letters written home at the time, one by Pitcairne, the other by an unidentified Boghall. The authenticity, however, remains doubtful – the anecdote too closely resembles one about the Florentine Neo-Platonist, Marsilio Ficino (1433–99) (Ficinus in the anecdote) told by the later author also mentioned, the Cambridge Platonist, Henry More:

> But of any private person that ever appeared upon design after his death, there is none did upon a more noble one then that eximious Platonist, *Marsilius Ficinus*; who having, as *Baronius* relates, made a solemn vow with his fellow-Platonist *Michael Mercatus* (after they

had been pretty warmly disputing of the Immortality of the Soul, out of the Principles of their Master *Plato*) that whether of them two died first should appear to his friend, and give him certain intimations of that truth; (it being *Ficinus* his fate to die first, and indeed not long after their mutual resolution) he was mindful of his promise when he had left the Body. For *Michael Mercatus* being very intent at his studies betimes on a morning, heard an horse riding by with all speed, and observed that he stopped at his window; and therewith heard the voice of his friend *Ficinus* crying out aloud, *O Michael, Michael, vera, vera sunt illa* [Michael, Michael, those things are true, are true]. Whereupon he suddenly opened the window, and espying *Marsilius* on a white steed, called after him; but he vanisht in his sight. He sent therefore presently to *Florence* to know how *Marsilius* did; and understood that he died about that hour he called at his window, to assure him of his own and other men's Immortalities.

(More 1659: 293–4*)

On 13 August 1680 Pitcairne graduated MD in the University of Rheims. On his return home, the great event, so far as he was concerned, was the foundation in 1681 of the Edinburgh Royal College of Physicians. The guiding spirit was Sir Robert Sibbald, MD of Leiden, with whom Pitcairne was to maintain an uneasy relationship for the rest of his life. Something of this has already been indicated (above, p. xxx). To make plans for the College, Sibbald and Pitcairne, together with three other eminent physicians, Dr Thomas Burnet (1638–1704), Dr Archibald Stevenson (1630–1710), later to be Pitcairne's father-in-law, and Dr Andrew Balfour (1630–94), met at Sibbald's lodgings 'once a fourthnight or so, wher we had conferences' (Sibbald 1833: 28; quoted in Craig 1976: 61). All but Pitcairne later received knighthoods.

Of the twenty-one original Fellows, Pitcairne was the youngest, probably, too, the most advanced in medical theory and practice. The masters whom he chiefly acknowledged were the Englishman, William Harvey (1578–1657), who had discovered the circulation of the blood, the Italian iatrophysicist G. A. Borelli (1608–79), and the anatomist, Lorenzo Bellini (1643–1704).

From 1683 to 1685 he was Depute Honorary Librarian of the College, and from 1684 to 1695 Secretary. In 1685 he became one of the three newly established professors of medicine in the University. Unfortunately, the posts received nothing from the funding body, the

---

* For the more general relevance of More's writings to the play, see above, pp. xxiv–xxv.

Town Council, and none seems ever to have lectured or demonstrated in University precincts. Notes by students on lectures undoubtedly delivered by Pitcairne are now preserved in the Library of the Royal College of Physicians, and in the Wellcome Library in London.

It seems likely that by 1680 Pitcairne had met David Gregorie (1661–1708), nephew of the great James Gregorie (1638–75), professor of mathematics at St Andrews 1668–74, and thereafter briefly at Edinburgh until his untimely death. James Gregorie was probably 'the most original and versatile mathematician Scotland has produced'. He discovered the binomial theory independently of Newton, the interpretation formula, a wealth of results on expansions in infinite series, in which he made use of what was essentially Taylor's theorem, and made many contributions to the development of the differential and integral calculus 'to name but a few' (Schlapp 1973: 1–16).

On James Gregorie's death, his unpublished papers were left to his brother, David Gregorie's father, also called David. Together with Pitcairne, the younger David set to work on them. 'Amongst the Gregory MSS in Edinburgh University Library are innumerable sheets of calculations, some begun in Pitcairne's writing and finished in Gregory's, others the other way about' (Shirlaw 1975: 24).

In 1683 Pitcairne issued a public challenge (Pitcairne 1683) to John Young (who had taken over James Gregorie's responsibilities for mathematics in the university, although not himself appointed professor) to solve a problem for which, unknown to Young, a solution already existed in the published works of Descartes. Young's failure to find the solution led to his dismissal and, although David Gregorie had not yet completed his degree, such was his brilliance that he was elected to his uncle's vacant chair. Pitcairne may have issued his challenge with this outcome in mind.

In 1687 the two briefly shared lodgings. They were together when Gregorie received a copy of Isaac Newton's great *Philosophiæ Naturalis Principia Mathematica*, published that year by the Royal Society. Pitcairne shared Gregorie's excitement and admiration.

In or about 1685 Pitcairne married Margaret Hay, daughter of Colonel James Hay of Pitfour, Aberdeenshire. They had a daughter Anne and a son who died in infancy. Margaret herself died in 1690 and was buried in Greyfriars churchyard. Anne was still alive in 1694; how long she survived thereafter is uncertain. Pitcairne commemorated both mother and daughter in Latin verse (Macqueen and Macqueen 2009: 140).

During this period nearly all of Pitcairne's written work is in Latin, much of it verse. The earliest, probably, is an expanded translation, in hexameters and elegiacs, of the second section of an English poem, *A Description of the King oof Fayries Clothes, brought to him on the New-yeares day in the morning, 1626, by his Queenes Chambermaids* (London, 1634), a poem usually attributed to Sir Simon Steward (d. 1629), a friend of the poet Robert Herrick (1591–1674). Herrick is sometimes regarded as himself the author. It may contain political undertones. Pitcairne's version was first published in London in 1670, when he was eighteen years old and an undergraduate (Macqueen and Macqueen 2009: 276–89). At much the same time he wrote a Platonic epigram addressed to Robert Lindsay (Macqueen and Macqueen 2009: 176). Later he produced an inscription for the new house built by the golfer John Paterson on the proceeds of a wager on the outcome of a match in which Paterson successfully partnered the duke of York against two English noblemen (Macqueen and Macqueen 2009: *ut cit.*). Pitcairne composed an ironic inscription for the tomb of the politician, John Maitland, 1st (and only) duke of Lauderdale (d. 1682; interred at Haddington, East Lothian, 1683), a member of the notorious Cabal (Macqueen and Macqueen 2009: 212). An epigram on Isaac Newton (Macqueen and Macqueen 2009: 178) is probably to be associated with the publication of the *Principia* in 1687. Another epitaph (Macqueen and Macqueen 2009: 180), this time for the bishop of Whithorn, James Aitken (1613–87), belongs to the same year, as may a poem on his daughter Anne (Macqueen and Macqueen 2009: 140).

In 1688 he published in Edinburgh a prose pamphlet, *Solutio problematis de historicis; seu de inventoribus dissertatio* (Resolving a historical problem, or, a dissertation on discoverers), primarily a vindication of William Harvey's claim to the discovery that blood circulates through the arteries and veins of the body by means of the pumping action of the heart. This may have been aimed at a Dutch humanist and physician, Theodoor Jansson van Almelooven (1657–1712), author of *Inventa novantiqua. Id est brevis enarratio ortus & progressus artis medicæ, ac præcipue de inventis vulgo novis ... in ea repertis* (New-old discoveries. That is, a short account of the rise and progress of the art of medicine, and especially of the new discoveries allegedly made in it; Amsterdam, 1684), in which he claimed, and sought to demonstrate, that modern medical discoveries, such as the circulation of the blood, had been anticipated by physicians of the ancient school of Hippocrates of Cos. In his reply, Pitcairne referred to mathematics as well as medicine and, in particular, to the new techniques introduced by James and David Gregorie, John Craig and himself. In his refutations, Pitcairne used humanistic scholarship as well as his wide knowledge of modern medicine and mathematics. Almelooven and he stood on opposite sides in the battle between Ancients and Moderns which at that time split the republics of letters and science, and which also makes an appearance in *The Phanaticks*.

At much the same time Pitcairne wrote a satire, *Epistola Archimedis ad Regem Gelonem, Albæ Græcæ Reperta. Anno Æræ Christianæ 1688* (Letter of Archimedes to King Gelo, discovered at Alba Græcæ in the Year 1688 of the Christian Era). It takes the form of an edition of a manuscript, supposedly a Late Latin translation of a Greek original, discovered in the year 1688 at a place otherwise unknown. In form it is a reply by the great ancient mathematician Archimedes (c. 287–212 BC; the name, incidentally, is deliberately close to that of *Archi*bald, *Archie* Pitcairne) to a query proposed by the king, whether mathematics might be used to solve religious difficulties. The relation of this to work by Pitcairne's contemporaries has already been mentioned. Pitcairne's satire is directed, for the most part, at Roman Catholic and presbyterian beliefs and practices, but a feeling persists that it is directed at all forms of organized religion, perhaps that Pitcairne, at bottom, was no more than a deist. Originally it circulated in manuscript; it was not printed until 1710 (possibly 1706; Simpson 1966: 67) and even then anonymously.

The uneasy relationship between Pitcairne and Sibbald surfaced in a vernacular pasquil, 'Pitcairn's Roundel on Sir Robert Sibbald, 1686', preserved in a corrupt nineteenth-century printed version (item 12 of Reliquiae Pitcairnianae, Edinburgh Room, Edinburgh Central Library, call-number qy R489P68, accession-number 36553). Sibbald began life as a Presbyterian, possibly an extremist – he witnessed the sack of Dundee (1651) by General Monck – but turned to more moderate courses under the influence of the eirenic Robert Leighton (1611–84), at that time Principal of Edinburgh University. Later, during the 1680s, he developed good relations with the Roman Catholic duke of York, later James VII, and with his Chancellor, James Drummond, 4th earl of Perth (1648–1716), also a Catholic. In 1685 Sibbald briefly converted to Catholicism. Neither his original Presbyterianism, nor his later conversion, pleased Pitcairne, who was also unfavourably impressed by *Scotia Illustrata sive Prodromus Historiæ Naturalis* (Scotland Illuminated, or The Advance-Guard for Natural History; Edinburgh, 1684), a massive work, partly based on circulated questionnaires, in which Sibbald attempted a survey of Scotland's natural resources, particularly the flora (in 1670, with Andrew Balfour, he had founded the Edinburgh Physic Garden, later to become the Royal Botanic Garden). The aim was scientific, but the approach was not rigid and entirely non-mathematical. On the title-page the work was described as *opus viginti annorum* (the work of twenty years). The title-page contains no indication of authorship, but Sibbald appended his name to the dedicatory epistle, addressed to that great patron of science, the king, Charles II.

The pasquil is not a roundel in the strict French sense, but, in the way of that verse-form, it makes use of repeated lines and rhymes, usually with some slight alteration of meaning. Formally it is a dialogue between speakers identified only as A and B. The first does not mention Sibbald by name (as indeed neither speaker ever does), but makes unmistakeable references to him as Catholic convert, Fellow of the Royal College of Physicians, and author of the apparently anonymous *Scotia Illustrata*:

> There is lost, there is lost
> On the Catholic coast,
> A quack of the college's quorum.
> Tho' his name be not shown,
> Yet the man may be known
> By his *opus viginti annorum*.   (1–6)

B takes up rhymes and lines from the first stanza, but ironically pretends to question the identification, not least because *Scotia Illustrata* falls well beneath the standard appropriate to a Fellow of a learned Society. If he were such a Fellow, he would have to be diabolic. A then declares that he is diabolic, because he has been a Whig and a Covenanter, and because he is a religious and political turncoat, who has 'split on ambition' (21) – a reference to his relationship with the earl of Perth. B takes the point immediately. A comments, both on his abandonment of extremism under Leighton's influence and his signing of the oath required by the 1681 Test Act. B makes the final damning summary:

> From the Whigs he did run
> In a by-way to Rome,
> But ne'er from our prelates found shelter.
> They could not endure
> To protect or secure
> Such rogues as he from the halter
>
> For his taking the Test,
> Which he forswore at last,
> A pardon he'll get from the Pope;
> But though he so do,
> I confess it to be true,
> He very well merits a rope.

> 'Tis not the way to appear
> A true cavalier
> To quit the protestant road;
> To the king, I avow,
> He can never be true,
> That so oft has played booby with God.   (61–78)

Dialogue form and subject-matter both show in miniature some affinity with *The Phanaticks*.

Pitcairne maintained his assault on Sibbald in a Latin mock-epitaph, *In Robertum Sibbaldum M.D.* (Macqueen and Macqueen 2009: 148), written, possibly at much the same time as the roundel, or possibly in conjunction with his own later criticism of *Scotia Illustrata*, the *Dissertatio de Legibus Historiæ Naturalis* (Monograph on the Laws of Natural History; Edinburgh, 1696). The criticism was somewhat belated, as was Sibbald's anonymous reply, *Vindiciæ Scotiæ Illustrata, sive Prodromi Naturalis Historiae contra Prodromomastiges* (Vindication of *Scotland Illuminated, or The Advance-Guard for Natural History* against the Scourger of the Advance-Guard; Edinburgh, 1710). In this last Sibbald professed to believe that Pitcairne had not written the *Dissertatio*. Pitcairne refers sourly to this in a letter dated 6 January 1711 (Johnston 1979: 65–6). The grudge clearly was life-long.

For James VII's fifty-fifth birthday on 14 October 1688 Pitcairne wrote a congratulatory Latin poem, which also celebrated the birth of the king's son and heir on 10 June of that year (Macqueen and Macqueen 2009: 212). The timing was unfortunate. Less than a month later William of Orange had descended on England and, by Christmas, James VII had reached Paris. The subsequent course of events has already been described.

The Phanaticks, together with some of Pitcairne's best Latin poems – two examples are the epitaph on Viscount Dundee and the poem on the Edinburgh taverns (Macqueen and Macqueen 2009: 72, 108–12) – show his reactions to the situation as it affected Scotland. Not so well known is *Ad Rob. Lindesium, 1689* (To Robert Lindsay, 1689; Macqueen and Macqueen 2009: 66–8), in which he summons his old friend back from the dead to witness what has happened. He begs Lindsay to return, appropriately accompanied by his 'great-grandfather', Sir David Lindsay of the Mount, scourge of the pre-Reformation Catholic hierarchy in Scotland. The presbyterian equivalent deserves the same treatment:

> Te nobis, te redde tuis, promissa daturus
>   Gaudia; sed Proavo sis comitante redux.

Namque novos cives mutataque regna videbis,
  Passaque Teutonicas Sceptre Britanna manus,
Legatosque Deûm Populo mandata ferentes –   (5–9)

(Restore yourself to us, to your own, to give us promised joys, but
come back accompanied by your great-grandfather. For you will
see a new citizenry and changed kingdoms, the British sceptre
suffering the grasp of a German and the deputies of the Gods
transferring their commission to the people)

'Promised joys' ('promissa ... gaudia') refers to the pledge given in
the dream related above. Pitcairne wishes to die rather than live under
the new order. 'Redux' in line 6 has Virgilian associations, the return
to earth of the virgin Astraea in the messianic *Eclogue* IV, most notably
applied to the 1660 Restoration of Charles II, as in Dryden's *Astræa
Redux. A Poem on the Happy Restoration and Return of His Sacred
Majesty Charles the Second* (London, 1660). *Redux* and the imperative
Reddite, 'Return!', 'Restore!', both later became Jacobite catch-phrases.
The 'new citizenry' are the presbyterian exiles who returned with
William, who is styled 'German' because he was prince of Nassau
(Wiesbaden, Germany) as well as Orange (France). In *The Phanaticks*,
1.1, 218, he is called 'the bullie of 20 or 30 german Lairds'. The 'deputies of the Gods' are the presbyterian clergy and ruling elders, demo-
cratically 'called' or elected by the congregation, a process of which
Pitcairne disapproved; cf., e.g., the words of the Moderator to Whigridne
in 1.3, 90–93: 'My Lord, by his providence, we've gott a Comission
from the zealous websters, souters and godlie women in St Andrews
for your Lordship to represent them in this Judicatorie.' For the most
part, indeed, Pitcairne's poem is aimed at presbyterian ministers and
elders, regarded as diabolic figures, with whom only David Lindsay and
Rhadamanthus, Judge of the Underworld, are competent to deal.

Pitcairne's parody of Horace, *Odes* 1.12, *Proceres Scotorum Anno
MDCXC* (Scots Worthies in the Year 1690; Macqueen and Macqueen
2009: 216–21), reads almost like a preview of the cast in *The Phanaticks*. *David Veneri/ Venus Davidi* (David to Venus/ Venus to David;
Macqueen and Macqueen 2009: 102–7) tells of an episode in the career
of David Williamson, in the play Mr Solomon Cherrietrees. Further
parallels are noted in the Commentary.

The rest of Pitcairne's life may be treated more briefly. On 26
December 1691 he accepted an invitation from the Senatus to join the
professoriate of the distinguished University of Leiden. This seemed
likely to be the culmination of his medical career and, initially, he was

very successful. His inaugural lecture, *Archibaldi Pitcarnii oratio qua ostenditur medicinam ab omni philosophorum secta esse liberam; et exemplo docetur quantam utilitatem medicis offerre possit mathesis* (Lecture by Archibald Pitcairne which demonstrates the freedom of medicine from all metaphysical dogma and by example demonstrates the great utility of mathematics to medicine) was published at Leiden in 1692. His salary was twice substantially increased. In the summer of 1693, however, he left after only three semesters. In August of that year he married Elizabeth Stevenson, daughter of Sir Archibald Stevenson already mentioned, and settled in Edinburgh. Five children of the marriage, four daughters and a son, survived to maturity. During his time in the Netherlands, or shortly after his return, he wrote a hudibrastic poem about the 1692 General Assembly, with a tongue-in-cheek title, *Babell; or The Assembly; a Poem, MDCXCII. Written in the Irish Tongue and Translated into Scottish for the Benefite of the Leidges. By A.P. A Well Wisher to the Cause.* This now survives, so far as I know, only in a Glasgow University Library manuscript, although others once existed (Kinloch 1830: xiv).

In 1694 he and his friend the surgeon Alexander Monteith (d. 1713) successfully petitioned the Town Council for the provision of bodies for public dissection. 'I doe propose, if it be granted, to make better emprovements, in anatomie, than have been made at Leyden these thrittie years' (Johnston 1979: 19).

Pitcairne and his father-in-law headed a faction in the College of Physicians which disagreed, politically and scientifically with the other Fellows. The division came to a head in 1695–96 with the suspension of Pitcairne and a subsequent unsuccessful attempt at a take-over by his party. Pitcairne blamed Sibbald for the debacle. It was not until November 1704 that he figured once more at a meeting. He was never again elected to office.

The affair does not seem to have affected his professional standing. In 1699 he received the honorary degree of MD from King's College, Aberdeen. By an accident of weather on his way home he met a young country schoolmaster, Thomas Ruddiman (1674–1757), who so impressed him that he invited him to Edinburgh. There Ruddiman, an accomplished Latinist, eventually became Keeper of the Advocates' Library, in addition to being a printer and publisher who, among much else, printed many of Pitcairne's poems as broadsheets and, much later, edited his *Selecta Poemata* (Edinburgh, 1727). Pitcairne helped Ruddiman in the preparation of the latter's edition of Gavin Douglas's *Aeneid* (Edinburgh, 1710) and his edition of George Buchanan's

Opera (Edinburgh, 1715), for which he received effusive posthumous thanks.

In January 1700 an intercepted letter from Pitcairne to his London friend Dr Robert Gray was regarded as seditious and in consequence he was arrested and briefly imprisoned in the Edinburgh Tolbooth. Two days later the Privy Council released him under the condition that he should 'live peaceably under and with all submission, to the present Government of his Majesty King William, And that he shall not Act Consult or Contrive any thing in prejudice therof, nor shall not Converse or Correspond with any Rebells' (Johnston 1979: 28). Obviously he was regarded as a Jacobite sympathizer and potential rebel, as indeed he was, and remained so for the rest of his life.

In the same year a discreetly Jacobite and episcopalian poem, *Gualteri Dannistoni ad Georgium Buchananum Epistola et Buchanani Responsum* (The Letter of Walter Dennistoun to George Buchanan and Buchanan's Reply; Macqueen and Macqueen 2009: 188–31) was published in Edinburgh, anonymously, but with the suggestion that it is the work of the recently deceased Walter Dennistoun – as indeed was partly the case. Also in 1700, as part of the Edinburgh celebrations for the birthday on 10 June of the exiled Prince of Wales and in condemnation of King William's failure to support the Darien scheme for Scottish foreign trade, Pitcairne wrote the innocuously named *Fabula 2. Lib. 1. Phaedri Metaphrasis* (Paraphrase of Phaedrus, Fable 2, Book 1; Macqueen and Macqueen 2009: 88–93), the story of King Log, King Stork and the Frogs. King Log is James VII, King Stork is William, and the Frogs are primarily the Scots, now suffering intolerable tyranny under the Stork.

There is less to record of Pitcairne's latter years. In 1701 *Archibaldi Pitcarnii Dissertationes Medicæ* (Medical Writings by Archibald Pitcairne) was published at Rotterdam. The death of King William in 1702 occasioned brief but heartfelt celebrations (Macqueen and Macqueen 2009: 224–7), while an address to the departed Charles II, celebrating the return of the Stewarts in the person of Queen Anne, daughter of James VII, at the same time suggested that, as soon as her half-brother came of age, the Queen should hand the sovereignty over (Macqueen and Macqueen 2009: 86). In 1703 he wrote a short satirical play or interlude, *Tollerators and Con-Tollerators* (Kinloch 1830: 70–78), dealing with the parliamentary obfuscation of a bill, proposed by John Lyon, 2nd earl of Strathmore (1663–1712) and supported by the joint Secretary, George Mackenzie, 1st earl of Cromartie (1630–1714), allowing toleration of episcopal clergy and congregations. Pitcairne only refers in passing to the 1707 Union of the Scottish with the English parliament and to the abortive Jacobite invasion of 1708.

In 1709 *Poemata Selecta*, a collection of seventeen Latin poems with a coded subtitle, was printed, perhaps to mark the Prince's 21st birthday. The sheets appear never to have been bound and were distributed in loose form, but appear to have had a wide circulation. The Bodleian exemplar (Antiq.d.X.7(1)) contains holograph alterations, incorporated elsewhere in an errata slip, which indicate that, although Pitcairne had long held to the ancient origin of the Scottish kingdom, his opinion had now changed.

In *The Phanaticks* the mere mention of a saint's day is enough to make the presbyterian Old Ladie faint (5.2, 113). The establishment had anathematized any observation of the festivals of the Christian Year. Pitcairne took early advantage of this in poems which usually also endow the festivals with a covert Jacobite significance. The feast-day of Margaret, Queen of Scotland, on 10 June was peculiarly appropriate. Like many others, he treated 30 January, the anniversary of the execution of Charles, King and Martyr, and 29 May, the birthday of Charles II and anniversary of his Restoration, as religious occasions. In later life he found many other more or less appropriate possibilities (Macqueen and Macqueen 2009: 78, 92, 94–5, 142, 144, 158 and 246–62).

In the later poems he often hints at the dangerous possibility of a Hanoverian succession. One poem, *Ad Annam Britannam* (Macqueen and Macqueen 2009: 238) is explicit:

> Anna *Stuartorum* Decus et Spes altera Regum,
>> Quos Sibi, quos reddi prisca *Caledon* avet,
> Este bonae, Faustaeque Tuis Rex *Anna Stuartis*,
>> Et nos *Teutonico* non onerate jugo.

> (Anna, ornament and second hope of the Stewart Kings, for whose Restoration ancient Caledonia longs, may you, Anna, and the King, together be good and favourable to your Stewarts. Do not burden us with a Teutonic yoke!)

By 'Rex' (the King) Pitcairne intends the Old Pretender, but the status of Anne as *de facto* monarch is indicated by the feminine gender of the plural adjectives 'bonae, Faustaeque' (good and favourable).

Pitcairne died on 20 October 1713, well before the accession of George I. A few months earlier the last of his books, an expanded version of *Dissertationes Medicæ*, had appeared (Edinburgh, 1713). It was dedicated, appropriately on the tenth of June, to his God and his Prince, 'Deo suo et Principi opus hoc consecrat Archibaldus Pitcarnius

Scotus, 10 Junii, 1713' (Archibald Pitcairne, Scot, dedicated this work to God and his Prince, 10 June 1713).

After his death his extensive library was purchased by the Czar Peter the Great of Russia (1672–1725) and included in the Library of the Russian Academy of Science, opened in 1714.

David Gregorie*

David Gregorie was born in Aberdeen on 5 June 1659, the fourth child of the physician David Gregorie (1625–1720) and his first wife, Jean (d. 1671). At least according to legend, the Aberdeen Gregories had originally been MacGregors, the royal, but notorious clan, descended from Girig or Grig (d. 889), king of Scotland. Their savage victory (1603) over another clan, the Colquhouns of Luss, at Glenfruin in Dunbartonshire, led to an Act of Council abolishing the name and commanding those who bore it to adopt another. Despite this and subsequent measures taken against them, the MacGregors remained loyal to the Stewart line up to and beyond the 1688 Revolution. 'The MacGregors to a man attached themselves during the Civil War to the cause [of Charles I] ... Upon the Restoration, King Charles, in the first Scottish Parliament of his reign (statute 1661, chap. 195) annulled the various acts against the clan Gregor, and restored them to the full use of their family name ... setting forth, as a reason for this lenity, that those who were formerly designed MacGregors had, during the late troubles, conducted themselves with such loyalty and affection to his Majesty, as might justly wipe off all memory of former miscarriages ... Upon the Revolution, an influence inimical to this unfortunate clan, said to be the same with that which afterwards dictated the massacre of Glencoe, occasioned the re-enaction of the penal statutes against the MacGregors' (Scott 1818: Introduction).

If there is any truth in the legend, the adoption of the name Gregorie shows that at least one branch of the clan was prepared to submit to the penal ordinances and, later, make no attempt to take advantage of the act of 1661. Gregories and MacGregors were alike Episcopalians.

The young David probably began his education at Aberdeen Grammar School, followed by entrance to Marischal College, Aberdeen, where he remained from 1671 to 1675. As was a not unusual practice at the time, he left without taking a degree.

---

* This section is based almost entirely on the biography by Dr Anita Guerrini in *OxfDNB* and on material from Dr David Money's study, *The English Horace* (Money 1998). I am grateful to both for permission to use their material.

It has already been noted that David was a nephew of the mathematician James Gregorie, on whose death in 1675 his papers came into the possession of his brother, David's father (James Gregorie's son was still an infant). The young man made good use of them; between 1675 and 1683 he turned himself into a very competent mathematician. The family medical tradition, however, remained strong. In September 1679 he went abroad and matriculated as a medical student at Leiden. Some months later mathematics resumed its domination and, while travelling by way of Rotterdam and Paris to London, he acquainted himself with the achievements of Descartes, the Dutchman Johann van Waveren Hudde (1628–1704) and Pierre de Fermat. His interests included the application of mathematical concepts to natural philosophy; in Paris he sketched several instruments in the Observatory; in London he attended a meeting of the Royal Society and made notes on Boyle's air-pump and Newton's reflector telescope (his uncle had already invented one, the Gregorian, but the grinding of mirrors to the required accuracy had proved beyond the skill of the workman to whom it had been entrusted). He returned home in 1681 and spent most of the next two years in further close study of his uncle's papers. By this time he and Pitcairne were well acquainted.

In October 1683, under the circumstances already mentioned (above, p. xxxiv), he was elected to the Edinburgh chair formerly held by his uncle. He was granted the degree of MA in November and shortly afterwards delivered his inaugural lecture, *De analyseos geometriae progressu et incrementis* (The progress and growth of analytic geometry). A year later his first book appeared, *Exercitatio geometrica de dimensione figurarum sive specimen methodi generalis: dimetiendi quasvis figuras* (A geometric approach to the measurement of series, or, a proof of a general methos for establishing a limit for all kinds of series). This was a development of his uncle's work on limits and infinite series, important in the development of the differential calculus.

Gregorie sent a copy to Newton, acknowledging his debt to the latter's work. This prompted Newton to begin preparing his own work for publication. Gregorie wrote Newton a laudatory letter on receipt of a copy of the *Principia* in 1687 and began a voluminous commentary, *Notae in Isaaci Newtoni 'Principia'* (Notes on Isaac Newton's *Principia*), on which he worked intermittently for the rest of his life.

In 1684 John Craig (above, pp. xxiv–xxv) became one of Gregorie's students, publishing in London in 1685 his own first work, *Methodus figurarum lineis rectis & curvis comprehensarum quadraturas determinandi* (A method for determining the squares of figures bounded by straight lines and curves), which probably owed something to Gregorie's influence. In it he made use of Leibnitz's differential calculus (the Newtonian version had not yet been published). Craig graduated MA in 1687.

As much as Pitcairne, Gregorie disliked the 1688 Revolution and its aftermath. One pleasing incident, however, was that in 1690 his father handed over to him the paternal estate of Kinnairdy, Banffshire. Gregorie survived the purgation of the university, but his position obviously became uncomfortable. He became a candidate for the Savilian chair of astronomy at Oxford, which fell vacant in 1691. He went to England in the summer of that year and succeeded in gaining support from Newton and the Astronomer Royal, John Flamsteed (1646–1719).

Newton 's letter of support read:

> Being desired by Mr David Gregory Mathematick Professor at the Colledge in Edinburgh to certifie my knowledge of him, and having known him by his printed Mathematical performances, and by discoursing with travellers from Scotland, and of late by conversing with him, I do account him one of the most able and judicious mathematicians of his age now living. He is very well skilled in analysis and Geometry both new and old. He has been conversant in the best writers about Astronomy and understands that Science very well. He is not only acquainted with books, but his invention in mathematical things is also good. He has performed his duty at Edinburgh with credit as I hear and advanced the mathematicks. He is reputed the greatest mathematician in Scotland, and that deservedly, so as my knowledge reaches, for I esteem him an ornament to his country, and upon these accounts recommendable to the Electors of the Astronomy professor into the place at Oxford now vacant.
>
> (Bodleian, MS Rawl.D.742, fo. 7, quoted in Money 1998: 136)

Gregorie was appointed to the chair in December 1691 and, early in 1692, took the Oxford degrees of MA and MD on admission as a Fellow of that home of Scots in Oxford, Balliol College. In 1692 he was made a Fellow of the Royal Society. As his papers and his correspondence with Pitcairne indicate, he retained his medical interest and, in a small way, even practised. In 1705 he was elected an Honorary Fellow of the Edinburgh Royal College of Physicians, as were two other friends of Pitcairne, the London physician Dr Robert Gray and [Sir] Hans Sloane (1660–1753), whose collections were later to become the basis of the British Museum.

Most summers Gregorie returned to Scotland and it was there, in 1695, that he married Elizabeth Oliphant, a marriage celebrated by the

Oxford scholar and Latin poet, Anthony Alsopp (1669–1726), in an epithalamium which emphasizes Gregorie's Jacobite and Episcopalian leanings:

Tu conjugali mollior in toro
Spectas tumultus, et miserabiles
   Ecclesiæ jam jam ruentis
      Relliquias, dubiumque regnum

Vides (obortis non sine lachrymis)
Tristes minas Cæsariæ Domus
   Pulsosque principes avitis
      Sedibus, atque iterum exulantes.   (Money 1998: 285–6)

(More relaxed in your marriage bed you watch the tumults [of the Nine Years War against Louis XIV] and see (not without tears springing up) a doubtful reign [that of King William] the miserable relics of a church on the point of collapse [the Church of England as well as the Episcopal church in Scotland is probably intended] and threats to the Imperial House, princes thrust from their ancestral seats and once more in exile.)

On his way back to Oxford with his bride, he wrote an ironic letter to Arthur Charlett (1655–1722), Master of University College, from Edinburgh which contrasts city circumstances with these in his native North-East. It might well serve as an illustrative footnote to *The Phanaticks*:

Nothing less than dragoons can displace them [the Episcopalian clergy] in those malignant Northern places. But heir in the city the Episcopal meeting houses are shut, and indeed the Magistrates of the Town bid as fair to be Canonized in the Church that has no use for a Calendar [of Saints] as any ever did. The only commendable piece of government that I have observed since I came from the North, is that this day sailed from Leith Road, half a dozen ships to Bordeaux, to fetch Claret, of which we continue very well provided.
   (Bodleian, MS Ballard 24.23, fo. 38; quoted in Money 1998: 137)

Gregorie and his wife had nine children, two of whom survived to maturity. During his Oxford tenure, he published several important works and edited classical mathematical texts. He was popular with his students, several of whom later achieved some distinction. During his last years he suffered ill-health. On 12 October 1708 Pitcairne wrote in a letter to Colin Campbell: 'Mean tyme my dear doctor is, in my opinion and in his owne, dying of a palpitation and polypus cordis [malignant growth on the heart]. He's advys'd to goe to Bath for it, a ridiculous advyce' (Johnston 1979: 54). Events had already anticipated Pitcairne.

On returning to London after less than a week at Bath, Gregorie had
died at Maidenhead, Berkshire, on 10 October. Pitcairne commemorated
him in an ode addressed to Robert Gray (which, incidentally, shows that
he believed the Gregories to be MacGregors and of royal origin):

Ille qui terris latitat Britannis
Solus, aut nullo sapiens amico,
Ille quam debet miser inquefelix
        Vivere, Grai?

Namque nos liquit decus ille ævi
Scotici, sic Di voluere, liquit
Regiæ stirpis decus atque fama
        Gregorianæ.

Ille Neutonum incolumem lubenti
Narrat Euclidi Siculoque Divo,
Miraque augusti docet almus Angli
        Cœpta stupentes,

Deinde Pergæum reducem novumque
Acris Halleii studiis; sed ipse
Quam graves nuper tulerit labores
        Dicere parcit.

Ista necquicquam memoramus: Ille
Immemor nostri, patruoque gaudens,
Nos ope & cura sapientis orbos
        Liquit amici.

        (Macqueen and Macqueen 2009: 160–3)

(He who lurks in Britain, alone or as a friendless savant, what
obligation has he, Gray, to live in wretched unhappiness? ... As
the Gods have willed, that ornament of the era in Scotland, that
ornament and renown of the royal race of Gregor, has left us. He
is now giving news of Newton, still with us, to a delighted Euclid
and the divine Sicilian [Archimedes]: he graciously instructs his
astonished audience in the wonderful work undertaken by the
great Englishman. Then [he tells how] the Pergean [Apollonius
of Perge, third-century BC author of *Conics*] has been recovered
with new material produced by the labours of acute Halley: but he
modestly refrains from talking about the important tasks recently
undertaken by himself. We bring those things to mind in vain.
Forgetful of us, and happy to see his uncle again, he leaves us
bereft of the support and attention of our learned friend.)

Pitcairne refers to Gregorie's edition of Euclid (Gregorie 1703) and to the edition of the *Conics* of Apollonius of Perge (third century BC) undertaken by him in collaboration with Edmund Halley (1656–1742; Halley 1710), but only published after Gregorie's death. Even at this point Pitcairne's emphasis on the close intellectual relationship between James and David Gregorie should be noted.

[Sir] Bertram Stott

To the best of the editor's knowledge, Stott is known only as author of a single Latin poem (Appendix II), by references in Pitcairne's own Latin poems and by a single reference in his letters. He appears, nevertheless, to have had a lively personality.

He first appears, c. 1690, as the recipient of Pitcairne's verses on the Edinburgh taverns (Macqueen and Macqueen 2009: 108–13). He is the *Advena*, the stranger visiting Edinburgh for the first time, described simply as 'Mr B. Stote'. There is no hint of rank beyond that of MA in some university. The poem, supposedly by the recently deceased Walter Dennistoun and addressed to John Ker (c. 1680–1741), 5th earl and 1st duke of Roxburghe, has Stott and Pitcairne together enjoying the nobleman's hospitality and drinking his health: 'Jamque bibit nectar pleno Pitcarnius ore,/ Jam Kerum læti Stotus et ille canunt' (13–14) (Now Pitcairne drinks his fill of nectar. Now Stott and he sing joyously of Ker). Stott's rank is not mentioned.

In the course of a letter dated 20 September 1707, addressed to John Erskine (1675–1732), 22nd earl of Mar, Secretary of State for Scotland, Pitcairne remarks: 'I send Your Lordship poor Stote's epitaph made by Wattie Danniston [Walter Dennistoun].' The text which follows also occurs, with small variations, in two other sources, a broadside preserved in NLS, and the 1727 *Selecta Poemata* (Macqueen and Macqueen 2009: 194):

> Stote Tuae moerens astat Pitcarnius urnae,
> > Qui sibi tam plausit se placuisse Tibi.
> Ille Tuos animi mores veneratus, & artes
> > Reddere, Quae Superis Te valuere parem.
> Te jubet invitus, jubet invitusque valere,
> > Dimidiumque animae, Deliciasque suae.

> (Pitcairne, who so applauded himself because he had pleased you, Stott, mourns as he stands at your tomb. He who venerated your character and your arts, unwillingly bids you give back the qualities which had the power to put you on a par with the gods. Unwillingly he bids you farewell, the darling half of his soul.)

In the NLS print the epitaph is headed 'Ad Bertramum Stotum Equitem Anglum' (To Bertram Stott, Knight, Englishman); in *Selecta Poemata*, however, for 'Equitem' (Knight), we have a word which does not imply a title, 'Armigerum' (Squire, Esquire). Ruddiman may have deliberately corrected the wording of the earlier print. We have thus no certain knowledge whether or not Stott had a title.

Sources and Influences

Because the action of *The Phanaticks* is so closely linked to the religious and political developments of the late seventeenth century, it is not possible to indicate any single literary source. On the title-page of the 1722 prints the play is described as 'A Comedy, by a Scots Gentleman', but it is difficult to see any significant influence by either of the two earlier Scots comedies so designated, *Philotus* ((Mill 1933) or *Pamphilus d Amore* (Burel 1590/1). Sir David Lyndsay's earlier *Ane Satyre of the Thrie Estaitis* offers a closer parallel; it too deals with contemporary religious and political affairs and one might even see, in one, the entry of the Captain of the Guard (5.3, 103) as corresponding to that of Divyne Correctioun in the other.

In *The Phanaticks*, however, characterization is more complex; even the least individual among the persons – Mr Shittle, Mr Turncoat, Mr Orthodox – are less abstract, farther removed from the Moralitie tradition, than Wantonnes, Sensualitie, Flatterie, Falset and Dissait. Less abstract still are Mr Timothie Turbulent, Mr Salathiel Littlesense, Mr Covenant Planedealer and Mr Solomon Cherrietrees, in whom a suggestive biblical first name is combined with a more particular and less flattering second. As the **Drammatis Personæ** indicates, each is modelled on a living person, well-known to the original audience. The names of Lord Whigriddne and Lord Huffie are simpler and, although no identification is given, the disguise is easy to penetrate.

Quotations are sometimes revealing, as, for instance, that in **Prologue** 35–6, 'Critiks for need, as ther ar many such/ Quhom art & nature hav not betterd much', an adaptation of the opening couplet in Ben Jonson's prologue to the anglicized version of *Every Man in His Humour* (Jonson 1960: 1, 559). In conjunction with lines 27–9,

> True Comedie should humore represent.
> We think for ones we've weall enough hitt on't.
> No character too wyld nor yet extravagant,

xlix

it becomes probable that the authors intended the play to be a Jonsonian comedy of humours, featuring

> deeds and language, such as men do use,
> And persons, such as comedy would choose,
> When she would shew an image of the times,
> And sport with human follies, not with crimes,
> Except we make them such, by loving still
> Our popular errors, when we know they're ill.
>
> (Jonson 1960: 1, 560, 21–6)

Pertinent to this is a remarkable passage from the Induction to Jonson's late comedy, *The Magnetic Lady* (1632; Jonson 1960: 2, 507), which first appeared posthumously in the 1640 *Works*:

> *Boy*: The author beginning his studies of this kind, with *Every Man in his Humour*; and after *Every Man out of his Humour*; and since, continuing in all his plays, especially those of the comic thread, whereof the *New Inn* was the last, some recent humours still, or manners of men, that went along with the times; finding himself now near the close, or shutting up of his circle, hath fancied to himself, in idea, this Magnetic Mistress: a lady, a brave bountiful house-keeper, and a virtuous widow; who having a young niece, ripe for a man, and marriageable, he makes that his centre attractive, to draw thither a diversity of guests, all persons of different humours to make up his perimeter. And this he hath called HUMOURS RECONCILED.
> *Prober*: A bold undertaking, and far greater than the reconciliation of both churches; the quarrel between humours having been much the ancienter; and, in my poor opinion, the root of all schism and faction both in church and commonwealth.

When Jonson refers to 'both churches' and 'schism and faction both in church and commonwealth', he probably intends the struggle, in 1632 not yet approaching its climax, between Charles I and the largely Calvinist (Presbyterian) English Parliament, which eventually led to the English Civil Wars (1642–80), the execution of Archbishop Laud (1645) and of Charles himself (1649). The play is in some sort an allegory of the English political and religious scene, with reconciliation of the two factions the over-hopeful intention. The phrase 'Humours Reconciled' is thus eirenic. In *The Phanaticks*, however, reconciliation is impossible. The play ends with the two sides farther apart than ever.

The names, as well as the words and actions, of the male characters indicate the humour, the dominating aspect, of the character, obviously with Lord Huffie and Mr Timothie Turbulent, still palpably with Will and Frank. The same applies to the newsmongers, Novell and Mr Abednego Visioner, the latter presumably a Presbyterian minister. The major debt lies elsewhere (see below), but the two owe something to Cymbal and Fitton, managers of the Staple of News in Jonson's play of that name (Jonson 1960: 2, 347–425). Parody of the language and manner of the English Puritan (usually a Calvinist) appears in such figures as Tribulation Wholesome and Ananias (*The Alchemist*) or Zeal-of-the-Land Busy and Win-the-Fight Littlewit (*Bartholomew Fair*).

Attacks on Puritans and Presbyterians, of course, make a regular appearance both in Jacobean and Caroline, and in Restoration drama. One might instance, as a minor example, an anonymous play brought to my notice by my friend Professor J. J. McGavin. The title conveys the substance: *The Scottish politike Presbyter, Slaine by the English Independent. Or, The Independent Victory over the Presbyterian Party. The rigour of the Scotch Government, their conniving and bribing: the lewdnesse and debaucherie of Elders in secret. A Tragi-Comedie Printed in the Yeere 1647*. The date is significant. By 1647 Oliver Cromwell, an Independent, had sufficient power to act against the Parliament which had pledged itself by the Solemn League and Covenant to abolish Episcopalianism, in England, and in its place establish Presbyterianism on the Scottish model. In Act 3 Liturgie (the Church of England) is put on trial and condemned by Directory (Presbyterianism, imported from Scotland). In Act 5 Anarchie (the Independents) finds Directory in bed with his (Anarchie's) wife who represents the treacherous English Parliament. He kills both.

A speech during this scene suggests, oddly enough, that Anarchie, despite his name, is on the side of the old order:

> O my fine Directory cams't thou from Scotland hither, to cheat us out of our Religion, our lives, our King, and covering thy ills with vertue's cloak, act even those crimes, which but to heare them nam'd, would fright the Caniballs; and shall we not strive to circumvent thee?

King Charles was in the hands of the Scots, from whom Cromwell and his followers hoped to ransom him, although not with any view to his restoration.

A similar suggestion appears in the brief, but somewhat incoherent, Prologue:

> Presbyterie and Independencie
> Have long time strove for the precedencie:
> Here one kills t'other, when we see him die,
> With his destroyer fell by Liturgie.

If this reading is correct, the anonymous author badly misread the situation.

There is no evidence that this play had any direct influence on *The Phanaticks*. I quote it because it offers a distorted image of an earlier political and religious situation, resembling that of 1691, but seen in an English mirror.

In the **Preface** (Appendix I; below, pp. 229–30; cf. too Clancy and Pittock 2007: 261) Pitcairne defends the dramatic unity of the play against two charges. The first is 'that our play is made up of two plots. The one of Love and the other about the General Assembly ... reasone will sufficiently defend us. Our Intire and uniform plot is to represent the villanies and follies of the Presbyterians in their publickt meetings and private transactions of their life' – a defence which (see below) seems entirely adequate. The second charge is that the part played by Lord Huffie is superfluous.

Pitcairne responds obliquely: 'And I doe not see but this Scene agrees also well with the principall plot, as the Reconcilment of Thais and Phaedria in Terences Eunuch with the marriadge of Chairea and Chremes's sister, which is principally intended by the Poet Yet it is thought Regular eneugh by all the Judicious Criticks.' The reference is to the *Eunuchus* (161 BC), a comedy by Terence (184–159 BC) with a plot that at first sight seems far removed from that of *The Phanaticks*. Phaedria and Chairea are brothers, both citizens of Athens. Phaedria loves the courtesan Thais, a Rhodian, and she him. When Thais was still a child, her mother had been given a little Athenian girl, Pamphila by name, who had been kidnapped by pirates. The child was reared as a sister to Thais. After the latter had grown up and left Rhodes for Athens, her mother died, bequeathing Pamphila to her unscrupulous brother, who, in turn, sold her to one of Thais' former lovers, the braggart soldier Thraso. In Athens, meanwhile, Thais and Phaedria have met and fallen in love. She has also discovered Pamphila's family, and is eager to restore her to the only surviving relative, Chremes, her brother. On his arrival in Athens with the girl, Thraso offers to return her to Thais, on condition that he be restored to her favour. To the great distress of Phaedria, and despite his counter-offer to her of a eunuch and an Ethiopian slave-girl, Thais agrees. She also sends Chremes an invitation to visit her on an important, but unspecified, matter. He is suspicious, but accepts. Chaeria sees Pamphila as she is being delivered to the house of Thais, and immediately falls desperately in love with her. During the absence of Thais, he disguises himself in the clothes of the eunuch promised by his brother, and so enters the house. The household servants have no suspicions and leave him alone with Pamphila. He rapes her, an experience which gives him such pleasure that he wishes to repeat it again and again. After various subsequent complications, Pamphila's relationship to Chremes is satisfactorily established and she and Chaerea become engaged. Thais and Phaedria are reconciled – but Thraso receives certain concessions.

Terence based his play on a Greek comedy by Menander (342/1–293/89 BC), now lost, also called *The Eunuch*, but added two characters, Thraso and his slave Gnatho, from another Menandrian comedy, also now lost, called *The Flatterer*. One result of this 'contamination' was the minor share in the happy ending obtained by Thraso, a share which has led to much critical discussion both in antiquity and in modern times. It is this to which Pitcairne refers. Like Thraso, Lord Huffie is a *miles gloriosus*, but one who at the conclusion is left humiliated. His part is included because he is 'a great Hero in the Reformation, and that all the matters of fact said about him are very trew' (Appendix I, *ut cit.*). He fits perfectly, that is to say, into the general pattern of the play.

Pitcairne does not mention the main point of resemblance between *The Eunuch* and *The Phanaticks*, that in both plays the lover, or lovers, approach the beloved in a harmless-seeming disguise, in the first, that of a eunuch, in the second that of two Presbyterian clergymen just back from exile in Holland. The Presbyterian approach to sexual and marital relationships is presented as sterile, for instance, in Violetta's bitter remark (3.1, 43–6), 'some revrend Spark in a band and short Cloack, with the patrimonie of the good gift of prayer (quich perhaps he will putt in exercise 2 hours on his bridall night, quhen I would wish he wer looking after some other thing)'. Even the assault on Laura by Mr Solomon (3.2) is essentially voyeuristic, as Laura herself points out: 'You have not the things cane allow for pressing into a Ladie's retirement so earlie. I mean Youth and Gallantrie' (3.2, 31–3). Solomon, in other words, is past it. Rachel's premarital pregnancy does not demonstrate the contrary; it shows that she and Mr Wordie are hypocrites – neither is truly a Presbyterian. Terentian overtones provide dramatic irony in Will's words (2.2, 78), long before Violetta has proposed the disguise, 'And if I faill, I wish I turne Eunoch'.

Although Wycherley's character, Mr Horner, represents an expansion and elaboration of the eunuch theme, I see no trace of *The Country Wife* (Weales 1966: 255–362) in *The Phanaticks*. The name Mr Covenant Planedealer, however, does imply a reference to Wycherley's last play, *The Plain-Dealer* (Weales 1966: 377–516). Some aspects of the character, or 'humour' of Manly, the Plain-Dealer, resemble those of

Mr Covenant. Novell, in *The Phanaticks* the name of 'a Jacobite news monger', appears in *The Plain-Dealer* as that of 'a pert railing Coxcomb, and an Admirer of Novelties'.

Earlier in this Introduction (above, pp. xxix–xxx) I have indicated that *The Phanaticks* owes something to an earlier comedy, *Tarugo's Wiles*, by Pitcairne's relative, Thomas Sydserff (Sydserff 1668), itself a free rendering of *No puede ser el guardar una mujer* by Agustin Moreto y Cabaña. The debt to a later version of the same play is greater. John Crown (c. 1640–1712) was a prolific dramatist, one of whose plays, *City Politiques* (Crown 1683), offers a slightly disguised but extremely hostile account of the Popish Plot, with 'Dr' Titus Oates figuring as Dr Sanchy. His later comedy, *Sir Courtly Nice: or, It Cannot be* (Crown 1685) is less political. It was first performed shortly after the death of Charles II, who had himself suggested an adaptation of the Spanish play. The Prologue laments the king's death and celebrates the accession of his brother (in English terms James II) an event which the Popish Plot had been designed to frustrate:

> What nation upon Earth besides our own,
> But by a loss like ours had been undone?
> Ten Ages scarce such Royal worths display
> As *England* lost, and found in one strange day.
> One hour in sorrow and confusion hurld:
> And yet the next the envy of the World.   (5–8)

The Popish Plot had finally been exposed and Titus Oates publicly flogged:

> To stop the blessings that oreflow this day,
> What heaps o' Rogues we pil'd up in the way?
> We chose fit tooles against all good to strive,
> The sauciest, lewdest, Protestants alive.
> They would have form'd a blessed Church indeed,
> Upon a Turne-coat Doctor's lying Creed.   (11–16)

The play was extremely successful and continued to be performed well into the next century (Owen 2001: 389). For Pitcairne and his associates both this play and its 1668 predecessor had an immediate appeal.

Sir Courtly Nice is the story of two young women, Leonora and Violante, who are close friends. Leonora is the sister of Lord Belguard, who intends that she should marry the fop, Sir Courtly Nice. He also uses his fraternal authority to forbid her the company of any other young man, appointing as her governess their Aunt, an elderly, would-be-amorous spinster. As additional guardians, Crown interpolated two elderly men, Hothead, a Tory, 'A choleric Zealot against Fanaticks', and Testimony, 'A Canting, Hypocritical Fanatick', whose mutual animosity will, he thinks, prevent either from any improper approach to Leonora. In Act 5, however, Testimony contrives, as he mistakenly thinks, an opportunity to seduce Leonora. This turns out to be unsuccessful. She loves, and is loved by, Farewel, a young man whose family are hereditary enemies of the Belguards.

Belguard himself loves Violante, who returns his love, but refuses to marry him so long as he persists in his tyrannical ways with Leonora. The situation appears hopeless until the clever manoeuvres of Crack (the figure corresponding to Tarugo in Sydserff's play) enable Farewel to walk off with a masked Leonora, and so marry her. Sir Courtly Nice does likewise with another masked woman, who, to his horror, turns out to be the Aunt. Belguard finally sees the error of his ways and so is able to marry Violante.

Some details in *Sir Courtly Nice*, it will readily be noticed, stand in close correspondence to names or incidents in *The Phanaticks*, for the most part, naturally enough, in the love-story. In both, the plot turns on relations between two young men and two young women. Although Violante and Leonora are friends rather than sisters, their names resemble those of Violetta and Laura. Leonora has for guardian her maiden Aunt; their widowed Aunt, the Old Ladie, is guardian to Violetta and Laura. The fanatic, Testimony, tries to rape Leonora. The fanatic, Mr Solomon, tries to rape Laura. The religious and political opposition of Hothead and Testimony provides both background and comic relief in one, as does that of Novell and Visioner in the other. The appearance in both plays of such a pair of antagonists is particularly striking.

Tobin notes (Tobin 1972: 9) a number of earlier plays as possible analogues to *The Phanaticks* – *The Rump* (1660) by John Tatham (fl. 1632–64), *Cutter of Coleman Street* (1661) by Abraham Cowley (1618–67), *The Committee* (1662) by Sir Robert Howard (1626–98), and *The Roundheads* (1681), an adaptation of *The Rump* by Aphra Behn (1640–89). He singles out *Cutter of Coleman Street*, where he claims to find 'a definite parallel in courting by clerical guising', a parallel which I fail to see. There is evidence, however, that our authors had at least some acquaintance with the play; the name of the newsmonger, AbednegoVisioner, is based on a passage in which Cutter, in Puritan dress, seduces Tabitha by claiming, not to be a clergyman, but to have had a vision: 'Sister *Barebottle*, I must not be called *Cutter* any more, that is a name of *Cavalero* darkness, the Devil was a *Cutter* from the beginning, my name is now *Abednego*, I had a Vision which whisper'd to me through a Key-hole, Go call thy self *Abednego*' (Cowley 1663: 38). He continues about his visions for several scenes thereafter.

Howard's *The Committee* has perhaps a greater relevance. The group of ministers and elders in *The Phanaticks* is usually styled 'The Comitie'; see 1.2, 49, where it first occurs, and especially the earlier part of 4.2.; on one occasion (l. 30) it is called 'a sub-comitee' (a sub-committee, that is, of the General Assembly). Howard's play is set in the Cromwellian Commonwealth and the action turns on the attempt made by 'the honourable Committee of Sequestration' to dispossess two royalist gentlemen, Colonel Carlesse and Colonel Blunt, of their estates. The Committee are carrying out the work of the Parliamentary Commission for Sequestration. The members are Nehemiah Cacib (?), Joseph Blemish, Jonathan Headstrong and Ezekiel Scrape (again note the combination of a biblical first name with a less complimentary second), under the chairmanship of Mr Day, and with Obadiah as Clerk. While the Colonels are by no means inactive, their resistance to the Committee is masterminded by two women, Mrs Ruth and Mrs Arbella, both themselves Committee victims. With their success, at the end of the play, Mrs Ruth becomes the wife of Colonel Carlesse, Mrs Arbella of Colonel Blunt.

The Prologue implies that the term 'Committee', with the sense Parliamentary Committee or Commission, has a significance immediately recognizable by everyone in a Restoration audience:

> Not that the name Committee can be new,
> That has been too well known to most of you:
> But you may smile, for you have past your doom;
> The Poet dares not, his is still to come.   (17–20)

In *The Phanaticks*, the use of the word suggests that the instrument of Cromwellian oppression has returned. In Howard's play the Committee works against the former secular establishment, the gentry; the Comitie works against the former ecclesiastical establishment, the Episcopalians. In both, the purpose, self-aggrandizement, is identical. It may not be coincidence that in both plays two couples are involved, that the names of the male partners indicate their contrasting humours, and that the initiative is usually taken by the women.

The Play

The Phanaticks has the usual five acts, together with a Prologue and an Epilogue. Each act has three scenes, with the exception of the fourth, which has one more. One scene of each act is devoted to the Comitie (1.3, 2.3, 3.3, 4.2, 5.3). The appearance in each of Mr Solomon (David Williamson), not officially a member, suggests that the meetings take place at the West Church of Edinburgh, now St Cuthbert's, where he was minister. Lord Whigridne is inducted as a lay-member, an elder, at the first meeting and is present at the others, apart from that in 5.3, where his absence is explained by his membership of the Privy Council.

Will and Frank appear in 1.1, Violetta and Laura towards the end of 1.2. This latter scene also introduces Rachiel and Wordie, the lovers against whom the others are counterpointed. All the young women are set to disappoint the expectations of the Presbyterian Old Ladie, mother of Rachiel, aunt and guardian of Violetta and Laura. Will introduces himself to Violetta in Mr Solomon's church (2.2), where arrangements are made for them to meet in Lady Murray's 'yeards' (3.1). Here Violetta proposes the approach to the Old Ladie's lodging under clerical disguise, a device accepted by Will. In 4.1 Laura and Frank meet in Heriot's 'yeards', where Frank reluctantly accepts that such a disguise is necessary. In 5.2 the disguised Will and Frank pay a visit to the Old Ladie, from whose lodging they eventually walk off with Violetta and Laura, returning, now married, to confound the Old Ladie's hopes and also probably those of Mr Solomon and Mr Covenant. To add to the Old Ladie's distress, there is also the revelation of the consummated union of Rachiel and Wordie.

The two opening scenes serve to introduce the major characters, other than the members of the Comitie. The love affairs occupy four of the sixteen scenes in the play. The affairs of the Comitie occupy another five. The five that remain (2.1, 3.2, 4.3, 4.4, 5.1) seem at first sight to deal with quite extraneous matters. The first and third feature Lord Huffie, the second Mr Solomon's abortive attempt to seduce Laura. Fourth is the 'discourse' between Will and Frank in Parliament Close, which accompanies a dumb-show of politicians entering Parliament; fifth the argument at the Cross between Novell and Visioner. In this last, Lord Huffie makes a brief appearance.

Although apparently quite separate, these five scenes are nevertheless thematically linked to the main action. The opening scene, for instance, involves not only Will and Frank, but also Novell and Visioner, who occupy a considerable part of it and who expand the theme of Williamite versus Jacobite, introduced earlier by Will. They also make a brief appearance in 3.1, 174–80.

Although Lord Huffie makes no appearance at any of the later meetings of the Comitie, he is actively present during the first. In 3.1, 127–68 he becomes a willing accomplice in the nefarious schemes of Lord Whigridne.

Parallel to the discourse of Will and Frank in Parliament Close are their earlier discussions in 1.1, 41–105 (on the general state of the country under Whig government) and 3.1, 120–159 (on Presbyterian ministers and university teachers). The second of these is also accompanied by a dumb-show.

In 5.1 Novell and Visioner argue about the state of Scottish education. The focus is on mathematics and Latinity.

These anomalies fall into place with the realization that the play is built, not simply on the love-story or the actions of the Comitie, but, more generally, on the state of Scotland in 1691. Politics, churchmanship and education are the main themes. The play, in effect, is an extension of such Latin poems as Pitcairne's *Scotia Martio. 1689* (Scotland in March 1689), or *Proceres Scotorum Anno MDCXC* (Scots Worthies in the Year 1690) (Macqueen and Macqueen 2009: 68, 216–21). In place of a single developed action, it presents a series of tableaux, which present the overall tragicomic situation. In the primary love-story, for instance, the driving force is the determination of the girls to escape the yoke of the Kirk establishment, immediately represented by their aunt and the prospect of marriage to Mr Solomon, Mr Covenant or some such other. Violetta asks, 'but, Cusine, what thinke you of oure life & conversatione at our godlie Aunt's house? We see nothing but Whigge Ministers & old Phanatick Ladies, we hear nothing but long prayers and sensless tedious sermons and lecturs.' A little later she adds, 'I'le be ryd of this Impertinent nonsensicall Clatter by the first conveniencie, I assur you', to which Laura replies, 'And if I doe not the lyk, may I be made a Nun, a thing as Cross my nature as it is unbefitting my Complexioun' (1.2, 52–67). Their motivation is the need to escape.

That they are successful is evident. Violetta quickly gets the better of Will – that experienced rake finds himself helpless to do anything but fall in with her schemes. Laura realizes that Frank has a different temperament; her treatment of him differs accordingly, but to the same result. At their moment of triumph, Violetta ironically assumes an air of innocence when she asks, 'What think you? May we trust ourselves to these reverend Sparks?' Laura recognizes the truth and replies 'Lead on, Sister – you ar eldest. I will follow Instantlie.'

As their discourses indicate, Will and Frank share many of the girls' opinions. They are less concerned, however, with religious matters, more with political. Will's major concern is himself and his pleasures; he is inclined to take things easy, make the best of the world which he sees so clearly. Frank is less inclined in this direction, less at home with words; his tendency is towards action, as his encounter with Lord Huffie (5.2, 189–207) finally proves. Almost the sole indications of their ecclesiastical leanings occur in Will's description of the ministers (3.1, 121–159) and their choice of 'ane honest Curat', an ousted Episcopalian priest, to perform the marriage ceremony – 'a Guynea or two will be Charity to him perhaps' (3.1, 65–6). The girls, of course, would have refused any other.

Frank and Will's discussion of the state of the country in 1.1, 51–108 is essentially political and Jacobite. In 4.2 Will presents Frank with a series of portraits of the politicians under whose misrule the country is now suffering, although, for the most part, these politicians play no direct part in the action of the play. There are two exceptions, Lord Whigridne and Lord Huffie. Frank has already met the first, but neither has so far come across Lord Huffie, although, as has just been indicated, a meeting does occur later in the same day. Whigridne is not only an influential lay member of the Comitie, he is also the unscrupulous President of the Parliament and a Privy Councillor. Huffie is Governor of Edinburgh Castle, in effect commander-in-chief of the Scottish army, but with traits reminiscent of the Plautine and Terentian *miles gloriosus*. He too is a Privy Councillor, son of another important politician presented in the dumb-show, George, 1st earl of Melville (1636–1707), the Secretary of State, who had been Commissioner to the 1690 General Assembly.

Will and Frank belong to the class with the greatest attachment to the House of Stewart and Episcopalianism, the gentry and their tenant-farmers. The rougher boatmen, hirers and fiddlers (2.1) share something of this loyalty. Lay Presbyterian Williamites are the great landowners, aristocrats like Whigridne and Huffie and (among those presented in the dumb-show) the earl of Melville and viscount Stair. Linked with them are the more prosperous trades people, such as 'the zealous websters, souters and godlie women in St Andrews' (1.3, 91–2).

Successive scenes, 1.3 and 2.1, show Huffie under two aspects, both dubious. In the first he is the zealous Protestant champion and gatekeeper, scourge of the Lord, using the famous hunting whip with which he had lashed the lady of Mortonhall, near Edinburgh, when she attempted to stop him hunting in her grounds. In the second, despite his whip and protests of nobility, he is made to submit to the humble boatmen, hirers and fiddlers whom he has refused to pay for services rendered. The action takes place within the bounds of his seat of authority, Edinburgh Castle. The whip reappears in 3.1, when Huffie, on a hunting expedition, agrees to help Whigridne hunt after the Curates. In 4.3, Huffie makes a ridiculous use of his military authority in an attempt to prevent others from hunting in the area which he has specified, two miles around Edinburgh. Again the whip appears. In 4.4 he is *persona muta*, and in 5.2 he receives his comeuppance at the hands (and feet) of Frank. The treatment throughout approaches farce, but the targets, Huffie's abuse of his position, his hypocrisy and cowardice, are made abundantly clear.

In 5.1 Novell and Visioner discuss some of the intellectual, as opposed to theological, issues which divided opinion at the time. One is mathematics. I have already (above, pp. xxi–xxviii) discussed its importance. The Renaissance doctrine of a pure classical Latin style was accepted by Episcopalians, rejected by the majority of Presbyterians. So long as Latin remained the language of literature, science and learning generally, the acceptance or rejection of that tradition remained an important educational issue (see, e.g., Durkan in MacQueen 1990: 130–60). At a later date, the Episcopalian Thomas Ruddiman kept the tradition alive; Dr Johnson reveals the aftermath in his brief but mordant comment on Boswell's Latinity, 'Ruddiman is dead' (Boswell 1949: 1, 324).

I have described the play as a series of tableaux, but, of course, there is plot development in the love-story and a peripeteia in the actions of the Comitie, a peripeteia which strikingly evokes the doctrine of the Two Kingdoms. At the beginning of the play the Presbyterian ministers are Williamite, by the end they have abjured all secular kingship and called down divine vengeance even on King William. Their loyalties lie elsewhere.

The play offers itself as a comedy and the scenes are often very funny. Cameron (in Hook 1987: 195) singles out the dialogue between the Old Ladie, Will and Frank in 5.2, 54–74. My favourite is the scene of administrative chaos at the beginning of 4.2. Readers will choose their own favourite.

Staging

As has already been shown, diction and plot in *The Phanaticks* imply considerable familiarity with the work of earlier dramatists. Correspondingly the action fits with what is known of the Restoration theatre – the fore-stage with boxes above the doors: the proscenium arch and curtain: behind it, inner stage wings, shutters and borders to establish place and scenic effects. The earliest London theatres of the period were converted indoor real tennis courts, seating perhaps 400 (Langhans in Owen 2001: 3); in Edinburgh correspondingly the tennis court at Holyroodhouse was used as a theatre. It has now disappeared, but the surviving example at Falkland Palace in Fife will give some idea of the structure.

Stage directions sometimes indicate how scenes were to be played. An actor delivers the **Prologue** from the fore-stage, with the proscenium curtain drawn. On his exit, it opens with painted shutters revealing that the scene is a corner in the Bull Tavern. The back-shutters may have figured a representation of St Giles, as seen through a window. Scene 2 has the opening stage-direction 'Discovers Mr Wordie sitting by Mrs Rachiel and his hand about her neck, ane bible in ther hands. The old ladie walking beside.' 'Discovers' implies that the back-shutters for the first scene have been pulled aside, revealing a room in the Old Ladie's lodging with the actors already in position. A shutter probably represented book-shelves and another the entrance to a closet, both important for later scenes in the same setting. At the end of the scene, Violetta and Laura exit towards the front of the stage, with shutters closing behind them, allowing the stagehands to set up scene 3 rapidly and the actors to take their places. At the end of 1.3, the stage direction 'Sceane closeth' indicates that the front shutters close behind the proscenium arch to signify the end of the act (the 'Sceane' is the part of the stage behind the proscenium arch). This stage direction is repeated at the end of each act save the last, where, in place of shutters, the curtain descends and an actor enters the fore-stage to deliver the **Epilogue**.

The directions for the opening of 2.1 are not entirely explicit. I suggest that the front shutters are drawn back to reveal another closed pair on which Edinburgh Castle is depicted. The dialogue between Boy and Huffie 'in his nightgowne' takes place in a box above a side-door to the proscenium, from which both make their exit (2.1, 8). Boatmen, hirers and fiddlers flood onto the stage from one side, while Huffie with his whip appears from the other.

At the end of the scene, the shutters would be drawn back to reveal the church setting of 1.3. The only props necessary would be stools at the front for Violetta, Laura, Will and Frank. The remainder of the congregation stand or move about. Mr Solomon and the Fornicatrix, I suggest, would each occupy a box, one stage right and one stage left. These would represent the pulpit and the raised stool of repentance. Solomon, no doubt, would give some indication when the service came to an end (2.2, 30), at which point both he and the Fornicatrix would disappear from their places. Most of the congregation, with Frank, exeunt left and right. The Old Ladie and her entourage linger in conversation, then exeunt right, leaving Violetta and Will. Violetta presently follows her aunt, as does Will after a brief soliloquy.

As the setting is the same for both, no change is required for the beginning of 2.3.

In the Commentary I discuss the management of later scenes in the play. All fit stage conditions of the 1690s, so far as these are known.

When the play was written, the stage, apparently, was very much in the authors' minds. MS A could be a prompt copy for a performance. No production, however, whether in 1691 or later, is on record. Presbyterian hostility to the stage is well known and, as late as 1756, affected the production of John Home's *Douglas* at the Canongate theatre (Parker 1972: 8; cf. Cameron, in Hook 1987: 195–202). It is thus usually assumed that no production during Pitcairne's lifetime would have been possible. I am not so sure. Private theatres existed elsewhere in Britain: *The Phanaticks* may have been played in such a house. There might even have been a surreptitious performance in Edinburgh.

The Preface

The **Preface** appears in MS C and in the 1752 and later printed editions. Tobin doubted its authenticity on the grounds that it first appeared in the 1752 edition and that 'The identification of characters in the preface is incomplete. Had Pitcairne provided the key one wonders why he withheld the impulse to identify the public figures Will and Frank observe in Act IV, scene iii' (Tobin 1972: 21). We now know that the **Preface** occurs much earlier than 1752 and that there is a reasonable possibility that it was already in existence by 1692. Political and personal expediency may have led the author, in dangerous times, to omit the identification of prominent figures. No identification is provided for Whigridne or Huffie, probably for the same reason. Elsewhere Pitcairne provided keys to his literary work (Macqueen and Macqueen 2009: 44–6).

It seems likely that the **Preface** was written, probably by Pitcairne, for a later version of the play. It is of some historical and critical interest. It is included here as Appendix I (below, pp. 223–231).

Language and Style

This section will, I hope, demonstrate that the language indicated by MS A is throughout Scots and that consequently, because a translation from English to Scots is unlikely, *The Phanaticks* was originally written in Scots, whether very late Middle Scots, or very early Modern Scots, it is difficult to say. The orthography has been affected by English practices, but already in the opening lines of 1.1, such forms as *Ane* (3), *hes* (6), *sex* (8: English 'six'), *brack* (13), *wes* (17) indicate the underlying Scots, as also does the regular occurrence of spellings in *quh* (English 'wh'). Scots idiom, sometimes profane, is found in phrases like *Wha a devill* and *Deill take me*. The spelling *Deill*, incidentally, indicates the probable pronunciation of *devill*. *Take* is elsewhere more often spelled *tack* or *tak*, while *Wha* suggests the presence of a final glottal stop, both features indicating Scots pronunciation.

The evidence from later scenes is similar. In 1.2, for instance, we find such phrases as *the day's morning* (32: English 'this morning'), *So expects you* (49: 'So I expect you'), *Her coms my 2 Cusins* (54: 'Here come my 2 cousins), where *2* probably indicates *twa*, and Violetta's ironic *she canna sleep in the nycht* (57) for 'she can't sleep at night'.

In a brief discussion of language in *The Phanaticks*, Caroline Macafee states that 'Pitcairne's play ... represents the speech of the gentry as StE [Standard English], apart from some of the older generation' (*DOST* XII, lii). In terms of the printed texts this is true, but in terms of A it must be rejected. The Scots forms and phrases quoted above are all found in the mouths of the gentry; one of the most obvious is assigned to Violetta, co-heroine of the play and a young woman of good birth and moderate fortune. Another instance may be adduced from a snatch of dialogue in 3.1:

> *Violetta*: You wes better at preaching yesterday. What, not one word? It seems ye want a text.
> *Will*: Faith, Madam, I have a text I would handle closelie here.
> [*Offers to kiss her*
> *Violetta*: Bear of, Sir! It's Superstitious to Kiss the bible. Forbear a little. You'l find this text somquhat hard for you & you must pray ere you medle with it, I assur you.

> *Will*: Hungrie people, madam, forgett to say grace. I shall not faill to say one therafter.
>
> *Violetta*: Div ye value not the meat, if ye'l not prove the cetshin, you mein?
>
> *Will*: I must Contradick you, Madam, and, to lett you see how conscientious, I'le eat of this dish as long as I live. Gad, it's too good a morsell for a Sply Mouth. (22–34)

Violetta's final words quoted are proverb-like ('Hunger is good kitchen'), but the language is vernacular Scots and the sense differs considerably. The marriage-ceremony is the *cetshin*, the kitchen or relish added to a humdrum meal to make it more palatable (a Scots usage). If a man wishes a sexual relationship with a woman not involving marriage, he must have a very low regard for her – he values not the meat, the plain bread, i.e. possession. The words are vulgar, one might say, not least in the use of the emphatic hybrid form *div*, otherwise unrecorded until 1816 (*SND*, s.v. **DAE**). The remark is one of Pitcairne's insertions, but Will's dignified response, 'I must contradict you, Madam', indicates that it properly belongs as part of the text.

The lost source of the 1722 print may also have had a gap; alternatively the vernacular Scots so shocked the printer that he omitted it altogether; his text combines into one, and also somewhat expands, two of Will's remarks:

> Hungry People forget, Madam, to say Grace. I shall not fail to say a good long one, after I have eaten my Belly-full. I must contradict you, Madam, and to let you see I'm conscientious, I'll confine myself to eat of this Dish so long as I live, rather than it should spoil; Gad it's too good a Morsel for a splay mouth. (Tobin 1972: 60)

In other sources, Violetta's remark is deprived of any Scots quality and becomes 'But it seems you value the meat less if you count it not worthy that Ceremonie' (B, followed by C and the later printed sources).

In scenes like this, involving the gentry, the language may be described as pointed-colloquial. The passage just quoted, for instance, plays, first, on the equation of *text* (i.e. biblical text) with the person of Violetta. A minister in his sermon 'handles' a biblical text. Will wishes to 'handle' Violetta. In response she transforms *handle* to *medle*, which she subordinates to *pray*, the marriage ceremony. The basic sense of *medle* is 'mix, mingle', often sexually. Semantically, as the Thistle motto, 'Wha daur medle wi' me?' shows, the word in any sense is stronger than modern English *meddle*. It retains, nevertheless, some suggestion of impudence and interference.

In this context, *pray* suggests to Will both a particular form of prayer, grace before meat, and a proverb-like saying, 'Hungrie people forgett to say grace.' Violetta's riposte gives new point to the metaphor and transforms the tone of the dialogue.

Another form of the pointed-colloquial, involving different rhetorical techniques, is to be found in Will's hostile description of the great Whig lawyer, James Dalrymple, 1ˢᵗ Viscount Stair (1619–95);

> That's a trew-blew rogue as ever pisht, whose Conscience hes as great a wry as his Neck. He's as much sense and philology as to make himself a fool in print, as much honestie as to make him a Whig & a rebell, as much law & justice as from on decisione to give occasne for 7 new ons. He's begott a generatione whose legittimacie non questions, they have so many marks of the father & so true a westerne brood that, if the[y] live, they'll be old Sir Haries. Evry on of them hes his turn of pettship & he's so carefull to have unjust gaine delt so equallie amongst them that at least in on caice he's for suum cuique. Thou sees he's a fresh, vigorous old fellow & perhaps may live to be hangd yet. (4.4, 90–8)

English orthography is here slightly more evident; *make*, for instance, rather than the more usual *mack* or *mak*. The verbal form *hes* remains, however, both in its full form and abbreviated in *he's begott* ('he has begotten'). Scots idiom appears in 'a trew-blew rogue as ever pisht' (this last too is a Scots form; English *pissed*), and the omission of any form of the verb 'to be' introducing 'so true a westerne brood'. The phrase *Sir Harries* for 'devils' seems not to be paralleled elsewhere, but *Harry* for 'devil' is at least northern in origin (*OED*, s.v.).

The rhetorical balance of the *as ... as* construction in the opening clauses is enhanced by the deliberate clash between the first and the second elements introduced – 'as much honestie as to make him a Whig & a rebell'. The climactic 'as much justice as from on decisione to give occasne for 7 new ons' introduces Stair as judge, manufacturing new business for himself and for his sons, an account of whom follows. A more complex balance is found in the later reference, 'so carefull to have unjust gaine delt so equallie amongst them that at least in on caice he's for *suum cuique*'. The phrase *unjust gaine* echoes the biblical Proverbs 28. 8, 'He that by usury and unjust gain increaseth his substance ...', and is balanced against *dealt equallie*, 'dealt equably, fairly, in terms of the law of nature'; one instance of which is the principle *suum cuique*, 'to each his own', basic to Stair's conception of law (Stair 1981: 74). Properly this has universal application; here, however, it matters only *in on caice.* Incidentally, but not accidentally, it was also a Jacobite rallying-cry for the restoration to his hereditary rights of James VII.

The proverbial 'live to be hangd' is obviously and powerfully effective when applied to the holder of the highest Scottish legal office, the Lord President of the Court of Session. Like a caricaturist, Will emphasizes his main physical peculiarity, a wry neck.

The portrait inverts the traditional style of panegyric, as a comparison with Pitcairne's Latin epitaph for Stair, composed a few year's later, will reveal. I quote it in translation (Macqueen and Macqueen 2009: 185):

> If virtue, if the spirit of law and equity, have been able to grant you a name which will live all over the world, your reputation will grow, untouched by the passage of time, and either Apollo will recite your praises. But even if the spirit should not bear witness to your merits, nor either Apollo recite your praises, let those four luminaries of the Scottish bar, your sons, soon going to give even greater brilliance to our courts, celebrate your deserts and the fourfold soul which Jupiter destined you, as a single person, to have: for you carried out with distinction all your services to the robe, and in your single person were what your four sons now are.

The sequence is the same; the references are similar, the style is again carefully balanced with much use of anaphora and anadiplosis, there is the same emphasis on the close relationship of father and sons. The total effect in one, however, is totally reversed in the other.

The controlled and consistent Scots used by the gentry contrasts markedly with the language of the presbyterian clergy, the phraseology of which is often English which tends to stumble into vernacular Scots. Linguistic insensitivity of this latter kind mirrors indifference in other matters. An example is an early speech of the Moderator:

> My lord, I cannot but Commend your zeal. I am sure amongst all our nobls, ther is non fitter to scurge the malignants out of the house of God – But to our wirk, bretheren. Ther is two sort of people who have takne ther hand from the work of the Lord, first, the Torries, who nevir putt ther hand to it, 2dly, the Court partie, so wee poor men Man e'n putt our shouldere to it & take a good lift of the cause of Christ, for, I assur you, a pek ne're brack on of your backs. (1.3, 17–24)

The opening is English, somewhat pompously reminiscent of the language of the Authorised Version; *commend*, for instance, in its various senses, and *zeal* are favourite words in the Pauline epistles; *zeal*, together with *scurge the malignants out of the house of God* refers to John 2. 15–17: 'And when he had made a scourge of small chords, he drove them all out of the temple ... and said unto them that sold doves, Take these things hence: make not my Father's house an house of merchandise. And his disciples remembered that it was written, The zeal of thine house hath eaten me up', a reference to Psalm 69. 9: 'The zeal of thine house hath eaten me up.' *House of God* recalls 'my Father's house'; the actual phrase is recurrent throughout the Old Testament and is found in the New. *Malignants* has a rather curious origin in the Old Latin version of Psalm 25. 5, *odivi ecclesiam malignantium*, 'I have hated the congregation of evil-doers', interpreted by the Church Fathers as a reference to the followers of Antichrist. This in turn English Puritans and Scottish Presbyterians understood to refer primarily to Roman Catholics and members of the Church of England, and extreme Presbyterians Scottish Episcopalians.

The stylistic and linguistic transition comes when the Moderator turns from Lord Huffie to address his colleagues on the Comitie. The first trace of Scots is the word *wirk*, soon followed by *Ther is two sort of people*, then by a Scots reminiscence of Luke 9. 62, 'No man having put his hand to the plough, and looking back, is fit for the kingdom of God', this leading to the anticlimactic, *ffirst, the Torries who nevir put ther hand to it, 2dly, the Court partie*. Thereafter Scots continues with a garbled combination of the proverbial 'Put your shoulder to the wheel' (Wilson 1970: 729) and 'God shapes the back for the burthen' (*ibid.*: 312*): so wee poor men Man e'n putt our shoulders to it & take a good lift of the cause of Christ, for, I assur you, a pek ne're brack on of your backs*. The proverbial element is strong in the speech of the clergymen, particularly the Moderator, and it is perhaps worth noting that these examples are early in terms of what is quoted by Wilson.

The playwright's target is not so much the use as the misuse of Scots and English, and the inability of the Moderator in either to maintain a consistent level of discourse. His failures in speech mirror a failure of intellectual grasp, a point also illustrated by an exchange in 5.3. Turbulent begins by making a sensible point, grasped by none of the others, and scorned by the Moderator:

> *Turbulent*: I think we should Consider how to fill the Curats' places ere we lay so many congregations wast, since we have not men to plant the 6th part of them.
> *Moderator*: Had your tounge! Let us doe our duty. God will e'ene provide.
> *Ruling Elder*: A west quintra beleever. Moderator, ma werk better than any Keerate in the north, and he'll ben sheen leir to baptiz and marry.

Covenant: I think We should tak a word of the common whore, the Church of England, for we have drest our owne gaylie already.

Salathiel: In truth, Moderator, of old the first thing evr the Generalle Assemblie did wes purge the K's armie of malignants. Now I think we have as good reasone as ever to purg K. Wm's armie of prelatists and papists and atheists quhilk abound in it, seing they are feighting for a good cause: *nam ubi finis est brevissimus, ibi media debent esse proportionalia.*

Moderator: Outts, Mr Salathiel, with your Greek – we know ye ar a Primar in the Colledge! I tell you we must not put our hand further then our slive cane reach. I fancie it's best and fittest for us to medle with them that hav no pouer to resist us, I mean the Curats who have not mynd to defend themselves.   (7–27)

Turbulent's language comes closest to English, but *lay ... wast* is Scots; compare the pronunciation indicated by rhyme and spelling in Burns' 'To a Mouse': 'Thou saw the fields laid bare an' *wast*,/ An' weary Winter comin *fast*' (Kinsley 1968: 1, 127, 25–6). As always, the words of Ruling Elder are in North-Eastern dialect, while general Scots idiom is to be seen in Covenant's *tak a word* and *drest our owne gaylie*. Salathiel attempts an Anglified diction, defined nevertheless as Scots by his use of *wes* and *feighting* (*fechtin*, English 'fighting') and the relative *quhilk*. He ends in bathos with some bad (and irrelevant) Latin. Although Salathiel is *Primar* (English 'Principal') of the College, the Moderator dismisses his Latin, which he takes to be Greek, with *Outts*, later Scots 'Hoots', and introduces another proverb (Wilson 1970: 780) to strengthen his policy of expediency. The speakers are in complete disagreement with each other; the proposals, for the most part, are impossible; one with a modicum of sense is summarily dismissed. The Moderator's policy is finally accepted with a minimum of dissent from Covenant.

The Scots of the ministers is capable of vivid presentation of temperamental differences, albeit in the form of caricature. In 4.2, 87–8 Turbulent makes the outrageous but straightforward proposal that there be 'ane more exquisitive forme of depositne, that ther be a *libella Universalis*, that's as much as to say ane Universall lybell'. Covenant's elaboration of the proposal shows a more scholastic, legalistic subtle and malicious turn of mind, combined with a certain inability to separate the relevant from the irrelevant:

To what our brothr hes said I have two queries, two difficulties, on fear, and a proposall. Or rather two proposalls, two queries, on difficultie and a fear. My proposall is that ther be ane act prohibiting all ansring of Lybells, either by word or work, and that the Curats be

Lybellit in falts as weall to be done as done. My first question is, whither we should plant ther kirk er we depose them or depose them er we plant ther kirk. My 2d is how it is possible to wark the Curats who ar nether in thiis side nor the other sid of Tay? (93–101)

Ruling Elder's attempt to contribute also reveals his mathematical inadequacies: 'Let them come in by a class of ther owne, which with the othr two – lett me sie, two and on mak just three' (102–3).

Turbulent finally shows a blasphemous impatience with Covenant's latter subtleties:

> What – will not Christ be judge in his owne cause at the last day? Did Josua, quhen he extirpate all the Idolaters Citt evry man to personall apperance & give him a Copie of his lybell befor hand? Did Christ, quhen he whipt out the buyers and sellers out of the temple tack evry particular huckster wyff be the lug? I trow not. (107–111)

His outburst meets with general approval.

Both Turbulent and Covenant have an impressive mastery of Scots legal terminology – *depositne, lybell, compeirance, indirect dealing & judging my owne caice, Citt*. The contrast which makes so startling Turbulent's implied identification of a summons to the Episcopal clergy with taking *evry particular huckster wife be the lug* is more than anti-climax. It is a revelation of his character.

There is an interesting contrast between the use of the Song of Solomon by Will and Violetta (2.2, 24–80) and that made *passim* by Mr Solomon. The pair use it as a code conveying information about a proposed clandestine meeting. With the success of their scheme it is dropped. Solomon, however, uses it on all occasions, even when speaking about church administration (3.3, 35–41). His fellow divines recognize it (1.3, 62–80) as a weakness built into his mental fibre. In effect, his personality is split. Laura's summary is precise:

> I warne you, no more of your Cant. I'le pardon quhat's past, but in tyme comeing if I hear on word of beds, bear brests and sweets of love & such Gibberish that becoms your wry mouth as ill as that fair wig does your monkie face I'le reveall all and Spoyle your trade; In stead of a mortified sant & preacher of the Gospell of Christ, a most prophane Lustfull and Impudent Villane. (3.2, 54–60)

The Scots of the gentry is pointed-colloquial, that of the clergy is mixed, pompous, anti-climactic, even bathetic. The speech of the nobility stands a little apart from either. Whigridne and Huffie are lay Presbyterian extremists and so have a marked tendency to include biblical reminiscences in their diction. These are usually to the Old Testament. Huffie's desire, for instance, to be *on of the scurges of the lord* (1.3, 16) refers to Isaiah 10. 26: 'And the Lord of Hosts shall stir up a scourge for him according to the slaughter of Midian', a reference diplomatically changed by the Moderator to the expulsion by Christ of the traders from the Temple (above, p. lxvi). In defence of his actions, or rather his failure to act, against an obnoxious parliamentary measure, Whigridne refers to the Lamentations of Jeremiah and Psalm 127. 1 when he says 'We have now reasone to lament with Jeremiah, and with David to sing "Except the Lord build the house"' (2.3, 122–3).

Huffie's idiom is Scots, for instance in 4.3, 12–13: 'Goe, sirra, we'll be follow. I have Catcht his dogs hunting two myls within the toun.' I have found no parallel elsewhere for the phrase *we'll be follow*, but *Catcht* is certainly Scots, as is the phrase *two myls within the toun* (English 'within two miles of the town'). The spelling *toun* is also distinctively Scots. Already in MS B, the process of anglicization is under way; the first phrase mentioned is absent; the final *-t* of *Catcht* has become *-ed*; the passage now reads: 'Go Sirrah tell the Colonell I have catched his Dogs hunting within two miles of the toun.'

Whigridne's remarks are sometimes taken verbatim from his published speeches, in which he makes a use, not always happy, of rhetorical topoi, as: 'If I should add to what hes bein said at this tyme upon this subject, It would be lyk a rash tuch of ane pencill upon a Compleat pictur by an unskilfull hand' (2.3, 28–30). The relevance is not obvious – as Turbulent remarks (33–4), 'Ther hes bene nothing at all said on this subject at this tyme' – and the follow-up is anticlimactic.

There is a distinction between his clumsy and hesitant language as a member of the Comitie, and his freer style of private conversation:

> *Whigridne*: But I goe a hunting today too, my Lord.
> *Huffie*: Wher's your dogs? We'il goe togather.
> *Whigridne*: [*Pulls some papers out of his pocket*] Thers a brass of weall pointed lybells. I hunt the Curats, my Lord, the wolvs out of Christ's vyne yeard. I'm ane old tyk for them, ha-ha-ha.
>
> (3.1, 159–64)

In *brass* (English 'brace'), *weall-pointed*, *hunt the Curats*, the mock-modest *tyk*, he plays variations on the metaphor of hunting, one appropriate for a member of the aristocracy, turning it into a conceit, or rather a mixed metaphor, by his combination of two biblical figures, the church as sheepfold, threatened by wolves (John 10. 7–16), and the church as vineyard (Isaiah 5. 7, John 15. 1). The idea of wolves occupying vine-yards is, of course, ridiculous.

A few Scots words and idioms are obvious in the passage, although not so prominently as in one of his earlier utterances in the Comitie:

> Who would have thought that, in so good ane act as this, rescinding severall acts of parliament, as that of keeping the 29th of May, they should have foisted in these wicked acts anent Excommunicatne, for, to tell you the truth, I nevir considered mare of the act but its title and that, I thought, sounded weall enough. But I have since syne bein consulting with Sir Wm Littlelaw, a lawyer and friend of our.
>
> (2.3, 102–7)

Several words, *ane, rescinding, anent, mare, friend,* are Scots, as are some phrases: *weall enough, since syne, bein consulting with, friend of our,* all serving also to indicate that other words – *thought, foisted, sounded* – were pronounced in Scots rather than English fashion. A little of this survives, although most has been anglicized, in other sources; MS B, for instance, reads:

> Who could have thought that in so good an act as that rescinding several wicked Acts of Parliament, as that for keeping the 29th of May, that they should have foisted in these wicked acts anent Excom-munication, for to tell you the truth I never considered more of any act than its title and that I thought sounded well enough. But I have since been consulting with Sir Will. Littlelaw a Lawier and friend of ours. (Gathering 6, leaf 2)

The use of Scots permits subtle linguistic differentiations of char-acter, differentiations often obscured in later, more anglicized versions of the text.

Bibliography

Abbreviations

APS	T. Thomson and C. Innes (eds) 1814–75 *Acts of the Parliament of Scotland*, Edinburgh: HMSO
DOST	*Dictionary of the Older Scottish Tongue*, available at: www.dsl.ac.uk/
EETS	Early English Text Society
GA Acts	*Acts of the General Assemblies of the Church of Scotland*, available at www.british–history.ac.uk/source.aspx?pubid=59
GUL	Glasgow University Library
NLS	National Library of Scotland
ODCC	*Oxford Dictionary of the Christian Church*, ed. F. L. Cross, London: Oxford University Press
ODEP	F. P. Wilson, *Oxford Dictionary of English Proverbs*, 3rd edn, Oxford: Clarendon Press
OED	*Oxford English Dictionary*
OxfDNB	*Oxford Dictionary of National Biography*
Proceres Scotorum	Archibald Pitcairne, *Proseres Scotorum Anno MDCXC* in MacQueen and MacQueen 2009
RPS	*Records of the Parliaments of Scotland*, available at www.rps.ac.uk
SHS	Scottish History Society
STS	Scottish Text Society
SND	*Scottish National Dictionary*, available at www.dsl.ac.uk/

Account Book of Sir John Foulis of Ravelston 1671–1707, 1894. Ed. A. W. Cornelius Hallen. Edinburgh: Scottish History Society

Acts of the General Assemblies of the Church of Scotland. Available at: www.british–history.ac.uk/source.aspx?pubid=599

Aldis, H. G. (ed) 1970. *A List of books printed in Scotland before 1700*. Edinburgh: National Library of Scotland

Alexander, J. H. (ed.) 1986. *Walter Scott: A Legend of the Wars of Montrose*. Edinburgh: Edinburgh University Press

[Allestree, Richard] 1659. *The Whole Duty of man Laid down In a Plain and Familiar Way for the Use of All, but especially the Meanest Reader: Divided into XVII Chapters, One whereof being read every Lords Day, the Whole may be read over Thrice in the Year. Necessary for all Families*. London: Timothy Garthwait

——— 1673. *The Ladies Calling in two parts By the Author of The Whole Duty of Man*. Oxford: At the Theater

Bacon, Francis 1620. *Francisci de Verulamio Summi Angliae Cancel-larii Instauratio Magna.* London: Ioannes Billius

Baker, H. C. 1952. *The Wars of Truth. Studies in the decay of Chris-tian Humanism in the Earlier Seventeenth Century.* London, New York: Staples Press

Balfour, Sir James 1963. *The Practicks of Sir James Balfour of Pitten-dreich*, vol. II, ed. Peter G. B. McNeill. Edinburgh: Stair Society

Bankton, A. M. 1994. *An Institute of the Laws of Scotland in Civil Rights*, vol. 2. Edinburgh: Stair Society

Bawcutt, P. J. (ed.) 1998. *The Poems of William Dunbar.* Glasgow: Association for Scottish Literary Studies

Bawcutt, P. (ed.) 2003. *The Shorter Poems of Gavin Douglas* rev. ed. Edinburgh: Scottish Text Society

Boece, Hector 1527. *Scotorum Historia a prima gentis origine.* Paris: Badius Ascensius

Boyle, R. 1744. *The Works of the Honourable Robert Boyle: in five volumes.* London: Printed for A. Millar

Broadie, Alexander 1983. *George Lokert: late scholastic logician.* Edin-burgh: Edinburgh University Press

Browne, Sir Thomas 1643. *Religio Medici.* London, Andrew Crooke

Buchanan, George 1578. *De Ivre Regni apud Scotos.* Edinburgh: J. Ross for H. Charteris. (See also Smith and Mason 2006)

———— 1582. *Rerum Scoticarum historia, auctore Georgio Buchanano Scoto.* Edinburgh: Alexander Arbuthnot

Burel, John 1596? *To Lodwick duke of Lennox.* Edinburgh

Carlyle, Thomas (ed.) 1845. *Oliver Cromwell's Letters and Speeches.* London: Chapman and Hall

Chambers, R. 1847. *Traditions of Edinburgh.* Edinburgh: W. & R. Chambers

Childe, F. J. 1885. *The English and Scottish Popular Ballads*, part III. Boston: Houghton and Mifflin

Clancy, T. and M. Pittock (eds.) 2007. *The Edinburgh History of Scot-tish Literature*, vol. 1. Edinburgh: Edinburgh University Press

Clyde, J. A. (ed.) 1938. *Hope's Major Practicks 1608–1633.* 2 vols. Edinburgh: Neill and Co

Cockburn, J. 1691. *An Historical Revelation of the late General Assembly, held at Edinburgh ...* London: J. Hindmarsh

Cope, Jackson I. and Harold Whitmore Jones (eds.) 1953. *History of the Royal Society by Thomas Sprat.* St Louis: Washington University Studies

Cowan, Ian B. 1976. *The Scottish Covenanters 1660–1688.* London: Gollancz

Cowley, A. 1663. *Cutter of Coleman Street. A Comedy. The scene London, in the year 1658.* London: Henry Herringman

Craig, John 1699. *Theologiae Christianae Principia Mathematica*. London: John Darby

Craig, W. S. 1976. *History of the Royal College of Physicians of Edinburgh*. Oxford: Blackwell Scientific

Craigie, J. 1982. *Minor Prose Works of King James VI and I*. Edinburgh: Scottish Text Society

Cramond. W. (ed.) 1903. *The Records of Elgin 1234–1800*. Aberdeen: New Spalding Society

Cranstoun, J. (ed.) 1896. *The Poems of Alexander Scott*. Edinburgh: Scottish Text Society

Crawford, W. L. 1690. *The Speech of William Earl of Crawfurd, president to the Parliament of Scotland, the 22d of April, 1690*. Edinburgh: Heir of A. Anderson

Crown, John 1683. *City Politiques A comedy: as it is acted by His Majesties servants. Written by Mr. Crown*. London: R. Bently and Joseph Hindmarsh

—— 1685. *Sir Courtly Nice: or, It cannot be A comedy, as it is acted by His Majesties servants. Written by Mr. Crown*. London: H. H. Jun. for R Bentley and Jos. Hindmarsh

Cruikshanks, Eveline and Edward T. Corp (eds.) 1995. *The Stuart Court in Exile and the Jacobites*. London: Hambledon Press

Curate, Jacob (pseudonym) 1692. *Scotch Presbyterian eloquence; or, the foolishness of their teaching discovered from their books, sermons, and prayers; and some remarks on Mr Rule's late vindication of the kirk*. London: Printed for Randal Taylor

Curtis, E. 1964. *A History of Ireland*. London: Methuen

Curtius, E. R. 1953. *European Literature and the Latin Middle Ages / translated from the German by Willard R. Trask*. London: Routledge and Kegan Paul

Davie, George Elder 1964. *The Democratic Intellect*, 2nd edn. Edinburgh: Edinburgh University Press

Dickinson, W. C. (ed.) 1928. *The Sheriff Court Book of Fife, 1515–1522*. Edinburgh: Scottish History Society

Dictionary of the Older Scottish Tongue. Available at: www.dsl.ac.uk/

Donaldson, G. 1965. *Scotland: James V to James VII*. Edinburgh: Oliver & Boyd

Donaldson, G. and R. Morpeth 1977. *A Dictionary of Scottish History*. Edinburgh: John Donald

Dow, F. D. 1979. *Cromwellian Scotland 1651–1660*. Edinburgh: John Donald

Dryden, John 1660. *Astraea Redux. A Poem on the Happy Restoration and Return of His Sacred Majesty Charles the Second*. London: Henry Herringman

Extracts from the Records of the Burgh of Edinburgh, 1927–67. Ed.

Marguerite Wood and Helen Arnet, 9 vols. Edinburgh: Scottish Burgh Record Society

Farmer 1987. see *ODCC*

Ferguson, W. 1968. *Scotland: 1689 to the Present*. Edinburgh: Oliver & Boyd

Fergusson, D. 1924. *Fergusson's Scottish Proverbs*. Edinburgh: Scottish Text Society

Ficino, Marsilio 1496. *Commentaria in Platonem*. Florence: Per Iaurentium francici de Venetiis

Figgis, J. N. 1922. *The Divine Right of Kings*. Cambridge: Cambridge University Press

Forbes, John et al 1638. *Generall Demands, Concerning the Late Covenant; Propounded by the Ministers and Professors of Divinitie in Aberdene*

Forbes, J. and T. Davidson 1662. *Cantus, songs and fancies. To Thre, foure or five partes*. Aberdeen: John Forbes

Fox, D. (ed.) 1981. *The Poems of Robert Henryson*. Oxford: Clarendon Press

Geddes, W. D. 1892. *Musa Latina Aberdonensis – Arthur Johnston*. Aberdeen: New Spalding Club

Gericke, Bradley T. 2008. 'Newburn 1640: Scotland Triumphant', *History Scotland* 8.5, pp. 27–33

Glanvill, Joseph 1681. *Saducismus Triumphatus: or, Full and Plain Evidence concerning Witches and Apparitions*. London: J. Collins and S. Lownds

Goodwin, W. W. 1894. *A Greek Grammar*. London: Macmillan

Goold, G. P. (ed.) 1977. *Metamorphoses / Ovid, with an English translation by Frank Justus Miller*. Cambridge, Mass.: Harvard University Press; London: Heinemann

Gordon, Ian A. (ed.) 1976. *John Galt, The Last of the Lairds*. Edinburgh & London: Scottish Academic Press

Gosse, E. (ed.) 1932. *Restoration Plays from Dryden to Farquhar* new edn. London: J. M. Dent

Gregorie, David 1684. *Exercitatio geometrica de dimensione figurarum sive specimen methodi generalis: dimitiendi quasvis figuras*. Edinburgh: Kniblo, Solingen and Colmar

———— (ed.) 1703. *Euclidis quae supersunt omnia*. Oxford

———— 1710. See Halley 1710

Guibert, Jacques Antoine Hippolyte, Comte de 1770. *Essai géneral de tactique*. Paris: n.p.

Halley, Edmund (ed. with D. Gregory) 1710. *Apollonii Pergaei Conicorum libri octo et Sereni Antissensis de sectione cylindri & coni libri duo*. Oxford

Hamer, D. 1931. *The Works of Sir David Lindsay of the Mount 1490–1555*. Edinburgh: Scottish Text Society

Harvey, P. and J. E. Heseltine 1959. *The Oxford Companion to French Literature*. Oxford: Clarendon Press

Herd, D. (ed.) 1776. *Ancient and Modern Scottish Songs, Heroic Ballads etc*. Edinburgh: Printed by John Wotherspoon, for James Dickson and Charles Eliot

Hobbes, T. (1651). *Leviathan* London: Andrew Ckooke

Hobbes, T. 1973. *Leviathan*, ed. K. R. Monogue. London: J. M. Dent

Hogg, J. 1983. *The Private Memoirs and Confessions of a Justified Sinner, edited with an introduction by John Wain*. Harmondsworth: Penguin

Hook, Andrew (ed.) 1987. *History of Scottish Literature, 2, 1660– 1800*. Aberdeen: Aberdeen University Press

Howard, Sir Robert 1665. *Four New Plays, viz, The Surprisal, The Committee, Comedies. The Indian Queen, The Vestal-Virgin, Tragedies. As they were acted by His Majesties Servants at the Theatre-Royal. Written by the Honourable Sir Robert Howard.* London: Henry Herringman

Howie, John, of Lochgoin [1902]. *Scots Worthies*. Edinburgh and London: Oliphant, Anderson & Ferrier

Hughes, M. Y. (ed.) 1957. *Complete Poems and Major Prose of John Milton*. New York: Odyssey Press

Hume, D. 1960. *Treatise on Human Nature*, ed. L. A. Selby-Bigge, 1888, reprinted 1960. Oxford: Clarendon Press

Hume Brown, P. (ed.) 1892. *Vernacular Writings of George Buchanan*. Edinburgh and London: Scottish Text Society

Jack, Ronald D. S. 1971. *Scottish Prose 1550–1700*. London: Calder and Boyars

James VI and I, King 1598. *The Trve Lawe of free Monarchies: or, The Reciprock and Mvtvall Dvtie betwixt a free King, and his naturall Subiectes*. Edinburgh: Robert Waldegrave

Jameson, John 1808. *An etymological dictionary of the Scottish Language*, 2 vols. Edinburgh: University Press

Jeans, Sir James 1931. *The Mysterious Universe*. Cambridge: Cambridge University Press

Johnston, W. T. (ed.) 1979. *The best of our owne letters of Archibald Pitcairne 1652–1713*. Edinburgh: Saorsa Books

Jonson, B. 1960. *Ben Jonson's Plays*, 2 vols. London: Everyman's Library

Kennedy, M. 1980. *The Concise Oxford Dictionary of Music*. London: Oxford University Press

Keynes, G. (ed.) 1968. *Sir Thomas Browne: Selected Writings*. London: Faber & Faber

Kinloch, G. R. (ed.) 1830. *Babell; a satirical poem on the General*

Assembly in the year M.DC.XCII / by Archibald Pitcairne. Edinburgh: Maitland Club

Kinsley, J. 1968. *The Poems and Songs of Robert Burns / edited by James Kinsley.* Oxford: Clarendon Press

Kirk, Robert 1976. *The Secret Common-Wealth [of Elves, Fauns and Fairies] & A Short Treatise of Charms and Spels,* ed. Stewart Sanderson. Cambridge: Folklore Society, Mistletoe Series

Koestler, A. 1959. *The Sleepwalkers. A History of Man's Changing Vision of the Universe.* Harmondsworth: Penguin

Linton, C. M. 2004. *From Eudoxus to Einstein: A History of Mathematical Astronomy.* Cambridge: Cambridge University Press

Lovejoy, A. O. 1936. *The Great Chain of Being: A Study of the History of an Idea.* Cambridge, Mass.: Harvard University Press

Mack, D. (ed.) 1993. *Walter Scott: The Tale of Old Mortality.* Edinburgh: Edinburgh Edition of the Waverly Novels 4b

Mackenzie, Sir George, of Rosehaugh 1684. *Jus Regium; or, The Just, and Solid Foundations of Monarchy in general, and more especially of the Monarchy of Scotland: Maintain'd against Buchanan, Naphthali, Dolman, Milton, &c.* Edinburgh: Heir of A. Anderson

———— 1684. *Institutions of the Law of Scotland.* Edinburgh: John Reid

———— 1685. *Defence of the Antiquity of the Royal Line of Scotland. With a true Account when the Scots were Govern'd by Kings in the Isle of Britain.* Edinburgh: Heir of A. Anderson

MacQueen, J. (ed.) 1990. *Humanism in Renaissance Scotland.* Edinburgh: Edinburgh University Press

MacQueen, J. and W. MacQueen (eds.) 2009. *Archibald Pitcairne: The Latin Poems,* Bibliotheca Latinitatis Novae. Assen: Royal Van Gorcum; Tempe, AZ: Arizona Center for Medieval and Renaissance Studies

Matheson, William (ed.) 1970. *An Clarsair Dall. Orain Ruaidhri Mhic Mhuirich Agus a Chuid ciuil. The Blind Harper. The Songs of Roderick Morison and his Music.* Edinburgh: Scottish Gaelic Texts Society

McDiarmid, M. P. (ed.) 1954–56. *The Poems of Robert Fergusson.* Edinburgh: Scottish Text Society

———— 1973. *The Kingis Quair of James Stewart.* London: Heinemann

McGrath, Alister 2001. *In the Beginning. The Story of the King James Bible.* London, Sydney, Auckland: Hodder & Stoughton

Mill, A. J. (ed.) 1933. *Ane verie excellent and delectabill Treatise entitulit Philotus.* In *Miscellany Volume,* 81–158: Edinburgh and London: Scottish Text Society

Money, D. 1998. *The English Horace: Anthony Alsop and the Tradition of British Latin Verse.* Oxford: Oxford University Press

Montgomerie, A. 2000. *Poems / Alexander Montgomerie; edited by David J. Parkinson*. Edinburgh: Scottish Text Society

More, Henry 1652. *Conjectura Cabbalistica, or, a Conjectural Essay of Interpreting the minde of Moses, according to a Threefold Cabbala*. London: James Flesher

——— 1653. *Antidote against Atheisme, or, an Appeal to the Natural Faculties of the Minde of Man, whether there be not a God*. London: J. Flesher

——— 1656. *Enthusiasmus Triumphatus, or, A Discourse of the Nature, Causes, Kinds, and Cure, of Enthusiasme*. London: J. Flesher

——— 1659. *Immortality of the Soul, so far forth as it is demonstrable from the Knowledge of Nature and the Light of Reason*. London: J. Flesher

Nairne, J. (ed.) 1830. *A Relation of Proceedings concerning the Affairs of the Kirk of Scotland from August 1637 to July 1638 / By J L Rothes*. Edinburgh: [s.n.]

Newton, Sir Isaac 1687. *Philosophiae Naturalis Principia Mathematica*. London: Joseph Streater for the Royal Society

Nicoll, John 1836. *Diary of Public Transactions and Other Occurrences, Chiefly in Scotland from January 1650 to June 1667*, ed. D. Laing. Edinburgh: Bannatyne Club

Otway, Thomas 1682. *Venice Preserv'd, or, A Plot Discover'd. A Tragedy. As it is Acted at the Duke's Theatre*. London: Jos. Hindmarsh

Owen, Susan J. (ed.) 2001. *Companion to Restoration Drama*. Oxford: Blackwell

Oxford Dictionary of the Christian Church, ed. F. L. Cross. London: Oxford University Press

Oxford Dictionary of National Biography

Oxford English Dictionary

Pascal, Blaise 1670. *Pensées*. Paris

Parker, G. D. 1972. *Douglas / by John Home*. Edinburgh: Oliver and Boyd

Patrides, C. A. 1969. *The Cambridge Platonists*. London: Edward Arnold

Pegis, Anton C. (ed.) 1945. *Basic Writings of Saint Thomas Aquinas*, 2 vols. New York: Random House

Pennant, T. 1774. *A Tour in Scotland and Voyage to the Hebrides; 1772*. London; J. Monk

Pitcairne, Archibald 1683. *Exempla additionis, subtractionis ... ad quorum reflectionem Joannem Young invitat Archibald Pitcairne*. Broadside, Edinburgh University Library, Dc.1.61/187: Edinburgh: [n.p], 1 March 1683

———— 1688a. *Epistola Archimedis ad Regem Gelonem Albae Graecae reperta 1688.* [n.p., n.d., s.n.]

———— 1688b. *Solutio problematis de historicis; seu de inventoribus dissertatio.* Edinburgh: John Reid

———— 1692. *Archibaldi Pitcarnii oratio qua ostenditur medicinam ab omni philosophorum secta esse liberam; et exemplo docetur quantam utilitatem medicis offerre possit mathesis.* Leiden (Edinburgh: John Reid, 1696)

———— 1696. *Dissertatio de Legibus Historiae Naturalis.* Edinburgh: John Reid

———— 1701. *Archibaldi Pitcarnii Dissertationes medicae.* Rotterdam: Typis Regneri Leers

———— 1709: *Poemata Selecta.* [n.p., n.d., s.n.]

———— 1713. *Archibaldi Pitcarnii Dissertationes Medicae.* Edinburgh: Robert Freebairn

———— 1727. *Selecta Poemata Archibaldi Pitcarnii Med. Doctoris, Gulielmi Scot a Thirlestane, Equitis, Thomae Kincadii, Civis Edinburgensis, et Aliorum.* Edinburgh: [Robert Freebairn]

Platnauer, M. 1976. *Claudian with an English Translation by Maurice Platnauer.* Cambridge, Mass., and London: Loeb Classical Library

Prior, Matthew 1721. *Selected Poems,* 2 vols. London: J. Tonson and J. Barber

Records of the Parliaments of Scotland. Available at www.rps.ac.uk

Reid, D. (ed.) 1982. *The Party-Coloured Mind: Prose Relating to the Conflict of Church and State in Seventeenth Century Scotland.* Edinburgh: Scottish Academic Press

Riley, P. W. J. 1979. *King William and the Scottish Politicians.* Edinburgh: Donald

Ruddiman, Thomas 1710. *Virgil's Aeneis, Translated into Scottish Verse by the famous Gawin Douglas Bishop of Dunkeld.* New Edition. Edinburgh: Andrew Symson and Robert Freebairn

———— 1715. *Georgii Buchanani Scoti, Poetarum sui seculi facile Principis, Opera Omnia, ad optimorum Codicum fidem summo studio recognita & castigata.* 2 vols. Edinburgh: Robert Freebairn

Rule, Gilbert 1680. *Answer to Dr. Stillingfleet's Irenicum by a learned Pen.* London: Richard Janeway

———— 1689. *Rational Defence of Non-conformity wherein the Practice of Nonconformity is Vindicated from Promoting Popery, and Ruining the Church, imputed to them by Dr. Stillingfleet in his Unreasonableness of Separation.* London: John Salusbury

———— 1691a. *Vindication of the Church of Scotland Being an Answer to a Paper, intituled Some Questions concerning Episcopal and Presbyterian government in Scotland.* Edinburgh: George Mosman

———— 1691b. *Second Vindication of the Church of Scotland being an*

Answer to five pamphlets, the Titles of which are set down after the Preface. Edinburgh: George Mosman

—— 1693. *Just and Modest Reproof of a pamphlet called The Scotch Presbyterian Eloquence.* Edinburgh: George Mosman

Runciman, S. 1947. *The Medieval Manichee. A Study of the Christian Dualist Heresy.* Cambridge: Cambridge University Press

Rutherford, Samuel 1646. *The Divine Right of Church Government and Excommunication: or A peacable Dispute for the perfection of the holy Scripture in point of Ceremonies and Church Government.* London: John Field for Christopher Meredith

—— 1649. *Free Disputation Against pretended Liberty of Conscience.* London: R.I. for Andrew Crook

—— 1671. *Joshua Redivivus, or Mr Rutherfoord's Letters, Divided in two Parts.* [Edinburgh, s.n.]

—— 1982. *Lex, Rex, or The Law and the Prince.* Harrisonburg, Virginia: Sprinkle Publications

Schlapp, R. 1973. 'The Contribution of the Scots to Mathematics'. *Mathematical Gazette* LVII, pp. 1–16

Scott, W. 1818. *Rob Roy. By the author of 'Waverley'...* 4th edn. Edinburgh: Archibald Constable

Scottish National Dictionary. Available at www.dsl.ac.uk/

Sherlock, William 1691. *Case of the Allegiance due to Soveraign Powers, Further Consider'd and Defended: with A more particular Respect to the Doctrine of Non-Resistance and Passive Obedience, Together with a Seasonable Perswasive to our New Dissenters.* London: W. Rogers

[Shields, Alexander] 1687. *A Hind let loose, or An Historical Representation of the Testimonies, Of the Church of Scotland, for the Interest of Christ, vvith the true State thereof in all its Periods.* [s.p., s.n.]

Shirlaw, L. 1975. 'Dr Archibald Pitcairne and Sir Isaac Newton's "Black Years" (1692–1694)'. *Royal College of Physicians, Edinburgh, Chronicle* 5 (January 1975), pp. 23–6

Sibbald, Sir Robert 1684. *Scotia Illustrata sive Prodromus Historiae Naturalis.* Edinburgh: Kniblo, Solingen and Colmar

—— 1710. *Vindiciae Scotiae Illustratae, sive prodromi naturalis historiae Scotiae, contra prodromomastiges, sub larva libello de legibus historiae naturalis latentes.* Edinburgh: Andrew Symson

—— 1833. *Autobiography of Sir Robert Sibbald, knt., M.D., to which is prefixed some account of his MSS.* Ed. James Maidment. Edinburgh: T. Stevenson

Simpson, S. M. 1966. 'An Anonymous and Undated Edinburgh Tract'. *The Book Collector* 67

Sinclair, George 1685. *Satans Invisible World Discovered: Or, A choice Collection of Modern Relations, proving evidently against the*

Saducees and Atheists of this present Age, that there are Devils, Spirits, Witches, and Apparitions, from Authentick Records, Attestations of Famous Witnesses, and undoubted Verity. Edinburgh: John Reid

Smith, Martin S. and Roger A. Mason (eds. and trs.) 2006. *George Buchanan. A dialogue on the Law of Kingship among the Scots*. Edinburgh: Saltire Society

Sprat, Thomas 1959. *History of the Royal Society*, ed. Jackson et al. London: Routledge & Kegan Paul

Spinoza. B. 1663. *Renati Des Cartes Principiorum Philosophiae Pars I et II More Geometrico Demonstratae*. Amsterdam: Iohannes Riewerts

———— 1979. *Spinoza's Ethics, translated by Andrew Royle, Introduction by T. S. Gregory*. London: Everyman's Library

Stevens, William 1859. *History of George Heriot's Hospital*. Edinburgh: Bell & Bradfute

Stewart, Sir James 1669. *Jus Populi Vindicatum, or, The People's Right to Defend Themselves and their Covenanted Religion vindicated. Wherein the Act of Defence and Vindication which was interprised anno 1666 is particularly Justified*. [London]: [n.p.]

Stewart, R. (ed.) 1992. *A History of the Church of Scotland 1660– 1679 / James Kirkton*. Lewiston, N.Y.; Lampeter: Edwin Mellen

Stillingfleet, Edward 1662. *Irenicum. A Weapon-Salve for the Churches Wounds or the Divine Right of Particular Forms of Church-Government*. London: R.L. for Henry Mortlock and John Simmon

———— 1681. *The Unreasonableness of Separation, or, An Impartial Account of the History, Nature, and Pleas of the Present Separation from the Communion of the Church of England*. London: T.N. for Henry Mortlock

Sydserff (S'Serfe), Thomas 1668. *Tarugo's Wiles: or, The Coffee-House. A Comedy. As it was Acted at his Highness's, the Duke of York's Theater*. London: Henry Herringman

Szechi, D. (ed.) 1995. *'Scotland's Ruine': Lockhart of Carnwath's memoirs of the Union*. Aberdeen: Association for Scottish Literary Studies

Thackeray, H. St. J. *et al.* (eds.) 1926–65. *Josephus*, 9 vols. Cambridge and London: Harvard University Press, William Heinemann

Thompson, Stith 1932–6. *Motif-Index of Folk Literature. A Classification of narrative elements in folk tales, ballads, myths etc.* 6 vols. Bloomington, IN: Manumissa

Tobin, T. (ed.) 1972. *The Assembly, by Archibald Pitcairne. A Critical Edition with Introduction and Notes by Terence Tobin*. Lafayette, Ind.: Purdue University Studies

Tod Ritchie, W. (ed.) 1928– . *The Bannatyne manuscript writtin in tyme of pest 1568 / by George Bannatyne*, 2 vols. Edinburgh: Scottish Text Society

Tucker Brooke, C. F. (ed.) 1954. *The Elegies of Ovid from the translation by Christopher Marlowe*. Surnford: Fantasy Press

Vickers, Brian (ed.) 1996. *The Oxford Authors. Francis Bacon*. Oxford: Oxford University Press

Walker, D. M. 1980. *The Oxford Companion to Law*. Oxford: Clarendon Press

——— (ed.) 1981. *The Institutions of the law of Scotland / by James, Viscount Stair*. Glasgow: University Presses of Edinburgh and Glasgow

Weales, Gerald (ed.) 1966. *Complete Plays of William Wycherley*. New York: Doubleday

Wendel, F. 1965. *Calvin: The Origins and Development of his Religious Thought / translated from the French by Philip Mairet*. London: Collins

Whitehead, A. N. 1939. *Science and the Modern World*. Cambridge: Cambridge University Press

Wilson, F. P. 1970. *Oxford Dictionary of English Proverbs*, 3rd edn. Oxford: Clarendon Press

Wood. W. (ed.) 1847. *The Memoirs of Walter Pringle of Greenknow*. Edinburgh: William P. Kennedy

The Phanaticks

Prologue

*It's a long whyle since any play heth been,
Except rope dancing, in owre natione seen.*
Our northern cuntre seldom tasts of witt.
Our too cold Clime is justlie blamed for itt.
Nothing our hearts cane move, our fancie bribe   5
Except the Gibberish of the canting tribe.
But now in this our all reforming age
We've gott a play, the pulpite turnd the stage
& Jack the actor does appear devout,
The only way to catch the sensles rout.   10
With hums & sighs & Ha's & whineing tone
He preaches nonsense & rebellion
& to obtine his interest & designe
To brack the church & abdicate the King,
Insted of tears & prayers he uses lyes,   15
Impostures, Shams & horrid forgeries.
He uses Canons in the literall sense
And calls the worst rebellion selff defence.
Kirk discipline he seemeinglie doth prize,
Useing in privat VENUS exercize.   20
He teaches Children how to disobey
And shaks the laws of all moralitie.
Yet notwithstanding he slurs o'er the same
Evn with Religions all atoneing name.
These arms & weapns fairlie represent   25
The presbiterian CHURCH MILITANT.

True Comedie should humore represent.
We think for ones we've weall enough hitt on't.
No character too wyld nor yet extravagant.
But ther is no thing treated in our play   30
But quhat all know the whyggis doe act & say
So we've a teast of ther new Gospell way.

Our author gentlie doth beseech & pray
The Criticks' favor for his first essay.
Sure they have reason, for the Scottish witt   35

3

Is only givn to Censur not to writt,
Critiks for need, & ther are many such
Quhom art & natur have not betterd much.
Yet if this play but tack, we'al promise more,
For of this kind we have laide up ane stoir,   40
Matter enough to mack at least a scoir.

Drammatis Personæ

Will: a discreet smart gentleman

Frank: his comerad, not weall seen in divinity, new come from his travells

Novell: a Jacobite news monger

Mr Abednego Visioner: a whig news monger

Lord Whiggridne: an emptie fool   5

phanatick peers

Lord Huffie: a meer mad cape

Mr Timothie Turbulent: Mr Frazer of Brae

Mr Salathiel Littlesense: Mr Gilbert Rule

Mr Covenant Planedealer: M^r Ja. Kirktoun   10

All members of the Commitie

Mr Solomon Cherrietrees: M^r Da: Williamson

Moderator: Mr Hugh Kennedy

Cleark: Mr John Spalding

Ruling Elder: Laird littlesense, a north cuntrie man   15

Mr Shittle: a complying Episcopall minister

Mr Orthodox: a non complying Episcopall Minister

Mr Turncoat: ane Episcopall Expectant turned phanatick

Mr Wordie: a presbiterian Chaplain to the Old Lady

Old Ladie: a bigott   20

Mrs Rachel: her daughter

Mrs Violetta:

neces to the old Lady

Mrs Laura: 25

a Captaine of the Guard

Maid

1. Act ffirst. Scene First. Bull Tavern.

Will and ffrank

Will: Dear ffrank, dare I trust myne eyes? Wha a devill hes brought you hither?

Frank: Ane Borrowstouness ship and a good protestant wynd. Dear Will, howe glad am I to see you. And St Gyles so nigh Convinces me that I am in Embro.　　　　　　　　　　　5

Will: Why, hes your sea viyage so distempered your head that you doubt on't?

Frank: No, but I have walked about the streets since sex incompased about with so many strange faces that I imagined my self cast upon some new plantatione in the othir sid of the Globe,　　10
for they looke not lyke the inhabitants of the world.

Will: Nether indeed they ar, for they came from hevne and some of theme brack their necks in the falling. But how long hest thou bene in toune?

Frank: Short whyle as yet – Upon my first arrivall I was charged　　15
to sie My Lord Whigeridne. All the way the croud gased on me as one some America Monster. This peire wes encompased with a dozen of Grammaceing fellows drest up in cloackes, Cringeing and boweing to him lyke so many beggars seking supplie from a cuntrie presbitery. Asked me on when the seidge of Mons wes　　20
raised.

Will: What anser made you then?

Frank: I said, as the truth wes, the 28th of March *Stilo novo*. Replys on of the Reverend Gentlemen, We ask not about the seidge of Stilo Novo in Savoy but Mons upon the Rhyne. Said　　25
another, how many lost K.W. in that interprize? Not many, said I, for it wes done ere he came. It's wonderfull providence, says he. It's the doing of the lord, says another. There's nothing impossible to God, says a thride. *On fears they'l say wer thyng or 2 if it should be writtn or printed.*　　30
[fo. 162v]

Will: What said you all the while?

Frank: You may be sure I hade little to say in this new way. Why (says this shadow of nobilitie) Is KW ther at present in Mons? No indeed, says I, But Lowis is, quhich quhen I hade scarce uttered　　35
quhen, with the universall consent of the wholl company, I wes

6

sentenced to the prisone for a certaine Animal called a Suspected person and hardly after ane Ingenuous relatione of the wholl storie escaped with the libertie to take a glass of good claret with you, my old freind, here. 40

Will: Good claret say you? Faith, that's hard without the Miracle of the marriage of Cana of Galilee. We have gott a sett of men who call themselvs Christ's discipls but methinks they ar most unlyke ther master, for the first effect of his power wes to give good wyne & the first of thers is to tack it from us. 45

Frank: In quest of good wyne Comend me to Hippocrates' discipls. I always found their advyce suitable in that. Come – lets taste what you have.

Will: Thy health, ffrank! Deil take me if K.J. will be more walcome to a starveing Curat than you are to me! 50

Frank: Canst thou give me no accont of my freinds in the Cuntrie?

Will: Little or non at all.

Frank: Then I think ther is nothing more hard to avoyd then speacking of the tyms, as they call it. 55

Will: Except it be speaking good of them – tho for my part I have no reason to Complain, ffor I find them as good whoreing drinking tyms as evir, for quhairas befor we wer most Christian Drunkards, now we ar most Catholik. And the Complements quhilk befor we touck out of *Cassandra* & *Cleopatra* for Courting 60 our mistress, we ar now beholdn to the song of Solomon for them. The money quhilk [befor] we gave befor to bauds, we give it now to phanatick ministers' wives and quhairas befor honest fellows Coyned new oaths at a glass of Wyne, we now send our representativs to parliament to doe it for us. 65

Frank: A wonderfull reformatne indeed! But what new oaths ar these, pray you?

Will: The alledgiance & Assurance. That is, to swear KW hes right to what he possesses, or els I can no longer possesse quhat I have right to.

Frank: Faith, ther's no danger in the Consequence, for I 70 confesse I should think it a subtile parliament could contrive ane oath quhich the natione would not first scruple at, then take and lastly bracke. But I admyre such a change, for the phanaticks wer turned mightie loyall Gentlemen befor I parted hence.

Will: Yow might have admired justly if it hade bein otherwase. 75 Who thinks strange if a pykpocket runs away with your money

7

quhen yow trust him, or that ane old rogue cheats a young
Cuntrie Squyer? I'le tell thee, man, for to belive a presbiterian
protestatione is as much as to think a man cannot cheat because
he Lyes. I'm resolvd never to trust a phanatik till I gett him on   80
his chear of verity, the stone at the Grass mercate. The villan is
then tempted to say something of the truth, that is, that he dyes a
rogue and a rebell.

Frank: Tell me sincerly, Will, what think you of the state of
the natione? My concerne about some freinds therine maks me   85
so inquisitive.

Will: Gad, it's a most monstruous hydeous body politick.
Nothing so Unruly as our rulers. I have nether tyme nor yet
rhethorick to describe it. You may have ane abridgement of it with
conversing with people in toune. A man that had walked betwixt   90
the Strait Bowe and the Cross could Imagine by ther converses
that he hade marched out of KW's territories to KJs – they have
both ther kingdoms in this toune, i' faith, only with this difference,
KJ domineers in the Taverns, KW's at the Councill table.

Frank: That must oblidge a man to ane Italian strickness in his   95
Conversatione.

Will: In that you may doe as you list, for I assure you sincerity
is a qualitie as much out of fashon as it's improsperous. Gad,
you'd sweare it haise beine abdicate in the late conventione with
K. James & declared a rebell to the stat. For my owne part, I   100
am forced to turne Torrie, for a man cane hardlie gett a good
Comarad or a Woman of Discretion or witt. On the othr syde, out
among our Whiggs, a man who hes as much sense as would keep
him from being disinherited of his faither's fortune is Compted
to statsman.   105

Frank: Pox on the Rascalls then! I'm resolved to have no more
to doe with them. It's a mean Ambition for a man to be the best
in his Company.

[*Enter Drawer*

Drawer: Ther's on Mr Novell, Gentlemen, desirs to speack
with you.   110
[fo. 163r]

Frank: Bid him come forward. Perhaps he will informe me of
my freinds in the Cuntrie.

[*Enter Novell*

Novell: Sir, your humble srvant. Dear sir, hegh – I have bene

8

anquireing for you in alle the taverns in the toune. Deare sir, quhen wes Mons takne? 115

Frank: I'm glade to see you weall. How does my father?

Novell: And how many men hes the K of ffrance ther?

Frank: I asked you, man, how all my freinds in the Cuntrie did. I have hade som ill report.

Novell: Nay, for we have hade such reports about the halfe 120 moon of Talemount & that damned Portiguise skipper.

Frank [*aside*]: The deil tack him for a damned eternall fool! – Will you resolve me as to my relativs in the Cuntrie & I shall give the thy belly full of that afterward.

Novell: Na, but the Marques of Buffliers, how does he? If thou 125 hadst not come, my 5 guyneas –

Frank: Woud I hade payd 4 of them, if thou wouldst but avys me quhen did you sie my freinds in the Cuntrie.

Novell: Cuntrie, say you? I'de have you to know – for I never went to the Cuntrie since the Revolution – I'de sooner goe to 130 Purgatorie, for why a man cane have no more Intelligence in the Cuntrie then good liquor her. News as sophistical as the wyne is, aye, Gad! But still concerneing Mons –

Frank: Then I'le tell. The summe of it is this, that upon the 28 of March It wes surrendred. 135

Novell: And all the Garisons putt to the edge of the sword, wer they not?

Frank: That had bein prettie indeed, faith, fully as ill as feighting and the artickles of peace in the generall's pocket.

Novell: Ther's ane honest fellow cane informe me. 140

[*Exit Novell*

Drawer: I have bene so plunged keipeing a Gentleman out of your Company. I told 1000 lys, but nothing will serve his turn – Ther he coms! He calls himselfe Mr Abednego Visoner.

[*Enter Visioner*

Visioner: I have not the honour of your accquantance, but I remember I wes in Company with your father, but I know his 145 minister, sweet Master Violene, wonderfullie weall – for you know Mr Hugh bade me putt up some Interrogatory about the affairs abroade.

Frank: I ask you pardon, for I nether know your Moderator, Mr Hugh, nor your K's affairs. 150

Visioner: The moderattor of the Generall Assemblie, Sir – not that I mean it as ane title of dignitie, for the place, yow know, is

9

ambulatorie, but no doubt, Sir, You cane informe me if ther be
any thing – I say, Sir, yow cane resolve me if the King is to be
conjunct Emperour –   155

[Reenter Novell]

Novell: Conjunct, say you? He will be sole Imperour or nothing.
I'le pawn myn ears he beis at the gates of VIENNA ere a monthe.

Visioner: I ask you pardon, I beleve he intends to be at the
gates of PARIS first.

Novell: Yes, I know he is alreadie at VERSAILLS.   160

Will [*aside*]: Ther two Gentlemen ar in a Mutuall mistack. We
must keep them ther, i' faith, for if they discover an another, they
will putt fyre in the house.

Visioner: Weall, Sir, but, think you, will our king have his
Court at VERSAILLS or at London, still meaneing, you know,   165
after he hes vanquished his enimies, you understand me?

Novell: Why not at London? – Yet, when I think bettir on't, If
he stays at VERSAILLS & if ther hapne to be another Revolusion,
they will not have desertion to lay to his charge – besids, it would
prevent frequent changes at Courte and a treasurer might make   170
himselfe riche ere a Cancellour Went to Versaills & back agane to
discount him. Weall, I'm satisfied. Lett it be at Versaills.

Visioner: Nay, ther would be this further inconveniencie in
it. My Lord, you know, hes nede ane Cotch. Now, ye know, he
might get ane Anstruther bark & hoop o'r to Versaills. But our   175
moderator, poor man, it would be too far a voage for him.

Novell: What a deil, would you not ventour to see the king?

Visioner: ffaith, I think it would ee'ne be too farr for him to
ventur.

Novell: Gad, I don't question but he would, if ther were anothr   180
Indulgence. I should hasord a new address, i' faith.

Will [*aside*]: Damn the fool, it will out!

Visioner: I'me sure the K. will never Indulge those he knows
to be enimies to his goverment. It's true the Q. is a little more
hereticall.   185

Novell: That's to say, she's a little more adicted to poprie.

Visioner: Indeed, for you say right, I can call it no other thing –
I see you undirstand matters, As on would say. Her's your health!
– But that Church of England! I hope in God to see it ruined.
[fo. 163v]

Novell: If it should, ther clargie only ar to be blamed. Gad,   190 these bishops of England ar a pack of odd fellows! They'd rathr part with heavne or they parted with ther benefices.

Visioner [*aside*]: A rare Gentleman this! – But have you heard nothing of King James his being ill?

Novell: If it be so, some people may be sorrie.   195

Visioner: The prince you mean? Yet I cane hardlie call him a prince, being sett up to defraud our present King of his just right.

Novell: And for that he deservs not the name of ane prince. A meer robber & usurper, i' Gad!

Visioner: I woud say that the poor babe hade no blame.   200

Novell: That's most certaine. But to defraud a poor Innocent Child of his just right!

Visioner: What child?

Novell: The prince of Wales – i' Gad, what othr?

Visioner: The prince of Wales! A shittne bastard! A meer   205
Imposture!

Novell: Are you ther, you Rottne Phanatick, you! I might have knowne you be your feindlyk face. Her's King James his health to you – drink it ere I'le be the Catt's Gutts of you!

                                    [*Drinks*

Visioner: Her's King Wm's health! See whou dare refuse it.   210

Will: Sitt doune, Gentles. We'v no quarrells heir.

Novell: King Willie, that Monkie in royall robs, that Cretur of the Giddie rable, that blasing Star of a Dutch fog, which will goe away in Smoack!

Visioner: King Jamie, a meir emptie title, by the grace of God   215
king of Great Limerick, Athlone and Galloway! A deserter, a runeaway, the ffrench king's first pensioner of State!

Novell: King Willie, the bullie of 20 or 30 german Lairds, guardiane of the protestant league betuixt the pope and the Emperour & the K. of Spaine and the Duck of Savoy, Genirall of   220
the most high & potent Cowsteallers of Inskilen & president of ane assemblie of mad men in this his Antient Kingdome of Scotland! A poor meane thing, within two months' march of Miserie!

Visioner: That's of K. James and his armie.

Novell: Dost thou know thy owne stat creed & Ministers'   225
Litany, ane Inglish Gazet?

Visioner: I'l have you! We use no creed or litany more than Carnall sense & reason in our religione.

Novell: It's a damn'd lye, for your Ministers' prayers ar all stuffd with the Gazet & I doe belive it's for no othr reasone they   230

11

have Shutte up the Coffe-houses on Sunday but least people
should know quhat they cane say and so stay from the Church.

Visioner: Weel, but what of the Gazet?

Novell: Mons is ten, i' Gad.

Visioner: That's a mistack. The garison of Mons have taken the   235
ffrench & detaind them within the toune & Compells them to keep
Garison for them there.

Novell: O God, such a notorious forgerie! The baltick kings
have forsaken the protestant legue – that's no true either, I'le
warrant.   240

Visioner: No matter, for ine ther sted we are to have the King
of Morroco, the K. of Mogull & prester John, who is presbiterian,
i' faith, & I cannot tell many Grand Czars & ducks & all that – I
tell you more, the French fleet is frozen in at Brest and Cannot
gett out this year.   245

Novell: All damnde phanatick lyes, i' Gad.

Visioner: I'le warrant. My Lord's man of Strutherdyks & the
[Erle] of Annandaill's vision of the 3 heads, all lys, I warrand, and
the torries will belive nothing at all.

Novell: And these phanaticks belive evrie thing. But I'le teache   250
you to speack truth, you silly rogue, you.

> [*Boxes him on the ears*

Visioner: I think thou'rt a messenger from Satan sent to buffet
me. Weall I'le mynd you the next rabling.

> [*Runs of, Novell*
> *chasing him*

Will [*to Frank*]: We've gott a bottle, now we'il to Church,
quhair perhaps we'il meet with a wench.   255

> [*Exeunt*

12

2. Act first, Scene 2ᵈ, The old Ladeis Lodging.

Discovers Mr Wordie sitting by Mrs Rachiel and his hand
about her neck, ane bible in ther hands.
The old Ladie walking beside.

[fo. 164r]
Old Ladie: Indeed, Mes James, I hope she will learne to expone
scriptur, will she not?
Wordie: She will be able to understand the hiddne misteries in
a short tyme In these words: three things be condiserable –

> [*Quhen the old Ladie*
> *turns, he kises Mrs*
> *Rachiel*

Rachel: So, three things. I understand that, *and, in hearing   5
work sincer Milk, shew secur base of grace-inbeareing, soul-
refreshing –*
Old Ladie: Blessed be God, Mes James, quho sent you to my
house. Great wes the scarcitie of family exercise we Laboured
under. But I hop shortly my daughter shall understand it, and   10
practise it as weale –

> [*Mes Ja: rises quhen*
> *the Lady speacks*

Sitt doune, Mes James.
Rachel: No, Madam, he exercises best standing. It's more
convenient, I thynke.
Old Ladie: But it's wearisome for Mes James.
Wordie: No, Madam, I'le give o'r in tyme.   15
Old Ladie: I know such is the frailtie of her natur that she will
wearie first.
Rachel: Indeed no, Madam. Mes James cane tell I Love it
very weall. I could hear him about the 3 things considerable 24
hours, but much exercise maks him dry, mother, and then he's   20
ei'ne forced to give o're, God knows sooner then I wished, many
a tyme.
Old Ladie: Teach her, Mr James, to drink in the sincere milk
of the word that she may grow therby.
Wordie: The truth is she is a verie plyable scoller.   25

> [*Exit old Ladie*

Rachel [*aside*]: The truth is, mother, I know my selfe growing

13

by it these 6 months bypast extremlie. My petticoat will hardlie meit by a quarter. He has used me so to it that I feare I shall hardlie ever live without it againe.

Wordie: How gravelie Lookt I, my dear, all the whille? 30

Rachel: You out did me not ther more then at the 3 things considerable. I wes at your chamber doore the day's morning, but you wes out.

[*They kiss*

Wordie: I wes at Mr Solomon and told him the caice, and he bade us not to fear but be cherfull, for he would assur me the old 35 Ladie would consent to the match & he would give it out that we wes maried more then 6 months agoe rather then to opne the mouths of the wickd, deboshd malignants by the scandall of your being with child.

Rachel: I hope the generall assemblie will give you a call. 40

Wordie: Doubt never that. I cane gett a dozen whenn I please. What tyme shall we meet at night?

Rachel: I'le come to your Chamber about 12 or 1. My two wanton Cusins, Violetta & Laura, begine to suspect my being with child. They would be glad of this to task me with, for many a fair 45 Lectur have I read to them against the scandalous custome of the speaking of men & looking over the windows at them.

Wordie: They shall know nothing of it. We must now part. I must goe heir what the Comittie does today. So expects you according to your promise. 50

[*Kisses*

Rachel: Yow never knew me faill yow. I ever hated lying. It's a most damnable sin.

Wordie: Indeed. It's a most vyle sin.

[*Rachel*:] But Mum! Her coms my 2 Cusins.

[*Enter Laura & Violetta*

Violetta: Methinks, Mr Wordie, you keep my Cusine under too 55 strick disciplin. She hes quit lost her complexion of Late & seems to be so takne up with your exercise that she canna sleep in the nycht.

Wordie: Verilie, Madam, your Cusine, Mrs Rachel, may be a pattern, for I am always exhorting her to watch and pray and It 60 seems she's very observant – but e'n God bie with you.

[*Exit Wordie*

Laura: Your Cusin, my sister, and I am come to see if you will hear Mr Solomon preach today.

14

Rachel: It wer a sin to slipe the goldne opportunitie of heareing
so pretious a man. I'le goe mak my selfe readie.   65

[*Exit Rachel*

Laura: Weel, this congress is brock up. Faith, methinks my
Cusine Rachiel is not nyce on't, quhen she trucks up with this *jure
divino*. He promises not much, I'm sure.

Violetta: But he performs better, else Rachel would have
nothing adoe with him – but, Cusine, what thinke you of oure   70
life & conversatione at our godlie Aunt's huse? We see nothing
but Whigg Ministers & old Phanatick Ladies, we hear nothing
but long prayers and sensless tedious sermons and lecturs, save
sometyms for our divertisement we read to *The Call to the
Unconverted, Tormenting Tophet* & such profound pieces that, in   75
faith, I understand no more then our old Lady hears quhen they
are read no louder then the bellman crys.

Laura: Methinks *The Ladies Calling* will suit us better. But,
faith, sister, if the whiggs be sants, I will tack ther Communion
out of my Creed, for I'le belive nothing I hate.   80

Violetta: I'le be ryd of this Impertinent nonsensicall Clatter by
the first conveniencie, I assur you.

Laura: And if I doe not the lyk, may I be made a Nun, a thing
as Cross my natur as it is unbefitting my Complexion. But I heir
the bell. Come, lett us goe.   85

[*Exeunt*

3: Act first, Scene thrie. A Church. The Comittie Dabatinge.

Moderator, Mr Salathiel, Mr Turbulent, Mr Solomon, Mr Covenant,
Lord Whigridne, Ruleing Elder, Lord Huffie
with his whippe in his hand.

[fo. 164v]

Moderator: I see many malignant spys heir to day. They ar
come for ill & not good. I have sein the day when a malignant
ey Gott not leave to look upon the work of the lord. The greatest
nobles in the natione thought it the greatest honour to stand at the
doors of the house of God with drawne swords to keep out the   5
malignants whom they would have knowne be the virie first Glisk
of ther faces.

Turbulent: It's better to be a doorkeeper in the house of God
then to dwell in the tents of the wicked. I think it both ther honour
& duty & I think we should comand the nobls of our tym to doe   10
the lyke *in the Name of Xst our Mr.*

> [*Lord Huffie starts up*
> *& shacks his quhip*

Huffie: Since I am not thought worthie to be a member of this
godlie & learned assembly, & heir offer my self and whip to be
on of your noble guards at the doore & beg you to belive that ther
is no title with quhich I am dignified I would be prouder of then   15
being on of the scurges of the lord.

> [*Clackis his whippe*
> *againe*

Moderator: My lord, I cannot but Commend your zeall. I
am sure amongst all our nobls ther is non fitter to scurge the
malignants out of the house of God – But to our wirk, bretheren.
Ther is two sort of people who have takne ther hands from the   20
work of the Lord, ffirst, the Torries, who nevir putt ther hand to it,
2dly, the Court partie, so wee poor men Man e'n putt our shoulders
to it & take a good lift of the cause of Christ, for, I assur you, a
pek ne're brack on of your baiks.

Covenant: It's your owne cause, your owne cause, aye forsuith   25
is't.

Moderator: I Would faine ken fat ye wad doe.

Turbulent: Why, moderator, I think we have a thanksgiveing
for the defeat of the duk of Savoy.

Solomon: Rather a fast, for he wes on the Confederate syde.   30

Moderator: I think rather brother Turbulent he hes the right end
Of the string, for he wes but a burden to the confederats & God's
jugment came upon him for persecuting the poor protestants.

Covenant: Indeed, Moderator, he's a[s] good a prisbiteriain as
King William.   35

Moderator: Outs, brother Covenant, had your toung o' that. We
must not be too severe, we wont rip up old sores.

> [*All the Comitee speek
> togather, some for a
> fast & some for a
> thanksgiving*

Moderator: Let's pray to drowne the noise and quiet our spirits.

Covenant: Quhat needs all this fool praying?

Moderator [*prays*]: Our mynds ar disordered and we doe not   40
know quhat we ar doing or saying. Lord, giv's grace, or thou
shall not gett glory, and see what will o' that – Now, since be
his providence the Din's done, I would propose ane dilemma, I
mean ane alternative, whither ye will plant the kirk of Scotland
or England first?   45

Covenant: Trewely, Moderator, I think Charitie should bigine
at home.

Salathiel: Of a truth, Moderator, I think ye should plant the
kirk of England, for ther is no minister ther and we have a Call
to preach the Gospell throw out all the world. That place is all   50
o'rgrowne with bryers and thorns & the'l o'rgang Scotland too,
except we send able men to trad them out. Yow know I wrott
a book proveing that Kingdom to be guiltie of Scandall, error,
Ignorance, will-worship and, besids, many of them have a sprituall
seekness and pastorall relation with some of us.   55

Moderator: Will the folk of England call you, or will ye goe
back againe?

Covenant: What needs all this pouder about Mr Salathiel's
going back againe? The've got a good enough lend of him already,
I know. Lykways he dare not goe back, for ther's ane order from   60
a Justice of peace to apprehend him.

Solomon [*from ane corner*]: Tho' I am not a Member of this
meeting of Christ's kirk, Yet I am a prive member. I am Concerned
for the kirk of Scotland, *sweet Clark*, that pure virgine *with
dove's eyes*. Her lips ar lyk threeds of Scarlet, her speech is   65
comlie, her panting breasts & doves eyes ar lyke two young Roes

17

that ar twinns & feed amongst Lillies, her navill is lyke a round
Goblet & wants no liquor, her bellie is as ane heape of wheat sett
about with Lillies. She hes bein defyled these 28 years by the
curats. I then intreat yow, bretheren, for the merces of Christ, Get   70
able men with soul-refreshing & inbeareing gifts to doe duity to
her seasonablie & aboundantly, ay, ay, forsooth.

Turbulent: Moderator!

Salathiel: Moderator!

Solomon: ffortificatne –   75

Covenant: ffornicatione with the virgine – that's as ill as the
Curats' hobling on the houer of Babylon and getting the 14 black
birds – No more about that!

Ruling Elder: Cleense out the Keerats that the Gospell may be
preached. Lett that be deen, that the work of the Lord –   80

> [*On knocks. Opns.*
> *Enter a Webster*

Webster: My Lord Moderator –

Moderator: Away with these proud prelatick – call me brother
in the Lord J.C.

Webster: Weel then, My lord brother Moderator in the Lord
J.C., I have brought a Covenan from our owne people in S^t   85
Andrews to mack the worthie Earle a ruling Elder.

Moderator: Brother, you should ca' that paper a Comission.

Webster: Covenant or Comission, that's a' on, but I think the
word Covenant stands best. But ye'r book leard.
[fo. 165r]

Moderator: My Lord, by his providence, we've gott a Comission   90
from the zealous websters, souters and godlie women in S^t
Andrews for your Lordship to represent them in this Judicatorie.
It's gravaminous for you to have wanted it swa long & e'ne give
us your opinion about what we wes speacking.

Whigridne: I have done as good service to this honorable   95
Judicatorie as any man living by ruineing and rabling the Curats.
I have manadged the wholl civill interest with much wisdome,
yet, As Nehemias says, it requireth much mor to be ane office
bearer in the house of God. Therfor I desir ye will pray for me
six moneths without ceasing that I may be fitt for this great work.   100

Moderator: It's not dishonorable & e'en seeks god's blissing
and he nevir gave a burthen but he fitted the back for bearing of it.

Whigridne: Though I be Conscious to my selfe of my owne
imbicillitie, Yet I Shall ofer 3 things about plantations that ye wer

speaking of: first, It's the only tyme to delve in order to plant; 2dly, 105
It's the fittest month now for planting; 3dly, It's the only tyme of
the said month now to plant.

Moderator: My Lord, we know not what ye would be at. We
wer speaking about planting of kirks and ye ar speaking about
planting trees and hedges. 110

Whigridne: The matter is the same, for it's the fittest tyme to
delve out the Curats by the spade of the sprid.

Moderator: Let us adjurne now till afternoone and speack
about these things then at more leanth, at that tyme quhen we
meet againe. 115

[*Sceane closeth*

4. Act second, Scene first. My Lord Huffie in his nightgowne.

Enter Boy

Boy: The deil tack me, my Lord, if ther be not a wholl battalia
of boatmen & fidlers that hath besidged the house. I hardly escaped
with my liffe to tell you.

Huffie: You dog, wherfor must I be pestered with you too, you
rascall? 5

Boy: Good faith, my Lord, it's best your Lordship mak a civill
warr within, quhen the enemie threatin us without? They'l be hard
enough for us both, and besids we ar farr 5 from the guard.

Huffie: You damned Villainie, gett a whip, you damned rascall.

> [*Boy brings whip. Huff
> throws it at the boy*

Did I not brack it on the Lady the othr day? Gette me the great 10
whipe

> [*My Lord appears
> armed with his whip.
> Boatmen, hyrers &
> fidlers throng about
> him*

What would you have, you Villains?

All: We would have our money –

1ˢᵗ Boatman: I have sailed this boat these 15 years & the deil
tack me, my Lord, If ever I wes so guided be any man, Gentle or 15
semple. How shall poor men live quhen you, & the lyk of you,
will not give us our money but abuse us lyk dogs this gate?

Huffie: This to me, ye Villains?

> [*Offers to beat them*

2ⁿᵈ Boatman: God damn me, my Lord, if we'l be so used. Off
hands is fair play, 20

As John Moncur said to the Deil. Be my Sale, my Lord, And
your head wer as whyte as Willie Miln's beard, I'le ha' my fraught,
and that I will.

3ʳᵈ Boatman: God nor boat wer at the boddom of the Sea if
I'le not be payd. What needs all this? I served the Duk of Rothes 25
(his saul praise God!), Earle of Marshall & my Lord Dundee. God
gie'n the deil blawe me in the air lyk pilens of onyons if ever ane

of them offered the lyk to me since I crossed bruntIsland water,
or goe, gie me my hindmost –

Huffie: Gett you gone, you dogs! I'le slash you. Call the Guard!　　30

3ʳᵈ Boatman: What needs all this? Where wes all this slashing
at Gillichrankie?

Iˢᵗ Hirer: Dill a guard nor guard till we be payd! It's much to
your Lordship's Credit to abuse a poor lad this way. If you will
not pay my hors, pay the plaster for my head!　　35

　　　　　　　　　　　　　　　[*Shows his head*

Huffie: You damned rascall, you shall gett the Stocks to keep
for offering such a horse to a nobleman.

2ⁿᵈ Hirer: Rascall heir, rascall ther, it's a shame to abuse a poor
Lad's horse who hes no othr way to win his living by.

3ʳᵈ Hirer: Mack a dish of Kail of my pounie, As ye please –　　40
he is lying at the dyk syd. Tuix me & god, I payd 50ˡᵇ of god
silver for him not 8 days agoe – Noblemen! The deil made sutors
seamen, we have gott so many lords & earls now, in the deil's
name. God nor Belzebie had a backburden o' them.

Huffie: Villans, rascalls! – o God! to be abused for half a dozen　　45
of men – ther's no help. Quhat wod you say, Sirs?

Fidler: God bliss your Lordship! It wes not willinglie your
Lordship did it.

　　　　　　　　　　　　　　　[*Shows his nose*

But loock to our instruments. Here's a violon brock just at the
neck – all the toune will not putt her togather againe. Ther's the　　50
bais of ane old bess viol als god as e're man laid bow on – look
you, my Lord.

Huffie: Why the deil would you not play the tune I desired?

Fidler: Indeed, my Lord, I Knew it not.

Huffie: Must I give you money, you Catterwalin, obstreporous　　55
villains, baboun, to people who cannot play? Goe, all of you!
[fo. 165v]

All: We'l know for what we came first.

Huffie: Tack you heir your fraught, dogs!

Boatman: Ay, but what for cutting the Cable & leaking the
great bumper?　　60

Huffie: Tack you ther. What must you have, rogue?

Hirer: You know, my Lord, ther's so muich for the horse.

Huffie: Quhat? Your horse, ye dog?

Hirer: God damn him beis me Looks after him againe – that's
a good on, indeed! – besids the bracking of the great manger &　　65

my owne head. A baillie would have allowd me 4^{lbs} of assithment besid the fyne.

Huffie: Come to me afterwards & you shall gett a bill on the Minister of Weem's stipend.

Fidler: My Lord, mynd us now. Ye see my nose heir & my   70
sunday's Cravat worth 20 Pense spoyld with Claret wyne in the glass ye threw at me – Ye see, our fidles ar useless. The blind harper, your Lordship had a fling at him.

Huffie: Damn your heads & instruments, they ar so confundedlie tendre! Tack you ther!   75

Fidler: God bliss your Lordship and all your noble familie!

[Exeunt boatmen, hyrers
and fidlers

Huffie: Hencefurth, you dogs, I ordre you to learn to cur wounds & cary a box of plaisters along with you & not putt me to all this neidless expences – and gett 20 ells of whippcoards. I have not a wholl on in my Custodie.   80

Boy: Indeed, it's no wonder. Your Lordship used them so mercifullie on a Ladye yee brak your whipe upon her –

[Exeunt

5. Act Second, Scene Second. A Church

Mr Solomon absolving a fornicatrix, the Congregatione Looking on.
Will & ffrank sitting by Violetta and Laura, old Lady
& Mrs Rachel neir by.

Solomon: O the wickedness of man's heart! For once or twyce
to be surprised with the temptatione is no wonder, Alas! But for
one of the people of God to opne the mouths of the wicked & to
wallow lyk a filthie swyne long in the filthy sin of fornicatione –
O, it ssould be for a lamentatione! Say quhat wes, woman, that   5
tempted thee so long to ly in this filthy fact?

Fornicatrix: Oh, fra once this filthie abominable flesh of myne
had rebelld against the spirit and the deivill had gottne possessione,
what cared I for it? Let him doe with it what he pleased. It wes
not warth the keeping any more but preserved my heart cleane to   10
my blessed maker.

Will [to *Violetta*]: Fair cretur, would I hade the possession of
thy bodie.

Violetta: If you had, Sir, I wish you should deall more lyke a
Gentleman then it Seems the devil hath done with this poore girle,   15
after you have used it a whyle to give it up again.

Will: Why not, if ye wer so impertinent as to demand it?
[*Aside*] Weall, this is a happie encounter. She is a handsome
Cretur. I'faith, I find I am lyk the devill! Indeed, I have a vast
appetit for holie flesh.   20

> [*Mrs Rachell looks &*
> *frowns & warns Will*
> *be pinch to forbear*

But I see I have that monster to conquer ere I catch my Goldn
Fleece. Weale, I have fallne in a stratagem of Love wes ner
practised befor.

> [*Will tacks the Bible,*
> *throws up a passage*
> *to Violetta, quhich*
> *she reads*

Violetta: 'Behold, thou art fair, my Love.'

Frank: I am as weall stated heir as your selfe. I intreat you,   25
show me a place to show up to this Lady. I vow she is young
and pretty.

Will: Wish, fool! – thou canst not act this.

23

[*Violetta poynts to Will
& he reads*

'That thow wart as my brother quho suckt the breasts of my
mother, I should Lead the and bring the unto my mother's house.'   30

[*The Congregatione
dismisseth. Will offers
to Convoy the old Ladie
home.They stand &
discourse. ffrank goes
away with the Croud*

Old Ladie: Weall, I wish all the Nebuchadnazers & Balshazers
of the age wer lyke this young gentleman.

Violetta: Tell me, what may be the sense of the 8 chapter, 1
verse, of the Song of Solomon?

Will: The best Comentars say that Solomon alluds to the   35
Metaphor of a man Courting his mistres and, non being admitted
amongst the Jews be strict mothrs to Converse with ther daughters
save brothrs & such near relations, the bryde wishes her Gallant
wer as her brother that She might converse more familiarlie with
him. But since that cannot be, She wes forced to gett out and   40
seik him amongst the feilds and the toune Guard meet her &
maltreated her.

Old Ladie: That sense, it's verie Ingenuous and ther may be
severall uses of Consolatione and Instruction drawne from it.
[fo. 166r]

Will: Come, my beloved, lett us walk in the feilds, lett us lodge   45
in the villages, such as the Cannogat in respect of Embro, and
vineyeards, such as the Lady Murray's yeards, to use ane homelie
expressione.

Old Ladie: A wondrous young man this!

Rachel: He is so indeed – But I say you'l doe weall to tack your   50
Neice out of the way. Weall, if this be not a plott, then –

Old Ladie: Then hold your peace now – I could hear the
Gentleman expon Scriptur all the day long. He illustrats evriething
so weale with homelie expressions & applys so Naturallie to our
present Conditione that –   55

Rachel: That he will debouch your neice, no more but that –

Old Ladie: No rests, mistress, from your impious interuptions?
Thou art yet in the Gall of bitherness, for I see thou hast ane
aversione to edifieing discourse. Say on, Sir!

Will: The 8 Chapter, towards the closs: 'Thou that dwellest   60

in the gardens, mark and herkin my voyce', that is still alluding
to the metaphor of a gallant quho by some signe warns his Mrs
to make haist (a whisle or so), the sum with 'Early yn the next
morning be sex a'clock', with that in the former Chapter, that is to
say, 'mak hast in the morning to accomplish our Loves'.   65

Old Ladie: Thou art a hopfull young Girle. I hop god hes
blessed my panis takne on the.

Violetta: 'But I have a little sister that hes no breasts'.

Will: Most interpreters understand the Gentils by that.

Violetta: Just lyk this sister of myn heir, quhom you know,   70
Aunt, we had a great difficultie to bring to the rycht way. This is
the same metaphor caryed on a little further & the woman, after
that she hes bestowed her selfe, would give her gallant comand to
provid for her sister.

Will: Why, this is truelie the practicall meaning of the words.   75
Methinks it is but reasonable she should provid and be concerned
with her sister to be provided.

Maid: Mr Solomon & Mr Covenant ar waiting for your Ladyship.

Will [*asyde*]: I must be gon then – Your servand, Madam.

Old Ladie: I must wait upon Ministers. Your servant, Sir.   80

[*Exeunt Old Lady,
Rachel and Laura*

Will [*to Violetta*]: Madam, I hope you will be so much Christian
as to obey this word of prophesie. It wer a pittie a word & intrigue
begun in doctrine should not be brought in use.

Violetta: Good Sir, my divinitie is meir Speculatione. I belive
you think I had ane ill meaning?   85

Will: No, faith, but it's fitt ye converse some tyme with
practicall peices, besids that decorum requirs ye should practise
quhat ye preach, and for your little sister, my Comorade, who satt
next me in Church, hes as good breasts for her as any in toun &
will be glad to lead the stragling sister in the right way.   90

Violetta [*Is going & smyling on him*]: Weall, I'le try to obey
you for once. The will of god be done.

Will: And if I faill, I wish I turne Eunoch – This is the prettiest
way of Courteing presbiterian Ladie's daughters or neices (Gad, I
know not quhat she is yet) that ever I heard of. Let me be hanged,   95
but I shall Love it, the *bible the* better for it, as long as I live.
But I'le follow her at a distance that I may find her lodging – then
I'le soone know quho she is.

[*Exit after her*

6. Act Second, Scene Third. The Commitie.

My Lord Whigriddne, Mr Covenant, Mr Salathiel, Mr Solomon, Ruleing Elder, Clarke.

Moderator: Bretheren, It hath pleasd God of his good pleasur to allow us anothr opportunitie to show our zeall in his work. We'il call in the Curate with his petition. We'il cane on the Curat with his petition and dispatch him. But first let's resolve quhat ansr to give.   5

Salathiel: Resolve, my Lord, to give them Nothing at all, for give them ane insh & the'l tack a span.

Ruling Elder: I eedg it geed for the sekiritie of the protestant religion that na Keerat gett leive to sett his foot within this bigging.

Moderator: Mr Salathiel, quhat say you?   10

Salathiel: *Bona certe*, Moderator, if you have a mynd to hear quhat he hes to say, it's best to call him in, but if othrways, I think it best he be not called in.

Turbulent: I say, Moderator, If he beis admitted within these walls, Lett him not come Nie on of us. Tuch not the unholie thing,   15 saythe the Lord. Let us not Salute him or give any testimonie of respect or favour.

Ruling Elder: Or jeestice, Moderator, for it would ofend God.

Moderator: Shall we call him in that he may come in?

Ruling Elder: But see the dors be not opnd to him.   20

Moderator: Officier, Call in Mr Shittle.

> [*Officier calls. Enters
> Mr Shittle*

[fo. 166v]

Shittle: I bring a petition and address from my bretheren of the episcopall persuasne, desireing it may be read and ansred, upon which I tack Instrument.

> [*Throws money to the
> Clerk quho taks out
> his Spickticles & looks
> to it & putts it in his
> pocket*

Moderator: I shall just now call you in and give you your ansr.   25

> [*Exit Shittle*

26

Now, bretheren, what shall be done? – Now, My Lord, your advice in this junctur?

Whigriddne: If I should add to what hes bein said at this tyme upon this subject, It would be lyk a rash tuch of ane pencill upon a Compleat pictur by an unskilfull hand – Curats, not being the Ministers of Christ, it's fitt ther should be a subcomitie ordined to draw up articles against the petitione. 30

Turbulent: Ther hes bene nothing at all said on this subject at this tyme And I hope ye will not ansr it er it be read, will ye?

Moderator: Whither shall it be read ere it be ansred or ansred ere it be reade? 35

> [*All the Commitie crys
> at once*]

A vot! A vot!

Moderator: That our Spirits may be composed, Let us pray – Hem – Hegh – o Lord, who art the Author and finisher of all our disorders, who directs us in all our Confusions to doe thy holie will, Setle our Sperits and e'en gi's thy best advice to thy ain wark, or it shall goe on the war. 40

Covenant: Ein reid a lyne of it quietlie to see what they would have.

Clerk reads: 'To the ministers and others who by Law have pouer to constitute Church judicatories, the humble petition of the Ministers of the episcopall persusion' – 45

Moderator: Stop ther, Cleark, read no more.

Turbulent: We not heir it. They call's not Ministers of Christ.

Covenant: I belive they think us ministers of Iniquitie. 50

Solomon: And besids they say 'pouer constitute by law'. I hope ther's non heir thinks that he's constitute by law.

Covenant: Cane Law constitute judges of Christ's Church? No! And they call themselvs 'Ministers of the Episcopall persuasne'. We'il give no favour to any such people. We'il root out the Canaanits and not leave on of them alive in the land. 55

Ruling Elder: Indeed, wee should make ane act of transportabilitie ordineing the civill magistrate to banish them out of the kingdome beyond the lyne.

Moderator: Call in the Curate. 60

> [*Officer calls. Enter
> Mr Shittle*]

We'il have nothing to doe with your petition, Sir. Tack it to you againe. We'l give you our reasons afterward.

27

Shittle: We are Clear in our consciences to joyne with you in purgeing the kirk of all Scandalous, Ignorant and hereticall Ministers of all sorts and cheiflie of all such of our persuasne as 65 refuise to owne your comitie, for we auknowledge your pouer *de facto* over us all. And all pouer is of God, that's certaine, for it is of the 39 new artickls. But consider, it's not long since we wer in possessione of the pouer. God pulls doune on & setts up another. The inclinations of the people ar verie changable and let 70 that be a *Memento Mori* to you, Moderator. Besids, we propose verie reasonable termis of Comunion. We ar readie to subscribe the confession of faith, be in it quhat will. We are convinced in our consciences as much as any heir that no faith is to be keiped to a popish king and we both pray and preach heartily against the 75 late K. James, & K. of ff. to, with all ther accomplices. We ar as much against the dangerous principle of non-resistance & passive obedience as either yourselvs or the new Church of England, and we are clear for judgeing and deposeing of kings whenever they displease us. In short, Moderator, ye shall find our Consciences 80 as tractable in all things as your owne, exept on scruple we desir to be solved in.

Moderator: What's it, Sir?

Shittle: It's this. You, Moderator, you have all assurance & promises, you know from quhom, that your kirk shall be the 85 kirk triumphant and the Church of England thinks that she hes as faithfull promises, and as good grounds to think that she shal prevaill. Now, we ar not clear in our Consciences quhilk of the promises shall be keeped. Therfor, Moderator, all our hopes is that ye would lett us sitt at our owne fyreside and preach for 90 our stipends till this weightie case of Conscience be decided & resolved, and then we'il know quhat to doe.
[fo. 167r]

Moderator: Sir, in a word, for all your long speeches we'il have nothing to doe with you.

> [*Exit Shittle Shaking*
> *his head*

Turbulent: Better the house of God ly in Rubbish then be built 95 be Samaritans.

Moderator: Now, bretheren, it may be cause of Lamentatione to us this day to see that the stats doe not goe on hand in hand with us in the work of the Lord.

Covenant: It setts them weall indeed to be as farr forward in the 100

work of the lord as his own servants. Na, Moderator, if they keep
sight of us and be readie at our call, we'il seek no mor of them.

Salathiel: Alas, Mod., they ar so farr from that that the[y] seem
now to have turned ther back on us. Quhat, have they not be act of
parliament takne away the verie thunderbolt of excommunicatne   105
from us, have they not takne away all the Civill and temporall
effects of it?

Ruling Elder: Fat ha they don? If that be true, we ar but a beech
of dron bees without stings.

Covenant: Indeed, brothr, you say verie ryt. What will   110
malignants care for our curses if we can doe na mair? Ye ken
the'r better at that than we ar. Na, herry them & Sham them wes
the good old way.

Salathiel: But what wes my lord Whigridne & the rest of our
eld who ar members of parliament doing when that act past?   115

Moderator: In truth, they cannot be blamed for that, because
it would have lookt too prelatick lyk in them to have watched &
guarded that the Church sustined no prejudice. You know yt wes a
reasone givne for prelats being in all Courts. Morover they know
if any such act wes made, it wes ane Impious Law & therfor of no 120
force – But, my Lord, quhat say you for yourselff?

Whigridne: We have now reasone to lament with Jeremiah, and
with David to sing 'Except the Lord build the house' – And the
Kirk of Scotland in my Lord My father's tyme wes so fortified
with Canons, pyks and Guns that ther wes no Suppriseing of her.   125
But now she's lyk a garden without eithr hedge or defence. We
ar left to our selvs evry way & that's a hard caice, for who would
have thought that, in so good ane act as this, rescinding severall
acts of parliament, as that of keeping the 29 of May, they should
have foisted in these wicked acts anent Excommunicatne, for, to   130
tell you the truth, I nevir Considered mare of the act but its title
and that, I thought, sounded weall enough. But I have since syne
bein Consulting with Sʳ Wᵐ Littlelaw, a lawyer and freind of our,
quha tells me the claime of ryt will secure weall enough as to
that –   135

Ruling Elder: If we be na better servisd but be the claime of
ryt, I fear we ha a cail coal ta blaw at. I wad eins siker the quitray
fra fre quarters & the rest o' the abeeses mentioned in it & syn
we ma expect some geed o't. Bat good feeth, my Lord, Sr Wᵐ
Littlelaw hadna a's witts about him fan that Clause wes drawn,   140
an' sal seme at this day, for they se he taks fitts.

Solomon [*from a corner*]: Quhat fitts? Fitts of the mother? I have ane Infallible cure for that.

Covenant: That's a helsom disease, to be trubled in Spirit. I wish ther wer more seek a' that Disease.   145

Salathiel: If that be all, little matter. *Semel Insaniving omnes.*

Turbulent: What needs all this din about the act of parliament? Canna we make ane act rescinding & annulling that act of parliament, and ther's an end o't? This is no the first tyme we've done yt.   150

All: Weall thought! Most reasonable!

[*Commitie applauded*

Moderator: It's best we adjurn till tomorrow morneing. At quhilk tyme let's meet. Tyme's pretious.

[*Scen closeth*

30

7. Act Thrid, Scene 1. My Lady Murray's yeards.

Will and Violetta meet in a walk.

Will: I see, though west not the first Challenger, yet ye ar first in the feild.

Violetta: You see I'm a Woman of honour. [*Will offers to kiss her*] Off hands, good knight! It's too soon to graple yet. Since I wes not the challanger, I have the Choice of the weapns. 5

Will: I beg you pardon, Madam. Mutherers ar not to be treated according to the law of arms. You wounded me ere I did draw, and that in the Church too. I'm resolved to repay you er we part.

Violetta: Peace, Sir. I'le warrand you think me one of the Conventicle sighing sisters whom, if ye Catch be the bible, you 10 ar as sure of them as of othr maids quhom ye catch be the smock.

Will: Quhat more would you hav? Our love first begune in the Church befor the preist.

Violetta: Ay, but we must be ther againe er it be ended.

Will [*aside*]: Too much beutie, witt and Innocence! I cane 15 bear off no longer way – But this proud heart of myne! damne, whineing, sygheing, humble love – bear it out Stoutlie once mor.

Violetta [*aside*]: Weall, this is a fair pass, I find – trusting my person to a stranger, no wonder he think me a good one! Since I have rashlie ingaged my forces ther, next thing I must think on is 20 a safe retreat. I must keep a good rear guard.

[*to Will*] You wes better at preaching yesterday. What, not one word? It seems ye want a text.

Will: Faith, Madam, I have a text I would handle closelie heir.
[*Offers to kiss her*

[fo. 167v]

Violetta: Bear of[f], Sir! It's Superstitious to Kiss the bible. 25 Forbear a little. You'l find this text somquhat hard for you & you must pray ere you medl with it, I assur you.

Will: Hungrie people, madam, forgett to say grace. I shall not faill to say one therafter.

Violetta: Div ye value not the meat, if ye'l not prove the 30 cetshin, you mein?

Will: I must Contradick you, Madam, and, to lett you see how Conscientouse, I'le eat of this dish as long as I live. Gad, it's too good a morsell for a Sply Mouth.

31

Violetta: If you mynd to mack your daylie bread of it, Sir, 35
I'le be so much your freind you shall never tast it till I see grace
fairlie said.

Will: To be plaine, Madam, ar you not wearie of your godlie
aunt (for I have gottne ane account of your geneologie alreadie),
her eternall whineing and lectureing, all the Nonsensicall religious 40
Cant of the ryt revrend godlie blockheads of the phanaticall order?

Violetta: I wes never verie fond of these, Sir, & truly I think I
have e'en fooled too much tym that way already.

Will: Woud ye not be oblidged to any that woud deliver you?
I swear it's hie tyme for you now to be looking after the busnes 45
of your Creatione.

Violetta: I would gladlie know how that might be done. I belive
I should not be wanting to doe my part.

Will: I'le mary you at the rycts, if you'l find in your heart to
give your selfe to ane honest fellow of a mean fortune. 50

Violetta: Truth, Sir, I think it wer fullie as much for my futur
confort to bestow my selfe, and my little fortune I have, upon
you as some revrend Spark in a band and short Cloack, with the
patrimonie of the good gift of prayer (quhilk perhaps he will putt
in exercise 2 hours on his bridall night, quhen I would wish he wer 55
looking after some othr thing) And with as little as his father (who
wes hanged in the Grass mercatt for killing the king's officers)
had of honestie.

Will: Then I must acknowledge, Dear Madam, I am most
damnablie in Love with you and must have you by foull or fair 60
play, chiese you whither.

Violetta: I'le give you fair play in ane honest way.

Will: Then, Madam, I cane Command a person quhen I please,
and if you'l be so, or halfe as, kind as I woude wish, we'il tack
our haickney & troat out to ane honest Curat's house. Besids, a 65
Guynea or two will be Charity to him, perhaips.

Violetta: Hold a little, I am not readie for that yet! I intend
to parley, not to yield at first attempt, and my little sister is not
provided yet, according to the 2nd part of the lectur.

Will: Gad, I had forgott that. I wes tyed to you that I had no 70
mynd to think on my freind ffrank, who is most dangerouslie in
Love with her.

Violetta: Iff he belie not his nam, Sir, that may be a Match, too,
for she hes Laboured long enough in this purgatorie & would be
thankfull to her deliverer, I think – But by this tyme my Aunt will 75

32

be calling Loudlie upon her Chaplane, Mr Wordie, her apparent
sone-in-law, for familie exercise. If I wes absent, the absolut
decree would pass against me. I should be shut out of the verge
of grace.

Will: Why Call you him hir apparent son-in-law?   80

Violetta: Faith, it's apparent in her belly. But I must be gon.

Will: I hop one quha hes bein so Christianly bred will not leave
her first Love so soon; that's indeed a falling back, but in the
wrong sense, and besids how shall we meet againe? The Canticles
will furnish us with no mor occasion. I said all I coud on the last   85
one.

Violetta: I shall putt to a task, may perhaps fright you, to see
me, but it's the only way. Goe, get a double-necked cloack and
hie-Crownd hate and all the othyr appertinencies of a presbiterian
Minister, not forgetting the true tone, smaickering and sighing   90
decentlie, & in this disguise you may venter up to my Aunt's
house. Faith, you need not doubt your welcome fra hir. Faith, I
think It best you bring your freind ffrank with you, least Laura's
mouth water & she Spoil the plott. I'le prepar your way & tell
my Aunt I inveeted two goodlie ministers to dyne with her that   95
ar just now come from Holland. I'l say I sawe you at my Lady
Conventikl's loging this morning.

Will: By the Lord, I'le doe it! I could transforme my selfe to a
stranger monster for yor deare sak.

Violetta: But hardly to a greater beast. Sir, Laura will be at   100
Heriot's yeards after prayr, meditating, but I should not wish yor
freind ffrank know this. He would perhaps disturbe her privat
thoughts –

[fo. 168r]

Will: I belive he may, for he uses to walk ther to shun the
Impertinencies of Streite fops quho prosecut a man as unreasonablie   105
as evr a dragoon did a Freinsh protestant.

Violetta: Or a Cameronian a Minister & his gowne. But I must
goe. Adieu. Do you know our lodging?

Will: ffaith an that I doe. ffareweall, my dear. I am thy devoted
servant, I assur you.   110

[*Exit Violetta*

Now I'le goe to ffrank & send him to meet the little sister and
in the mean tyme I'l indeavour to lay by any little sense I have,
that I may the better fitt the Character I am to putt on – But ther
he comes.

[Enter ffrank

Good news for you, freind! It will doe, man! The Ladies ar   115
plyabl, be the Lord!

Frank: I'm truely restless till I speack with this Laura.

Will: She'l be just now in Heriot's yeards.

Frank: Gad, I'le attend her.

> *[They walk toward the*
> *street. They meet*
> *people as they goe,*
> *with hatts*

What Grave reverend People ar those, dost thou No?   120

Will: Gad, that's a parcell of Prisbyterian Ministers. Faith,
ffrank, these may be called the foolishness of preaching in a
litterall sense. Both in ther prayers & sermons, the'r mightie
Pindarick, for this sentence hes no more Coherence with quhat is
past, nor connexion with quhat is to follow, then the *Ave Maria*   125
hes on the *Lord's Prayer*. They hate confinement to sense and
Reason, but freelie give such confused notions as the spirit of
giddines dictats to them (as they use to preface it). This is the
only thing I know them keep ther promise in. What grasce they
may have, I canno tell, but for gifts, methinks they cannot be verie   130
throng about them. They have not, In my opinion, many talents
to ansr for (as truely they ar not wanting to cry doune carnall and
humane learneing), For indeed they are as scarce of thatt as off
candour and honestie.

Frank: Gad, methinks Christ's vyneyeard is butt ill tenent-sted,   135
as we say of our lands.

Will: If I had such tenents on my little interest, I vow to
Gad I should rayther lett it ly lay. Besids, iff my tenents wer as
impertinently homlie with me as they ar with ther Master, I should
not endur it so patientlie – But ther's a Convention of universitie   140
men who may be truelie divided into two Clases, ffools and knavs.
They ar all of the letter sort & the greatest part of the former; the
most of them ar so ignorant that it wer hard to tell ther *primum
Cognitum*. They ar for the old Heterogeniall principls, for they
speack on on thing, think a second, and mantaine a thrid & profess   145
a fourth. Says one fellow, Why should I loss my place for 2 lyns
of ane oath? Says another, I'le swear, but I'le be the old man still.
Says a thrid, I have a family must be mantained. Says a fourth,
I'le keep my place meirly to dispit my Colleogue who would have

me outted. So doune goes the oaths as weall as tender Claikns a   150
prysbiterian's throat after a long Sunday's exercise.

Frank: I thought these bretheren had agreed better & that ther
wes no gangling with them.

Will: Gad, these sparks can nevr agree quhill ther interests ar
divided. If they can cheat one another of a scoller, that's ther great   155
plott. Quhen once he is gott behind his nightbour's back, he'il
tell his conscience is as wyde as hell, so that, throwing dirt at his
nightbour, he bespatters himself. In short, honesty and Ingenuity
is banished far fra them. Dissembling is ther chifest qualitie.

                                          [Exeunt discoursing
Enter Lord Huffie, Lord Whigridne meeting him. Lord Huffie
hes ane whipe in his hands and dogs following him.

Huffie: Ho–ho-ho-ho etc. Good morrow to you, my Lord.   160

Whigridne: Your Lordship's servnt. Whither so tymely with all
this beastly eguipage, ha-ha?

Huffie: A hunting, my Lord. A little divertisement after the toyl
& fatigue of business.

Whigridne: Upon my honour, my Lord, I am mightly burthened   165
& born doune truely with weighty affairs of the nation. I'le tell
thee, man, I had not so much tyme as to kiss my wiffe these 12
months for publick business. My concerne with the State maks
me forgett my duty to my family. But I goe a hunting today too,
my Lord.   170

Huffie: Wher's your dogs? We'il goe togather.

Whigridne [Pulls some papers out of his pocket]: Ther's a brass
of weall pointed lybells. I hunt the Curats, my Lord, the wolvs
out of Christ's vyne yeards. I'm ane old tyk for them, ha-ha-ha.
[fo. 168v]

Huffie: A good Jest, I'faith. I think I cane rune doune a Curate   175
too, but I hope shortly we shall have non of that sort of Cattle to
hunt. Then your Lordship's dogs ly idle, ha–ha–ha-.

Whigridne: If it be othrgate, it shan't be my falt – I'le worrie
all I see. My dogs ar sure matines, ha-ha-ha. I'm told K. Wm.
will interdict the forest. He says he will protect the Curats *they   180
tacking the formula* they behaving themselves as becoms.

Huffie: Which if he doe, my father, my brother & I will lay
doune our Comissions. I shan't say much – but mum–

                                  [Enter behind them
                                  Visioner and Novell

Visioner: Let them fill them againe with frish men in haist. I'm
sur they shan't –   185
     Novell: Such beasts, you woud say.
     Visioner: Beasts or men, it's all one; butt speack disorderlie.
Lett me tell you, I had be sorrie K.W. losed such fellows. Faith,
they'l mak our natione famous for –
     Novell: ffor produceing monsters lyk the Indies.   190

[*Exeunt Visioner*
and Novell

     Huffie: If I whip not out the buyers and sellers out of the temple
of the Lord, lett my right hand forgett its cuneing.

[*Clashes his whip*

     Whigridne: I have Curate in chass today. My Lord, you must
returne befor the Counsell sitt doune. I'le need assistance; the
fellow hes complyd & may gett freinds. Quhen his busines is   195
called, I'le make me as if I never heird o't befor, so out pull I my
pocket book and, finding his name ther *ordine Alphabetico*, ther
say so that the Curat, such a man, wes drunk such a day, beat his
beaddall at such a time, plaid at Cards on such a Company, swore
such ane Oath, a bloodie-mindd mad rogue causd Imprison one   200
of the people of God for no other falt save his being at Bothwell
Bridge. Your Lordship must ansr The verie same, ye must avou
the whole Storie.
     Huffie: In faith, I shall assur the Lords I heard it this morneing
from your Lordship's own mouth.   205
     Whigridne: Weel, your Lordship's servant. I will goe to the
Comittie. If you be neir the Minthouse, accquant my Lord Garless
of the plott. You know he's a confederat – ha-ha.

[*Exit laughing*

     Huffie: I shall. Your servant, my Lord. Ho-ho-ho-ho.

[*Exit with his tranie*

8. Act Thrid, Scene second. Old Ladie's loging.

Old Ladie & Mr Solomon.

Old Ladie: Mr Solomon, have you not convinced my Neice, My stubborne, obstinat Nice, that ther should be Union & Comunion twixt the members of the said kirk and that, for the better performance of this, ther should be parity twixt the members?

Solomon: Indeed ther should be twixt Ministers, but no twixt   5
Minister & his 2 lay Elders.

Old Ladie: But as to the first postur in tyme of exercise?

Solomon: Indeed, I cane hardlie persuad her that a falne member will evir rise agen – But as for these things, nothing but experience. Wait but a whyle till she feel the inbearing work about   10
her owne heart.

[*Exit Old Ladie*

I am resolved to visit and deall with hir. She is in her Chamber, I hope –

[*Rushes forward to her*
Chamber. Laura retirs
in disorder

Maid: Pray stay a little. She is just now dressing her selfe.

Solomon: No matter. I must be present in season & out of   15
Season.

Maid: You'r in a prick haist, I'faith –

[*Exit Maid*

Solomon: I'm resolved to be Impudent for once. Madam, tho' ye wold be ne're so obstinat, these two fair breasts of yours [*handls her brests*] evidentlie prove a paritie in Church members. Look   20
you now, does the one of these insult or tirranize over the other, thus or thus? They live in brotherlie unity & concord togather. Doe not Imagine that the naturall bodie is thus orderlie and that the wise Creatur would suffer a blemish in the misticall

Laura: Good Mr Parson, you must fetch your similies elswher.   25
I assur you I'le ne're be parable nor Metaphor to your Church Government.

[*Laura retires*

Solomon: Dear Madam, fforbear that Antichristian name of parson. Curst prelacie runs still in your head. But this leads me to discours of bear breasts [*handling her breasts*] and Gaudie   30

apperrel. O what a hydeous thing this is for a protestant Woman
to have her breasts
[fo. 169r]
strowting out thus [*still handling*]. Some will discover them thus
farr to ther eternall shame [*thrusting his hand doune her breast*].

Laura: Men of such mettall as you cannot endure it, but   35
however me thinks you are a little too familiar. I'm sure you never
use to handle your text so closlie.

Solomon: It may be. You'l never know the difference till you
find me in the pulpitt.

Laura: I say once more, Good Mr Parson (if that will fright   40
you), forbear. You have not the things cane allow for pressing
into a Ladie's retirement so earlie. I mean Youth and Gallantrie.

Solomon: Nay, Madam, I think soul concerns. Yet I am not so
old nethr [*Looking in the Glass*]. But, Madam, the Concerne I have
for your bodie – Your mynd, I mean. And it wer a pitty such a   45
fear peice of the Creatne should parish and these bright eys quhich
shyne lyk the stars of the Sanctuarie. Putt your Confidence in me,
Madam, trust to my conduct. I'le cure all your fleshie appetits that
warr against the sprit. I'le carie you to a bed of roses, perfumed
with Lillies, wher you shall teast the sweets of Love. O, the hight,   50
the depth, the breadth & leanth of true, active Love!

Laura: Hold, Sir, fforbear! Gad, I'le not trust my little Spaniel
Bitch in your bed of roses amongst your perfumes and things.
Marke me, Sir – Foch, you sent strangelie of tobacco and saik! – I
warne you, no more of your Cant. I'le pardon quhat's past, but in   55
tyme comeing if I hear on word of beds, bear brests and sweets of
Love & such Gibberish that becoms your wry mouth as ill as that
fair wig does your monkie face I'le reveall all and Spoyle your
trade, In stead of a mortified sant & preacher of the Gospell of
Christ, a most prophane Lustfull and Impudent Villane.   60

[*Exit Laura*

Solomon: I'le gett me gone and tell her Aunt she is a good
proficient in the Lessons of grace. If I irritat her, she'il marr all &
reveall me to the olde Matron. She hes my thoumb under her belt
for once. I wish my whole hand wer ther indeed also, for, as old
as I am, she should find that I would –   65

[*Exit, shaking his headd*

9. Act thride, Scene thrid. A Church.

The Commitie: Moderator, Mr Salathiel, Mr Turbulent, Mr Covenant, Mr Solomon, Mr Whigridne, the ruling Elder and his Cleark.

Moderator: By his providence, we have gott the hardest of our work ower. We've den The Curats, who wer never planted in Christ's Vynyeard. Lett us now proceed to planting, for now all things are as they wer in the begineing.

Salathiel: Thanks to his predestinat Majestie for that, *Nam*   5
Reges ad exemplos totos Compositur orbos. But in truth, Moderator, I must tell you our Colledge is doing its duity to send out excellent men to the vineyeard. Thanks to M^r M–sie, who teaches them to dispatch *Cattigorietuaclie* and *Sincategormatice*, and Dispise vane philosophie & Mathematicks & Instruct them   10
in many things quhich the Malignants, who want grace, say are contraire to reasone – Indeed, Moderator, they ar above Reasone, and what they are contrarie to it? Quhat hath Carnal reasone or humane learneing to doe with Christ's Spouse?

Moderator: Wei've heird mickle good of him indeed, brother.   15

[*Salathiel*]: Truely, if all our proffessors wer lyke him, we should be as happie a Colledge as in Scotland this day, but you know some of them perjured themsels to dissapont our good doings. An' yet, far a' that, I man say, give we bie quit of one man, we wer e'en Niper-lyke yet. It's the Lad's doings that hath   20
purged the fountains and seminaries. They wer all o'rgrowne with Cart's Mathematicks & humane Reasoneings. Yea, some of them wes so Blasphemous as to Mantainie that the King wes supreame & unaccomptable.

Moderator: That's a' true, Mr Salathiel, but I think we've tein a   25
course with'm for that, be sicker of them. But as to the planting –

Turbulent: Truely, Moderator, I would have some of the Malignant expectants hooked, if we cold.

Covenant: The Curats ar bulls of Bashan & therfor I will speak a word about dogs and so have done. Ye know quhair ther ar bulls,   30
ther is Bull-beating, & quhair ther is bull-beating, ther ther are dogs. Now ther ar two sorts of dogs, God's dogs & the Devill's dogs. If ye latt in the Devill's Mastivs, they will worrie all God's messins. No mor o't.

Solomon [*from a Corner*]: I would have able divins to dress   35

39

the Spouse aboundantlie, in season and out of Seasone, and to
satisfie her Creavings & longeings, for, poor virgine, she heth bein
starved these 28 years. These

[fo. 169v]

Malignants are people who have good naturall gifts. I think if
they had grace to wait closs on her wark, we might admitt them   40
to the bryd's bed.

   Moderator: I know people that ar ryt good judges of gifts that
say the malignants ar as weall indued with them as any and they
may gett share from they come to our syde of the house; therefore,
officer, call in Mr Turncoat.   45

> *[Officer calls. Enter M^r*
> *Turncoat, bowing and*
> *cringeing*

Sir, What say you to me?

   Turncoat: If it please your godlie wysdome, I would know
quhat ye wold say to me.

   Moderator: It's cause, Sir, of murneing and Lamentatione to
you for ever, as long as you live, that you have dwelt so long in   50
the tents of Sin & have so publicklie committed uncleanness with
the whore?

   Turncoat: My Lord – I meane Moderator – I never in my liftyme
on the repenting stoole and consequentlie I never Committed
adulterie.   55

   Moderator: O, Mr Turncoat, I see out of the aboundance of
the heart the mouth does Speack. I see you a great kindness and
hankering after prelacie quhen you speak so the language of the
beast & doesno know the leed of the Sancts.

   Clerk: Sir, Doe you not know that Mr Covenant provd that the   60
Curats lay with the whore of Babylon and begott 14 Black birds,
viz., the prelats, out of that text of Revelatne, I laid her in a bed
&c.?

   Covenant: Ryt! But how come you to Comply with the
adulterous laws?   65

   Turncoat: O, the Iniquitie, Tirrany and wickedness of the
former tyms! I wes e'en forced to Communicat with them as I
would have done with a Turk or Jew, yea a papist, but I wes still
a good prisbiterian in my heart & I think that's enough.

   Moderator: Very good, Sir, and Guid ministers wer e'en forced   70
to doe the same. But ther hearts wer richt and that's all we or God
seeks of them. But quhat say you about prelacie?

Turncoat: I say it's a most Superstitious, Idolatrous order & Antichristiane, reprobated be God befor the foundatione of the world.   75

Whigridne: Mark, Moderator, he says Episcopacie's foundatn's in the world. He calls it ane order. I think he should raythr call it ane confusion, or else we'el tack order with him.

Salathiel: That's all na matter, my Lord, Whither it be a Confusion or not, so it be no order. But, as tucheing the *Confession*   80
of Faith–

Turncoat: I think It the best book in the world and that the penmen therof wer more then Spirittuallie inspired.

Ruling Elder: Nae more, my Lord Moderator. He calls the *Confession of Faith* a book. I think it should be called a bible,   85
for the *Whole Duty of Man* is called a book.

Covenant: No matter whither it be called a book or bible, for the word *Biblia, Biblie* may signifie both, so it be not a *Wholl Duty of Man*.

Moderator: Weall, Sir, you'l subscribe it without qualifications   90
or restrictions & assent to it Not only *materialiter* but *formaliter*?

Turncoat: Yes. I think ther's ane argument against the perfection of the Scripturs, becaus they contradict the *Confession* in the points of Universall redemption & reprobation.

Solomon: A rar gifted brother this! He looks not to have the   95
twe Corner Stones, the twe Cardinall graces, the good gift of preaching & lectureing togather and the long gift of prayer.

Covenant: I'le give you ane advice about reading, (1) what books ye should not read, (2) what books ye should read. (1) Read not prelaticall, papisticall authors, heathine, Jewish or morality   100
books. (2) Read Gray, Guthrie's sermons and Rutherford's letters, the *Covenant* and the *Confession of Faith*.

Moderator: The bennieson of the Covenant light upon you, Sir, for now and ever.

[*Exit Turncoat bowing
and Crengeing*

Weel, Sirs, I see this will not doe except we fall upon some   105
way to cause all the rich nobles & wise gentils concurr with us in the wark of the Lord. If they knew them selves, they would e'en come and lend us a fist without bidding. But, Sirs, what shall we doe with that?

Turbulent: As the Lord livs, I think we ar better without them,   110
for ye know the apostle says, not many nobles, not many learned,

Ritch, or wise. And think that the only mark our kirk hes of the true kirk.

Moderator: Lett us meet agen at 10 a'clock, bretheren, for I hear some ill reports that ther ar enimies to the kirk, so we'il doe   115 as much as we cane and leave the rest that we doe not undon.

                                        [*Scene closeth*

[fo. 170r]

10. Act Fourth, Scene First. Heriot's yeards.

Enter Laura and Violetta in a walke.

Laura: Sister, you told me your servand used to walk her to
shune the tedious Impertinancies to the toune fops, but it seems he
ethyr Shuns the opprtunity of meeting me or his freind wes dull.

Violetta: No, faith, sister. I find you in Love with him alreadie,
you'r so impatient. But if they be what we'r Certainly informed,   5
they ar nethr such sotts nor so ill-natured.

Laura: I would Love better a Conversatne with this brave young
fellow, that cane spaik sense & doe his Courtesie rycht, then of
the presbiteran blookheads, these haters of reason & these Creeres
doune of good manners as much as sett forms, who nothing know   10
mor of ther duty to a Ladie then to ther soveragne.

          [Exit by a walk. A little
          after, Enter Frank solus

Frank: Damm these phanatick dogs! Hed it not bene for their
long prayers, she had bein heir er now. I'm all Impatient to see
her. It wer more for her edificatne, and confort to her, to heir me
assur hir in due tyme I am hir humble servant Then a fellwo, after   15
so many wry mouths as might have feared a Necromancer, And as
many pangs as his mothr had when she bear him, tell his master
with ane Emphasis that the K of ffrance is a bloodie Tyrant and
ought to be rooted out – But heir she is – I'm all in a fyre! By the
heavns, she's fair! Gad, she's young!   20

          [Re-enter Laura, sola

Laura [*aside*]: He's ther. It's nou for gravitie – Let me sie –
I'le think on damnatne, as my Aunt bids me, quhen I'm inclined
to laugh.

Frank: Madam, may I have the honour to accompany you in
your walk?   25

Laura: If you would, Sir, It might prove scandalous and I'm
raithr resolved to hazart my owne Reputatne then ruine any title
you may hav.

Frank: No great scandall, Madam, for the place is publick –
Methinks It should ruine my reputatne to walk by a handsome   30
Lady, lyk a merchant on the Exchange – I'm sure it would in some
places wher I hav bene.

43

Laura: If it be only, Sir, a generall peice of gallantrie that I belive you ar readie to pay to all in toune, it hardly merits my thanks, so assur yourself I'le nethr laugh at you nor tell it for a jest and nobody sees to confuse you.   35

> [*Laura's going, but he detains her*

Frank: Gad, Madam, you escape not so. Since you had the patience to heir on (Mr Solomon I belive they call him) mangle so cruelly ane Innocent peice of scriptur yesterday, me thinks thou art nonsense-proffe. So ye must e'en beir with me a little. Besids, 40 it's Charitie to administer alle confort to me, for I am in Love.

Laura: I find it will out. I'me content it should [*aside*] – On Conditione you'l leave me, I'l promise you my best helpe. I'le pray for you, Sir.

Frank: If you be my intercessor, I hope I shall be soone happie, 45 for the lady is young, Ritch and handsome and may have many othr good qualities. Besids, she's ane Intimate of yours, I'm sur.

Laura: Mack your demands reasonable & assur yor selfe I'le doe all I can for you.

Frank: I tack you at yor word, madam. Gad, you'r the fair on. 50

Laura: I'm oblidged to you, sir, if all these good things be truely said of my selfe, for still belived them so, yet you ar the first flatterer that evir told me of them.

Frank: Then, at least, I have no declared rivall.

Laura: Nay for that, Sir. This is the way to gett you on, and a 55 very dangerous on too, for you'l make me fall in Love with my Selfe, to tell me of so many good qualities. But you must speak good things of yor selfe, er I cane love you, if ye wold be at that.

Frank: Ther I would be, indeed, but would be intirely beholdne to yor goodness for yor Love, for I disclame Merit.   60

Laura: But this is ane age quhairin Charity waxeth cold.

Frank: I'le only ask Libertie to serve you.

Laura: You'l 10 to 1 Exept wages in the end.

Frank: Ay, Madam, yorselfe or nothing – I could be Content to have earnest in hand.   65

> [*offers to kiss her*

Laura: Holde of, Sir! You'r a Saucy fellow! Besids, I would have not agreed. I must know quhat we can doe ere we swap a bargane. Coud you come evry day to church & be condemned, without ethr sleeping or whisling, to sitt gravelie to heir 2 hours of a sermon?   70

Frank: I could, evry Sunday in the week, to see you.

Laura: And to heir 10 or 12 verses of a plasme to a pittifull tune?

Frank: I could heir from the first of *Revelatn* to the end of the *Genesis* to hear you sing as on of the quiristers.   75

Laura: It seems you ar ane ill Divine. But these ar two mortifiing peices of sservice, are they not?
[fo. 170v]

Frank: fflat tirrany, as I shall ansr to Gad. But, after all that, could you Love, mary, live with me and begett sons and daughters?

Laura: If I would promise to live at home, read the scriptures,   80
sing psalms & pray in yor familie, I might doe my duty, perhaps.

Frank: Gad! I shall be very glad at familie exercise, I'le warrand you. It's not rallery on my part. Faith, I'm resolved I'le have you. I have a Camrad hes a plott on your sister, too. I can't tell if you know on't?   85

Laura: I belive I doe. I must try your fidelity & Curag, as my sister does yor Camrad. Goe putt me on a presbiterian's garb & meet me in my Aunt's against denner. Your freind is to doe the same for my sister. I'le accompany you & instruct you further. If you Love me as much as he does her, you'l ventur as far for me.   90
I'm generous and will reward you.

Frank: ffaith, that's hard, Madam. Gad, it's a monstruous disguize!

Laura: No more words – I see people coming & it's my first Comand. Adieu.   95

Frank: Madam, your servand –

[*Exit Laura*

Gad, I'le keep it most religiouslie, I'le endeavour to have as little sense and as much Hippocrisie as the best of them. But what if I should be ordined to say prayers or grace? – stay, quhen I wes yongue, my mother taught me a word or two –   100

[*Exit*

11. Act fourth, Scene Second.

*The Comitee: Moderator, Mr Turbulent, Mr Salathiel, Mr Solomon,
Mr Covnant, Lord Whigridne, Ruling Elder, Clark.*

Moderator: Bretheren, we ar meet togather heir in this place
by God's providence about his wark. We hop ther is non heir but
will go chearfully & willniglie on with the work & designe of
reformation. Indeed, our hands ar as much weaknd, for the Court
e'en begins to forget the house of God. Therfor we ought to goe   5
on with the more streanth, Curage and zeall in the work we are
going about. Cleark, read the assemblies act about plantations, for
that the thing we ar to madle with at this tyme.

Clerk: 'The ryt Reverend *Moderator & the* Genirall Assemblie
of the Kirk of Scotland, taking to their serious Consideration the   10
groath of prophanity for want of the Gospell & Aboundance
of hippocrisie through the preaching of the same, have with
Unanimous consent ordined the respective synods & presbiteries
to mak diligent search After all vagabounds and Randie beggers
& to give up ther names to the Kirk sessions' –   15

Turbulent: The Clerk knows not what he reads.

Clerk: If you heir it out, ye wold be Convinced.

Moderator: Say on, Sir.

> [*Turbulent offers
> to speack*

Don't disturbe the Comittee, Sir.

Clerk: 'The Assemblie appoynts ther nams to be delated to   20
the respective Kirk's Sessions and in Cace they be Contumatious
ordins the Civill magistrates to notice them ay and whill they give
Obedience to the Kirk.' *Extractum per me, John Spalding*.

Turbulent: I say, Moderator, that's not the act we ar seeking.
Not on word in that about plantations.   25

Clerk: Will you hear it read ower againe?

Moderator: Ther is no need of this. I think the wholl Comitie
seems to be satisfied that this is the act. Sir, you should not speak
against the wholl Comitee. Sitt doun, Sir.

Turbulent: The plantation act nams a sub-comitee who ar to   30
call befor them the Prelats and Curats that preach in the Cuntrie
and, unless ye mean them be vagabounds, I do not see that this
is the act.

Moderator: What if we doe, Sir? Ther's no great hazard. But will ye have a vott whither this be the act or not? Speak out, Sir.   35

Covenant: I think this debate needless. Lett Mr Turbulent tell quhat the act wes or else acquisce to the Comittee. I think the Clerke should be belived.

Moderator: Mr Salathiel, wes you present quhen this act wes made? Is this the act the Clerk hes rid just now, Sir? – Say, Sir,   40 and rid our feet out of this difficalty.

Salathiel: As the truth is in me, I cannot tell positively if this be the act or not, but for anything I know this may be it. *Nam de futuris glingentibus non dabitur determinata verytas.*

Moderator: What think you then? Must we referr it to ane vott?   45

Clerk: Now I have found the act.

Moderator: Sir, you ar to be blamed for putting the Comittee to all this trouble. Read it out, Sir, and see that you be ryt, Sir & not wrong this tyme once mor.

[fo. 171r]

Clerk: 'The generall Assemblie of the Kirk of Scotland,   50 Considering the great damage the kirk hes sustind, and dayly sustines thorow, from severall persons who call them selvs the Ministers of God, by venting the soul-destroying and Gospell-overturneing doctrine principly of Arminianism, Pelagianism, Arianism, Nestorianism & doe with ane Unanimous vott forbid   55 all such Ministers to preach in any place within or without this Kingdom, ay & till such tyme as they profess repentance to the Comittee for receiving Apostats.' *Extractum per me John Spalding*

Moderator: Now you have heird this act, what is the best way to treat with these prelatists who will not joyne with us in duity?   60

Salathiel: Ther ar 3 things in that busines would be narrowlie considered, (1), how we ar to treat, (2), with whom we ar to treat, (3 and lastly), if we shall treat or no.

Moderator: Sitt doune, Mr Salathiel. Let's ask my Lord's opinion – My Lord, what think your Lordship of the busines now   65 in hand for the present under our consideratione?

Whigridne: Such is the sence of my owne infirmitie, Moderator, that I need more then ane ordinarie stock of Confidence without your desir to declar my opinion. I perceive the thing befor the burd is Communion terms with the prelatick partie about quhilk   70 I shall speack but 3 words and have done. I shall begine with the last first. First then of the last. I think the Institutione of the Sacrament by our Lord J.C. to be the great work of Comunion in

the Catholick Church & that quhilk does distingish Protestants
from Papists & Prisbyterians from both. And, (2d), I think the   75
postur of sitting is mor decent then kneeling, quhilk is Idolatrous,
or standing, quhilk is superstitious and the most prophane postur
in that ordinance. Lastly, Moderator, The admitting persons to the
holy table is a matter of great Import & deservs consideration &
ought not to be rashly don, quhilk wes the error of prelacy.   80

Moderator: Will your Lordship be pleasd to explane yourselfe,
for some heir doe not understand you?

Solomon: Though I be not a member of this Comitee, yet I'le
give my opinion as if I wer a member in a Caice that Concerns
Christ's kirk. Get able, gifted men to doe duty to her for fortificatne.   85

Moderator: Sitt doune, Sir. What say you, brother Turbulent?

Turbulent: I advise that, for ane more exquisitive forme of
depositne, that ther be a *libella Universalis*, that's as much as to
say ane Universall lybell, & that two days compeirance on the
fornoon & afternoon of the same day be alloted for the wholl   90
Curats on this syde and the othr syd of Tay, that he be cited at the
instance of the Comittee to compeir befor it.

Covenant: To what our brothr hes said I have two queries, two
difficulties, on fear, and a proposall. Or rather two proposalls, two
queries, on difficultie and a fear. My proposall is that ther be ane   95
act prohibiting all ansring of Lybells, either by word or work, and
that the Curats be lybellit in falts as weall tto be done as done. My
first question is, whither we should plant ther kirk er we depose
them or depose them er we plant ther kirk. My 2d question is how
it is possible to wark the Curats who ar nethr in this syde nor the   100
othr sid of Tay?

Ruling Elder: Let them come in by a class of ther owne, which
with the other two – lett me sie, two and on mak just three.

Covenant: Weel, my difficultie is whither this lybell should be
writne or printed, and my fear is that the Curats call this indirect   105
dealling & judging my owne cause.

Turbulent: What – will not Christ be judge in his owne cause
at the last day? Did Josua, quhen he extirpate all the Idolaters
Citt evry man to personall apperance & give him a Copie of his
lybell befor hand? Did Christ, quhen he whipt out the buyers and   110
sellers out of the temple tack evry particular huckster wyff be the
lug? I trow not.

All: Strange sense!

Moderator: But as to all these, what say you, my Lord?

Whigridne: ffirst, to Conclud, ther being a standing relation   115
twixt pastors & ther flock, & Churches being comprehended in
synods & synods in presbitries, I would say that Churches being
Comprehended in presbiteries & these in provinciall assemblies &
these againe in Generall Assemblie, this would breed a kind of a –
a – you understand me now? Thus beyng joyned to the badness of   120
the wather & planting   100 following depositions either Imediatly
befor or Imediatly behynd, It would be Considered that ther be no
Stope, but Imediatlie to the work of the Lord.
[fo. 171v]

Moderator: Wher ar your doubts now, Sir? I fear they ar gon,   125
Sir.

Covenant: But still, as tuching the proposalls –

Turbulent: A Committee for the proposalls, anothr for the
questions, anothr for the fears.

Ruling Elder: We Cana vote a Comittee till we see wha shall   130
be on't.

Covenant: But as to privat Baptisme and Comunion –

All: Comittee or no Comittee!

Moderator: To appease this Multitud, Lett us pray. O Lord, the
Confusion of our mynds shows that our spirits ar in disorder &, as   135
we wer orderly befor our confusion begane, so we entreat we may
be so quhen it is ane end. And we thank Thee for so great order,
harmonie & Comunion that's amongst us, for, be we orderly or
confused, we ar all on gate –

Turbulent: I hear we ar to be dissolved, that this sunshyne will   140
not last. This should be takne notice of –

Moderator: I heir no less, brother, but I doe not belive it.
However, Sir, lett us adjurne till the afternoone, at quhich tyme
we'il meet againe & give a home stroack at least. I'the mean
tyme I think ther should be Comitties appoynted for appealls,   145
declinators and depositions, with plantations, pastorall relations,
spirituall seekness and acts of transportabilitie.

[*Ex. omn.*

12. Act Fourth, Scene thrid. The Abbagate.

Enter Lord Huffie kiking and whipping two dogs led be two
shouldiers. A huntsman with his hands bound. A boy.

Huffie: You damned Currs, I'le teach you to hunt contrar my
orders! & for you, Mr huntsman, I'm sure you must be dissaffected
to the present Government both in Church and State – Carry him
to the Guard!

> [*Ex. shouldier and*
> *huntsman*

Boy: But the poor Currs understand not your Lordship's orders.   5
Huffie: Peace, you rascall! I'le teach you & them both to
understand. Carry in the dogs & putt them in closs prisone. Lett
no body sie them unless ane officer be present.

> [*Exit shouldier leading*
> *dogs*

Boy [*whispers Huffie*]: Collonell's dogs, Sir.
Huffie: Devill's dogs, Sir! If the best Collonell in the armie   10
wer hunting contrair to my Commands (and wer a doge), he
should find no better treatment – Goe, sirra, we'l be follow. I
have Catcht his dogs hunting two myls within the toune contrar
to my orders & have layd them in prison till he give surtie for ther
better behaviour –   15

> [*Enter shouldier*

What, from your post, son of a whore, you!

> [*whipping him*

Shouldier: An't please your Lordship, dog hes brock thorow
the prison window and escaped thorow the gate.
Huffie: You villane, persue him, raise the huy & cry! If you gett
him not back, I'le cause Shuitt you for your neglect. Damned cur,   20
brack the King's prison! – Quhat, you rascall, littering? Persue!
Make hast!

> [*Exit Huffie, whipping*
> *a shouldier*

13. Act fourth, Scene fourth. Parliament Closs.

enter Will & ffrank discourseing. People passing by.

Frank: I cannot bear the thought of the disguise – rid me of it,
Dear Will, if it wer possible. I'd almost loss my new mistres as be
behold to lying, dissimulatione, sighing & double-necked Clock,
the *Covenant & Confession of Faith* for her.

Will: It must be. 2000 lb. and a handsome young Lady – the   5
end's pleasant, tho' the means be rough and odd – But see you
there!

Frank: That fellow looks weall.

Will: Indeed, ye have takne the best prospect of him first. He
looks big, as if he hade a mind to doe something, Gad, quhen the   10
man hes no more ill meaneings then the silliest cobler in toune.
He'l bluster & make a noise & tell it must be so and he will –
Why, nothing at all. After a pause or two, 3 or 4 sawis, a long
declaratne of his interest in the peerage & his concerne for the
good of the natne, he sitts doun & tells he's satisfied and will say 15
no more. In short, no party could e're fixx him, no favour oblidge
him, no stat of liffe content him. He's exactly lyk a Lady's petted
dog who snarls at evry thing but can byt non, except you thrust
your hand into his mouth.

Frank: Or lyk ane old Leacher, whos toung is the unruliest   20
member about him.

Will: Ay, a stat Hector with the spirit of a Chiken, who hes
bein all his lifetyme strouting & branking at Courtiers & each of
them, from the hiest to the lowest, hes trampled & pist on him.
His wholl honour lys in his title & blazon, his loyaltie as weall   25
as his religion is compounded in the want of all principls and his
Lady's Whigrie. He talks bigly of his Contry, but never did it
any othr service then to help to putt it in confusion to serve his
owne insatiable avarice, quhilk is the thing in the world that he's
constant to. If God & the Deil wer personallie in competition for   30
the Government, 100 lbs. odds Carry's him to ethr syde, and I
doubt not but if he had bein ane apostle but he had underselled
Judas. He's no man's freind & evry man's & yet no man's foe. In
short, he is a blazing nothing and below historie – Lett him goe
there.   35

Frank: I perceive, Will, thou'rt prettie fre in thy descriptions.

Quhat he that he seems to look evry wher and yet no way? He
turns so suddenly as if the De'l wer at his heels.

Will: Consider him, Frank. Thou mayst look as many ways as
he seems to doe and travell as farr as he hes don er you find it   40
out such anothr on. Befor his Cuntry wes curst To have him for
a magistrat or statsman, I'le pass for a pleasant sort of whoreing,
painting, talking, fidling, lewd fellow & a hero of fighting, fineness
& Bells letters, but he's made such a damned figur since he wes
Clad in silk and Ermine that a body would think that he had e'en   45
conjured the good old Gentleman of Hell himselfe to judge of our
livs and fortuns.

Frank: Is not this the mightie fox that made so long pedant
speech against his predicessors and for purposse to his praise
about shelvs & splitting & of adding the graine weights to the   50
ballance of equitie & all that? I remember I have seen abroad by
that speech.

Will: Ay, but ther's a difference twixt pedantry & madness. He'il
tell you the Government cannot thrive because it's not bloodie
enough. He's mad at witnesss that will not damm themselvs to   55
destroy the panall & sitting doune gravly in his robs he'l tell you
(in mokerie of all laws and government) that a good swird & a
stout heart is e'en a Lawyer or pleader's best securitie.

Frank: Then methinks we'v gott our livs & liberties as weall
secured if we wer in old Thomas of Mamsbury's State of Natur   60
– But, hark ye, what's he that comes with his gresie-cutt fingered
Glovs, Staff & Cravat string quhilk befor the happie Revolution
hes bein of Scarlett – protest to God, my old phanatick inquisitor!
But ha! His mouth's gon to the othr sid since I had the honour
to sie him.   65

Will: A Saint, and one as sure of worldlie wisdome as any othr
dyed a Callender. Gad! he hes not so much witt as dissemble.
Ask justice of him, he'l tell he's sworne to the contrair. Pray God
save you from his pocket. He hes as much ther as would keepe
the hangmane imployd this 12 months at the raet of 3 Curats and   70
as many Jacobits a day. His mouth, you sie, follows his word in
quest of his meaneing, but it now only returne to its proper place,
dispaireing to find it. That Staffe is a great Supporter of the true
kirk and his arse is more able to support it then his head. He hes
just as much mother witt as would serve him to be a provost of   75
a toune of 20s. of Comon good, as much religion as is necessr in

a lay Elder, as much Curagge as he may look on a snail's horn
without fainting,
[fo. 172v]

as mutch learneing as mack duity planie, As much honestie as
is required in a member of the present privie Councell, and finallie,   80
beloved, as much grace as is needfull in a Scots reformer, with
no More estat then cane be reasonablie expected in a presbyterian
peer & can secur him from the hazard of forfalting, the next
revolutne.

Frank: Hold! hold! – too much of him – he's below the dignity   85
of Consideratne – bliss me, quhat for a shittine monster is that
came Crawling out of that Coatch ther? He looks as if he wer
in great perplexitie, lyke some underclark second *man second*
bearing a burden of informatne.

Will: That's the spane of a nobleman, the true type of the   90
bodie politique. Ye see how confoundedly the head sitts and these
excressents reppresent the kirk that defams & burthens the state
extreamly. The pillars of both ar extraordinarie waik, you sie,
& crocked. That's the *Covenant* on his breast and in on of the
bunshes on his back, that's the *Confession of Faith*, in the other,   95
Calvin's book to prove *jure Gladii Coercendos esse hereticos*. If
he hes little of human Shape, he's as little of human natur & it's
impossible to tell if his mynd or his body be more deformed.
He breaths stink, spits venome, speaks vengence and Crueltie &
begets monsters. In short, ther's nothing lyk him but the rest of   100
his owne kindred.

Frank: – Rest! – Good God, cane ther be more then on of these
Creturs in a Natione at once?

Will: Faith, ther's a wholl familie of them, ffrank, and I'le
tell thee more, they ar the rulers & governours of this antient   105
kingdome.

Frank: Antient! – dam't for ane old sensless monster of a
kingdome, to be ruld be monkies and Monsters. Gad, that's to
burlesque Government & to affront humanekind to all intents &
purposes, to mak them governors.   110

Will: Thow grows angry, ffrank, I think, & therfor no mor
of these Catterpillars – Come along & tack a view of this old
wry-necked fellow with the fraudulent Countenance.

Frank: Anothr pillar of the government, I'le warrant. I shall not
say this government is against God, but I'm sure it's against natur.   115

Will: Weall, that's a true-blew rogue as ever pisht, whose

Conscience hes as great a wry as his Neck. He's as much sense &
philologie as to make himselfe a fool in print, as much honestie as
to make him a Whig & a rebell, as much law & justice as from on
decisione to give occasne for 7 new ons. He's begott a generatione 120
whose legittimacie non questions, they have so many marks of
the father & so true a westerne brood that, if the[y] live, they'l be
old Sir Haries. Evry on of them hes his turn of pettship & he's so
carefull to have unjust gaine delt so equallie amongst them that
at least in on caice he's for *suum cuique*. Thou sees he's a fresh, 125
vigorous old fellow & perhaps may live to be hangd yet.

Frank: But yonder's a serious Caball –

Will: Yes, about ther last night's intrigue for procureing a
whore or so. These are zealous reformers, I' faith. Base romish
popist *jads* – the'r not for them but for a singing, goodlie sister, 130
a Godlie, groaneing, prisbiterian sweet singer (whore in Inglish)
– that's ther good old cause, in faith. On of them is the strangest
mangrell between a brute & a man that cane be. He nethr speaks
nor thinks, and wer it not for his long wig,
[fo. 173r]
hate & black coat, he might pass for a horse in the grass mercat. 135
There's something of human shape, but nothing of human reason.
They nevr plott abov lying with a Chamberlin's wiff or picking
up a Street whore in caice of Necessitie.

Frank: And who ar these, Will? Gad, thou'rt mytie at epithets
this fornoone! 140

Will: That's a pack of Jacobitish Williamits, the strangest
monsters of the kingdom, with Jacobit hearts & Williamit hands
– Jacobit heads & Williamit tongues. They ar just now rewarding
the favors done the[m] be K.J. on his duty full sone and lawll
successor, K.W. They on the othr syd ar to restor K.J. They never 145
made a further plott to restore him then to writt a misticall letter,
drop in some ambiguous words without ethr sense or meaning, as
swapt up, give cautne, tack ane oath or 2 to the king. In faith, the'r
good for nothing but to be noble men & bear the title of Duks,
Marquises, Earls, Viscounts & Lords. 150

Frank: Cane thou tell me who are these with papers in on of
ther hands?

Will: ffaith, Sir, that's a parcell of people that ar nethr Jacobits
nor W^mits & yet woud be thought mightie with both. Gad, it's
the *Clame of Ryt* in on of ther hands! They love mightilie to be 155
suspected &, rathr then fail in that, they'l plott & reveall. Tell

them any thing & you may as weall placate it on the Cross. They
are a Company of discontented blockheads at best, with more
modells in ther head then some of them hav 1000 Merks.

Frank: Gad, I nevr saw such a congregatne of fools & Knaves   160
all my liff! I'm damnably wearied of this politiq exchange &
besids I long mightily for Laura. Pray thee, lett's begon & as
we walk along that mob of politicks, give me a hint of the most
remar[k]able of them.

Will: Thene, in the first place ther, a Calfe in human shap, a   165
long north Quintra feil young nobleman who hes no mor sense
then to be greedie and trublsome & no more Curag then he hes
witt & discretne. After he wes Shamfully chast weeping from his
own Cuntrie, he went to London, and since he came doune he's
gott a declaratione that he heth not a pocks, but it's thought he   170
stood more in need of a testimonie of his abilitie to gett on –
Ther's a pack of disbanded Collonells who raisd new regements
to thrust out ther old Master and ar now mocked be ther new on.
Ther's on of them too stamped in the deil's Coyn & non of them
saw, & some of them woud never have seine, & deil a on of them   175
woud e'r hav looked the enimie in the face – Ther's a young,
emptie fluttering spark of 22 Created a hero who wes sent to
dragoon ane Universitie to Whigrie & rebellion. Ther's a Collnell
fights Duells in buff. He brought the first news of Killickrangie,
tho he wes not neir the place & that all his Nightbors wer dead   180
upon the Spott, tho they ran away as Cowardlie as himselfe. But
tack notice, ffrank, heir's a bress of revrend, stearcht Villans, two
new doctors of Aberdeen refuting the old ons and Contriveing a
new address out of Sharlock, *Case of Alledgiance.*

Frank: Dam them & Sharlock too! Preists of all religions ar   185
the same, ther God is ther bellie & they ar Villans from generatne
to generatne – But, faith, it's dennertym. Lett's goe out. Gad, this
place smells of treasone & Infidelitie! I shall bespeack the Curate
that livs next door to the Ladies.

Will: And I am sure the Cloaths are ready.   190

> [*Exeunt. Scene Closeth.*
> *ffinis.*

[fo. 173v]

14. Act Fyfth, Scene First. The Cross. People walkinge.

Novell and Visioner meet.

Visioner: Good morrow, Mr Novell! Sir, I'l warrand you have not heard, or, quhat is all on, doe not beleive, the news about the late battle in fflanders, quhair the ffrench K's routed to all intents and purposes & the Dauphin takne.

Novell: O God! Unsupportable impudence, *Cuius Contrarium* 5
est Verum!

Visioner: It's true, upon my honestie, that the Dauphin is to be sent over to his godly wisdom, Mr Salathiel, to be bred protestant. He's the fittest Mr for a young Prince. It had bein Much for the protestant interest that he had bred the present tyrant off ffrance. 10

Novell: Methinks we should not have had so formidable ane enimie of him. The Dauphin is happie in this, that he hath learned his Latine er he came, for I'm perswaded he would have bein under ane ill Mr for that quhill under Salathiel's tutorie, who is so professed ane enimie to poor Prisciane (God help him!) as he 15
is to K. James, and hes no true Latine to himselfe.

Visioner: No Latine! – why, that's a Mistack. Did you not hear him speak ane oratne halfe-an-houer long, all Greek and Latine, just the othr day?

Novell: All the Latine and sense both in it myht have bein so 20
in a much shorter tyme. Ther wes never a sentence of Roman Latine in it.

Visioner: Roman Latine, qoth he – I know quhair I should find you. A presbyterian, protestant man to speack filthie Roman popish Latine! 25

Novell: I say that barbarous Ignorance. I' Gad, thou understands not. I mean such Latine as the auntient Romans spock.

Visioner: Still worse! That's my positne, that a presbyterian ought to speack presbyterian Latine, and ther should be ane act of the assemblie against all Roman Latine, *The language of the 30
whore*. I hop in God to heir non of it spak except K. James come back againe, quhilk God for his owne glory will not permitt.

Novell: Who cane endure this? What think you of this Latine, *Si aliquis virus colebit fasum Deum aut verum Deum, ut non scryptum est, iste virus est guiltus Idolatrie*? 35

Visioner: That may be good enough presbyteriane Latine. *Ye may as soon Induce him to Mass as to speack Roman popistic Latin.*

Novell: Damn me! *Si aliquis virus* speackes such Latine, *iste virus* should be hanged. But what think you of *Biblia potest*   40
apprehendi cum mediis extraordinaribus et supernaturalibus?

Visioner: Why, that's easie understood. *Biblia*, 'the Bible', *potest apprehendi*, 'cane be apprehended', *cum mediis extraordinaribus et supernaturalibus*, 'with supernaturall & extraordinarie means'.
It wes ay good Latine that runs smooth *with -bus & -orum* &   45
sounds weall. I must tell you plainlie he's a discreet, worthie, learned Gentleman & hes as much witt as –

Novell: I might tell you he hes much originall and habituall follie. He looks as if he had not o'rcome the freight of the late persecutne, or as if he had bein dryed sevine years at the devill's   50
Cichen fyre. He speak lyk a nurse counterfitting a bougle to fright ane ill-natured Child. He walks lyk a night Ghost, as if he feared at evry step the Jugements of his forfathers, Cora, Dathan & Abiram and, in fine, he thinks not att all –

Visioner: All Damned lys and Calumnies!   55

Novell: All true stories, I' faith. He'l make a Speech about *media vox, sinecategormatice* argueing with such bombastick words that he as little understands as you doe your *Confessione of Faith*. This he thinks sufficient plea for the reputatne of ane learned author. He not only plagues people to heir his nonsense,   60
he hes Spoyled
[fo. 174r]
      much good *paper* in his tyme that might have beine much better imployd to weip you know quhat – and all this of no other designe thane to writt that whilk he nethr cars nor knows, so it be against some books of Credit and sense & some author of   65
renoune.

Visioner: These are but false reports & slanders of the malignants, for he's a grave, wiss and proudent man and, to Justifie quhat I say, consider but the Government of the College.

Novell: Which is no Government at all. I' Gad, I shall swear,   70
It's no arbitrarie on. Ther's nothing done ther without the consent of the people.

Visioner: People, say on! Ther's nothing but ane pack of Malguided, rambling *Yo*uths, misled by malignant Masters & I fear the[y] begott a wrong *warp* alreadie, and if it had not bein   75

of the wysdome of Mr Salathiel, I think most of the fool's scollars
might have bein Changed as weall as ther masters.

Novell: They ar fyne young Gentlemen, the flour of the nobility
& Gentrie, the hope of the sinking state. They have more witt and
discretne then a whole Conventione. I hope in God to sie them   80
have as much pouer in the State & kirk as now they have in the
Colledge. Then, Thou Dog – you –

Visioner: Then I, and all my persuasne, will be forced to leave
the kingdome, for I'm sure they have severall tyms huft and hist
out of the Colledge lyk so manie Jesuits. I always found the old   85
Masters could have hindred the affronts be the Authoritie, but
now, I must confess, we ar in a worse conditne then ever. I see
the newe ons *Can't doe it*.

Novell: Nether indeed they cane, but it's no wonder that young
men of sense should disobey Masters that want abilitie to teach,   90
witt to Governe, honestie to be exampls and paterns. There are
few Youths in the Colledge who have not more Latine then ther
Primar and more logick and Mathematicks, *Philosophie*, then
the Masters who know nothing but Metaphisicall jargone.

Visioner: Ther wes never so many Tumults and uproars in the   95
Colledge as this year, such as bonefyrs *Mac*king and windows
braking.

Novell: And good reason for that. They scurvilie thrust out
the old masters, who had sense to overrule the students with
proudence and discretione. The Government might have as weall   100
sent in a Mountebank to the Colledge as that old fope Salathiel
to play the fool to the *boyes* – and, faith, I belive I have lyhted
on't. Would ye Kno the reasone why the government hes mad Mr
Salathiel Primar?

Visioner: Why, I think I know as weall as any puny Torrie.   105

Novell: Damn you for a rottne Whyg! I shall tell you the true
reasone. It wes to be even with Balls for abusing them. They've
sett up this anti-Ball; that's *strenuis strenua opposita*, I'faith, and
for evry boy of poor Boulis's, Mr Salathiel will have twentie.
That's Boulis *enervatus*, I' Gad.   110

Visioner: That's but the effect of the insolence of the students
that must be damed.

Novell: Insolence it's not, for they use it frequentlie. It's as
familiar with them now to play the fool with ther Primar as it
wes befor with ther porter. They persecute him most unmercifullie   115
and hunt him and his divins from Chamber to Chamber, lyke the

dissolveing of a Phanaticall Assemblie or Conventicle, or ane
terrier hunting a Tod and his puppies.

Visioner: It's better for him to goe to his Chamber then to be
hunted with a Number of extravagant Mathematicall Atheists.   120

   Novell: Just Contrair, for all ar Atheists Except Mathematicians.

   Visioner: O Intollerable Impudence! Show me a Mathematician
among a hundred that cars for the *Confession of Faith*! I'm told
that the first propositne in Euclid is to prove that the world is
eternall and the 2ᵈ that ther is no God. Besid that, on must have   125
a Compact with the devill er he understand them. I putt it to the
tryall and, upon my honestie, I could not learne to speak on word
of them, so I really beleive it's true.

   Novell: I' Gad, the height of Ignorance & desirvs no anser –
But, as tuching the worthie Primar, lyk ane old horse, cure him   130
in on place and
[fo. 174v]

                              he'il brack out in anothr.
He's now upon a project of making a German randy beggar ane
extraordinarie proffessor of theology.

   Visioner: I must confess I wes against that. My reasin is, we   135
must be rid of the Mathematicks. I would not Willinglie disoblidge
a man who cane raise the devill, so I'm clear the present professor
of the Mathematicks be made ane extraordinarie prophessor of
Theologie – Ther coms Huffy.

                         [*Enter Huffie. Visioner*
                              asyde to him

My Lord, this is the Malignant news-monger I told your   140
Lordship of.

   Huffie: I'm informed you gett rebellious news writt to you
quhilk ye vent throw the toune.

   Novell: Your Lordship's misinformed.

   Visioner: Upon my honestie, my Lord, he told me he had it   145
from a good hand that the K. of ffrance hade 50,000 men in arms,
God save, in armis (God save us! that's enough to cutt all our
throats).

   Huffie: Weall, Mr Novell, I'le warne you to tack notice that
you nethr heir, relate nor belive any things, any stories, contrair   150
to the Civill or Ecclesiasticall Government or you shall be lodged
in a Certaine place that shall be namless & your news both, and
lett me tell you that.

Novell: I assure your Lordship I shall nether relate nor belive
any thing that may offend your Lordship.   155
                              [*Exit Huffy*
                    Imprison me – not amongst your Collonell's
dogs, the Collonell you cured last year of the Clap! He advanced,
I' faith, to be Comander in Cheiffe for murthering of a dozen or
two of women and baggage boys. Gad, he hes hardly so much   160
sense as your selfe.

Visioner: But his being, as you know, dogs of the Government,
they ought to have givne good example.

Novell: But I'le make you ane Example for a rogue. To be ane
Informer against ane honest man – take the wages ye deserve!   165
                              [*Kiks him agane and*
                              again
And so fareweall for ever!

Visioner: Lett me be brunt for a witch, if e'r I doe the lyk
againe.
                              [*Exeunt*

15. Act Fifth, Scene Second. Old Lady's Loging.

Will and ffrank Dressed up lyk phanatikall Ministers in the hall.

Will: It's a strange Metamorphosis indeed! I'm sure it's next to that of Jupiter turneing himselfe into a toun bull. But that's all a matter. The Ladys assure us it's the only way to doe the business, ffrank.

Frank: Ay, and ane succesfull way too, I'le warrand. It will be   5
as puerfull as when Jupiter turned himselfe into a golden shower, if the sweet godlie ladies Can no more resist the Charms of this black velvet neck and that sneking meane then your maids cane the tinkling of a Guynea.

Will: Methinks I begine to turn phanatick all over. I could   10
raill most devellishly at Antichrist, the Whore of Babylon & the Government, Curse prelacie, solve the Caices of Conscience, devour pigeon pyes & Gulp up wholl boulls of Sack.

Frank: For my part I must fear I bisheheave. We might have hade some tyme to have acted our parts befor we had ventered   15
on the Theatre.

Will: Then I'le give thee my sincere advice. First, thou must forbear that Sparkish mean. 2ᵈ, beloved, Thou must banish farr from thee ffrench fashions & phrases. 3ᵈ, Thou must mortifie thy Corrupt inclinatns to speak sense. 4ᵗˡʸ, Thy ton must be grave &   20
affected, evry sillabe pronunced to the lenth of a breiffe, or semi-breiffe at least. Thou must Wearie the Company er they catch thee at the end of a period and then be sure they find no sense at all. 5ᵗˡʸ, lye *Incessantly* and sweir non. 6ˡʸ and lastly, beloved, Eate Chikne pyes as if thou had come from the seidge of Jerusalem.   25

Frank: I shall observe your instructions as far as I cane, but I am mightilie distrustfull of my gifts that way.
[fo. 175r]

> [*Rachell looks in &
> Crys*

Rachel: The Godlie Ministers, mother, Mr John and Mr Samuel, whom your Nices invited to denner ar come. They are the Godliest, bravest men, mother.   30

> [*Old Lady runs and
> hugs them*

Will: Grace, mercie and peace be multiplyed on this familie.

Old Lady: Wealcome to me, Gentlemen, and all your Mr's men.

Frank: We'd beg your pardon, Madam. We owne no masters.

Old Lady: I know, but the Master of masters. How could you
be so long in toune & never ask for me? Tho' I say it myselfe, I   35
have fedd many of the prophets of God in the days of tribulatne.
Look you, in this press were three or 4, in this Closett honest Mr
Covenant & Mr Solomon.

> *[She weeps*

Frank: But your two Neices, how did they?

Will [asyd to ffrank]: Pray thee, hold thy peace. Thou'l Spoyle   40
all.

Old Lady: You shall see them anon – But, look you heir, such a
rare Collection of Books I wes buying! Ther's Dickson's *Sermons*.
Ther's *11 Pynts to Bind up a Beleiver's Breeches*. Ther's *Bessie
of Lanerk*. Ther's Saml. Rutherford's *Letters*. Ther's *Good News*   45
from Heavn. And ther's *Satan's Invisible World*. What think you,
Mr John, of *Satan's Invisible World*?

Frank: Indeed, I think it's the best Sermon evr I heard.

Old Lady: Sermon say you, Sir?

Will: Everie thing May be called a Sermon insofar as ye gett   50
uses of Consolatne and instruction from it and all that.

Old Lady: Ther you say right. Bring a Botle of Sack.

> *[Sack gos round*

O but it's a sade world, Mr Samuel!

Will: Ane abominable, Curst, unjust, malicious, ill-natured
world.   55

Old Lady: A praying-Sensorious, soul-seducing, *wordlie
Wor[l]d*. A Gospel-renouncing, *Minister-Mocking, filthie,
Sabbath-breaking* world. A Malignant, back-slyding, Covenant-
braking, parents-disobeying World.

> *[Enter maid*

Maid: Ther's a poor man, Madam, says he lost his means by   60
the west cuntrie rable.

Old Lady: Came you to tell me that, you baggag? Beat him
doune stairs – But, Mr Samuel, It's a troublesome, beggarlie,
officious world. Vaine, guadie, prayer-slighting and reformatne-
overturneing world!   65

Will [aside]: Now I cane say no more. She's rune me out of
breath. She's a longer practitioner of this trad then I.

Old Lady: But how coms that Mes John says nothing heir?

Frank: Then I'le tell you, Madam. It's ane abominable –

whoreing – drinking – reformatione-overturneing world – And all   70
that –

Old Lady: That's said alreadie, Sir.

Will: Nay, madam, you must excuse my freind. He uses to be
deep in his meditatne.

> [*Enter two neices*
> *singeing & laughing*

Old Lady: I wes just going to call you, Neices.   75

Will: Is this the way to use the ambassadors of Christ – to mock
us? I expected to have meet with non of this within these walls.

Old Lady: Settle me a Serene Countenance. Ye'l laugh in hell
yet.

Violetta: Indeed no, Madam. We'l weep ther.   80

Old Lady: I recommend you both to the Caire of these 2 revered
Gentlemen. They ar to infuse unto you good and wholsome
principls.

Frank [*offers to lead Laura*]: Indeed, Madam, we shall doe our
duty to infuse the best we cane.   85

Old Lady: Nay stay, Sir. Since we ar heir, you must call the
servants togather. You must speak a word. Our ordinarie is in the
Revelatione about the beast with the sevne heads and ten horns –
Bring the Bible and Psalme book heir, Maid.

> [*Maid brings them both*

Frank [*aside*]: Lord, how I sweat & trimble! This is the worst   90
of all. God damn brought him in this *premunire*! – Would I wer
fairlie louse of this Character! I make a vow ne'ir to try the lyke
experiment againe – Indeed, Madam, My brothr Samuel is better
gifted that way.

Will: Not, Madam. Besids, he's the oldest Minister & ought to   95
have the place.

Old Lady: That's nothing. I have knowne young Ministers
better gifted at such familie exercise then the old. Indeed for a
caice of Conscience or so the old should be consulted.

Will: But, Madam, if it be about horns, ther is this further   100
reason. Mr John her understands the busines of horns better then
any man in the Kirk of Scotland. Indeed, he hes a peice in the
press relating to't.

[fo. 175v]

Frank: God damn thee, when –

> [*Old Lady starts*

Will: He's telling the oath he heird a Curate swear when he   105 came up the stairs. I belive he wes drunck too. But *God damn him*, blissed be His holy Nam, wes ar evry third word.

Old Lady: Indeed, these Curats are a prophane, Godless generatne. But I pray you, goe on, Sir. We shall keep back denner ane hour or two.   110

Frank [*Aside*]: O Lord, what shall I doe? I will rune for it and leave the rascall in the lurch. Ther's the disadvantage of the want of divinitie. If I had but learned the *Who made man?* by heart, it might have helped me a dead lifte at such a pinching occasne as this.   115

Old Lady: Perhaps you doe not use to exercise standing? Sitt doune, Sir.

Violetta: The Gentleman looks as if he wer indisposed, Madam. I woud hav you forbear at this tyme.

Old Lady: Peace, you Bagage! I know thou hast aversione to   120
evry thing that's serious. Bring a bottle of sack, lass.

> [*Sack goes round. She
> throws up the Bible.
> Frank looks to it
> accordinglie & says*

Frank: Ten horns, say you? I say that Bibl's quite wrong. The old translatne hes more then twentie heads and four*ty 4* horns and I knowe not how many Crowns and all that.

> [*Throw the Bible from
> him and sheaks his fist
> at Will*

Weall, Sir, if I be not revenged on you for this!   125

Laura [*Aside*]: Now I pitie him. He's *too* farr ingaged in my Service now to disert him in his greatest extreamitie. I'le try my Invention. Pox on't, methinks it's not a true womone cane forme ane excuse befor she cane putt her hand to her apron string. I'le say the denner will be Spoylit – but that will not doe, for she'd   130
rathr fast then loss a lectur. I'le Counterfitt my selfe seek, but then he must pray – that's worse still –

Old Lady: I thought this hade bein the best Edition, but I'm resolved to have on of the old versione, for I always thought that Antichrist should have more horns than ten. But We'el tak some   135
othr place that's ryht, or send for your Bible.

Laura [*Aside*]: Stay, I have it! – Madam, I think fitte the lectur should be about St. Peter's keys, for this is his day – Show me the Bible.

Old Lady: O Abominable! Nameing ane Saint's day! 140

[*She faints*

Violetta: Would S⁺. Peter wer heir to raise her from the dead! But till he come, Maid, bring the bottle of Cynnamon water in the further end of the press.

[*They putt something in
her mouth. She revivs*

Old Lady: Stand off, Stand off! Lett me gett a little air – So I have no Lectur heir this day. 145

Frank: Indeed, Madam, I wes neigh the poynt of fainting too. And now, quhen I doe rytlie remember, this is not only S⁺ Peter's day, But S⁺ Mathew's and S⁺ Andrews and S⁺ John's too. I wold be sooner brunt at a Staik then to Lectur in a privat familie this day.

[*Enter Solomon*

Solomon: I'm e'en come to Enquire if the oft-talked-of match 150 betwixt thy Neices and the Lord or holds or no.

Frank [*Asid to Will*]: Still worse then. It seems we have rivalls, and a Lord too!

Old Lady: It will faill on her if they doe not, for I'm sure the bans wer proclaimed long since. 155

[*Solomon*]: Indeed, Madam, I came to tell you in my Master's name he is weall pleased to mary them. He hath filled up the blanks of the contract, but he will not putt too the ring and say Amen to ane Imagination.

Frank [*Asid to Will*]: All meer stories & will on man Mary 160 them both? He'l have aneugh a doe, faith.

Will: Dull and Insensible! Dost thou never understand, will thou not distinguish, twixt these peopl's meaneing and ther words? The sens is Sprittuall, faith, and the words carnall.

Frank: Pox tack them, must a man travell as farr as the thrid 165 heavns to Catch ther meaneing? After this I shall be as wise as to hold my toung at least.

Covenant: I'm e'en come to tack a part of your denner, Madam, and to ask you if the ship be come yet.

Frank: Who deil cane guess the meaneing of that? My liff on't, 170 it's something about Noah's ark or S⁺ Paul's ship.

[fo. 176r]

Covenant: If she be not come yet, you may expect her shortly, for she sett saile from heavne ladne with goldne comforts for yourselfe and familie.

[Mr Solomon and M^r
Covenant Look to Will
and ffrank and putt the
o. La. in a Closett

Frank: Now, my Dear, I hope ye ar Satisfied as to my   175
Obedience. Gad, I'd rather have Courted you in a Civill way these
twelve moneths.

Laura: Methinks that Garb becoms you weall, Sir. Ye'r ane
excellent divne. Pray a word about horns.

Will: No tyme to be fooled now, Madam. Resolve and goe with   180
us. Ther's a Curate dwells next doore and, Gad, our Cloacks will
Conduct you doune undiscovered.

Violetta: It's e'en best to be Resolute. *[To Laura aside]* What
think you? May we trust ourselvs to these reverend Sparks?

Frank: Gad, We'il deall most discretlie and honestlie with you.   185
For first, Let's goe to the Curat's house and, efter he hes mumbld
o'r the matrimonie, ye have no more to say.

Laura: Lead on, Sister – you ar Eldest. I will follow Instantlie.

[As Will's leading
Violetta and ffrank
Laura and goeing
toward the Curat's,
they meet Lord Huffie,
who justles ffranke

Huffie: Zounds, Sir, no respect to a man of my qualitie? Why,
Sir, not craving pardon ethr?   190

Frank: No great offence, Sir. I forgive you.

Huffie: O God, you forgive me! I'l teach you breeding.

[Offers to beatt ffrank
who letts his Cloack fall

Frank: Faith, you'l find me a good enough Scollar at that trad!

[Kiks Huffie o'r stair
& looks at him

Fy, man, run away from your Scollar? I thought first he should
run o'r us.   95

[Frank taks up his Cloak
& is putting it on the
wrong sid upmost
quhill Will says

Will: No bodie needs fear his wrath, save Ladys, Boatmen,
hyrers, dogs, or anything that cane bid a beating patiently.

66

However, he's more then a gentleman, in faith (as he told a Lady
once quhen he beat hir), he's a nobleman. I'le warrand we shall
have 20 Laques about or ears just now.   200

Frank: If they be no better mattle then ther master, it's no great
hazard.

Violetta: Good Sir, you ar a turnecoat. The wrong side of your
Coat is outmost.

Frank: Then at least I have on qualitie of ane presbiterian   205
Minister. But it matters not. We have not farr to goe.

> [*Exeunt. Enter old Lady,*
> *Mr Solomon and M^r*
> *Covenant*

Covenant: We never knew them, Madam, yet perhaps they are
come over to work in the vyneyeard, for the work is great and the
Labourers but few.

> [*Enter maide*   210

Old Lady: Wher ar they gone? Laura, Violetta, *Mr John, Mr
Samuel* and all is gone.

Maid: Whom'd your ladyship have?

Old Lady: My Neices. Sawe you them?

Maid: The(y) desired me to tell your Ladyship, to tell you that
they are gone, evrie on of them, to gett a Covenant from the Mrs 215
& will be back shortlie.

Old Lady: Goe se wher they ar.

> [*Exit Maide*

I don't Love this. But, Mr Solomon,
what wes it ye wes telling me about Mes James?

Solomon: Not much, Madam, only I think it Convenient he   220
marie your daughter, Mrs Rachel, for I fear ther hes bein foul play.
But marriag will mak all ods evne.

Old Lady: What, my daughter marrie a dominie! She sha'not.

Solomon: Then, Madam, to be plaine, she's with Child and it
must be so.   225

Old Lady: What hear? Is my daughter deboshed, my family
abused?

> [*She weeps*

Solomon: Hist, Madam, lett them be made on by marriage.
Ther's no great hurt, he's a weall-gifted man.

Old Lady: O, But the Shame and Scandall!   230

> [*She wrings her hands*

Solomon: This will evit both. I'le say I maried them 7 or 8 months agoe. Ther needs no mor.

Covenant: Good enough. Marriage, It's but a Ceremony as weall as baptisme. I have know many a good Cuple doe duty lyke man & wyff who wer nevir married and good Ministers preached   235
of God's word who wer ne're baptised all ther liffe.

Solomon: I'le call them in. Brother! Mes James!

> [*Enter Rachel and*
> *Wordie*

Old Lady: Since these two godlie men will have it so, I am Content.

[fo. 176v]

Wordie: Weel, no more words then. I'm sure your good sone   240
& I hope your daughter shall live as good a liffe with me as you or she could wish.

Old Lady: I'm sure she's bein Christianly educate. Many a good prayer have I causd her say, many a Chapter have I heard her reade, many a good Sermon and lectur hes she read in her   245
tyme. I hope they have not beine lost upon her.

Solomon: Indeed no, Madam. I ever thought her weal inclined. She's a constant hearer of Sermons.

Rachel: I hope I shall find the good of them as long as I live.

Solomon: Weall I wish God's blissing on the married Couple.   250

> [*Enter Will and ffrank*
> *Leading Violetta &*
> *Laura, undisguised*

Old Lady: Wher have you bein, Neices, and wher ar the two ministers?

Violetta: Heir they ar, Madam. They have Cheated us & causd us mary them.

Old Lady: Are you married then, without my Consent? I'm   255
cheated under that godly disguise – O horrid!

Will: Yes, Madam. Be not offended, for we have done them the favor to ryd them of the impertinent truble of these blockheads.

> [*poynting to the ministers*
> *who Snaick off*

Frank: The ladies think our familie exercise a little more pleasing then the sensless Cant they have been persecuted with   260
at your house.

Old Lady: O hynous, abuseing the Ambassadors of Christ

and the presbyterian religion at my house! Gett you gone, you
Impertinent Jads! Let me sie your face no more!

[*Exit old Ladie*

Laura: That's no great matter, Aunt, Considering what we gaind 265
by your seing us, but I'm sorrie poor Rachel should Languish
under the insupportable burthen of a Maidine head and not to
pity her.

Rachel: Spare your sorrow, Cusine. I think I have bestowed
myne as weall upon my husband heir [*poynting to Mr Wordie*] as 270
you are lyke to doe yours.

Laura: And as soon too. A wordie man Indeed! And ar you
maried to him?

Wordie: Indeed I have betrothed her with her mother's consent
& that I hav. 275

Laura: I beleive you have bein in bed togather about halfe-a-
year ago. Indeed, for I wes going to tell you that I thought your
maidnhead bucksome a little, Cusine.

Will: Gad, the old presbiterian ladie's sweet daughter is as sure
of the Chaplane as the waiting woman is of the gentleman. But I 280
wish you much Joy.

Laura: Methinks they have not wanted that. They have antidated
it a little. But, Cusine, wher ar all your Long Speeches against
Kissing of men and Speaking with them, these wicked Customs?
Ther hes bein more then Speaking and Kissing both heir, I' faith. 285

Violetta: But come, enough of that! Let's mynd the work of
the day.

Frank: And the work of the nyht too.

[*Exit Will leading
Violetta and ffrank
Laura on way, and
Wordie Rachell
another way*

16. Act Fyfth, Scene Thrid. A Church.

The Commitie: Moderator, M Salathiel, M* Covenant,
and M* Turbulent, Ruling Elder, Clark.*

Moderator: Bretheren, we ar againe assembled
[fo. 177r]
about his owne wark. I hope you will not weary at all our
interests to mack a Cleane house and we will be on the wing of
the prayrs of the godlie in Scotland and of the flour therof. My
Lord Whigridne hes sent me his excuse, for, as he wes comeing,
he's sent for to the privie Counsell to Considre of a letter that wes   5
sent be His Majesty in reference to our affairs.

Turbulent: I think we should Consider how to fill the Curats'
places ere we lay so many congregations wast, since we have not
men to plant the 6th part of them.

Moderator: Had your tounge! Let us doe our duty. God will   10
e'ene provide.

Ruling Elder: A west quintra beleever, Moderator, ma werk
better then any Keerate in the north, and he'l ben sheen leir to
baptiz and marry.

Covenant: I think We should tak a word of the comon whore,   15
the Church of England, for we have drest our owne gaylie alreadie.

Salathiel: In truth, Moderator, of old the first thing evr the
Generalle Assemblie did wes purge the K.'s armie of malignants.
Now I think we have as good reasone as ever to purg K. Wm.'s
armie of prelatists and papists & atheists quhilk abound in it, seing   20
they are feighting for a good cause: *nam ubi finis est brevissimus,
ibi media debent esse proportionalia.*

Moderator: Outts, Mr Salathiel, with your Greek – we know ye
ar a Primar in the Colledge! I tell you we must not putt our hand
further then our slive cane reach. I fancie it's best and fittest for   25
us to medle with them that hav no pouer to resist us, I mean the
Curats who have not mynd to defend themselvs.

Covenant: Outward persecutne is no signe of God's forsakeing
them, for we wer persecuted 28 years ourselvs.

Moderator: God only chastises his owne people, but he destroys   30
the malignants. We did thrive under our persecutne, but the Curats
ar starveing, quhilk evidently provs them to be wicked & I think

we sud ca in Mr Othodox, that Curat who stays on the east side of
Tay and pesters the Cuntry with errors.

Covenant: They say he's a discreet, sober man and good 35
enough at his owne trad.

Moderator: We have the greater reason to be affrayd of him, for
he will doe us the more harme, for I assur you he's a Malignant of
a deep dye, for he teaches prelacie or episcopacie, Arminianisme
or Arrianisme, for the'r all on, ye know, &, to (to) Conclud all, 40
he's much for dry moralitie.

[*All the Comittie cry*

All: Monstrous, damnable opinions! Huge error & soul-killing
doctrins! Out, away with the Keerat! Cutt him doune! Why
cumbreth he the ground?

Moderator: Weel, e'en Call him in. Officer, call him in! 45

[*Officer calls. Enter M^r
Orthodox*

This is a Court fenced in
Christ's owne Name, for ther's no appeall to be made. We designe
to be moderate. We'el only tack your kirk, that's a'. Mark, Sir, that
ye are to be accused on falts as weall to be done as done.

Orthodox: Not to medle with the authoritie of your Court, 50
It's blasphemous to accuse me on falts to be done, seing God
only knows them. It's as ridiculous to pretend moderatne by only
taking my living, seing it's the only injurie ye cane doe to me.

Moderator: Sir, You'v learnd much Carnall witt & policie, but
you have not so learnd Christ. Clerk, read the universall lybell. 55

Orthodox: I designe to know who are the informers that,
according to the Law of natur and nations, they may be punished
if these things be no made out.

Moderator: Sir, they'r honest men and you'r no more concerned.

Orthodox: I'm concerned that they be not made wittnesses. 60

Moderator: We ar not concerned ovir your questions. Clerk,
doe your duity.

[*Reads*

Clerk: 'Wheras, **1**, —, late incumbent at —, wes boirne & bred
under the hellish order of Episcopacie,

2, That he received ordinatne at the hands of prelats and 65
presbyters, for they ar as guiltie that add to the Scripturs as they
who diminish from them,

3, He concluds his stinted prayer with the Lord's Prayer,

quhilk, quhen our Saviour made, wes certainly drunk, if ever he
wes drunk in his liftyme,   70

    4, Grace does no accompany his ministrie,

    5, he reads & recommends erronious books, such as *The Whol
Duty of Man,*

    6, He is Supinly negligent , for he mispends 4 days a week
in Catechiseing, quhich might be more profitablie takne up in   75
lectureing,

    7, He administrats baptisme and the Comunion privatlie, quhilk
is charmeing & sorcerie, and since the blessed Revolutione,

    8, He has keept no fasts on Sunday, ordined by us for seeking
God's concurrance to the abolishing of prelacie & the K. of   80
ffrance,

    9, He would comply and swear alledgiance to that Tyrran, K.J,
(who is both forsakne of God and man), if he wer restored agane,

    10, And lastly, quhilk is wirst of all, he would joyne cordially
with antichristian ordr of prelacie, if it wer re-established, quhilk   85
God of his justice will not permitt.

    Mr —, being guiltie of all this, provs his evident breach of the
10 Commandments, for quhilk he ought to be degraded, deprived
and destroyed.'

[fo. 177v]

Moderator: Sir, you have herrd positively quhat you have don   90
& negatively quhat you have not done. These ar sins of the scarlet
dye and ar all sufficiently provne be honest men quha have the
fear o God in 'em.

Orthodox: Sir, I should have heard the depositnes of these
wittnesss, for I am sure I cane prove them all infamous or guiltie   95
of malice against me, for this is according to the acts of parliament.

Moderator: Mr Turbulent, quhat say you to this?

Turbulent: We ar not to be guided be your acts of parliament,
but by the Sparit of God.

                                            [*All Comitee Cry outt*

[*All*]: Away with the Keerat! He hes had too long a lend of a   100
fatt stipend!

                                        [*On knock at the door*

Moderator: That looks lyk a malignant rape. Sie who disturbs
us.

                                    [*officer opns. Enter
                                    Captan of the Guard*

Captain: I have brought the King's letter, which must be instantlie reade and obeyd. 105

Moderator: We're about his owne work.

Captain: Sir, You'r about your owne busines & making for your owne interest and nothing att all concerned in the King's affaires.

Moderator: Sir, you mistaik us. I say we ar about J.C. his owne 110 wark in purgeing out the Curats and when we have done with God's work, we shall then doe his Majestie's grace's work, for better obey God then man.

All cry: It's better to obey God then man first.

Captain: You must obey us for once, for we have God's 115 authority, seing we have pouer on our syd. Mak haste, else –

Moderator: Else we wer disloyall subjects if we diputt the K. Comands. Clerk, read the letter.

Clerk reads:

'Gentlemen, you know what favour I have showne you and 120 have supported you because I thought ye had the people on your syde. I'm told you lost them by driving so furiouslie. All the world repute you as people that are enimies to monarchie, who are mad in your adversitie and in prosperitie insupportablie insolent. I have oftine warned you to keep Ecclesiastick dominions within bounds, 125 for I wes not borne in a Cuntry of *jus divinianus*, but still ye go one without reins. And the Church off England, who hes a greater people on ther syde, hats you, so we find it of necessitie to our government , That ye must not exarcise your Villanie any longer under our name & therfor We Command you Immediatly 130 to dissolve on the reading of these. And We require you to doe it on your perrill, for we ar your master, we will be obeyd.

W.R.'

Moderator: Bretheren, What think ye of this letter?

Salathiel: We sitt by a Comission under the broad seall of 135 heavne. The K's right ys only accumulative and not objectivelie privative. I think we should sitt and doe our duity & no be affraid quhat man can doe to us.

[*all the Comittie Cry '
yes'*

Captain: Doe not truble me with your ridicolous Cant & Gibberish, for I shall doe my duity, that is, to cause my Shouldiers 140 draw you hence.

Moderator: Sir, we will not displease you. Lord, send the king

good & goodlie Councellers, who ar for The(e) and Thy interest.
He's but a young man yet & he hes mickle neid of wise men about
him – Gie's only leave to speack a word or two & sing a double   145
to God and sa we a done.

Captain [*he interrupts them*]: You must not sing doune a
summer sune nor speack a day-long a word – Mack hast!
                     [*Exit Captain*

Moderator: Bretheren, We have brought our hogs to a bra
mercate, have we na? We have joyned with & supported this   150
perfidious usurper, wicked limb of Antichrist. We compact with
the devill who hes dethroned his honest old father & Uncle and
his tender young brother and sett them a begging for his curst
Ambitione.

[fo. 178r]

He promised to   155
protect us against all deadlie but, lyk Judas, you see how he
guyds. Cause read our sentence at the Cross & peir of Leith for
Angus' regement. We sud no doe ill that good may come o't.

Salathiel: He hath *Conscientia Hollandia* indeed who can sett
up in Holland atheisme o'r all religions, In England prelacie, In   160
Irland poprie, In Scotland us, And joyn in duty with them all. *Infer
ergo, Si aliquis virus guiltus est Idolrie, iste virus est.*

Turbulent: He pretends to defend the protestant religion but
Joyns with the enimies of it, As, the Pope, the Imperor & K of
Spaine etc. and if the house be new built, I'm sur ther's many a   165
foul finger about it.

Covenant: That tyrant sais lykways that he has secured libertie
& propertie. It's true – they'r so secured that non can call his
fortoun or his head his owne, for ther's a man that's both true to
God & his K. in his own fassion, he's clapt up in prison, ther's a   170
man treacherous to both and he goes frie. Bra wark indeed!

Solomon: To be plaine, his Ambition's hellish Hypocarit is
worse the(n) Jeroboam and Ahab, who made Israel to Committ
adulterie, and his Q. is lyk the painted Jezebell – the dogs shall
lick her blood yet and they shall be sent with Nebigodnazer to   175
eat grass in the feild with beasts for the unnaturall theu he brings.

Moderator: All kings ar tyrants and the Church never thrivs but
when it is founded on ther bloods. Now togthr go pray for another
of these so did agane. It wold relish sweetly.

Salathiel: They ar the wicked of the earth & should be   180 destroyed. I proved 3 year agoe that all the kings in Scotland wer damned because they wer all papists, and I'm sure K.W. is on, or ane atheist, with the rest, as appears by the Confederatione.

Turbulent: The Scriptur sais expreslie that the kings of the earth ar sett against Christ and his Laws. We should then observe this following verse, *Lett us brack ther bonds asunder and cast ther cords from us*, that is to say, the Oaths of Allegiance and Assurance, and let us steir up our bretheren in the west cuntrie to shake the tyrant's throne and lett our Assemblie be called in Glasgow by the authoritie of Jesus Christ alone, Our Sprittuall pouer being intrinsicall to us from J.C. & extrinsick to all kings and potentats of earth.

> [*The wholl assemblie cry*

All: A most excellent overtur! We'il all follow it!

> [*Reenter Captaine*

Captain: Pack you of, rebells!

Moderator: We'ive ee'ine bein praying for the king, for as ill as he is to us.

Captain: Gett you gone, you damned rebells! Your Moderator, quhen he saw his Majestie's letter, out of derision desired the Clark to pyck the Scabb from the wound o't.

Moderator: Lett's sing a verse to God out of the 109 psalme.

> [*Exeunt omnes in confusion, singing*

> Set Thou the wicked over him
> And upon his ryght hand
> Give Thou his Cruel Enimie,
> E'n Satan, leave to stand.
> And when be The(e) he shall be judgd,
> Let him Condemned be
> And lett his prayar be turnd to sin,
> When he shall call on Thee.

185

190

195

200

205

Epilogue

Our play is done. The Circumstance, the plott
Our authors out of meer design forgott,
For the phanaticks, quham we represent,
Have no fixt plott nor regular intent.
They dash throu thick & thine; amongst the throng   5
They'r always right and all ther nibours wrong.
Ther interest drivs them on most furiouslie
Without the ruls of Comon policie.
   Perhaps our freinds they may some anger raise;
We cair not, since it's truth our author says.   10
We doe for truth with the same curage writt
That honest Torries for ther king do feight.
We fear not then a privat shott or stab,
Nor yet the furie of the westerne mob
Nethr the greater rable of the State   15
Quhilk did our owne King Jamie abdiceate.
   Some also quho have much more zeall then Witt
May think we doe burlisk the holy writt,
Because our heros sometyms mak address
In sacred prase unto ther mistresss,   20
But the intelligent will always say
We've but obsrvd decorum in our play,
For Jack without a scriptur phrase could never
His mistres court or Cheat without a prayer.
   And now, since prayers ar so much in vougue,   25
We will with on Conclude our epilogue.
Let the just heavns our King and peace restore,
And villains never wronge us any more.

Commentary

Prologue

1–2. *It's a long ... natione seen.**: the asterisks indicate that the words enclosed are insertions in the MS, probably in Pitcairne's hand. The layout of the Prologue in the MS is cramped almost to obscurity. Pitcairne has inserted numerals to indicate the order of couplets and, on one occasion, to indicate the appropriate point for a couplet. In B and the printed texts the couplet occurs after line 6.

long whyle: play productions in Edinburgh were sporadic. Besides that in the Tennis Court at Holyrood several stages had been erected in or near the city, most notably one in Blackfriars Wynd, near the Mercat Cross. These were used, not only for plays, but for other entertainments, such as rope dancing; see the references in *Extracts from the Records of the Burgh of Edinburgh* (1927–67) and the *Account Book of Sir John Foulis of Ravelston 1671–1707* (1894); cf. too the passage quoted by Tobin (Tobin 1972: 8–9) from John Nicoll's *Diary of Public Transactions and Other Occurrences Chiefly in Scotland* (1836), describing a show mounted by the quack-physician John Pontus in 1663: 'Thir playes and dancing upone the rop or tow continued by the space of mony dayis, quhais agilitie and nimbilnes wes admirable to the beholderis: ane of these danceris haifing dancit seven scoir tymes at ane tyme without intermission, lifting himself and volting six quarter heigh above his awin heid, and lichting directlie upone the tow as punctuallie as gif he haid bene dancing upone the playne stones.'

I have not been able to consult Terence Tobin, 'A Checklist of Plays Presented in Scotland, 1650–1705' (*Restoration and Eighteenth Century Theatre Research* 12, May 1973, 151 ff).

2. *rope dancing*: see previous note. The association (or confrontation) of plays with rope-dancing is a Topic of the Exordium, which goes back a long way; cf., e.g., Terence, *Hecyra*, first Prologue (c. 165 BC), 1–5:

> Hecyra quom datast
> Novae novom intervenit vitium et calamitas,
> Ut neque spectari neque cognosci potuerit:
> Ita populus studio stupidus in funambulo
> Animum occuparat.

> (At the first performance of *Hecyra*, a vicious new misfortune interrupted the new production, so that the play could neither be seen or heard. In fact the stupid audience turned its partisan attention to a rope-dancer)

Nearer Pitcairne's time is Sir Car Scroope's 'Prologue' to Etherege's *The Man of Mode* (1676), 1–2: 'Like dancers on the ropes poor poets fare,/ Most perish young, the rest in danger are'; cf., too, Jacob Curate (pseudonym) 1692, 41: 'Others frequent them [the Presbyterian preachers] for Sport and Diversion, as Men of little Sense and less Business run after Stage-Players and Rope-Dancers.'

4. *too cold clime*: the idea is a commonplace, at least as old as Aristotle, *Politics* VII, 1327ᵇ, 23–5: 'Those who live in a cold climate and in Europe are full of spirit, but wanting in intelligence and skill'; cf. almost a century after Pitcairne, Adam Ferguson, *Essay on the History of Civil Society* (Edinburgh, 1767), Part Third, Section 1, 'Of the Influences of Climate and Situation'.

6. *Gibberish of the canting tribe*: i.e. presbyterian sermons and conversation generally.

8. *We've got a play*: i.e. in Scotland sermons now perform the function once taken by plays.

9–16. *Jack the actor ... forgeries*: cf. *Scotch Presbyterian Eloquence* (Curate 1692), 7: 'Such is the Force that a loud Voice, and whining Tone, in broken and smother'd Words, have upon the Animal Spirits of the Presbyterian Rabble, that they look not upon a Man as endued with the Spirit of God, without such Canting, and Deformity of Holiness. A Person that hath the Dexterity of Whining, may make a great Congregation of them weep with an Ode of *Horace*, or Eclogue of *Virgil*, especially if he can but drivel a little, either at Mouth or Eyes, when he repeats them ... They are more concern'd at the reading the Speeches of their Covenant Martyrs, yea such Martyrs as dy'd for Rebellion and Murder, than in reading the Martyrdom of St. *Stephen*, or of any of his Followers.'

9. *Jack*: a representative name for a group of men of common rank; cf. *DOST*, s.v. **Jak, Jack 1**.

13. *designe*: note the rhyme with *King*, indicating a pronunciation now obsolete. The spelling *obtine* also indicates an archaic pronunciation.

14. *church*: the episcopal church in Scotland.

abdicate: depose.

King: James VII and II, a reference to recent events.

15. *Instead of ... lyes*: B and the later printed texts read *Instead of Prayers he makes use of Lies*; the 1722 print reads *For Tears and Pray'rs, he makest use of Lies*.

17. *uses Canons in the literall sense*: The covenanting forces had one small cannon at the battle of Bothwell Brig on 22 June 1679 (Cowan 1976: 98). Pitcairne may have had in mind the use of artillery by the covenanting armies of King Charles I's reign. It was decisive, for instance, in the defeat of the English royalists at Newburn in 1640 (Gericke 2008: 33). See also below, 124 and n.

Although, the two words are not, in fact, etymologically connected, Pitcairne is making a verbal play between *cannon*, 'artillery piece', and *canon*, 'rule, law or decree of the church'.

18. *calls ... selff defence*: a reference, primarily, to the covenanting classic by the lawyer Sir James Stewart, bt., of Goodtrees (1635–1713), *Jus populi vindicatum, or, the people's right to defend themselves and their covenanted religion* (1667, printed, probably, in Holland).

19–20. *Kirk discipline ... Venus exercize*: a recurrent complaint, culminating in Robert Burns' 'Holy Willie's Prayer'; cf. the behaviour of Mr Wordie and, more especially, Mr Solomon Cherrietrees in the course of the play. Compare too *Scotch Presbyterian Eloquence* (Curate 1692), 5: 'Generally their Conventicles produced very many Bastards, and the Excuses they made for that, was, "Where Sin abounds, the Grace of God superabounds: There is no Condemnation to them that are in Christ" [Romans 8. 1]. Sometimes this, "The Lambs of Christ may sport together: To the Pure all things are pure" [Titus 1, 15].'

20. *VENUS exercize*: a play on *family exercise*, 'family worship, prayers'; cf. below 1.2, 7n. Cf. too Pitcairne's Latin poem *David ad venerem* (supposedly addressed to Venus by the Rev. David Williamson, i.e. Mr Solomon Charrietrees), especially lines 18–22 (MacQueen and MacQueen 2009: 102, 103):

> Mirentur Mahometem Arabes, mirentur et Indi,
>   Europam alterius Numinis urat Amor,
> Ast ego furtivæ Veneris præconia dicam,
>   Illi sacra libens tempus in omne feram.

> (Let the Arabs and Indians wonder at Mahomet, let love of another divinity consume Europe; I shall sing the praises of a furtive Venus and gladly make sacrifices to her for ever.)

22. *moralitie*: cf. *Scotch Presbyterian Eloquence* (Curate 1692), 23: 'Morality with them is but old, out-dated, heathenish Vertue, and therefore such a Book as *the Whole Duty of Man* is look'd upon with wonderful Contempt by them. *Frazer of Bray*, one of the greatest among them, professes downright, that there is no Gospel, nor any Relish of it in that Book'; cf. below, 5.3, 33 and n.

The Whole Duty of Man, laid down in a plain and familiar way, for the use of all: but especially the meanest reader: divided into XVII chapters; one whereof being read every Lord's day, the whole may be read over thrice in the year. Necessary for all families, was published anonymously in London in 1659 and became an instant bestseller in the episcopalian community. The probable author was Richard Allestree (1621/2–1681),

Regius Professor of Divinity at Oxford University and a devoted royalist. For a reference in the play, see below, 3.3, 67.

Allestree is also the probable author of *The Ladies Calling, in two parts/ By the author of The Whole Duty of Man, The Causes of the Decay of Christian Piety, and The Gentlemans Calling* (Oxford, 1673), mentioned below, 1.2, 62.

25–6. *arms ... MILITANT*: a play on the word 'militant'. Technically, the Church Militant is 'the body of Christians still on earth, as distinct from those in Purgatory (Church Expectant), and those in heaven (Church Triumphant)' (*ODCC*). Pitcairne exploits the overtones – Presbyterians behave as if the term were directly military.

Pitcairne echoes Samuel Butler, *Hudibras* (1663), 1, 189–200:

> For his religion, it was fit
> To match his learning and his wit;
> 'Twas Presbyterian, true blue:
> For he was of that stubborn crew
> Of errant saints, whom all men grant
> To be the true Church Militant;
> Such as do build their faith upon
> The holy text of pike and gun;
> Decide all controversies by
> Infallible artillery;
> And prove their doctrine orthodox
> By apostolic blows and knocks.

27. *humore*: a technical term as used of character in comedy; see above, p. xlix.

31. *whyggis*: Presbyterians of the extreme sort. *Whig* is probably a shortened form of *Whiggamore*, 'originally one of the participants in the *Whiggamore Raid* of 1648, when Covenanters from the West marched on Edinburgh, dispersed the royalist party and put the Marquis of Argyll in power; later extended to mean any Covenanter' (*SND*).

33–8. *Our author ... much*: a convoluted passage. The word *critick* is used in a double sense, initially, apparently, that of the literary critic or judge, but predominantly thereafter as 'censurer, fault-finder, caviller' (*OED*). 'Sure they have reason' (35) implies 'reason to behave in their normal, cavilling way', an idea developed in the following lines. 'Critiks for need' (37) stands in apposition to 'the Scottish wit' (35).

33–4. *Our author ... essay*: in B this couplet reads: *Our authors gentlie do bespeak & pray/ The Criticks' favor for our first essay.*

37–8. *Critiks ... much*: a slightly clumsy echo of the opening couplet in the Prologue to the anglicised edition of Jonson's *Every Man in his Humour*: 'Though need make many poets, and some such/ As art and nature have not better'd much'.

The couplet is crammed into the first page of the MS, in a different ink from the rest of the **Prologue**. Not in B, C or the printed editions other than 1722.

35. *witt*: ability, talent.

36. *writt*: 'Something written; a chronicle or story; poetry or literary composition' (*DOST*), with the implication that genuine literary criticism is unknown in Scotland. Also subliminally present is the phrase 'Holy Writ', with the insinuation that the controversial writings of the Presbyterians have little basis in the Bible.

38. *for need*: 'in an emergency, at a pinch' (*OED*), here perhaps 'for want of a better term'.

Drammatis Personæ

The form *Drammatis* (for *Dramatis*) occurs only in A and the 1722 print.

1, 2. Will, Frank: the names indicate the dominant features of each character. Will is the will as a human faculty, often contrasted with **wit** (perhaps represented by Violetta); there is also the sense 'carnal desire or appetite' (*OED*, s.v. **Will 2**) – Will, at least to begin with, is a rake. **Frank** means 'ingenuous, open, sincere'; there is also a suggestion of 'French'; Frank has spent some time abroad. For the contrast between the two, see, e.g., the opening exchange in 4.4.

2. *not weall seen in divinity*: see especially below, 5.2.

weall seen: 'well-versed, proficient, very knowledgeable' (*SND*, s.v. **Weel-seen**). For *seen*, B and C, followed by the printed texts, reads the more familiar *skilled*.

3, 4. *news monger*: 'one who collects and retails news' (*OED*). The term is pejorative: cf. Shakespeare, *1 Henry IV*, 3.2, 23–5: 'many tales devised – Which oft the ear of greatness needs must hear/ By smiling pickthanks and base newsmongers'.

The treatment of Novell and Visioner as newsmongers may be influenced by Ben Jonson's *The Staple of News* (1625) and possibly by the coffee-house scene (Act 3, especially pp. 24–6, of *Tarugo's Wiles: or, the Coffee-House*, where the place becomes, in effect, another Staple of News. The idea is not uncommon in Restoration Comedy.

No historical original has been found for either Novell or Visioner. As noted above, p. liv, the name Novell is perhaps derived from a character in Wycherley's *The Plain-Dealer*; Abednego Visioner from an incident in Cowley's *Cutter of Coleman Street*.

5. Lord Whiggridne: i.e. William Crawford (1644–98), 18th earl of Crawford and 2nd of Lindsay, son of the covenanting and fiercely anti-episcopalian John Crawford (1596–1678), 17th earl of Crawford and 1st of Lindsay. William inherited his father's principles and as a consequence was forced to live in retirement during the decade before 1688. Under King William, however, he emerged to become a member of the Privy Council and to attend both council and parliament. In 1689 he became President of the parliament, a position which he retained until 1693. This made him one of the most powerful men in the kingdom, second only to the Secretary, George Melville, 1st earl of Melville (1636–1707; see below, 4.4, 66–84 and nn.). In 1690 Crawford became a commissioner for settling the government of the Church. He was a single-minded adherent of 'the old resolutioner policies' (Ferguson 1968: 1) and became 'the personification of official integrity whilst in fact creating a screen behind which zealous Presbyterians, with his connivance and even active cooperation, purged the Scottish church' (Riley 1979: 36).

In both versions of Pitcairne's parody of Horace, *Odes* 1, 12, *Proceres Scotorum Anno MDCXC* (Scots Worthies in the Year 1690 – hereafter *Proceres Scotorum*), Crawford, as President of the parliament, is ironically made the Scottish counterpart of the supreme god, Jupiter (MacQueen and MacQueen 2009: 214):

> Quid prius dicam solitis Parentis
> Laudibus, qui res hominum et deorum
> Turbat, et longi novitate monti[s]
> > Terruit urbem?
>
> Vnde nil majus generatur ipso,
> Nec viget quicquam simile aut secundum.   (9–14)

> (How shall I begin but with the customary praises of the Father who throws into confusion the affairs of men and gods and has terrorised the City [Edinburgh] with the novelty of the long mount, whence nothing greater than himself is born, nor does anything flourish his equal or second?)

The best-known episcopalian attack on presbyterianism is *Scotch Presbyterian Eloquence* (Curate 1692), ironically dedicated to the same earl of Crawford: 'If in this incredulous Age, some Men should charge the following Relations of any Falshoods; it were an Injustice done to your Lordship to pretend, that any Man is so capable to vindicate them as your Lordship, who, amidst the Throng of so much ecclesiastical and civil Business at Court (from which you are now fain to retire for Ease and Refreshment to your wonted Solitude in the Country) have been very constant and close in the Study of those extraordinary Books cited in this Pamphlet; and so unwearied a Hearer of those wonderful Preachers of whom I now treat, that you have every Day heard them with Joy for many hours together; and never failed, with your own Hand, to write those learned and elaborate Discourses I have here published, and many more of the like Nature; in which Zeal (to your Glory and to the Shame of other Professors be it spoken) you had no Equal, but one Reverend Ruling-Elder, a Bonnet-maker in Leithwind.'

In *Babell, a Satirical Poem on the Proceedings of the General Assembly in the Year M.DC.XCII* (1692; Kinloch 1830), almost certainly by Pitcairne, a long passage, 890–1001, is devoted to Crawford, 'whom Presbyterians justly call/ Ther Hector or ther Hanniball' (p. 35, 892–3); cf. too the epigram, 'Hectoris exuvias indutum cernite Mosen' (MacQueen and MacQueen 2009: 222).

The name 'Whiggridne' is modelled on such compounds as 'hag-ridden', 'priest-ridden'; for 'Whig' see above, **Prologue**, 31n.

6. *phanatick*: term used by Episcopalians to characterize extreme Presbyterians.

7. Lord Huffie: i.e. David Melville (1660–1728), 3rd earl of Leven and 2nd earl of Melville, born at Monimail, Fife, third son of George, 1st earl of Melville. He became a soldier of some distinction in the service of the Elector of Brandenburg and, while on the Continent, raised a regiment of Scots presbyterian exiles, which he brought to England with King William in 1688. Soon afterwards the regiment was posted to Scotland, where Leven had become William's envoy to the convention of March 1689. In June, on the surrender of Edinburgh Castle by the Jacobite and Catholic duke of Gordon, he became Governor of the Castle, a member of the Privy Council and a commissioner for the plantation of kirks. At the rout of Killiecrankie (27 July) his regiment, unlike others, did not break and covered the subsequent retreat.

Lockhart says of him (Szechi 1995: 60): 'David, Earl of Leven, in the beginning of his life was so vain and conceity that he became the jest of all sober men. But as he grew older he overcame that folly in part and from the proudest became the civilest man alive ... And though he had once the command of a regiment, and was at last created Lieutenant-General and Commander-in-Chief of the forces in this kingdom, yet his courage was much called in question upon sundry accounts not necessary to be mentioned here.' Leven was particularly celebrated for the whip with which he had 'switched the Lady Mortonhall ... when she reproved him for hunting in her park' (Kinloch 1830: 91). The lady was probably wife of one of the Trotters of Mortonhall, Midlothian, south of Edinburgh. The Trotters were Jacobites, which may have been a factor in the incident. Pitcairne refers to it, and to Leven's dealings with Fife boatmen elsewhere in the play (see below, 2.1), and in *Proceres Scotorum*:

Prœliis audax neque te Levine
Non canam, sævis metuende flagris,

Quem colunt nautæ per amena Fifæ
Littora sparsi.   (17–20)

(Nor shall I fail to sing thee, Leven, audacious in battle, fearsome with your savage whips, whom the sailors scattered across the pleasant shores of Fife cultivate.)

Note the suggestion that it is by whips alone that Leven is audacious in battle.

The corresponding verses in Horace (21–24), commemorate Liber (Bacchus), god of drink, Diana, ruthless hunter of monsters, and Apollo with his vengeful arrows, all figures whose properties find some ironic correspondence in the way Leven is presented in the play.

In another Horatian parody (*Odes* 3, 28), Pitcairne celebrated Leven's marriage on 3 September 1691 to the ultra-presbyterian Lady Anne Wemyss (MacQueen and MacQueen 2009: 220).

The adjective *huffie* means 'puffed up with pride, conceit, or self-esteem; haughty, blustering' (*OED*).

8–15. *Mr Timothie ... north cuntrie man*: with the exception of David Williamson, all the ministers mentioned were members of the Commission for Visitations on the South Side of Tay, set up under Article 15 of the 1690 General Assembly; see above, pp. xx–xxi.

8. Mʳ Timothie Turbulent: *Mʳ Frazer of Brae*: James Fraser (1639–99) of Brae in the Black Isle, Ross and Cromarty. His father, Sir James Fraser of Brae, died in 1649. During Fraser's minority the estate was mismanaged and after his graduation (MA, Marischal College, Aberdeen) in 1658 he found himself crippled by debts and litigation. A protracted spiritual crisis in 1665–66 eventually led him to accept ordination in 1672 by ministers deprived as a result of the 1660 Restoration. He was outlawed in 1675; in 1677–79 he was imprisoned on the Bass Rock, East Lothian, where he studied Hebrew, Greek and oriental languages. In 1681–82 he was imprisoned under harsher circumstances in Blackness Castle, West Lothian. On his release he went to England, but in 1685 found himself in Newgate prison. He returned to Scotland in 1687 and in 1689 became minister of Culross, Fife. He attended the 1690 and 1692 General Assemblies. He was very active in the purgation of churches in Fife. He died in Edinburgh on 13 September 1699, having witnessed an eclipse of the sun that morning.

His writings were all published posthumously. Best known is *Memoirs of the Life of the very Reverend Mr James Fraser of Brae, Minister of the Gospel at Culross, written by himself* (Edinburgh, 1730).

The **Preface** (below, p. 227) paints a rather different picture of his character. In *Proceres Scotorum* there is a brief reference. As is usual in Scots, he is called by the name of his estate:

et Breæum
Sæva paupertas, et avitus arcto
Cum Lare fundus.   (39–40)

(Harsh poverty and his hereditary farm with northern Lar [bore] Brae.)

Fraser figures as 'the Laird of Braes' in *Babell*, 220–70 (Kinloch 1830: 12–14).

In Horace the corresponding figure is Marcus Furius Camillus, appointed dictator when he was in exile and Rome had been captured by the Gauls (387/6 BC). He returned, defeated the invaders and recovered the gold which had been used to drive them from the city.

9. Mr Salathiel Littlesense: *Mr Gilbert Rule* : On 26 September 1690 Gilbert Rule (c. 1629–1701), minister of Old Greyfriars, Edinburgh, became Principal (*Primar*) of the Tounis College, the University of Edinburgh. His early life is only partly documented; in 1647 he was a student at St Andrews; by 1651 he had become a Regent (Tutor) at King's College, Aberdeen, where in 1652 he became Sub-Principal. Both positions imply that he was already a clergyman. The fact that in or about 1657 he became Church of England Curate at Alnwick, Northumberland, possibly implies that his ordination was at the hands of a bishop. At Alnwick, however, he refused to use the English *Book of Common Prayer*. One of his church wardens, Major Orde, charged him at Newcastle assizes with defamation of the prayer book. Orde died as the result of a fall from his horse (something regarded as a providential judgement), and in the absence of a prosecutor, Rule was acquitted. After the Restoration the 1662 Act of Uniformity led to his ejection from the parish. He returned to Scotland, but was soon forced abroad. He studied medicine at Leiden, graduating MD in 1666. In 1679 he set up as a physician in Berwick-on-Tweed, but in 1680 was imprisoned on the Bass Rock for preaching at conventicles in England and Scotland. There he fell ill and gained release on condition that he left Scotland within eight days. He retired to Dublin.

In 1688, after the Revolution, he was called to Old Greyfriars church in Edinburgh. In 1690 he was appointed to the commission for purging the University of Edinburgh from Jacobites and Episcopalians. On 26 September 1690 he was appointed Principal of the University in place of Alexander Monro (d. 1698), who had been purged on the previous day.

At a time when Latin, Greek and Hebrew were the only languages permitted in the University, Rule's Latin was notoriously bad. Pitcairne often comments on the fact.

Rule regarded himself as a theologian and controversialist. During his time at Alnwick he published *A Rational Defence of Non-Conformity* (London, 1689), intended as a reply to *The Unreasonableness of Separation: or, an Impartial account of the history, nature, and pleas of the present separation from the Communion of the Church of England* (2nd edn, corrected, London, 1681), by the distinguished English theologian, Edward Stillingfleet, then dean of St Paul's, later bishop of Worcester. Earlier he had published *An Answer to Dr Stillingfleet's Irenicum* (London, 1680). On these works Pitcairne remarked (below, **Preface**, p. 226): 'Ignorance, which is a fitter parent of impudence than devotion, made this fellow [Rule] attack the learned Dr Stillingfleet with an impertinent scribble on an impertinent subject, to wit, on the *Jure-divino*-ship of presbytery [Presbyterianism], which few men of sense or ingenuity ever pretended to maintain.' Rule followed the treatise with *A True Representation of Presbyterian Government* (Edinburgh, 1690) and *A Second Vindication of the Church of Scotland* (Edinburgh, 1691). *Scotch Presbyterian Eloquence* contains (Curate 1692: 79–98) a hostile criticism of this last, to which Rule responded with *A just and modest reproof of a pamphlet called the Scotch Presbyterian Eloquence* (Edinburgh, 1693). The value of these writings may perhaps be judged by David Reid's comment that 'There is no really interesting defence of the Presbyterian establishment' (Reid 1982: 178).

There is a brief but ironically apt reference to Rule in *Proceres Scotorum*, 21–22: 'an quieta/ Regna Rulæi memorem?' (should I call to mind the quiet kingdoms of Rule?). The immediate reference is probably to his reign in the University, which was anything but quiet; see below, 5.1, 55–96. In Horace, however, the corresponding figure is Numa Pompilius, the peace-loving second king of Rome, credited with the reformation of Roman religious beliefs and practices.

In the play Rule shares the surname Littlesense with the Ruling Elder, 'Laird littlesense, a north cuntrie man' (line 15 below). Possibly the two are to be regarded as relations, perhaps elder and younger brother. Ruling Elder speaks throughout in north-eastern dialect, traces of which sometimes also emerge in the speech of Mr Salathiel Littlesense.

10. Mr Covenant Planedealer: *M^r Ja. Kirktoun*: James Kirkton (1620?– 1699), MA (Edinburgh) 1647, became minister of the second charge in Lanark, 1655, then in 1657 minister of Mertoun, near St Boswells, Roxburghshire. In 1662 he was expelled under one of the statutes passed by the Scottish parliament of that year, 'formally restoring episcopal government, reviving lay patronage, declaring the covenants unlawful and forbidding private conventicles' (Donaldson 1965: 363). He was probably one of the 'young ministers who hade entered to the ministry since the beginning of the year 1649, when patronages hade been by law abolished: these they declared to have hade no right to their stipends at any time since their admission to the ministry' (Stewart 1992: 82). He then moved to Edinburgh, where he became a noted illegal preacher. In 1672 he opposed the second Indulgence, which would have allowed most presbyterian ministers to function officially, though under strict conditions. In 1674 he was declared a rebel and fugitive. He retired to England, but in 1678, when he had returned to Edinburgh, he had the curious brush with Captain Carstaires described in his *History of the Church of Scotland 1660–1679* (Stewart 1992: 211–14). He was intercommuned, i.e. he was not only himself outlawed as a rebel, but so was anyone else who ventured to speak to him. Kirkton spent two long periods in Holland, finally returning in the slightly milder ecclesiastical climate of 1687. From 1691 to his death he was minister of Edinburgh Tolbooth. He was a member of the commission for the purging of Edinburgh University and the Church in the south of Scotland. In 1693 he wrote the *History* already mentioned, partly as a counterblast to the *Scotch Presbyterian Eloquence* (Curate 1692). During the eighteenth century this circulated in MS, first appearing in print under the hostile editorship of C.K. Sharpe (Edinburgh, 1817), more recently by the friendlier Ralph Stewart (Lewiston, Queenston and Lampeter, 1992).

Mr Planedealer probably derives his name from the eponym of Wycherley's *The Plain Dealer*; see above, p. liii.

Kirktoun's son George was on friendly terms with Pitcairne, who described him as 'my good comrad, a merry fellow, no presbyterian, son to the famous Mr James Kirton' (MacQueen and MacQueen 2009: 367).

Kirkton, like most of the other ministers listed, belonged to the presbyterian Old Guard, in office before 1660, and, as such, is mentioned before Rule in the second version of *Proceres Scotorum*. His equivalent in Horace is Romulus, founder and first king of Rome.

11. *Commitie*: i.e. the Commission for Visitations on the South Side of Tay, established by Act 15 of the 1690 General Assembly; see above, pp. xx–xxi. The Commission had many more members than these mentioned, but any seven were sufficient to form a quorum.

12. Mᵣ Solomon Cherrietrees: *Mᵣ Da: Williamson*: David Williamson (c. 1634–1706) was minister of the West Kirk (St Cuthbert's), Edinburgh, to which Charles II presented him in 1661. He preached at conventicles, for which he was deprived in 1664. He continued to preach at conventicles in and around Teviotdale and later served as captain in the covenanting army defeated at Bothwell Brig in 1679. He escaped capture there, but in 1688 was imprisoned on the evidence of papers found on the person of the Cameronian, James Renwick (1662–88), who was taken in January 1688 and executed a month later – one of the last covenanting martyrs. Williamson was released after the flight of James VII to France in December 1688 and restored to the West Kirk in 1689. In 1702 he became Moderator of the General Assembly of the Church of Scotland. He was married seven times and fathered many children. His grave is in St Cuthbert's churchyard.

He is best remembered for the exploit recorded in *Scotch Presbyterian Eloquence* (Curate 1692: 5–6):

A Party of King *Charles* the Second's Guards being sent to apprehend Mr. *David Williamson* (one of the most eminent of their Ministers now in *Edinburg*) for the frequent Rebellion and Treason he preached then at Field-Meetings; and the Party having surrounded the House where he was, a zealous Lady, Mistress of the House, being very sollicitous to conceal him, rose in al Haste from her Bed, where she left her Daughter of about 18 Years of Age; and having dressed up the Holy Man's Head with some of her own Night-Cloaths, she wittily advised him to take her Place in the warm bed, with her Girl; to which he modestly and readily consented; and knowing well how to employ his Time, especially upon such an extrordinary Call, to propagate the Image of the Party, while the Mother, to divert the Troopers Enquiry, was treating them with strong Drink in the Parlour, he, to express his Gratitude, applies himself with extraordinary Kindness to the Daughter; who finding him to prove a very useful Man in his Generation, told her Mother she would have him for her Husband: To which the Mother, though otherwise unwilling, yet, for concealing the Scandal, out of Love to the Cause, consented, when the Mystery of the Iniquity was wholly disclosed to her. This whole Story is as well known in Scotland, as that the Covenant was begun, and carried out by Rebellion and Oppression.

Williamson apparently defended himself by quoting St Paul (Romans 7. 23): 'Verily I do not', said he, 'deny, But that with St Paul, I have a Law in my Members, warring against the Law of my Mind, and bringing me into Captivity unto the Law of Sin, which is in my Members' (*ut cit.*: 6).

According to the **Preface** (below, p. 228), and several other sources, the episode took place at Cherrytrees, near Kirk Yetholm, Roxburghshire – whence the pseudonym Solomon Cherrietrees. In the seventeenth century Cherrytrees was held by Kers, a cadet branch of the Kers, earls and subsequently dukes of Roxburghe. The name Solomon refers to the biblical King Solomon who 'had seven hundred wives, princesses, and three hundred concubines' (1 Kings 11. 3). Solomon is much given to quoting the Song of his biblical namesake.

Williamson is briefly mentioned (line 21) in the first version of *Proceres Scotorum*. The position is the same as that given to Kirkton in the second. In the second version, however, two stanzas (lines 21–28) are dedicated to him. In Horace the corresponding stanzas refer to Hercules and the Dioscuri, powers who extend protection to those, like Williamson at Cherrytrees, in danger of death.

Pitcairne also gives a mock-heroic elaboration of the episode in two brilliant Latin poems, *David Veneri* and *Venus Davidi* (MacQueen and MacQueen 2009: 100–105). There is a further brief reference in Mr Solomon's speech to the assembly in *Babell* (1140–98):

Before that Sol had rais'd his head
Vp from the fair Aurora's bed,
E're that bright star which all things sees;
Had cast it's eyes on Cherrytrees,
While I lay sweetlie by the side
Of her who after was my bride.   (1143–1149)

Compare too the song 'Dainty Davie'. David Herd published an expurgated version (Herd 1776, ii, 215). A more explicit version will be found on www.glasgowguide.co.uk:

Being pursu'd by the dragoons,
Within my bed he was laid doon,
And weel I wat he was worth his room
My ain dear dainty Davie.

My minnie laid him at my back,
I trow he lay na lang at that,
But turn'd, and in a verra crack
Produc'd a dainty Davie.

Then in the field amang the pease,
Behin' the house o' Cherrytrees,
Again he wan atweesh my thies,
And, splash! gaed out his gravy.

13. Moderator: *Mʳ Hugh Kennedy*: I have not been able to find much biographical information on Hugh Kennedy. He was born c. 1625. His surname suggests that his family belonged to Carrick (south Ayrshire), but this is no more than a guess. In 1641 he graduated MA from Glasgow. In 1643 he became minister of West Calder in West Lothian. He was an active Covenanter and is said to have received £100 as his share of the money paid to the Scottish army for the sale of Charles I to the English army in 1646. On the Restoration he was deprived of his charge. He returned in 1687 as a consequence of the proclamation of tolerance by James VII. In the same year he was translated to Trinity College church, Edinburgh. He was Moderator of the 1690 General Assembly, but illness forced his retirement before the 1692 Assembly; cf. below, 1.1, 337–9. He collapsed between 'the Cross and Fountain Well' (Kinloch 1830: 8, 102) and died soon afterwards. According to Robert Mylne, quoted in Kinloch, *ut cit.*, 62, 'His 2 sons wer banisht for poysening, and he fell doun dead on the street himselfe.'

In both versions of *Proceres Scotorum* Kennedy and the earl of Crawford are closely linked. In Horace the figure who corresponds to Kennedy is the emperor Augustus, supreme ruler in the world of men, subject only to Jupiter –in Pitcairne's parody Crawford:

Crescit occulto velut arbor ævo
Fama Crafurdii: micat inter omnes

Kennedis sydus, velut inter ignes
        Luna minores.

Gentis Albanæ pater atque custos
Orte Nassavo, tibi cura magni
Kennedis fatis data: Tu secundo
        Kennede regnes

Ille seu mistas pueris puellas
Egerit justo domitas triumpho,
Sive subjectos populos avari
        Præsulis iræ,

Te minor nostrum reget unus orbem –   (ii, 41–53)

(The fame of Crawford grows like a tree from a hidden age; the star of Kennedy sparkles, like the Moon among lesser fires. Father and Guardian of the Scottish race, risen from the Nassovan [King William, prince of Orange-*Nassau*], the care of great Kennedy has been granted to you by the Fates. May you hold sway, with Kennedy for deputy! He – whether he will have led girls, mingled with boys, conquered in a just triumph, or people subjected to the wrath of a greedy Moderator – Though less than you, he will be sole ruler of our world.)

Throughout the play the Moderator defers to Whigriddne.

14. Cleark: *M* *John Spalding*: On Sunday 11 May 1690 John Spalding (1633?–1699) delivered *A sermon preached before his grace, George Earl of Melvil, their majesties commissioner, and the nobility, barons and burrows, members of the high court of parliament: In the parliament-house* (Edinburgh, 1690). In October 1690 he was appointed Clerk to the General Assembly meeting that month. At this Assembly he became a member of the Commission for Visitations on the South Side of Tay. He prepared the minutes of the Assembly. In 1696 *A Sermon before His Grace John Earl of Tullibardine – by John Spalding minister at Dundie* was printed in Edinburgh. A posthumous collection, *Synaxis sacra; or, a collection of sermons preached at several communions – by the late Reverend Mr John Spalding*, was published at Edinburgh in 1703.

15. Ruling Elder: 'In the Presbyterian church "one who is elected and ordained to the exercise of government in ecclesiastical courts, without having authority to teach"' (*SND*, s.v. **Elder**). No historical original has been identified. As already noted, he is a North-country man, who speaks in dialect throughout.

north cuntrie: i.e. north-eastern Scotland, here probably Buchan.

16–19. *Mr Shittle ... Mr Wordie*: no historical original has been found for any of these characters.

16. *complying*: i.e. conforming (or wishing to conform) with the presbyterian establishment.

18. *Expectant*: 'a candidate for the ministry in the Scottish Church' (*SND*).

19. *Chaplain*: 'a clergyman who conducts religious services ... in the household of a person of rank or quality' (*OED*). Mr Wordie is thus not minister of a parish and so not a member of the General Assembly or any Commission or sub-committee. In hope of gaining a benefice, he is careful to attend the meetings of the Comitie.

The name Wordie, 'worthy', is applied ironically. Wordie takes full advantage of his privileged position.

20–25. *Old Ladie ... Mrs Laura*: no historical originals have been found. As already noted (above, p. lv) the names Violetta and Laura are probably modelled on Violante and Leonora in *Sir Courtly Nice*.

20. Old Ladie: i.e. 'dowager lady', a Scottish usage; cf. 'the auld ladye and young ladie of Grant', quoted in *DOST*, s.v. **Lady**. 4. The Old Lady is thus the widow of a landowner, whose male heir has succeeded to the estate; with her daughter and nieces, and her chaplain, she now lives in an Edinburgh 'land', a high tenement building on burgage land, where, as befits her status, she occupies an upper floor. A lower floor is occupied by an extruded episcopalian minister.

bigott: an alternative term for 'phanatick'.

26. Guard: the Edinburgh City Guard, 'supposed to have been established in the troubled minority of James V; reconstituted c. 1648 with captain, 2 lieutenants and 60 men; another body, numbering 126, was raised in 1689; disbanded early 19th century' (Donaldson and Morpeth 1977: 40).

27. *Maid*: B and C, followed by the later printed texts, read *Maids, a webster, Boy, Drawers, Boatmen, Hyrers & Fidlers, Fornicatrix, huntsmen & Dogs. Scene Edinburgh.* The 1722 print omits all.

Act 1, Scene 1

The inner stage represents the tavern. The back shutters include a painted representation of St Giles' cathedral as seen through either a window or open door.

The scene does more than introduce two leading characters, Will and Frank; it sets them in the context of domestic and European political and religious strife.

The stage direction lists only the speaking parts. Other drinkers, including Pitcairne himself, seem also to be present, and someone passes across the stage in the course of the action.

Bull Tavern: not identified, apart from its location near St Giles. It may be the same as the tavern nicknamed Greppa's or the Greping Office, also situated near St Giles and often mentioned in Pitcairne's Latin verse (MacQueen and MacQueen 2009: 80, 82, 106, 204).

It should perhaps be noted that the setting for a crucial scene in James Hogg's *Private Memoirs and Confessions of a Justified Sinner* (Hogg 1983: 46 ff) is a tavern called the Black Bull of Norway, situated on a close which ran from the Edinburgh High Street to the North Loch (since drained and now Princes Street Gardens). The tavern was close to the Guard House in the High Street. If not simply a product of Hogg's imagination, it may be the Bull Tavern of the play.

3. *Borrowstouness*: Bo'ness at the mouth of the river Avon, West Lothian, once a sea-port of some consequence.

good protestant wynd: on 7 May 1689 protestant England (but not Scotland) had declared war on catholic France, thus rendering the regular sea-traffic between England (or Scotland) and France impracticable. The only remaining practicable route was by protestant Holland or north Germany. Frank, it seems likely, had been on a visit to France from which he was forced to return via Holland and a good protestant wind. Tobin (Tobin 1972: 105) suggests an additional reference to the 1688 invasion of England by William of Orange. Less plausible is his suggestion that the mention of Bo'ness implies a reference to Muckle John Gibb, a Bo'ness shipmaster, who in 1680 'persuaded three men and 26 women to renounce a wicked world and to follow him into the wilderness of the Pentland Hills. There they spent their time fasting, praying and singing psalms' (Cowan 1976: 106). They were known as the Sweet Singers of Borrowstouness.

4. *St Gyles*: the High Church of Edinburgh, from 1633–8, and 1662–89 an episcopalian cathedral.

9. *strange faces*: cf. Pitcairne's Latin poem *Ad Rob. Lindesium, 1689* (MacQueen and MacQueen 2009: 66–8), addressed to a long-dead friend, whom he summons back to the an Edinburgh changed by the Revolution: 'novos cives mutataque regna videbis' (you will see a new citizenry and changed kingdoms) (7); 'Solus in obscœnas homines transire figuras/ cogit, & exutum scit revocare genus' (He [Satan] alone has the power to transform men into indecent shapes and knows how to call back a deprived race) (21–2).

plantatione: 'colony', but cf. the later use of the word, e.g. in 1.3, 104; 4.2, 7.

11–12. *came from hevne ... falling*: Presbyterians regarded themselves as having no intermediary in their contact with God and therefore as coming from heaven. By contrast, Will regards them as demons thrust down from heaven, like Satan and the other fallen angels.

braik ... falling: refers to their stance, with head to one side, like hanged criminals on the gallows.

necks: B and C, followed by the printed texts, have the less plausible reading *backs*.

15–16. *to see ... Whigeridne*: as noted above, Whigridne (Crawford) was President of the Scottish parliament and so had authority to summon Frank into his presence. The later importance of Whigridne and his clerical entourage is foreshadowed by this indirect appearance at an early stage of the action.

17. *Monster*: cf. below, 3.1, 190. The reference is probably to a native North American clad in feathers and war paint, put on exhibition as part of a travelling show.

18. *Grammaceing fellows ... cloackes*: Presbyterian clergymen in characteristic attire.

20. *on*: 'one'.

seidge of Mons was raised: reference to an episode in the Nine Years War (1689–97). The questioner characteristically assumes that the French forces besieging Mons in the Spanish Netherlands (modern Belgium) in the early spring of 1691 have been driven off by King William's army. In fact, by the reformed Gregorian calendar used on the continent (*Stilo novo*), on 28 March the French under Louis XIV captured Mons.

23. *28th of March*: B, followed by the 1722 print, reads *August* for *March*.

Stilo Novo in Savoy: Duke Victor Amadeus II of Savoy (1675–1730) for a time was allied to William in the Nine Years War.

The reverend gentleman shows his ignorance by assuming that *Stilo Novo* is the name of a Savoyan fort. Frank makes use of the mathematically more accurate continental Gregorian calendar. This, and the gross error on the part of the other, together illustrate one aspect of the struggle between moderns and ancients discussed above, pp. xxviii–xxxvi, on which see also MacQueen and MacQueen 2009: 246 and n.

25. *Mons upon the Rhine*: Mons is about a hundred miles from the Rhine.

26. *K.W.*: King William. So too C. I have retained the abbreviation as characteristic of the MS and perhaps of the speech of the day.

27–8. *wonderfull providence ... thride*: i.e. the fact that King William lost so few men in an action at which he and his army were not present.

There's nothing impossible to God: proverbial (Wilson 1995, 580).

29–30. *On fears ... printed*: MS insertion in Pitcairne's hand. Not in B, C, or the printed texts. For presbyterian dependence on the printed word, see below, 229–32.

35. *Lowis*: Louis XIV (1643–1715), the Sun King of France. He was in direct command of the French forces during the siege of Mons.

37–8. *Suspected person*: General warrants for the arrest of suspect persons received authorization from the Scottish parliament on several occasions; see, e.g., *APS* 1689/3/101.

42. *Cana of Galilee*: see John 2. 1–11, the changing of water into wine at the wedding-feast.

44–5. *first ... from us*: war with France meant that supplies of French wine, in particular claret from Bordeaux, became unavailable.

46–7. *Hippocrates' discipls*: the medical profession, physicians. The physician Pitcairne was well-known, even notorious, as a lover of fine wine and frequenter of taverns, especially the Greping-office, where he sometimes gave consultations (MacQueen and MacQueen 2009: 28–9). Pitcairne himself, or an actor made up to resemble him, may have played a silent part in this scene. A gesture from Frank would have made the point clear to the audience.

47. *suitable*: B and C, followed by the printed texts, read *most seasonable*.

Come: B and C, followed by the printed texts, read *Come, Drawer*.

49. *K.J.*: King James (VII and II).

50. *Curat*: '**Curate**: a clergyman who has the charge ('cure') of a parish ... From 1662 to 1688 the episcopalian incumbents of Scottish parishes were styled curates' (*ODCC*, 361). This reference introduces one of the main themes of the play, the successful attempt by extreme Presbyterians, after 1688, to drive episcopal clergymen, usually also Jacobites, from their parishes. Many of these expelled were reduced to extreme poverty. Will's assumption is that the process would be put in reverse by the restoration of King James and the Stuart male line, a restoration which he obviously favours.

51–52. *freinds in the Cuntrie*: i.e. his parents and other relatives who live on their estates rather than in Edinburgh. In Scots *freind* often means 'relative, kinsman'.

55. *speacking of the tyms*: regarded as primarily a presbyterian habit; cf. below, 5.2, 53–74; 3, 41 and n.; also Curate 1692: 17: 'This was an old custom among them to preach up the Times, and the Neglect thereof they call sinful Silence.' The phrase might also be applied to the play as a whole.

57–63. *as good whoring ... ministers' wives*: Will presents himself as a rake, who has adapted his technique of seduction to the manners of the time. For his final attempt to apply the technique, see below, 2.2, 21–97.

58–9. *most Christian ... most Catholic*: titles attached to the kings of France and Spain respectively. Spanish wines had now taken the place of French; see above, 44–45n.

60. *Cassandra, Cleopatra*: long, but much read, pseudo-historical romances by Gauthier de Costes de la Calprenède (1614–63). *Cassandre* appeared in 10 volumes, 1644–50; *Cléopâtre* in 12 volumes, 1647–56.

61. *song of Solomon*: see below, 2.2.

66. *reformatione*: an ironic use of the word. It is perhaps worth noting that B and the later printed editions of the play have as sub-title *Scotch Reformation*.

68. *alledgiance and Assurance*: the oath of allegiance is the final item in the 1689 Claim of Right by the Scottish parliament: 'I A: B Do sincerly promise and swear That I will be faithfull and bear true allegiance to their Majesties King William and Queen Mary So help me God.' All people of any substance were required, under heavy penalties, to sign the Assurance: 'I, A.B., do in the sincerity of my heart assert, acknowledge and declare that their majesties King William and Queen Mary are the only lawfull, undoubted soveraigns of this realm as well *de jure*, this is, of right king and queen, as *de facto*, that is, in the possession and exercise of the government, and therefore I do sincerely and faithfully promise and ingage that I will with heart and hand, life and goods maintain and defend their majesties' title and government against the late King James and his adherents, and all other enemies who either by open or secret attempts shall disturb or disquiet their majesties in the possession and exercise therof.'

The two were combined in the Act for takeing the oath of alleadgeance and assurance (*APS* 1693/4/50), but from the wording of the act it is clear that the Assurance was already in effect before 1693.

There were severe penalties for these who refused to take the oaths.

73–4. *phanaticks ... hence*: as a consequence of James VII's proclamation of Indulgence (June 1687) by which 'all the king's subjects were allowed "to meet and serve God after their own way, be it in private houses, chapels, or places purposely hired or built for that use"' (Donaldson 1965: 382).

77. *Rogue*: B and C, followed by the printed texts, read *Rook*, 'thief, cheat, swindler' (*DOST*, s.v. **Ruke, Ruik 2**). *Rook* in this sense is commoner in Scots than in English, where the dominant pejorative sense of the word is 'gull, fool'.

81. *the stone at the Grass mercate*: 'In a central situation at the west end of the Grassmarket, there remained till very lately a massive block of sandstone, having a quadrangular hole in the middle, being the stone which served as a socket for the gallows, when this was the common place of execution. Instead of the stone, there is now only a St Andrews cross, indicated by an arrangement of the paving stones' (Chambers 1847: 52). Condemned Covenanters, as well as many others, suffered here.

84–5. *state of the natione*: a curiously modern-sounding phrase. I have found no earlier example.

85. *therine*: B and C read *interests*, the printed texts *interested*.

87. *body politick*: An early example of the phrase, first noted by *OED* in 1634 and given some prominence by Thomas Hobbes (1588–1679) in part 2, chapter 22 of *Leviathan* (1657), 'Of Systemes subordinate' (i.e. 'to some central authority'): 'some are Politicall and some Private. *Politicall* (otherwise called *Bodies Politique* and *Persons in Law,*) are those, which are made by authority from the Soveraign Power of the Commonwealth ... In Bodies Politique, the power of the Representative is alwaies Limited: And that which prescribeth the Limits thereof, is the Power Soveraign ... And to give leave to a Body Politique of Subjects, to have an absolute Representative to all intents and purposes, wer to abandon the government of so much of the Commonwealth, and to divide the Dominion, contrary to their Peace and Defence, which the Soveraign cannot be understood to doe, by any Grant, that does not plainly, and directly discharge them of their subjection' (Hobbes 1973: 18).

The Soveraign is the head of the body politic and a body cannot have two heads. The Scottish body politic is 'monstruous and hydeous' because two kings reign over it, albeit one is at the Councill table, one in the Taverns. The duality is later exemplified by the opposed newsmongers, Novell and Visioner.

The Glorious Revolution and the question of sovereignty are obviously very much present in Will's mind.

88. *Nothing ... rulers*: added to the MS in Pitcairne's hand. Unruly rulers create havoc in Leviathan, the state. The words do not occur in B, C, or the printed texts.

91. *the Strait Bowe*: i.e. the West Bow, a street running downhill from the junction of Castle Hill and the Lawnmarket to the Grassmarket. The curvaceous course is now obscured by the later intrusion of Victoria Street, connecting George IV Bridge with the Grassmarket. As the adjective 'strait' implies, the street was extremely narrow; cf. *DOST*, s.v. **Strait, Strate**, *adj., adv.* and *n.*, C, **5.**

'In the latter part of the seventeenth century, the inhabitants of the West Bow enjoyed a peculiar fame for their piety and zeal in the Covenanting cause. The wits of the opposite faction are full of allusions to them as "the Bowhead saints", "the godly plants of the Bowhead", and so forth' (Chambers 1847: 81). They were, of course, Williamites.

the Cross: this monument was situated on the High Street, a little to the east of St Giles' and Old Fishmarket Close. It was 'the great centre of gossip in former days. The principal coffee-houses and booksellers' shops were close to this spot. The chief merchants, the leading official persons, the men of learning and talents, the laird, the noble, the clergyman, were constantly clustering hereabouts, during certain hours of the day. It was the very centre and cynosure of the old city' (Chambers 1847: 168). Taverns as well as coffee-houses, the patrons of which were Jacobites, or had Jacobite sympathies, were thick in the neighbourhood.

95. *Italian*: 'Machiavellian' or 'Jesuistic'.

strickness: 'rigorous accuracy or precision in statement' (*OED*).

99–100. *you'd sweare ... stat*: i.e. 'you'd swear it (sincerity) had been deposed with K. James in the late conventione & declared a rebell to the stat'.

99. *conventione*: the 1689 Parliament (Convention of the Estates).

101. *Torrie*: i.e Tory, '1. an outlawed or rebel supporter of Charles II, in arms against Cromwellian forces ... 2. a political supporter of the royalist cause [OIr *tóraidhe*, pursuer, implied in *tóraidecht*, pursuit]' (*DOST*). After the Revolution, the word came, as here, to mean 'Jacobite'.

103. *Whiggs*: see above, Prologue, 31n.

104–5. *Compted to*: 'counted as (a)'.

109. *Drawer*: 'one who draws liquor for customers; a tapster at a tavern' (*OED*).

109–110. *Mr Novell*: Novell and Visioner are newsmongers, a word found in Shakespeare, *1 Henry IV*, 3.2, 23–5:

> any tales devised –
> which oft the ear of greatness needs must hear
> By smiling pickthanks and base newsmongers.

Pitcairne, however, may have developed the concept more in terms of Jonson's comedy *The Staple of News* (1631), where the topics available include

> news of the faction,
> As the reformed-news; Protestant-news; –
> And pontifical news; of all which several,
> The day-books, characters, precedents are kept –   (I.2, 33–6)

The news is often sensational, but false, in the finest tradition of the yellow press:

> They write the king of Spain is chosen pope ...
> And emperor too, the thirtieth of February.   (III.1, 74–5)

Cf. too *Tarugo's Wiles: or, The Coffee-House* 3, pp. 24–7.

The two newsmongers, Novell and Visioner, serve to keep the conflict of Jacobite with Williamite, under almost every aspect, prominent throughout the play. As noted above (p. lv), they are probably modelled on Hothead and Testimony in *Sir Courtly Nice*.

Note how Frank and Novell talk only at cross-purposes.

111–12. *Perhaps ... Cuntrie*: Frank and Novell seem to be acquaintances.

113. *Dear sir*: after this, B and C, followed by the printed texts, have the stage-direction [*Embraces*].

hegh: an indication of breathlessness.

115. *quhen wes Mons taken?*: in Jonsonian terms, Novell's humour is his obsessive desire for information favouring the Jacobite cause.

120. *for*: B and C, followed by the printed texts, insert after this *Reports*.

121. *halfe moon of Talemount*: not identified, but perhaps the two batteries of twelve mortars which bombarded Mons from different sides in preparation for the assault.

121. *damned Portiguise skipper*: not identified.

125. *Marques of Buffliers*: Louis François, Duc de Boufflers, Comte de Cagny (1644–1711). At the siege of Mons he acted as Louis XIV's lieutenant-general and was wounded in an attack on the town, whence Novell's question, 'how does he?'

126. *my 5 guyneas*: presumably Novell had laid a wager, either on the outcome of the siege of Mons, or on the fate of the Marques.

135. *putt to the edge of the sword*: Novell assumes a continuance of the merciless killing during the Thirty Years War (1618–48); cf. Dugald Dalgetty on the Swedish capture of Frankfurt-on-Oder in 1631: 'I once saw a brigade of Irish, at the taking of Frankfort upon the Oder, stand to it with sword and pike until they beat off the blue and yellow Swedish brigades, esteemed as stout as any that fought under the immortal Gustavus. And although stout Hepburn, valiant Lumsdale, courageous Monroe, with myself and other cavaliers, made entry elsewhere at point of pike, yet, had we all met with such opposition, we had returned with great loss and little profit. Wherefore these valiant Irishes, being all put to the sword, as is usual in such cases, did nevertheless gain immortal praise and honour.' Alexander 1995, p. 23

139. *feighting ... pocket*: reference not identified.

140. *Ther's an honest fellow cane informe me*: a passer-by crosses the stage and is pursued off-stage by Novell.

141. *plunged*: see *OED*, s.v. plunge: 'to overwhelm, overpower, esp. with trouble or difficulty: to put to straits, embarrass'; cf. J. L. Rothes, *A Relation of Proceedings concerning the Affairs of the Kirk of Scotland from August 1637 to July 1638* (Nairne 1830: 170): 'two or three factors there which extreamlie plunged the noblemen'; Sir Thomas Browne, *Religio Medici* (Keynes 1968: 27): 'With another I was familiarly acquainted in France, a Divine and man of singular parts, that on the same point was so plunged and gravelled with three lines of Seneca.'

B and C, followed by the printed texts, read *plagued*.

144. *have not ... acquaintance*: unlike Novell, Visioner is unknown to Frank, but attempts to make some kind of link by way of the Church and even the Moderator.

The name Visioner indicates that his 'news', even more than that of

Novell, lacks any firm basis in reality. As noted above (pp. lv–lvi), the name is based on an incident in Cowley's *Cutter of Coleman Street*.

147. *Mr Hugh*: Hugh Kennedy, the 1690 Moderator of the General Assembly; see above, **Drammatis Personae** 13n. He figures prominently in the later stages of the play.

147–8. *the affairs*: B and C, followed by the printed texts, read *the King's affairs*.

149. *your Moderator*: although Frank has never met Mr Hugh, he knows that he is Moderator.

150. *your K's affairs*: i.e. King William's affairs. By calling him 'your' King, Frank plants himself squarely on the Jacobite side.

152–3. *title of dignitie ... ambulatorie*: Visioner is eager to point out that 'Moderator' as a title is not to be confused with 'Bishop' or such other episcopalian dignities conferred for life. The office lasted only from one General Assembly to the next.

ambulatorie: 'shifting, not permanent, temporary, mutable' (*OED*). The word is not recorded in *DOST* or *SND*.

154. *the King*: again, King William.

155. *conjunct Emperour*: i.e. together with the Holy Roman Emperor Leopold I (1658–1705), a catholic monarch joined with the protestant William during the Nine Years War. Visioner finds no difficulty in the idea of a protestant Holy Roman Emperor.

156. Novell re-enters in time to hear Visioner's remark, which he misunderstands.

He: King James – as a Catholic a more likely, but still highly improbable, Holy Roman Emperor.

157. *beis*: a distinctively Scottish form of the verb 'to be', = 'shall be'. 'Chiefly in subordinate clauses' (*DOST*).

158. *he*: King William.

162. *them*: King James and Louis XIV.

164. *our king*: King William.

165. *London*: for Novell, the capital city of a Britain regained by King James.

166. *he*: King James.

169. *desertion*: after William had landed at Torbay in 1688 and was advancing on London, James fled to France. This was termed desertion by his opponents. Novell seems to accept the charge.

170–2. *treasurer ... discount him*: a satirical reference to the hostile relationship between James VII's Chancellor in Scotland, the converted Catholic, James Drummond (1648–1716), 4th earl of Perth, and the Treasurer, the episcopalian William Douglas (1637–95), 1st duke of Queensberry. Douglas was deprived of overall control of the Treasury in March 1686 and ordered to remain in Edinburgh until the accounts were audited. Nothing was proved against him.

Novell takes peculation in high office very lightly.

172. *discount him*: apparently 'count him out', an unparalleled usage.

174. *My Lord*: Lord Whiggridne, as President of the parliament.

174. *Cotch*: coach. A reference to Whiggridne's lack of means.

175. *Anstruther*: sea-port in Whiggridne's part of Fife. Visioner assumes that Versailles is on the French coast.

hoop: hop. In *OED* this idiomatic use of the verb is not recorded before the twentieth century.

176. *too far a voage*: Kennedy's health was poor; see above, **Drammatis Personae**, 13n.

180–1. *Gad ... i'faith*: Novell suggests that the Moderator would flee to a continental refuge if King James were to be restored and there were a new act of Indulgence (see above, 73–4n).

183. *The K.*: King William.

184. *The Q.*: Mary II (1662–94), daughter of James VII, married to King William. Her father attempted to convert her to Catholicism, but she remained a devout member of the Church of England. From a presbyterian point of view, however, this meant that she was almost a Catholic. The Church of England, moreover, had failed to honour the 1643 Solemn League and Covenant.

Novell takes the reference as being to James VII's second wife, Mary of Modena (1658–1718) a devout Catholic.

187. *call call*: so in the MS. Dittography; B and C, followed by the printed texts, read *can call*.

190–2. *If it should ... benefices*: Novell agrees with Visioner, but on quite different grounds. For pecuniary motives, most bishops in the Church of England had failed in their sacred duty to support James, their anointed king and head of their Church.

193. *rare Gentleman*: Visioner begins to realize that he and Novell belong to opposite sides. His next remark is in effect a leading question.

192. *prince*: James Frances Edward, born 10 June 1688, son of James VII and Mary of Modena. Novell, however, understands it as the Prince of Orange, i.e. King William.

197. *our present King*: King William.

198. *he*: King William, the Prince of Orange.

200. *poor babe ... blame*: the violence of Novell's remarks startles Visioner into a momentary sympathy with the infant prince.

201–2. *defraud ... just right*: Novell agrees with the sympathy expressed by Visioner and takes it further, much to the latter's surprise.

204. *The prince of Wales*: the moment of truth.

206. *Imposture*: Whigs claimed to believe that Mary of Modena's pregnancy was feigned and that another woman's probably bastard child was smuggled in for the birth. It was almost impossible for them to admit that a legitimate heir male had been born to the catholic King James.

209. *I'le be the Catt's Gutts of you*: i.e. 'I'll stab you in the belly and let your guts fall out.' The 1722 print preserves the same reading. For *I'le be*, B, C, and the later prints read *I'le be with*. The term *Cat-* or *Cat's gut* was usually applied to the strings of musical instruments, perhaps with a derisive reference to the sounds produced. Novell offers to halt Visioner's flow of words by cutting out the strings which produce them.

211. *Sitt doune*: Will attempts, unsuccessfully, to make peace. Novell and Visioner had been sitting with Will and Frank, but now have sprung to their feet to confront each other.

215–16. *Great Limerick, Athlone and Galloway*: Jacobite strongholds in Ireland. King James landed at Kinsale, Co. Cork, in 1689, but returned to France after the battle of the Boyne in 1690. After his departure, Limerick, Athlone and Galway (*Galloway*) continued to hold out, Limerick the longest. The Treaty of Limerick was signed on 3 October 1691.

218. *german Lairds*: King William was prince of Orange-Nassau. Nassau is in Germany, on the Rhine, around Wiesbaden.

219. *protestant league*: the Grand Alliance, which fought the Nine Years War against Louis XIV. *Protestant* is used ironically; most of King William's allies were catholic powers.

221. *Inskilen*: Enniskillen, Co. Fermanagh, a protestant stronghold unsuccessfully besieged by James in 1689.

222. *assemblie*: the General Assembly or, more probably, the Scottish parliament.

223. *two months' march of Miserie*: reference unclear. Visioner derisively equates Miserie with King James's army.

226. *ane Inglish Gazet*: the MS reads *and* for *ane*. The emendation improves the sense. The reference is to the official organ of the English government, the *London Gazette*, which from 1666 appeared twice a week on Tuesday and Friday. The implication is that ministers often based their prayers on information taken from the gazette.

228. *Carnall sense & reason*: this separation of religion from common sense and reason is an extreme statement of what Dr Davie calls 'metaphysical intellectualism of an anti-empirical sort' (Davie 1961: xiv). It comes to the forefront at the beginning of 3.3, and figures in the struggle between ancients and moderns discussed above, pp. xxviii–xxxvi.

229–32. *your Ministers' ... from the Church*: there are three assumptions here, first that the (Tuesday) English gazette arrived in Edinburgh late on Saturday night or early on Sunday morning; second, that copies were destined, not so much for private individuals as for the coffee-houses, where patrons might read them; finally, that ministers surreptitiously obtained early copies, on the contents of which they based their prayers and sermons.

Presbyterians allegedly despised prayer in set forms. Novell insinuates that the gazette has become the presbyterian equivalent of the episcopalian *Book of Common Prayer*.

It is of some interest to the social historian that in the early 1690s coffee-houses already flourished in Edinburgh.

234. *ten*: 'ta'en, taken'.

235. *mistack*: an example of Visioner's visionary talents. After the surrender of Mons, the garrison was allowed to march out.

238. *baltick kings*: Charles XI, king of Sweden (1660–97) and Christian V, king of Denmark (1670–99).

forsaken: perhaps 'declined to have to do with' (*OED*).

241–5. *in ther sted ... this year*: more of Visioner's visions.

241–2. *King of Morroco*: Mulai Ismail 'the Bloodthirsty' (1672–1727).

242. *K. of Mogull*: the Mogul emperor Aurangzeb (1658–1707). His despotic rule roused much interest in the West; see, e.g., Dryden's rhymed tragedy *Aureng-Zebe* (1676). Both Aurangzeb and Mulai Ismail were devout, even fanatical, Muslims.

242. *Prester John*: mythical Christian monarch in Asia or Abyssinia. *Prester* is an abbreviated form of *presbyter*, 'priest' or 'elder', but is taken by Visioner to mean 'presbyterian'.

244. *French fleet*: Visioner attempts to counter fear of a French invasion after the English naval defeat off Beachy Head, Sussex, in 1690.

247–8. *My Lord's man ... 3 heads*: references not identified. My Lord is Lord Whiggridne, the earl of Crawford.

247. *Strutherdyks*: Cellardyke, near Anstruther, Fife.

[*Earl*] *of Annandaill*: William Johnston (1672–1721), 4th earl (and from 24 June 1701 1st marquis) of Annandale. In the MS the title is left blank. This may indicate that Annandale's title was known to be changing when the MS was written; i.e. that it was written in early 1701.

Annandale had conspired with Sir James Montgomerie of Skelmorlie (d. in Paris, 1694) for the restoration of James VII. He confessed, was pardoned and became a Williamite, but was never fully trusted. He is one of the characters in Pitcairne's play *Tollerators and Con-Tollerators* (Kinloch 1830: 70–78).

252. *messenger ... buffet me*: a characteristic presbyterian reaction.

253. *rabling*: verbal noun from '*Rab(b)le*: to attack (a clergyman) by means of a rabble or mob in order to drive him from (*out of*) his charge. Applied, spec., to the attacks made by bands of Presbyterians on the Episcopalian clergy following upon the Revolution settlement of 1688–9' (*DOST*).

Visioner's threat shows the intimate link of the episcopalian church with Jacobitism. The Presbyterians will not confine their attacks to churchmen.

254. *to church*: Will's attitude to attendance at a presbyterian church service is as relaxed as his motives are mixed.

255. *wench*: cf. above, 57–63 and n.

Act 1, Scene 2

The scene is a room in the Old Ladie's apartments on an upper floor of an Edinburgh land. Wordie and Rachel are sitting on a high-backed settle, mid-stage, partly concealed from the Old Ladie, who is walking 'beside' (B and C, followed by the printed texts, aside, 'to the side'). She speaks initially from that position.

Furnishings include a shelf with books and a wall-mirror. There are at least two doors, one to a closet and one to Laura's bedroom.

The Old Ladie is deaf (below, 60–61) and mishears or fails to hear much of the exchange between Rachel and Wordie.

1. *Mes*: shortened form of *Maister* (Master), indicating the university degree of Master of Arts (MA); usually applied to a clergyman.

expone: 'expound', 'explain'.

4. *these words*: i.e. words of Scripture. Wordie indicates a passage in the Bible which Rachel and he are holding.

4. *condiserable*: B and C, followed by the printed texts, correctly read *considerable*.

5–6. **and ... soul-refreshing -**: words inserted in Pitcairne's hand. A parody of the canting speech of the devout Presbyterian, intended to deceive the Old Ladie as to what is actually happening; cf. her remark below, 17–18. When the Old Ladie comes forward, Wordie rises in some confusion.

8. *Blessed ... house*: the Old Ladie is pleased by Rachel's remark.

9. *family exercise*: the Old Ladie intends 'family worship' (including exposition of biblical texts). Her unmeant *double-entendre*, however, leads to the sequence of others immediately following.

12–25. *exercises ... scoller*: sustained *double-entendre* on the part of Rachel and Wordie; cf. above, **Prologue** 20n.

26. *growing*: Rachel is six months pregnant.

28–9. *it ... it*: i.e. Venus's exercise.

30. *How gravelie ... whille*: Wordie is pleased and relieved by the success of their deception.

32. *the day's morning*: Scots usage; 'this morning'.

33. *wes*: regular Scots form of the preterite singular of 'to be'.

34. *Mr Solomon*: an appropriate person for Wordie to consult; see above, **Drammatis Personæ**, 12n.

38. *deboshd*: 'debauched'. Wordie characteristically projects his own failings on to the Malignants, the Episcopalians.

40. *generall assembly*: the ultimate ruling body in the presbyterian Church of Scotland.

call: formal invitation to become minister of a parish or congregation.

41. *gett a dozen*: i.e. when episcopalian clergymen have been extruded from their parishes; see following scene.

42–3. *What tyme ... 12 or 1*: the liaison has become routine.

42. *at night*: Scots usage. B and C, followed by the printed texts, read *to night*.

44. *wanton*: Rachel projects her own nature on to her cousins.

45–7. *many a fair Lectur ... at them*: Rachel is as much a hypocrite as Wordie. Compare Laura's words below, 5.2, 266–84.

49. *Comittie*: the executive sub-committee of the Commission for Visitations on the South Side of Tay, one of two Commissions set up by the fifteenth Act of the 1690 General Assembly, the main function of both being to extrude episcopalian ministers from their parishes; see above, pp. xx–xxi, and the scene which follows. Wordie, still only a chaplain, hopes to obtain one of the extruded parishes for himself.

expects: Scots first person singular, present tense, when the verb is not preceded by the personal pronoun.

51–2. *I ever hated lying ... a most vyle sin*: more hypocrisy by both parties; cf. below, 5.2, 24.

54. *coms*: Scots third person plural, present tense, when the verb is not preceded by the personal pronoun.

55–8. *Methinks ... nycht*: Violetta's first words are appropriately barbed.

56. *disciplin*: ironic; 'Instruction having for its aim to form the pupil to proper conduct and action' (*OED*).

57. *exercise*: see above 7n.

60. *pattern*: ironic; 'an example or model deserving imitation; an example or model of a particular excellence' (*OED*).

61 *observant*: 'careful to perform or practise duly' (*OED*).

61. *but e'n God bie with you*: embarrassment hastens Wordie's exit.

62–5. *Your Cusin ... readie*: omitted in B.

63. *Mr Solomon*: an appropriate preacher for Rachel to hear.

75. *pretious*: ironic; 'of great moral, spiritual, or non-material worth; held in high esteem' (*OED*).

66. *congress*: 'sexual union' (*OED*).

brock: 'broken'. A Scots form of the past participle.

67. *nyce*: 'fastidious, dainty, difficult to please' (*OED*).

trucks up with: '**truck** 5b: to have dealings or intercourse *with*, to have to do *with*, to be on familiar terms; *spec.* of sexual intercourse' (*OED*). The construction with *up* is on the analogy of *take up with*, 'to consort with (esp. with a view to marriage)' (*OED*).

67–8. *jure divino*: 'by divine right', the presbyterian claim, in ambitious competition with that of the monarch, to rule by divine right; cf., e.g., Samuel Rutherford's treatise *The Divine Right of Church-Government and Excommunication* (London, 1646).

68–9. *promises ... performs*: a proverbial opposition.

70. *adoe*: B and C, followed by the printed texts, has the later form *to do*; *adae* is still a familiar Scots form.

70. *Cusine*: B and C, followed by the printed texts, have the correct *Sister*.

71. *conversatione*: probably 'circle of acquaintance, company, society' (*OED*).

73. *lecturs*: much the same as *sermons*.

74–5. *Call to the Unconverted*: Richard Baxter (1615–91), *A Call to the Unconverted to turn and live* (London and Kidderminster, 1658), 'a classic of puritan evangelism' (*OxfDNB*).

Tormenting Tophet: Henry Greenwood, *Tormenting Tophet: or, A terrible Description of Hel*, 2nd edn (London, 1615).

77. *bellman*: town crier. The Old Ladie is extremely deaf.

78. *Ladies Calling*: an episcopalian work, probably by Richard Allestree; see above, **Prologue**, 22n.

79. *sants ... Communion*: the Communion of the Saints is an article of the Apostles' Creed. Her reference to the Creed provides more evidence that Laura is an Episcopalian.

81–4. *I'le be ryd ... Complexion*: anticipation of later events. Violetta and Laura are prepared to go to almost any length to escape their environment.

81. *Clatter*: B reads *Clutter*, the 1722 text *Blatter*.

84. *Complexion*: the word is probably used in the modern sense, 'the natural colour, texture and appearance of the skin, esp. of the face; originally as showing the "temperament" or bodily constitution' (*OED*). The black habit of a nun would not suit Laura's complexion.

85. *bell*: the bell summoning people to church.

Act 1, Scene 3

The painted shutters represent a church interior, with the boxes, stage left and right, representing the pulpit and the raised stool of repentance. There is probably some indication (a window, for example, painted on the back shutters, with a view of the Castle Rock) that the Edinburgh West church is intended.

This scene parodies a meeting of the sub-committee of the 1690 General Assembly's Commission for Visitations on the South Side of Tay, the members of which included Hugh Kennedy (Moderator), Gilbert Rule (Mr Salathiel Littlesense), James Kirkton (Mr Covenant Planedealer), John Spalding (Cleark), James Frazer (Mr Timothie Turbulent), and the earl of Crawford (Lord Whiggridne). As in the play, neither David Williamson (Mr Solomon Cherrietrees) nor the earl of Leven (Lord Huffie) belonged to the Commission, but their presence in this scene is easily accounted for. A Church, where the meeting takes place, is David Williamson's West Kirk (St Cuthberts) and Lord Huffie, with his whip, is an appropriate comic door-keeper. Wordie, it may be suspected, is persona muta, among other such present, some only initially. The introductory stage direction lists only speaking parts.

Structurally, this and the next episode of the play are clumsy. Act 1, scene 1, ends with Will and Frank on their way to church. In the middle of scene 2 Wordie leaves the Old Ladie's apartments to be present at a meeting of the Committee, the meeting, presumably, on which 1.3 opens; later in the same scene Violetta and Laura are summoned by the bell to hear Mr Solomon preach. Yet in scene 3 Mr Solomon is seated or standing in a corner, attending to the proceedings of the Committee. The Moderator brings proceedings to an end with the suggestion that the Committee reassemble in the afternoon. In 2.1, which immediately follows, Lord Huffie appears in his nightgown, indicating that it is at least late evening, more probably the morning after his spell of duty with the Committee. Yet in 2.2 Will, Frank, Violetta, Laura, Rachel and the Old Ladie are in church, hearing Mr Solomon absolve a fornicatrix, with no suggestion that at least a day has passed since their exits in 1.1 and 2.

1. *see ... malignant spies*: the words imply that more people are on stage than those listed in the initial stage direction; Wordie, for instance, is almost certainly present. Huffie later drives most of them out with his whip. It is not likely that dramatists or producer would have missed this opportunity for comic action.

The original audience would certainly have been made up of 'malignants'. Huffie may well have concluded by cracking his whip at them. *malignant*: 'Episcopalian'.

to day: B has *the day*, idiomatic Scots.

2. *for ill and not good*: a characteristic tautology by the Moderator, Hugh Kennedy.

For *not good* B has the Scots *no for good*.

2. *the day*: i.e. the period between the signing of the National Covenant in 1638 and the beginning of the Cromwellian administration in 1652.

6. *Glisk*: Scots; 'glimpse'.

8–11. *It's better ... Xst our Mr*: Not in B, but present in C and the later printed texts; cf. Psalm 84. 10: 'I had rather be a doorkeeper in the house of my God, than to dwell in the tents of wickedness.'

10. *comand*: Turbulent regards his Church as by right the ultimate authority in Scotland.

11. **in the Name ... Mr***: an addition to the MS in Pitcairne's hand. *Xst* is for 'Christ', *Mr* for 'Maister', 'Master'.

14. *beg*: B and the 1722 print have the older Scots form *begs*.

15. *no title ... prouder of*: notoriously the earl of Leven prided himself on his ancestry and rank, but he was also a Presbyterian of extreme views and a bully.

16. *scurges of the lord*: Huffie refers to John 2. 13–17, where Christ drives the traders and money-changers out of the Temple, using 'a scourge of small cords'. Cf. also Isaiah 10. 26: 'And the Lord of hosts shall stir up a scourge for him according to the slaughter of Midian.'

18–19. *scurge ... house of God*: Huffie drives out most of the spectators, thus allowing the Committee to proceed with business. Wordie, in his garb as a presbyterian minister, remains.

20–4. *takne ther hands ... your baiks*: cf. Curate 1692: 127: 'Mr *Areskine* in the *Tron Church* said "That the work of the Lord is like to be ruin'd; for there are two Sorts of People that have taken their Hands from the Work of the Lord. First, the Malignants, that never laid their Hands to it. Secondly, the Court-Party. But you Lasses and Lads put your Shoulders to the Work, take a good Lift of it, for it will not break your Backs; and you can never use your Backs in a better Work."'

23. *To take a great* or *good lift of* is 'to take a great deal upon oneself, to undertake much' (*DOST*, s.v. **Lift, Lyft**, n., **2. b.**)

21. *Torries*: 'Tories', Jacobites; see above, 1.1, 101n.

22. *Court partie*: the governing faction in the Scottish parliament after the Revolution. They supported King William but many members were lukewarm to the powers of the presbyterian church.

22. *Man*: i.e. Scots *maun*, 'must'.

24. *pek*: peck, a dry measure of capacity; for barley, oats, malt, 13.229 litres.

pek ... baiks: apparently proverbial, though I have not been able to trace the particular form of words; cf. below, 102 and n.

baiks: 'backs'.

27. *fat*: 'what'; Scots, NE dialect form. B and C, followed by the printed texts, read *what*; see above, p. lxviii.

28. *thanksgiveing*: 'an act or expression of thanks, esp. one taking the form of a religious service' (*DOST*).

29–30. *defeat ... Savoy*: in August 1690 Duke Victor Amadeus II of Savoy was defeated by the French at Staffarda in Piedmont. Savoy belonged to the Grand Alliance against Louis XIV – in other words, he and King William were allies; *he wes on the Confederate syde*, as Solomon remarks (23). Turbulent's proposal of a Thanksgiving is therefore a little surprising.

30. *Rather a fast ... syde*: Solomon is not a member of the Committee, but characteristically puts in his oar.

fast: 'A time or day of fasting; *spec.* one appointed to be observed by the General Assembly, or locally by a presbytery or kirk session' (*DOST*).

Confederate syde: the allied powers united against Louis XIV in the Nine Years War.

31–2. *right end Of the string*: perhaps a garbled version of the proverb (*ODEP*, 221), the usual form of which is 'wrong end of the staff, stick'. In *OED* the earliest date quoted for the phrase is 1886; it is glossed as 'to have got a story wrong, not know the facts of a case'. In *ODEP*, however, the first clear example is dated 1533.

Alternatively, *OED* gives examples of 'the better end of the staffe' as early as 1626, where it means: 'to come off best in a contest, disputation etc.' This comes closer to the sense intended by the Moderator.

33. *persecuting ... protestants*: during the 1650s Charles Emmanuel II of Savoy, father of Victor Amadeus, instituted a savage persecution of the Waldensian Protestants in his dominions (see Milton's Sonnet XVIII, 'On the Late Massacre in Piemont'). The persecution was renewed by his son after the revocation of the Edict of Nantes in 1685, but ceased when Victor Amadeus joined the allied powers.

34. *prisbiteriain*: B, C, and the printed texts (except 1722) read *Protestant*.

34–5. *as King William* : i.e. he is not a Presbyterian at all. The church in Holland was Calvinist, but William's partners in the Grand Alliance were predominantly Catholic.

36. *Outs*: 'Hoots!' (exclamatory).

had: *haud*, 'hold'.

had your toung o' that: keep quiet, hold your peace, about that.

37. *won't rip up old sores*: proverbial (*ODEP*, 678).

38. *pray to drown the noise*: this apparently was Kennedy's usual practice; see below, **Preface** p. 225: 'It is knowen that he prayed in the assemblie to drowne the noise and silence the bable of the brethren.' Apparently he had many occasions to use the method.

39. *fool praying*: Covenant sees through the Moderator's ruse; cf. below, **Preface** p. 227: 'he said their fool praying was Hipocritical, and the were seeking their own intrests.'

Our mynds ... saying: dramatic irony; the prayer applies as much to the Moderator as to the other Committee members.

40–1. *giv's grace ... what will o' that*: cf. below, **Preface**, p. 225: 'He uses hiw own words in all the prayers Except this on He desires Grace from God If he would Expect Glory which is indeed borrowed from one Mean a brother of his, who preaches just now att Dalkeith.'

will: B and C, followed by the printed texts, read *win*, subjunctive of *win*, 'become' (*DOST*, s.v. **Win, Wyn**, v. **16. b**).

44. *plant*: 'provide with ministers'.

45. *England*: in terms of the Solemn League and Covenant (1643), the English parliament agreed that presbyterian church discipline should be established in England, an agreement that came to nothing. Although Scottish Presbyterians retained some hopes and ambitions, neither Committee nor General Assembly had any authority in England. Covenant gives a sensible, Salathiel an unrealistic, response to the question.

46–7. *Charitie ... home*: proverbial (*ODEP*, 115).

48. *plant*: B and C, followed by the printed texts, read *first plant*.

51. *o'rgrowne with bryers and thorns*: i.e. dominated by the Church of England episcopate.

53. *book*: *A Rational Defence of Non-Conformity* (London, 1689).

54. *Ignorance*: after this, B and C, followed by the printed texts, read *superstition &*.

55. *seekness*: 'sickness'.

pastorall relation: Salathiel refers to his former charge at Alnwick; see above, **Drammatis Personæ**, 9n.

55–6. *Will the folk ... againe?*: a seemingly innocent question, put into context by Covenant's response.

58. *pouder*: 'pother', 'fuss about nothing'. The word is not recorded in *DOST* or *SND*.

59. *got*: MS *not*.

lend: loan.

61. *apprehend him*: B and C, followed by the printed texts, add 'if they can catch him'.

62. *Solomon [from ane corner]*: Solomon is not a member of the Commission and therefore has no right to speak at the Committee (he has already intervened; above, 30). Probably he is present because the Committee is meeting in his church, the West Kirk.

62. *prive*: 'with no official standing' (*DOST*). Note the *double-entendre* in 'prive member', peculiarly appropriate to Solomon.

sweet Clark: the clerk to the Committee, Mr John Spalding. Marginal insertion in Pitcairne's hand. Not in B, C, or the printed texts. The phrase fits the references to the Song of Solomon immediately following.

64–5. *with dove's eyes*: marginal insertion in Pitcairne's hand. Not in B or the 1722 print. C and the later prints have an expanded version: 'which is altogether lovely, who hath dove's eyes within her locks'.

65–9. *Her lips ... Lillies*: cf. Song of Solomon 4. 3–5; 7. 2–4. The text is a favourite with Mr Solomon, as with Will and Violetta (above, 1.1, 61; 2.2 *passim*). The latter pair, however, use the text simply as a code to convey arrangements for a secret meeting. Solomon uses it in the traditional terms of the mutual love between Christ and the Church, mingling this with his own subconscious fantasies. In doing so, he shocks even his clerical brethren.

69. *defyled*: 'sexually abused'.

these 28 years: from the Restoration in 1660 to the Revolution in 1688.

70–2. *Get able men ... aboundantly*: it seems likely that at this point Solomon gestures towards Wordie as an appropriately able man. Equally appropriate to his character is the undercurrent of sexual reference.

71. *inbeareing*: 'capable of producing a vivid impression on the mind, impressive, persuasive' (*DOST*).

73–4. *Moderator! ... Moderator!*: Both Turbulent and Salathiel object, not so much to Solomon's intervention, as to the style in which it is expressed.

75. *ffortificatne*: so also in the 1722 print. B and C, followed by the later printed texts, read *For Fornication*.

76. *ffornicatione*: the underlying drift of Solomon's words makes Covenant mishear *ffortificatione*.

hobling on: literally 'bobbing, jogging about on', i.e. 'copulating with'; cf. *Defence of Crissel Sandelandis*, 21–2 (Tod Ritchie vol. 2, 1928, 329–33): 'Had scho bene vndir, and he hobland abone,/ That was a perllous play for to suspect thame.'

77. *houer of Babylon*: 'whore of Babylon'; see Revelation 17. 3–6; interpreted by Protestants as the Roman Catholic church.

14 black birds: the fourteen Scottish bishops; cf. below, 3.3, 61–2 and n.

79–80. *Cleense ... Keerats ... deen*: NE dialectal forms for *Cleanse, Curates, done*.

80. *Webster*: weaver, in the seventeenth century a typical working man.

81. *My Lord Moderator*: although a Presbyterian, the webster addresses the Moderator in terms appropriate to a bishop.

82–3. *Away*: B, C, and the later prints read Scots *Awa*.

prelatick: 'a hostile term for episcopal' (*OED*), from *prelate*, 'bishop'. For the Moderator's reaction, cf. above, 1.1, 118 and n. B and C, followed by the later printed texts, read *prelatick titles*.

J.C.: 'Jesus Christ'.

84. *My lord brother ... J.C.*: the webster fails to take the point.

85. *Covenan*: Covenant. For the Solemn League and Covenant see above, 44n, under *England*, p. 109. For extreme Presbyterians this, together with the National Covenant of 1638 (see above, 2n, p. 107), held an almost mystical authority. For this reason the webster applies the term to a document which he regarded as of great religious importance.

St Andrews: the Fife royal burgh is mentioned, partly because it lay in Crawford (Whigridne) territory, partly because, before the Revolution, it had been the seat of the senior episcopalian archbishop in Scotland and an ancient university. The archbishopric had been abolished under the Claim of Right, and the university had subsequently been severely purged. The administration of church affairs was now democratic, in the hands of 'websters, souters and godlie women', a situation which Pitcairne deplored.

Whigridne's election to the ruling eldership, and consequently to membership of the Committee, does not fit historical fact. Crawford's appointment was by the 1690 General Assembly, of which he was a member. He must therefore already have been an Elder. Nor are Elders appointed by popular vote. For Pitcairne's own satirical purposes he is distorting the actual situation.

86. *ruling Elder*: for the meaning of the term, see above, **Drammatis Personæ**, 15n.

89. *stands best*: 'is best'; 'to be as described by the predicated adj.' (*DOST*, s.v. **Stand: 22**).

89. *book leard*: 'book-learned', 'educated'. B and C, followed by the printed texts, read *e'en call it what you pleas, ye'r book leard*.

90. *by his providence*: a customary phrase with the Moderator; cf. below, **Preface**, p. 225: 'every body who had the honour to see him in the Chair must confess that he begane his speaches with a By his providence we are met here in this place.' Here he is formally welcoming Lord Whiggridne to the Committee.

Kennedy and Crawford had a close personal relationship; see the Latin quotation above, **Drammatis Personæ**, 13n.

91. *zealous websters ... godlie women*: the grouping implies contempt for the more democratic aspects of Presbyterianism.

111

92. *Judicatorie*: both Moderator and Whigridne (74) regard the Comitie as a court of law, with powers of sentencing.

93. *gravaminous*: 'grievous, annoying, distressing', from late Latin *gravamen*, 'trouble, physical inconvenience'.

94. *wes*: Scots form of the 1st person plural.

96. *rabling*: cf. above, 1.1, 253n.

97. *manadged the wholl civill interest*: as President of the Scottish parliament; see above, **Drammatis Personæ**, 5n. The word *manage* often, as here, has pejorative overtones.

98. *Nehemias says*: no such saying is to be found in the biblical Nehemiah. The real point is that Nehemiah was the lay authority for the rebuilding of Jerusalem, and the reestablishment of the pure faith, after the Babylonian captivity of the Jews. Whigridne sees himself as playing the same role in Scotland after the Babylonian captivity of the reigns of Charles II and James VII.

Cf. too below, **Preface**, p. 224: 'He always mixeth together bitts of Nehemia and pieces of Arcadia.' Here Whiggridne purports to quote Nehemiah, but I detect no traces of Sir Philip Sidney's heroic romance, *The Countesse of Pembrokes Arcadia* (1590–93).

99–100. *pray ... ceasing*: cf. below, **Preface**, p. 224: 'That he sought moneths to advise and fitt himself for being a member of the assemblie when it was to sitt but one is Clear from the Historicall account of the Gen-Ass.'

102. *he nevir ... bearing of it*: proverbial; cf. above, 18n, *ODEP*, 312: 'God shapes the back for the burthen.' The examples quoted in *ODEP* are all of nineteenth-century date.

104. *imbicillitie*: 'incompetency or incapacity (*to do* something)' (*OED*); Latin *imbecillitas*. There is probably a play on the modern sense of the word.

Self-disparagement was a rhetorical topic of the exordium (Curtius 1953, 84). Whigridne has evidently received a humanist education, but makes poor use of it.

103–6. *Though I be ... now to plant*: cf. below, **Preface**, p. 224: 'That we make him take plantations of Gairdines for plantations of Kirks is naturall enugh for a man who understands nothing but Gairdenrie and frequently uses to mistake'; cf. too Curate 1692: 92: '*My Lord C–d*, who is deservedly honour'd by all the party, his godly Parks and Orchards are well planted already; and why then should the General Assembly be any farther concern'd about *Planting Work*? Purging Work *is their* great Business.'

108–10. *My Lord ... hedges*: despite his veneration for a peer, the Moderator is baffled by Whigriddne's remarks; cf. below, 4.2, 81–2.

112. *spade of the sprid*: a parody of St Paul's phrase, 'the sword of the spirit' (Ephesians 6. 17). Whigridne recovers somewhat from his previous blunder.

Act 2, Scene 1

The setting is the courtyard of Edinburgh Castle, the battlements of which are painted on the back-shutters. One of the boxes represents Huffie's bedroom in the Governor's residence, where Huffie is either preparing for bed or just risen; he appears in his nightgown, 'a full robe worn before dressing or for lounging' (*OED*). The Boy stands below in the courtyard.

The scene stands in sharp contrast to the previous, in which Huffie presented himself as the aristocratic guardian of the presbyterian church. In both, however, he is primarily a bully. The reference to his dealings with Fife boatmen in *Proceres Scotorum* (MacQueen and MacQueen 2009: 216; above, p. 84) suggests that the scene had some basis in fact.

1. *battalia*: 'a large body of men in battle array; Italian *battaglia*, Spanish *batalla*' (*OED*); cf. Shakespeare, *Richard III*, 5.3, 10–11: '*Norfolk*: Six or seven thousand is their utmost power. *K. Richard*: Why, our battalia trebles that account.'

The metaphor of military action, begun in *battalia*, continues in (2) with *besidged* and is further developed in *civill war* (4) and *enemie threaten us without* (5). The phrase *civill war* is particularly relevant; Edinburgh Castle had recently been under actual siege when the Roman Catholic George Gordon, 1st duke of Gordon (1643–1716), as Governor, held it for James VII, 1688–89 (*Siege of the castle of Edinburgh MDCLXXXIX*, ed. R. Bell, Bannatyne Club 23 [Edinburgh, 1828]). By contrast, Gordon's successor as Governor is now under siege by his creditors.

boatmen & fidlers: B and C, followed by the printed texts, read *Boatmen, Hyrers & Fidlers*.

6–8. *Good faith ... us both*: the boy speaks ironically; cf. below, 81–2.

8. *guard*: the City Guard (above, **Drammatis Personæ**, 26n). The Guardhouse was in the High Street, just west of the Cross, and some little distance from the Castle.

9. *Villainie*: 'a person or thing that is the source of discredit or disgrace' (*OED*, where this sense is classified as 'Obs., rare'). The printed texts read *Villain*.

9. [stage-direction]: Boy exits to bring whip, which on his return he passes up to Huffie. Huffie throws it at him.

10. *brack ... Lady*: refers to Huffie's assault on the Lady Mortonhall, on which see above, **Drammatis Personæ**, 7n.

11. [stage-direction]: Huffie retires and Boy exits to obtain the great whip; Huffie re-enters on the stage, where boatmen, hirers and fiddlers (i.e. string players) throng about him.

hyrers: '*hirer*: one who lets out something [in this case, horses] for hire' (*OED*, where this use of the word is classified as 'Obs. or Sc.'). Not in *DOST* or *SND*.

13 ff. The language of the *boatmen, hyrers and fidlers* is an idiomatic vernacular Scots, often elliptic, making much use of proverbial turns of expression.

15. *guided*: 'treated', 'used', 'handled'.

15–16. *Gentle or semple*: 'well-born or low-born'.

17. *this gate*: 'in this way'.

19–20. *Off hands is fair play*: proverbial; Fergusson 1924: 47, 'Hands off is fair play'; *ODEP*, 348, 'Hands off and fair play'.

21. *John Moncur*: not identified. Perhaps a Scots equivalent of English John a Cumber; 'This John a Cumber ... that went beyond the deuill, And made him serue him seuen yeares prentiship' (*ODEP*, 35).

22. *Willie Miln*: not identified, but probably proverbial; cf. 'as white as a bear's (hound's) tooth' (*ODEP*, 35).

fraught: 'passage money'. Lord Leven's (Huffie's) ancestral home was in eastern Fife; consequently it was more convenient for him to travel to Edinburgh by boat across the Firth of Forth. His route was probably by horse to Burntisland, from whence he would hire a ferry; see below, 29n.

24–5. *God nor ... Sea*: the phrase is idiomatic and ironic: 'God [let] my boat be at the bottom of the sea, unless –'; for the idiom, cf. Dunbar, 78B, 31–3: 'Ane souttar said, "In gud effek,/ Nor I be hangit be the nek,/ Gif bettir butis of ledder ma be"' (Bawcutt 1998: 252); a more elaborate example in Henryson, *Morall Fabillis,* 'The Fox, the Wolf and the Cadger', 2121–2: 'Than said the volff, "Nou God nor that I hang,/ Bot to be thaire I wald gif all my clays"' (Fox 1981, 81). See *DOST,* s.v. **Nor**, *conj.*[1], **3**. The clause introduced by *nor* also carries some such implication as 'which God forbid'.

B and C, followed by the printed texts, insert *my* before *boat*.

boddom: Scots for 'bottom'.

25. *Duk of Rothes*: 7th earl and 1st duke of Rothes (1630–81), the 'disso-lute Rothes' of 'Wandering Willie's Tale' in Scott's *Redgauntlet*. He was a friend of Charles II and an Episcopalian, whose policy, as President of the Privy Council and later Chancellor, was to use military force to discourage religious dissent. Rothes was Leven's kinsman and had in fact disputed the succession to the earldom of Leven.

26. *His saul praise God!*: i.e. '[Rothes is dead,] may his soul [now] be praising God [in heaven]'. Rothes' dissolute life makes the proposition at best dubious.

Earle of Marshall: William Keith, 8th Earl Marischall (1665–1712). The Jacobite memorialist Lockhart says of him, 'being a man of honour and capacity, he was always faithful to his prince [James VII and later his son, James Francis] and country, did them both great service and merited much from them' (Szechi 1995: 111). Pitcairne composed a Latin verse-epitaph for him (MacQueen and MacQueen 2009: 168).

The 3rd Boatman misunderstands the title.

26. *my Lord Dundee*: John Graham of Claverhouse (1648–89) was a soldier, originally on the Continent under William of Orange. He was commissioned in the duke of Montrose's horseguards to curb covenanting activity in Scotland. In June 1679 his troop was defeated in a skirmish at Drumclog, Ayrshire, but immediately afterwards he defended Glasgow and was on the winning side at Bothwell Brig in Lanarkshire. He became hereditary sheriff of Wigtown and steward-depute of Kirkcudbright with authority to prosecute recalcitrants in south-west Scotland. He used his power sparingly. In October 1688 he was second-in-command of the Scottish forces sent southwards to resist the invasion by William. In November 1688 King James made him Viscount Dundee and Lord Graham of Claverhouse. When the king fled to France, Graham returned to Scotland. On 18 March 1689 he withdrew from the Convention of Estates in Edinburgh and set out, accompanied by fifty of his own troop, to raise an army in the Highlands to fight for James. In a battle (27 July) at the head of the Pass of Killiecrankie, north of Pitlochry, Perthshire, he defeated the Williamite army under General Mackay, but was himself killed.

Pitcairne wrote a celebrated Latin verse-epitaph for Dundee (MacQueen and MacQueen 2009: 72).

The 3rd Boatman contrasts Huffie's behaviour with that of these other noblemen, all supporters of the Stuart monarchy.

26–7. *God gie 'n*: 'God [has] given', 'granted that –'.

27. *lyke pilens of onyons*: the 1722 print reads *like Peelings of Onions*. B, C and the later printed texts lack the plebeian simile.

pilens: 'peelings', 'rinds'. Not in *DOST*.

28. *bruntIsland water*: the Firth of Forth. Burntisland is a port on the Fife coast of the firth, from which ferry-boats crossed to Granton or Newhaven, near Edinburgh.

28. *hindmost*: 'last', probably intended to qualify some such noun as *fraught*. The Boatman, however, is violently interrupted by Huffie.

30. *Call the Guard*: B, C and the printed texts give Huffie this phrase after line 24.

32. *Gillichrankie*: Killiecrankie; see above, 26n. The remark is a little unfair. Leven's regiment did not break in face of the Highland charge and covered the subsequent retreat.

33. *Dill*: 'de'il', 'devil'.

35. *plaster*: more elaborate and expensive than a modern plaster; 'an external curative application, consisting of a solid or semi-solid substance spread upon a piece of muslin, skin, or some similar material, and of such nature as to be adhesive at the temperature of the body, used for the local application of a medicament, or for closing a wound, and sometimes to give mechanical support' (*OED*). The suggestion is ironic.

36. *Stocks*: 'an instrument of public and humiliating punishment by which the ankles and wrists of the seated offender were restrained by wooden bars in front of him' (*OED*).

37. *nobleman*: illustrates Huffie's overweening pride in his birth.

40. *Kail*: here 'broth' or 'soup'.

pounie: 'pony'.

41. *dyk*: 'ditch'; cf. Henryson, *Morall Fabillis*, 2063, 'The Fox, the Wolf, and the Cadger': ' "Heir lyis the Deuyll", quod he, "deid in ane dyke" ' (Fox 1981: 79).

42–3. *The deil made sutors seamen*: proverbial; Fergusson 1924: 103: 'The devil maid soutars shipmen that can nather steir nor row'; *ODEP*, 756: 'Souters shouldna be sailors, wha can neither steer nor row'.

sutors: 'shoemakers', 'cobblers'.

43–44. *gott ... earls now*: a satirical reference to the many new titles created in the reigns of James VII and William of Orange.

44. *God ... backburden o' them*: 'God grant that Beelzebub should carry them off on his back'. For *had* B reads *laks*.

Belzebie: 'Beelzebub', 'the Devil'.

46. *ther's no help*: Huffie's courage fails as he realizes that his domestic staff has disappeared and that he is alone.

46. *Sirs*: note the change to a more conciliatory vocative.

47. *God bliss ... did it*: the fiddler responds diplomatically.

49. *brock*: 'broken'.

50: *all the toun will not*: i.e. 'nobody can'.

51. *bais*: 'base'; here the belly of the instrument.

bess viol: 'bass viol or viola da gamba', held between the knees, like the modern 'cello.

56. *babouns*: 'baboons', celebrated for their howling.

56. *people who cannot play*: Professor McGavin remarks: 'I'm pretty sure that this could relate to the problems with eighteenth-century aristocrats wanting music other than the traditional repertoire of the (often Highland) musicians. The itinerants played from memory and by ear, and the nobles wanted the kind of music which was now represented only on sheets.' The date of the play is rather early for this to apply, but Leven (Huffie) had spent time on the Continent, where he may have acquired a sophisticated ear.

116

Scottish printed music, the Aberdeen *Cantus, Songs and Fancies. To Thre, Foure, or Five Parts* (Forbes 1662), had been published some thirty years earlier, but, outside the North-East, was not well known, and by 1691 the music it contained would have seemed old-fashioned.

59. *Cable*: 'the strong thick rope to which a ship's anchor is fastened' (*OED*).

leaking: apparently 'causing to leak', a sense unrecorded in *OED*, *DOST* or *SND*. The printed editions read 'breaking'.

60. *bumper*: obscure; perhaps *bomspar* ('boom-spar'), 'a large spar' (*DOST*). The *boom* was 'that part of a ship's deck where spare spars are stowed' (*OED*). B, C, and the printed editions read *pump*.

64. *beis me ... againe*: 'if it be me who shall attend to him again'; see above, 1.1, 157n.

65. *manger*: 'a trough from which horses feed'. Huffie, presumably, had run amok in the hirer's stable.

66. *baillie*: 'town magistrate'.

66. *assithment*: 'compensation'.

67. *fyne*: i.e. for assault.

68. *bill*: 'promissory note'.

69. *Minister of Weems stipend*: in September 1691 Leven had married Lady Anne Wemyss and perhaps, through her, became lay-patron of Wemyss parish in Fife. Alternatively, he is simply taking advantage of the new family connection. Either way, his action ill becomes the self-proclaimed champion of the presbyterian Church of Scotland.

71. *Cravat*: 'an article of dress worn round the neck, chiefly by men' (*OED*).

72–3. *the blind harper*: Professor McGavin suggests the possibility of a specific reference to Roderick Morison, *An Clarsair Dall* (the Blind Harper) (c. 1656–c. 1713). Morison was certainly in Edinburgh at some time between 1679 and 1683, and there is at least a possibility that he made another visit at the time of the Glorious Revolution (Matheson 1970: xlii–xlv, 184–5). He was an ardent supporter of James VII, something that would not have endeared him to the earl of Leven, if the two had ever met.

77. *you dogs*: the plural is unexplained, unless we assume that, with the departure of the boatmen, hirers and fiddlers, Huffie's domestic staff (including the Boy) has appeared on stage. Before *Hencefurth* B inserts *Boy!* and for *dogs* reads *dog*. The printed texts read *dog*. The plural may be no more than a slip of the pen.

81–2. *Your Lordship ... upon her*: B, C, and the printed texts have only *Your Lordship uses them so unmercifully.*

uses ... upon her: see above, 10n.

In A the text here is partly illegible, partly obscured because overwritten by the introductory stage-directions for the next scene.

Act 2, Scene 2

This scene completes the action begun at the end of Act 1, Scenes 1 and 2. As in Act 1, Scene 3, the stage represents the West Kirk, with the congregation sitting on stools or standing, with the fornicatrix in one box, representing the elevated stool of repentance and Solomon in the other, representing the pulpit.

2. *no wonder*: Solomon speaks from experience.

3–4. *opne ... wicked*: i.e. provide material for Episcopalians (and others) to mock the members of the presbyterian church.

7–11. *fra once ... maker*: the fornicatrix gives an admittedly comic, but at the same time antinomian and dualistic, defence of her past way of life; her heart remained devoted to her Maker, even while Satan had possession of her body. She implies the Gnostic tenet that there is an absolute dichotomy between the evil material body and the spark of true divinity, the heart or soul, imprisoned, as it were, in the body, from which it will eventually win release to rejoin its Maker. Bodily behaviour is irrelevant to the destiny of the soul. Remnants of such beliefs were widespread in the Middle Ages, e.g. among the Bogomiles and Albigensians (Runciman 1947: especially cc. IV, VI and VII). Certain Pauline passages, especially in Romans (3. 28, 'Therefore we conclude that a man is justified by faith without the deeds of the law'; 7. 23, 'But I see another law in my members, warring against the law of my mind and bringing me into captivity to the law of sin which is in my members') provided an opening for a post-Reformation version of the doctrine, later powerfully illustrated by James Hogg's novel, *Private Memoirs and Confessions of a Justified Sinner* (London, 1824). The fornicatrix, at least in her own opinion, is a justified sinner. Solomon appears to accept the defence; at least he makes no comment. Pitcairne and his associates thought otherwise. Both Will and Violetta make fun of the doctrine.

Solomon concludes the service by silently absolving the fornicatrix. While he is doing so, Will begins his campaign.

12. *Fair cretur ... thy bodie*: Will has strategically placed Frank and himself beside the two young ladies. He adapts the words of the fornicatrix in a rather crude beginning to his imagined campaign of seduction. He will play the part of the devil by gaining possession of Violetta's body. Her response is spirited and shows that although she too is willing to play the game, it will be only on her own terms.

17. *impertinent*: 'out of place', 'absurd'.

demand it: as the fornicatrix has by mounting the stool of repentance.

19. *lyk the devill ... holy flesh*: Will elaborates his own ironic version of the defence put up by the fornicatrix. Violetta's flesh is holy because she is attending church.

21. *that monster*: Mrs Rachel; the word *monster* may contain a reference to her advanced pregnancy (above, 1.2, 26). See following note.

Goldn Fleece: the Golden Fleece was concealed in a dense thicket, guarded by a dragon which, in bulk and length was vaster than a ship of fifty oarsmen (Pindar, *Pythian* 4, 245). Jason killed the dragon and so won, not only the Golden Fleece, but also the princess Medea.

21. *stratagem of Love*: cf. above 1.1, 58–61.

21 [stage direction]. *throws up*: the original meaning of *throw*, 'twist, turn', was retained longer than elsewhere in Scotland and northern England. The present usage in terms of turning over the pages of a book is not, however, recorded in *OED* or *DOST*. A single instance, dated 1743, is noted in *SND*: 'Throwing up the Presbytry register near thirty years back' (Ayr Presbytery Register MS, 19 January). The usage must however have been reasonably familiar; it is retained in B and the printed editions. The nearest parallel quoted in *DOST* (s.v. **Thraw(e 6**) is Barbour, *Bruce* 13, 658–60:

> And gif it fall yat fortoun throw
> The quheill about, it yat on hicht
> Was ere, it most doune lycht.
>
> (McDiarmid and Stevenson 1981: 75)

24. *Behold ... Love*: Song of Solomon 1. 15.

25–6. *I am ... Lady*: as the names indicate, Frank lacks the determination and ingenuity of Will towards attaining his purpose. He is wholly dependent on Will.

25. *stated*: 'placed', 'positioned'. Frank is sitting or standing next to Laura and is impressed by Will's technique, which he would like to try on Laura.

place: i.e. 'biblical passage'.

26. *this Lady*: Laura.

28. *Wish*: 'Wheesh!', 'Be quiet!' Will recognizes that Frank has no ability for this kind of game.

28 [stage direction]: after *poynts*, B, followed by the later editions, inserts *a place*.

29–30. *That thou wart ... mother's house*: Song of Solomon 8. 1–2: 'O that thou wert as my brother, that sucked the breasts of my mother! ... I would lead thee, and bring thee into my mother's house.' Violetta has been quick to catch Will's meaning.

30 [stage direction]. Will, the Old Ladie and her entourage advance front-stage; Frank and the other members of the congregation exeunt to the rear. Frank is obviously downcast.

31. *Nebuchadnazers & Balshazers*: Nebuchadnezzar and Belshazzar were successive kings of Babylon and oppressors of the Jews. Both received valuable advice from the prophet Daniel, advice which they tended to misunderstand; see Daniel 1–5. The Old Ladie implies that Will is a second Daniel. There is perhaps an ironic reference to Shylock's words, addressed to Portia, in *Merchant of Venice* 4.1, 223, 'A Daniel come to judgment! Yea, a Daniel'. Like Shylock, the Old Ladie will discover that her assessment is accurate otherwise than she had intended.

33–4. *8 chapter ... Song of Solomon*: see above, 29–30 and n.

35–6. *best Comentars ... Metaphor*: Will hypocritically presents himself as a learned biblical scholar, skilled in the interpretation of figures of speech. Violetta shows herself an apt pupil; for the effect see above, 1.3, 65–9n.

Comentars: commentaries, expositions; cf., e.g., Buchanan 1892: 9: 'Thys classe sal reid Terence, and sum of the maist facil epistles of Cicero, alternatim, and als the reulis of grammar assignat to thayme, without commentair, but only the expresse wordis and sentence of the reul.'

41–2. *seik him ... maltreated her*: Song of Solomon 3. 2: 'I will rise now and go about the city in the streets, and in the broad ways I will seek him whom my soul loveth'; 5. 7: 'The watchmen that went about the city found me, they smote me, they wounded me.'

toune Guard: Will is thinking of the Edinburgh City Guard; see above, **Drammatis Personæ**, 26n.

41. *meet*: preterite of **Met(e, Meit**, 'come or light upon, come across, find'; cf. the long vowel in the forms *mete, meit, meyt, mate* (*DOST*).

43. *Ingenuous*: a malapropism; the Old Ladie means *ingenious*.

feall: 'profound' (*SND*, s.v. **Fell** 4).

45–7. *Come ... yeards*: Song of Solomon 7. 11–12: 'Come, my beloved, let us go forth into the field; let us lodge in the villages. Let us get up early to the vineyards.'

46. *Cannogat*: the Canongate, literally 'street of the canons'; here the suburb of Edinburgh, originally a separate burgh belonging to the Augustinian canons of the abbey of Holyrood, built around the street of the same name.

Lady Murray's yeards: the gardens of Moray House, residence of the earls of Moray, in the Canongate. Lady Murray is Lady Margaret Home (d. 1683), who in 1627 became the wife of James Stuart, who later (1638) succeeded as 4th earl of Moray; see below, 3.1, opening note.

47–8. *homelie expressione*: presbyterian ministers deliberately cultivated a homely style of expression in their discourses, a custom deplored by Episcopalians; see Curate 1692: 23: 'the most of their sermons are nonsensick

Raptures, the Abuse of mystick Divinity, in canting and compounding Vocables, oft-times stuffed with impertinent and base Similies, and always with homely, coarse, and ridiculous Expressions, very unsuitable to the Gravity and Solemnity, that becomes Divinity'.

49. *Old Ladie*: B adds the stage direction [*aside to Rachael*.

51. *plott*: a recurrent word in the play; see below, 3.1, 94, 146; 4.1, 84; 4.4, 137, 146, 156; **Epilogue**, 4. The latter years of Charles II and the reign of his brother were characterized by plots, the Popish Plot, the Rye House Plot, etc. The authors of the play would have regarded the risings by Monmouth and Argyll, and indeed the Glorious Revolution itself, as 'plots'. Correspondingly, events in the play proceed by a series of plots.

53. *expon*: 'expound', 'explain'. B has *Dispone*, perhaps intended to mean 'deal with' (*DOST*, s.v. **Dispone 3**).

56. *debouch*: 'debauch', 'seduce'.

60–1. *'Thou ... voyce*: a partial misquotation; Song of Solomon 8. 13: 'Thou that dwellest in the gardens, the companions hearken to thy voice: cause me to hear it.'

61–5. *that is still ... Loves*: a series of clauses, intended to mislead the Old Ladie, and at the same time convey to Violetta that she is to meet Will the next morning in Lady Murray's yards; see 3.1. In B, C, and the printed texts, these lines are given to Violetta, who is thus made to propose the assignment.

62. *signe ... (a whistle or so)*: Will does not actually whistle; but intends to emphasize that his words have a special, lover's significance for Violetta. *Mrs*: 'Mistress'.

63. *sum*: i.e. Song of Solomon 7. 12: 'Let us get up early to the vineyards; let us see if the vine flourish, whether the tender grape appear, and the pomegranates bud forth: there will I give thee my loves', taken together with 8. 13, the whole summarised as 'mak hast in the morning to accomplish our Loves' (65).

68. *I have ... no breasts*: Song of Solomon 8. 8: 'We have a little sister, and she hath no breasts: what shall we do for our sister in the day when she shall be spoken for?' Violetta refers to Laura, who certainly has breasts; see below, 3.2. See also 3.1, 67–9.

69. *Gentils*: 'non-Jews': more generally, 'those outside the faith', interpreted by Violetta (70–1) as meaning 'outside the tenets of the presbyterian church'.

71. *great difficultie*: cf. above, 1.2, 78–9; below, 3.2, 1–11. Violetta demonstrates that Laura is likely to be as willing as herself.

76–7. *Methinks ... provided*: Will does not forget Frank.

78. *Mr Solomon & Mr Covenant*: the pair are on suspiciously close terms with the Old Ladie. It later becomes apparent that they have matrimonial designs on Violetta and Laura, perhaps with the Old Ladie's consent.

81–2. *Christian ... prophesie*: Christians accepted that Old Testament words and events were prophetic intimations of New Testament and later occurrences. Will urges Violetta to apply such a hermeneutics to the Song of Solomon.

82. *prophesie*: after this, B and C, followed by the printed texts, read *to morrow be Six*.

83. *doctrine*: 'biblical interpretation', 'hermeneutics'.

84–7. *divinitie ... Speculatione ... practicall*: Violetta and Will play with the terms speculative and practical divinity, for which see, e.g., *The Importance and Advantage of a Thorough Knowledge of Divine Truth* by the American Calvinist theologian, Jonathan Edwards (1703–58): 'There are two kinds of knowledge of the things of divinity, viz., speculative and practical, or in other terms, natural and spiritual. The former ... consists in having a natural or rational knowledge of the things of religion, or such a knowledge as is to be obtained by the natural exercise of our own faculties, without any special illumination of the Spirit of God. The latter rests not entirely in the head, or in the speculative ideas of things, but the heart is concerned in it ... In the former consists speculative or natural knowledge of the things of divinity, in the latter consists the spiritual or practical knowledge of them.' The distinction ultimately depends on the Aristotelian concept of the speculative and practical intellect, and of natural science as speculative knowledge. http://www.ccel.org/ccel/edwards/sermons.divineTruth.html

Violetta, however, insinuates that, for her, *Speculatione* means no more than 'conjectural consideration' (*OED*). For Will *practicall* means 'actively engaged in the practice of some occupation' (*OED*), for him, specifically the practice of love-making.

87. *peices*: 'persons', 'people', 'individuals'; cf. Jonson, *Bartholomew Fair*, 1.4: 'Gentlemen, you do not know him; he is another manner of piece than you think for.'

87. *decorum*: 'propriety'.

87–8. *practise quhat ye preach*: proverbial; *ODEP*, 643.

88. *Comerade*: 'comrade', 'companion'; French *camerade, camarade*.

breasts: 'the affections, private thoughts and feelings. (Commonly pl. in OE.)' (*OED*, s.v. **Breast** 1.5). The illustrative quotation is from William Cartwright, *The Royal Slave* (1636): 'That man of peace there, Hath been trusted with Kings breasts.'

Note the verbal play between *hes no breasts* (68) and *hes as good breasts for her as any*, also above, 68n.

B and C, followed by the printed texts, read *breasts and back both*.

90. *stragling*: 'wandering' (from presbyterian doctrine; cf. above, 70–1). B and C, followed by the printed texts, read *straying*.

96. **bible the**: MS insertion in Pitcairne's hand. The reading intended is probably 'but I shall Love the bible the better for it', with reference to Will's use of Song of Solomon. B and C, followed by the later printed texts, read *Love the Bible the better for it*. The 1722 text reads *love the Bible for it*.

Act 2, Scene 3

For the setting, see notes to 1.3. Solomon is again present, in a corner, not as a member of the Committee.

1–2. *Bretheren ... work*: a characteristic introduction by the Moderator.

3. *cane on*: i.e. ken [up]on, 'make judicial enquiry, take legal cognizance upon' (*DOST*, s.v. **Ken** 13b). The Moderator, with the other members, regards the Committee as a court of law, but not civil law; see below, 45–6n.

The words look like an auctorial correction, or revision, of the previous sentence, which differs only in having *call in* for *cane on*. The latter, as *lectio difficilior*, should be accepted.

dispatch: 'send away'.

4–5. *quhat ansr to give*: the Committee has not yet heard or read the Curate's petition; indeed it never does.

6. *Salathiel*: there is some confusion of speaker in the MS here: see below, 10. B, C and the later printed texts make Solomon the speaker.

Note too the curious use of 'my Lord', addressed to the Moderator; see above, 1.3, 81 and n.

6–7. *give ... span*: a more modest version of the proverbial 'Give him an inch and he'll take an ell' (*ODEP*, 303), probably influenced by other Scots phrases and proverbs in which inch and span are contrasted: a good example is the refrain of Montgomerie's 'A Counsell aganst Dispair in Love': 'Drie furth the inch as thou hes done the span' (Montgomerie 2000, 23–4).

7. *span*: 'the distance from the tip of the thumb to the tip of the little finger, or sometimes to the tip of the forefinger, when the hand is fully extended' (*OED*).

8. *eedg*: 'judge' (NE dialect).

geed: 'good' (NE dialect).

9. *foot*: representing Middle Scots *fute*. B and C, followed by the printed texts, have the later form *fitt*, the first instance of which recorded in *DOST* is dated 1627 (*Elgin Records* ii, 199) and which became standard in Modern Scots; see *DOST* 12, xcix, Figure 14a.

bigging: 'building'.

11. *Bona certe*: Salathiel probably intends the phrase to mean 'Of a good certainty', but the combination of the feminine adjective *bona* with the adverb *certe* makes for the impossible Latinity characteristic of Salathiel.

11–13. *if you have a mind ... not called in*: this meaningless balance of tautological phrases is characteristic of Salathiel's rhetoric.

15. *Tuch not the unholie thing*: 2 Corinthians 6. 17: 'touch not the unclean thing', adapting Isaiah 52. 11, 'touch no unclean thing'. In the latter, the speaker of the words is God, the Lord.

18. *jeestice*: 'justice' (NE dialect).

19. *call him ... come in*: another tautology.

20. *But see ... opnd to him*: Ruler Elder suggests that the Officier should call for Shittle, who is waiting outside, but should not open the door for him – a calculated insult.

21. *Officier*: from med. Latin *officiarius*, a term 'applied to certain petty executive officers ... of various authorities, as ... the sergeant of a court ... a church officer' (*DOST*, s.v. **Officiar**, 2b).

Shittle: i.e. 'shuttle': cf. Zachary Boyd, *Last Battell of the Soule in Death* (Edinburgh, 1629), 191, quoted in *DOST* s.v. **Schittle**: 'What is life? ... the working of a weever's shittle, which by winding here and there vnwindeth itselfe to an end'. A possible additional meaning of the word is 'shuttlecock'. The implication for Mr Shittle is that he shuttles between Episcopalianism and Presbyterianism. He is, or would like to be, a Scottish equivalent of the English Vicar of Bray.

24. *tack Instrument*: 'Instrument' means 'notarial instrument; a formal and duly authenticated record of any proceeding or transaction drawn up by a notary public; a similar record made by the scribe of a court'. To 'take instrument' is 'to call for the instrument, at the same time handing to the notary the conventional earnest-payment (often of fourpence, as it appears)' (*DOST*, s.v. **Instrument** 5a, c). Shittle wishes his petition and address to be treated as an instrument; cf., e.g., Lindsay, *Ane Satyre of the* Thrie *Estaitis*, 2815–16: '*Counsall*: To mak ane Act on this we ar content./ *Iohne*: On that sir Scribe I tak ane instrument' (Hamer 1931: 267).

24 [stage-direction]: *pocket*: 'pouch'.

28–30. *If I should add ... unskilfull hand*: an attempted mock-modest rhetorical proem by Whigriddne (Curtius 1953: 83–5, also 560–3). As Turbulent indicates (33–4), it bears no relevance to the actual situation.

The words are an adaptation of Crawford's 1690 speech to the parliament: 'What my Lord Commissioner spoke the other day, was delivered to such advantage that any enlargment I could make on it, would be like the rash touch of a Pencil, by an unskilful hand, upon a compleat Picture; So I forbear everything of that kind' (Crawford 1690: 2).

30–1. *Curats, not being the Ministers of Christ*: i.e. in terms of Calvinistic church order.

31–2. *subcomitie ... articles*: Whigriddne is thinking in terms of the recently abolished office of the Lords of the Articles, 'a committee of Parliament ... consisting of members drawn from all estates, plus the officers of state, which prepared business for the full house' (Donaldson and Morpeth 1977: 18). It was abolished in 1690. Whigriddne speaks with a politician's instinct for avoiding personal responsibility, yet he clearly implies that the petition should be rejected.

32. *articles*: 'the separate members or portions of anything written' (*OED*).

33–4. *Ther hes bene ... will ye?*: Turbulent (with Covenant, 36) is unusually the voice of commonsense.

35–6. *Whither ... ere it be reade?*: one of the Moderator's characteristic distinctions.

37. *A vot!*: the Committee's decisions, on a very minor matter, are democratic, to Pitcairne's disgust.

39–42. *That our Spirits ... on the war*: cf. 1.3, 30, 32, 33 and nn.

39–41. *o Lord ... holie will*: parody of the opening of the Collect for Peace in the episcopalian *Order for Morning Prayer*: 'O God, who art the author of peace and lover of concord, in knowledge of whom standeth our eternal life, whose service is perfect freedom'. The remainder of the prayer is in the homely style mentioned above, 2.2, 39 and n.

42. *goe on the war*: 'continue in a worse way'.

45–6. *by Law ... judicatories*: see Act Ratifying the Confession of Faith and settling Presbyterian Church Government (*APS* 1690/4/43), 7 June 1690. This authorised 'the general meeting and representatives of the foresaid presbyterian ministers and elders in whose hands the exercise of the church government is established either by themselves, or by such ministers and elders as shall be appointed and authorised visitors by them ... to try and purge out all insufficient, negligent, scandalous and erroneous ministers by due course of ecclesiastical processes and censures, and likewise for redressing all other church disorders. And further it is hereby provided that whatsoever minister being convened before the said general meeting, and representatives of the presbyterian ministers and elders or the visitors to be appointed by them, shall either prove contumacious in not compearing or be found guilty, and shall be therefore censured whether by suspension or deposition, they shall ipso facto be suspended from or deprived of their stipends and benefices.' In terms of the Act the members of the Committee were 'visitors'.

47. *persuasion*: 'religious belief or opinion; a form or system of religious belief, a creed' (*OED* s.v. **Persuasion** 3).

48–50. *Stop ther ... Iniquitie*: Moderator and Turbulent object to the idea that the jurisdiction of the Committee is based on anything other than divine right. Covenant makes a sardonic but realistic intervention.

51. *Solomon*: B and C, followed by the printed texts, read *Salathiel*.

51–2. *And besids ... by law*: Solomon's interjection complements Turbulent's. The jurisdiction of ministers of Christ does not depend on secular legislation. Covenant adopts the same position.

55–6. *root out ... alive in the land*: Covenant sees the Presbyterians as Israelites, returning from the Egyptian captivity of the reigns of Charles II and James VII and exterminating the Canaanites, the Episcopalians, who had seized possession of their heritage; see Joshua, 1–12.

58. *transportabilitie*: 'transportation', a common punishment at the time.

Ruling Elder shares the assumptions of Solomon and Covenant. In his opinion the Committee has the authority to order a particular course of action on the part of the civil powers.

59. *the lyne*: 'the Equator'. Ruling Elder exaggerates or shows his ignorance; in his time transportation was to North America or the West Indies.

64. *purgeing*: a rare use of the word by an Episcopalian.

64–6. *Scandalous ... comitie*: even by seventeenth-century standards of polemical divinity, Shittle's claim, that refusal to recognize the Committee is scandalous, ignorant and heretical, is remarkable.

67. *de facto*: 'in fact', whether legally or not, as opposed to *de jure*, 'by right'. Shittle is reserving his position. 'It was the execution of Charles [I] and the exclusion of his heir [Charles II] that led men to dwell upon the distinction between a *de facto* and a *de jure* authority' (Figgis 1922: 143). Cromwell as Lord Protector exemplified *de facto* authority. A similar distinction was applied by Scottish Episcopalians and Jacobites to the authority of William II and III as opposed to that of James VII and II.

67. *all pouer is of God*: Psalm 62. 11: 'power belongeth unto God'.

68. *the 39 new artickls*: The Thirty-Nine Articles of Religion (1573) form 'the set of doctrinal formulae accepted by the Church of England in its attempt to define its dogmatic position in relation to the controversies of the 16th century' (*ODCC*). Jacobites held that recognition by the Church of England of the Dutchman, William of Orange, as king in effect abrogated the Articles, in particular Article 37, which states: 'The King's Majesty hath the chief power in this Realm of England, and other his Dominions, unto whom the chief Government of all Estates of this Realm, whether they be Ecclesiastical or Civil, in all causes doth appertain, and is not, nor ought to be, subject to any foreign Jurisdiction ... that only Prerogative, which we see to have been given always to all godly Princes in holy Scriptures by God himself; [all pouer is of God] that is, that they should rule all estates and degrees committed to their charge by God, whether they be Ecclesiastical or Temporal, and restrain with the civil sword the stubborn and evil-doers'. The 39 New Artickls, apparently adopted by the compliant Church of England, but not by most Scottish Episcopalians, implied that might is right and that God was the source of such might.

68. *not long since*: i.e. from 1660 to 1688, the reigns of Charles II and James VII.

69–70. *God pulls ... setts up another*: semi-proverbial; cf., e.g., Henryson, *Morall Fabillis*, 'The Fox, Wolf, and Husbandman', 2418–9 and n. (Fox 1981, 90, 307): ' "Schir," quod the foxe, "thus fairis it off fortoun:/ As ane cummis vp, scho quheillis anr vther doun" '; *ODEP*, 282.

71. *Memento Mori*: literally, 'remember [that you are] to die', figuratively 'a reminder of death, such as a skull or other symbolic object' (*OED*).

72. *Comunion*: 'association', 'religious fellowship'.

73. *confession of faith*: enunciation for the three kingdoms, according to the Solemn League and Covenant, of Presbyterian doctrine, set out in 33 articles by the Westminster Assembly (1643–53). It was completed on 4 December 1646, ratified in Scotland by the 1647 General Assembly and approved by the English parliament on 20 June 1648. It at once established itself as the definitive statement of Presbyterianism; see above, pp. xvi and li.

73. *be in it quhat will*: i.e. for Shittle and his associates, the actual contents are of no importance.

76. *late K. James*: James VII who, until lately, had been king.

K. of ff.: Louis XIV, king of France.

77–8. *non-resistance & passive obedience*: central tenets in the doctrine of the Divine Right of Kings, central to the beliefs of Episcopalians and Jacobites. A hereditary monarch must be regarded as 'a loving Father, and careful watchman, caring for them' [his people] 'more than himselfe ... countable to that great GOD, who placed him as his lieutenant over them ... Their obedience, I say, ought to be to him ... obeying his commands in all things, except directly against God, as the commands of Gods Minister ... without resistance' ('The Trve Lawe of *free Monarchies*: or, The Reciprock and *Mutuall Dutie* Betwixt a free King and his *naturall Subiectes*', Craigie 1982: 61, 69). The rules hold, even if the king is a tyrant: 'God must first giue sentence vpon the king that breketh, before the people can think themselves fred of their oth [of allegiance]. What Iustice then is it that the party, shall be both Iudge & party, vsurping vpon himself the office of God?' (Craigie, 1982: 79). For a full discussion see Figgis 1922, especially pp. 177–266.

78. *new Church of England*: for the most part the English clergy accepted William of Orange as monarch, in Jacobite eyes thus forming a new Church of England. The old church was continued by the nonjurors, eight bishops, deprived of their sees by act of parliament, but still regarded as their lawful bishops by some 400 nonjuring clergymen. The nonjurors continued as a separate church until the late eighteenth century.

79–80. *judgeing ... displease us*: as in the case of James VII.

81. *scruple*: 'a doubt or uncertainty as to a matter of fact or allegation' (*OED* s.v. **Scruple** 2).

82. *solved*: 'resolved'.

85. *you know from quhom*: i.e. King William. Even under such circumstances, Shittle cannot bring himself to name the usurper.

86. *kirk triumphant*: ironic. The phrase is usually applied to the company of the redeemed in heaven; the church on earth is the church militant; cf. above, **Prologue**, 25–6n.

90–1. *sitt at ... stipends*: at last the real aim of Shittle and his associates becomes clear.

91–2. *decided and resolved*: Shittle thinks that the restoration of King James remains a possibility.

95–6. *Better ... Samaritans*: cf. the remark alleged to have been made by Frazer of Brae (Turbulent) in the 1690 General Assembly: 'it was better that the Temple of the Lord did lie sometime unbuilt and unrepair'd, than be reared up by Gibeonites and Samaritans' (Cockburn 1691: 9).

The Samaritans were the ten tribes who revolted against Solomon's son Rehoboam and attached themselves to his rival Jereboam, thus forming the northern kingdom of Israel. The Jews, the tribe of Judah, had no dealings with them.

The immediate reference is to the building of the second Temple in Jerusalem after the destruction of the first by the Babylonians (586 BC), by the Jews, the tribe of Judah, returning from captivity. The Samaritans were in fact hostile to the rebuilding (Nehemiah 4. 2).

For Turbulent, the Presbyterians correspond to the returning Jews, the Episcopalians to the Samaritans.

97. *Lamentatione*: a reference to the biblical Lamentations of Jeremiah over the state of the fallen Jerusalem and the destruction of the Temple.

98. *stats*: 'the Estates', the Scottish parliament.

100. *setts*: 'becomes', 'befits' (*DOST*, **Set** 8); cf. Henryson, *Morall Fabillis*, 'The Wolf and the Wether', 2613–14: 'It settis na seruand for to vphald weir,/ Nor clym sa hie quhill he fall of the ledder'. (Fox 1981: 97)

104–5. *act of parliament*: 15 April 1690, Act rescinding Severall Acts of Parliament, *APS* 1690/4/119. The first Act rescinded is 'anent a solemne anniversary thanksgiveing' (*APS* 1661/1/255), by which it was ordained that 29 May, the birthday of Charles II in 1630 and the official date of his Restoration in 1660, should be observed as a holy day to the Lord. Also rescinded is one 'anent sentences of excommunication' (*APS* 1661/1/294), by which excommunicated persons were to be treated as rebels and outlawed ('put to the horn'), suffering escheat of their property and any income, monetary or in kind, derived from it.

105. *thunderbolt of excommunicatne*: the Confession of Faith set out by the Westminster Assembly (above, 73n) gave extraordinary powers to the officers (i.e. ministers and Ruling Elders) of the Church: 'To those 191 officers the keys of the kingdom of heaven are committed, by virtue whereof they have power, respectively, to retain and remit sins; to shut that kingdom against the impenitent, both by the Word and censures; and to open it unto penitent sinners, by the ministry of the Gospel, and by absolution from censures, as occasion shall require' (c. 30, 'Of Church Government'). Excommunication involved civil penalties: 'Persons excommunicated by the church could not formerly pursue or defend, but such procedure, on excommunication, is now [1752] abolished' (Bankton 1994: 602).

The power to excommunicate was regarded as part of the *ius divinum*, 'divine right' of the Church, superseding the Divine Right of Kings; see Rutherford, *The Divine Right of Church-Government and Excommunication* (London, 1646), also the response by the Anglican, Edward Stillingfleet, *Irenicum. A Weapon-Salve for the Churches Wounds, Or The Divine Right of Particular Forms of Church Government* (London, 1662); cf. too above, **Drammatis Personæ**, 9n; below, 3.3, 80n; 5.3, 99n. For an earlier perspective see Hooker, *Of the Laws of Ecclesiastical Politie* (London, 1593), 3.11, 21. See too Figgis 1922: 267–92.

108. *Fat*: 'What' (NE dialect).

beech: probably intended as a NE dialectal variant, not found in *DOST* or *SND*, of *byke*, 'hive, nest', occasionally 'swarm'.

112. *herry*: 'harry', 'plunder'.

115. *eld*: 'elders'.

119. *reasone ... Courts*: perhaps a reference to *APS* 1662/5/4 (8 May 1662), Act for calling in the Bishops to the Parliament.

122–3. *lament ... build the house*: allusion to Lamentations (above, 97 and n.) and to Psalm 127. 1: 'Except the Lord build the house, they labour in vain that build it.'

124. *my Lord My father*: John Crawford (1596–1678), 17th earl of Crawford and 1st of Lindsay, one of the 'Covenanter lords' opposed to Charles I, particularly on the matter of the Prayer Book. He was a soldier, whose regiment played a part in the battle of Newburn (1640), in which the Scots presbyterian army defeated an English royalist force at a ford on the river Tyne and went on to capture Newcastle (Gericke 2008). He took a major part in the negotiations which led to the signing of the Solemn League and Covenant (1643; v.1.3, 35n), by which the Scots agreed to help the English Parliamentarians against the king, on condition that England accept a presbyterian system of church government. He fought on the winning side at Marston Moor (1644), but was partly responsible for the defeat of the Cove-nanters by Montrose at Kilsyth (1645). His regiment was almost totally wiped out in the battle. He signed the Act for the surrender of Charles I to the English army in 1647, but carried the sceptre at the Scottish coronation of Charles II at Scone in 1651. Later that year he was captured, together with other members of the Scottish parliament, at Alyth, Perthshire, and was imprisoned in England until the Restoration. He withdrew from public life rather than accept the revival of episcopacy and died at Tynninghame, East Lothian, in 1678.

129. *keeping the 29 of May*: see above, 104–5n.

133. *Sir Wm Littlelaw*: not identified; perhaps merely an allegorical name.

134. *claime of ryt*: in effect, the middle section of the Declaration of the Estates containing the *Claim of Right* and the Offer of the Croune to the King and Queen of England (*APS* 1689/3/108; 11 April 1689). The Claim laid down certain conditions in terms of which the parliament was prepared to accept the sovereignty of William and Mary, who had already (13 February) been accepted as joint monarchs by the English parliament. No article in it seems relevant to the process of excommunication.

137. *a cail coal to blaw at*: Scottish proverbial (*ODEP*, 132).

cail: i.e. 'caul', 'cauld', 'cold'.

blaw: 'blow'.

137. *siker*: 'secure'.

quitray: 'country' (NE dialect).

138. *fre quarters*: the quartering of troops at the expense of a recalci-trant populace, as the 'Highland Host' was quartered on the Covenanters of Renfrewshire and Ayrshire in 1678. The practice was forbidden by the sixteenth article of the Claim of Right: 'That the sending of ane army in ane hostile manner upon any pairt of the kingdome, in a peaceable tyme, and exacting of locality and any manner of fre quarters, is contrary to law.'

138. *abeeses*: 'abuses' (NE dialect).

geed: 'good' (NE dialect).

140. *a's*: 'all his'.

fan: 'when' (NE dialect).

141. *an' sal seme at this day*: 'as shall become clear this day'.

141. *se*: 'say'.

taks fitts: i.e, 'suffers from epilepsy'.

142–3. *Quhat fitts ... cure for yt*: an uncharacteristic intrusion by Solomon, who is not usually credited with medical skills.

142. *fitts of the mother*: 'hysteria'; 'mother' is used in the sense 'womb'; cf. Shakespeare, *King Lear*, 2.4, 56–7: 'O! how this mother swells up toward my heart;/ Hysterica passio! Down, thou climbing sorrow!'

144. *helsum*: 'wholesome', 'health-giving'. With 'disease' making up a presbyterian paradox; cf. below, **Preface**: 'Then when he prays for people troubled in spirit, he'll tell 'tis a wholesome disease, and wish that many more were so, because he was once bound himself'; Curate 1692: 20–21: 'And lately in *Edinburgh*, Mr. *James Kirton* (the everlasting Comedian of their Party) one of their famous Preachers in that City, praying publickly for a poor Woman much troubled in Spirit, said, *A wholesome Disease, good Lord, a wholesome Disease, Lord, for the Soul. Alas,* said he, *few in the Land are troubled with this Disease. Lord, grant that she may have many Fellows in this Disease.'* Mr James Kirton is, of course, Mr Covenant Planedealer.

146. *Semel Insaniving omnes*: for *semel insanivimus omnes*, 'we have all been mad once'. The distorted Latin is typical of Salathiel.

The corrected phrase is semi-proverbial; cf. *ODEP*, 229: 'Every man is mad on some point'. Perhaps intended as a medical apopthegm; Gilbert Rule (Salathiel) was MD of Leiden and had been in practice in Berwick-on-Tweed (**Drammatis Personæ**, 9n).

Act 3, Scene 1

Lady Murray's yeards: see above, 2.2, 46n. The back shutters show the rear of Moray House. The outer shutters show the yeards, the gardens. The front stage is a street, the South Back of Canongate.

'The gardens connected with the house of the Earl of Moray are spoken of as "of such elegance and cultivated with so much care, as to vie with those of warmer countries, and perhaps even of England itself" ... On the uppermost of the terraces there is a large and beautiful thorn, with pensile leaves; on the second there are some fruit-trees, the branches of which have been caused to spread out in a particular way, so as to form a kind of cup, possibly for the reception of a pleasure-party ... In the lowest level of the garden there is a little receptacle for water, beside which is the statue of a fishing-boy, having a basket of fish at his feet, and a clam-shell inverted upon his head. Here is also a small building, surmounted by two lions holding female shields, and which may therefore be supposed contemporaneous with the house: this was formerly a summer-house, but has latterly been expanded into the character of a conservatory' (Chambers 1847: 206, partly quoting and translating from a seventeenth-century Latin MS).

The time is early morning.

1–14. *though west not ... be ended*: a witty exchange in which Violetta more than holds her own against Will, who has mistakenly assumed that his technique of seduction is infallible. Initially the underlying metaphor is knightly combat, the duel of the sexes. Violetta, Will claims, is the challenged, not the challenger, despite which she is first to reach the lists. She must be eager for the fray – so he attempts to kiss her. Her quick response implies much: she is a woman of honour, punctilious in observing the rules, so long as they are honourably observed. Will is breaking them when he chooses a weapon, a kiss; the right to choose belongs to the person challenged. Will claims that she has forfeited her rights because, in terms of the old cliché of courtly love, she is a murderer, whose beauty has sacrilegiously wounded him in church, when he was utterly defenceless. In reply she points out that it was he, rather than she, who used a weapon, the Bible, in the mistaken belief that she was a Conventicle sighing sister. Will shifts ground by claiming that their love began in church before the priest. Violetta's swift response is that it must end there too, i.e. by marriage, about which she has already expressed her determination (1.2, 81–3).

1. *west*: Scots adaptation of the unhistorical analogical form of the preterite 2nd person sg. of 'to be', *wast*, found in the Authorized Version of the Bible: 'thou wast a bondman in the land of Egypt' (Deuteronomy 15. 15). The distinctive 2nd person form removes the need of a pronoun for subject. B and C, followed by the printed texts, substitute *thou art* or *thou wert*.

4. *graple*: 'come to close quarters' – a word here appropriate, but generally more used for naval combat than a duel on land.

6. *Mutherers*: 'murderers', from OE *morðor*, 'murder, homicide', with metathesis and *ð* preserved in *th*.

10. *Conventicle*: 'meeting or assembly of a clandestine, irregular, or illegal character … in Scottish History more especially associated with the field preaching of the Presbyterian ministers during the reigns of Charles II and James II' (*OED*). Here used adjectivally.

sighing sisters: Covenanting women who sigh hypocritically over their sins and the fate of the Church in Scotland. Violetta has the insight to see that Will imagined she belonged to this kind.

12–13. *Quhat more … priest*: Will is taken aback by Violetta's response and tries a new tack.

15–17. *Too much … once mor*: despite himself, Will is overwhelmed by Violetta's qualities as a woman, but pride impels him to continue his attempt to seduce her.

15. *Innocence*: 'moral purity' – the original sense of the word (*OED*). Violetta is certainly not 'innocent' in the modern sense; she knows the facts of life.

16. *bear off*: 'hold back'. A nautical term, continuing the metaphor in *grapple*, above, 4.

18. *fair pass, I find*: B and C, followed by the later printed texts, read *faus pans* (*faux-pas*) for *fair pass* and inserts *dangerous* after *find*.

19. *good one*: 'simpleton'. Under **Good 7c** *OED* gives examples of the word used 'in mildly depreciative sense implying weakness or trustful simplicity'; cf. in Wolsey's great speech (Shakespeare, *Henry VIII*, 3.2, 356–9): 'The third day comes a frost, a killing frost;/ And, when he thinks, good easy man, full surely/ His greatness is a-ripening, nips his root,/ And then he falls, as I do.'

21. *ingaged ... rear guard*: Violetta further elaborates the metaphor of conflict, this time in terms of land warfare.

22. *wes*: regular Scots 2nd person sg. preterite of *to be*.

better at preaching yesterday: i.e. by his use of Song of Solomon in church.

23. *text*: the biblical passage on which a minister bases his sermon.

24. *text I would handle closely*: i.e. Violetta. A minister in his sermon handles the text closely. The words accompany Will's second attempt to kiss Violetta.

25. *Superstitious to Kiss the bible*: this mock-Presbyterian response to Will's attempt maintains the textual metaphor. Kissing the Bible usually accompanied the swearing of oaths.

27. *medl*: 'to join battle, begin fighting with' (*DOST*, s.v. **Med(d)ill 1b**); 'to mingle in fight' (*OED*, s.v. **Meddle 6**); cf. Sir Toby's remark to Viola in Shakespeare, *Twelfth Night*, 3.4, 277–9: 'therefore, on, or strip your sword stark naked; for meddle you must, that's certain, or forswear to wear iron about you'. The metaphor of combat is thus continued. *Meddle*, however, also means 'to have sexual intercourse with' (*OED*, s.v. **Meddle 5**); cf. the quotation in *DOST* (s.v. **Meddil(l)ing 4**) from *Dundonald Parish Records* 8 (1602): 'Jonat Gibsoun ... confessit hir medling in fornicatioun with Thomas Michell.' Both meanings are appropriate to the situation.

28–9. *Hungrie people ... grace*: Will continues his attempt to seduce Violetta and introduces a new, rather crude, metaphor; the satisfaction afforded to an ardent lover by the consummation of his desire corresponds to the physical satisfaction afforded to a hungry man by a meal. 'Grace', that is, 'grace before meat', is a development of 'pray' in the preceding line.

The phrase sounds like a proverb, but I have failed to find a parallel.

therafter: 'after our love has been consummated'. B and C, followed by the printed texts, substitute *after I have eat my belly full*.

30. **Violetta: Div ye ... you mein**: inserted in MS in Pitcairne's hand. The transcriber of the MS appears to have missed out a line here; Will's subsequent remark (lines 31–3) certainly indicates an earlier one by Violetta. In the 1722 printed text Will's speech, ending with line 24, runs on directly into lines 31–3, followed by a version of Violetta's words in lines 35–7. B, C and the later printed texts give Violetta the intervening remark: 'But it seems you value the meat little, if you account it not worth the ceremony [of saying grace]'. The present insertion is more pointed; see above, p. lxiv.

div: emphatic interrogative, and interrogative negative, present tense of *dae*, 'do'. Not in *OED* or *DOST*. The earliest example quoted in *SND* is from c. 37 (IV, 7) of Scott's *Old Mortalitie* (1816): 'Div I ken onything o' Lord Evandale! Div I no?' There are two further earlier examples, not quoted, in c. 8 (II, 8); all are put in the mouth of Cuddie Headrigg, the ploughman, or of Mause, his mother. By Scott's time, it is clear, the usage had become vulgar. Violetta's words perhaps demonstrate that this had not always been the case.

meat: 'bread'; cf. below, 35, 'mack your daylie bread of it'.

prove: 'make trial of, try, test' (*OED*, s.v. **Prove 1**).

31. *cetshin*: 'kitchen', 'food, especially cooked food ... additional to a staple uncooked food such as bread, and serving as a relish to it' (*DOST*, s.v. **Kichin(g b)**

Metaphorically, *cetshin* is 'premarital sexual intercourse', i.e. an excitingly illicit trial run before any possible later legalizing ceremony; *meat* is the humdrum everyday matter of marriage itself.

33. *Conscientouse*: 'obedient or loyal to conscience; habitually governed by a sense of duty; scrupulous' (*OED*, s.v. **Conscientious 1**). Will is stung by Violetta's implication that he is a rake.

33. *as long as I live*: i.e. 'so long as ye both shall live' and 'till death do us part', in the episcopalian 'Form of Solemnization of Matrimony'.

34. *morsel*: 'bite'.

34. *a Sply mouth*: a Covenanting clergyman, regarded as characteristically wry- (*splay-*, *sply-*) mouthed; cf. the periodical *The Entertainer* (1717–18), 30, 202, quoted in *OED*, s.v. **Splay-mouthed**: 'The Splay-mouth'd Covenanters, that Sanctified Crew of Hypocrites'. Will dislikes the idea of Violetta marrying one of the frequenters of her Aunt's house. The food metaphor continues.

35. *daylie bread*: an echo of a clause in the Lord's Prayer, 'Give us this day our daily bread'.

36. *freind*: here meaning 'lover, paramour' (*OED*, s.v. **Friend 4**); cf. Shakespeare, *Measure for Measure*, 1.4, 29: 'He hath got his friend with child'; *Othello*, 4.1, 3–4: 'Or to be naked with her friend in bed/ An hour or more, not meaning any harm?' Not in *DOST* or *SND*.

36–7. *grace fairlie said*: i.e. after the solemnization of marriage. Violetta means that only then can Will and she physically become lovers.

45–6. *the busnes of your Creatione*: i.e. her business as a wife and mother; 'be fruitful, and multiply, and replenish the earth' (Genesis 1. 1, 28).

49–50. *I'le mary you ... mean fortune*: Will finally proposes, explicitly and modestly.

at the rycts: 'properly', 'rightly', 'aright'.

50. *honest fellow of a mean fortune*: i.e. 'respectable man of limited

134

means'. Will politely understates his position as a laird, one of the landed gentry.

52. *my little fortune*: Violetta too is modest about her wealth.

53. *spark*: 'a man, chiefly derogatory' (*DOST*, s.v. **Spark 2**), in Scots usage, unlike English, lacking any association with the fashionable and foppish; *revrend* indicates that the spark would be a presbyterian minister. Violetta has some sense of the English connotations and uses the word ironically.

band: 'short strip of white linen hanging down from the collar as part of the conventional clerical dress in the Scottish Church, used only by an ordained minister' (*SND*, s.v. **BA(A)ND**). Usually plural in later use. The examples there quoted are much later. Not in *DOST*. In *OED* (**Band** *sb.*² **4b**) the definition is more general: 'part of a conventional dress, clerical, legal or academical', with the earliest example given 'before 1700'.

54. *patrimonie*: 'property inherited from one's father' (*OED*, s.v. **Patrimony 1**). The father was a covenanting minister, acting and suffering during the Killing Times.

56. *little*: B and C, followed by the printed texts, after *little* insert *sense* – a reminiscence, perhaps, of Mr Salathiel Littlesense and Laird Littlesense, the Ruling Elder.

56–7. *hanged in the Grass mercatt*: The Grassmarket was the usual Edinburgh place of execution; see above, 1.1, 81n. The hypothetical father was hanged because he had killed a soldier during some scuffle between Covenanters and government troops.

60–1. *foull or fair play*: Will has not quite forgotten his role as a rake, but gives Violetta choice of the course to be taken.

chiese: 'choose'.

63. *Command*: 'to have at one's call or disposal' (*OED*, s.v. **Command** *v.* **12**).

person: 'parson', 'episcopal clergyman'; cf. below, 3.2, 28–9.

65. *our haickney*: a hackney is a hired horse. 'Our' is used in the vaguer sense noted in *OED*, s.v. **Our 1d**, 'with which we have to do'; cf. the satiric rhyme from the time of Richard III (1483–85): 'The Cat, the Rat, and Lovell our Dog,/ Rule all England under an Hog' (*ODEP*, 109).

65. *ane honest Curat's house*: Scots Law at this period followed Canon Law in requiring no more than that the parties should take each other as husband and wife in the presence of an ordained clergyman. No previous notice or parental consent was required.

66. *Charity to him*: because episcopal clergymen had been deprived of their livings by the Comitie. Many were starving.

68. *parley*: 'discuss terms of surrender, generally under truce'. Violetta maintains the earlier metaphor of military conflict, tactfully obscuring the fact that she has been the victor.

68. *attempt*: B and C, followed by the printed texts, read *trumpet*.

69. *2nd part of the lectur*: see above, 2.2, 56 and n.

lectur: 'exposition' (Will's interpretation of Song of Solomon). Violetta speaks ironically, as if Will had been a presbyterian clergyman.

73. *Iff he belie not his nam*: i.e. 'if he lives up to his name', is liberal, ingenuous etc; see **Drammatis Personæ**, 1–2n.

74. *purgatorie*: Violetta uses a distinctively Roman Catholic concept to characterize life in the Old Ladie's house. The concept of Purgatory was anathema to Calvinists and was also repudiated in Article XXII of the Thirty Nine Articles.

75. *by this tyme*: i.e. about seven in the morning. Will and Violetta arranged to meet at six; see above 2.2, 64–4.

76. *apparent*: 'manifest', 'evident', 'obvious', with overtones of 'heir-apparent'; cf. below, 81.

77–9. *If I wes absent ... verge of grace*: Violetta ironically uses the language of presbyterian devotion.

familie exercise: see above, 1.2, 9, 18–25 and nn.

absolut decree: 'In Scottish legal practice a decree ... is the term for a final order of the court granting or refusing the remedy sought' (Walker 1980: 343). 'Absolute' indicates that it is immediately of full effect and complete. Here the remedy sought, justification or election, is refused by the court of heaven, with the consequence that Violetta is 'shut out of the verge of grace'.

shut: B, followed by the later printed texts, reads *thrust*.

verge: 'area', 'territory', 'realm', from Latin *virga*, 'rod', in medieval Latin 'measuring rod'. The area indicated is usually small, suitable for the small group specially chosen by God for entry to the verge of grace, the state of the redeemed.

81. *her belly*: B and C, followed by the printed texts, read *her daughter's belly*.

84. *in the wrong sense*: i.e. when 'fall back' means 'apostatize'; here, 'abandon her lover'. For the right sense, cf. the Nurse's speech in Shakespeare's *Romeo and Juliet*, 1.3, 36–42:

> And then my husband – God be with his soul!
> A' was a merry man – took up the child:
> 'Yea,' quoth he, 'dost thou fall upon thy face?
> Thou wilt fall backward when thou hast more wit,
> Wilt thou not, Jule?' and, by my halidom,
> The pretty wretch left crying, and said 'Ay'.

84. *the Canticles*: the Song of Solomon.

87. *task*: Violetta, following the precedent set by folk-narrative and tales of courtly love, sets her lover a test of fidelity, what in Welsh is called *anoeth*, 'something difficult to obtain or achieve'. The task set, however, is one for which Will has already, by his behaviour in church, demonstrated some aptitude.

88. *double-necked cloack*: 'cloak with two layers of cloth at the neck'; a reference to the Geneva bands?

89. *appertinencies*: 'appurtenancies'.

90. *smaikering*: not in *DOST* or *SND*, and probably not related to the obsolete English verbal noun *smackering*, used uniquely by John Florio (?1553–1625) in his *A worlde of wordes, or most copious and exact dictionarie in Italian and English* (1598), where *Bacio* is defined as *a kiss, a smackering*, *Bichiacco* as *a smack or smacking with the toong*, and *Bichiacchie* as *iestes, toyes ... flim-flam, tales, smackrings*. The most probable connection is with the Scots noun *smaik, smake*, 'a low, mean, or contemptible fellow' and *smaikrie*, 'contemptible behaviour; roguery, trickery'. The Germanic cognates of these words usually include some shade of 'fawning, toadying, flattering, cringing' (*DOST*, s.v. **Smaik, Smak(e,** *n.*). The most probable meaning is 'fawning, cringing'; cf. 1.1, 12–13: 'a dozen of Grammaceing fellows drest up in cloackes, Cringeing and boweing to him lyke so many beggars'.

B and C read *Smack, Cringe*, the 1722 print *Smack Cring*, later prints *smack, cringe*, derived from an attempt to correct, or from a misreading of, *smaikering*. In this context, the word *smack* is meaningless.

91. *decentlie*: 'becomingly'. Ironic.

94. *mouth water*: metaphorical and specious; if Laura sees that Violetta's lover is present, but that she herself has no one, she will be unable to conceal her longing, and so may betray the entire plot. Violetta is actually intent on providing a suitor for her sister.

plott: second use of the word in the play; see above, 2.2, 51.

97. *Holland*: place of refuge for Calvinists, Scots and English, throughout the seventeenth century.

Conventikl: see above, 10n. The name indicates the lady's religious stance. Violetta is quite prepared to lie to further her schemes.

98–9. *transforme ... monster*: humorous reference to the folk-tale motif Beauty and the Beast (Stith Thompson 1932–6: D735.1). Recurrence of the monster theme.

100. *beast*: Violetta proclaims her opinion of presbyterian clergymen, based at least partly on her observation of Mr Wordie's behaviour in the Old Ladie's house. See too next scene.

Heriot's yeards: the grounds of Heriot's Hospital, on higher ground south of the Cowgate, separated from the remainder of the old town of Edinburgh by Greyfriar's churchyard. 'The garden connected with Heriot's Hospital ...

was a sort of public promenade or lounging-place' (Chambers 1847: 286); see below, 4.1.

101–3. *meditating ... privat thoughts*: Violetta knows that Laura's meditations and private thoughts are not religious, and that Frank will not disturb them. She uses allegory in the original Greek sense, by which one thing is said, but the opposite understood.

105. *Fops*: 'fools', 'coxcombs'.

prosecut: 'persecute', 'follow with hostile intent'.

106. *dragoon ... Freinsh protestant*: a reference to *dragonadde*, 'the practice of billeting dragoons or other soldiers on communities or individuals whom it was desired to punish; extensively applied against the Huguenots [French Calvinist Protestants] from 1680 to 1685' (Harvey and Heseltine 1959: 224).

107. *Cameronian ... gowne*: the Cameronians were extreme Presbyterians, followers of Richard Cameron (1648–80), who denounced presbyterian clergymen who accepted the Indulgencies of 1669, 1672 and 1679. In the Sanquhar Declaration (1680) he and his associates renounced allegiance to the King (Charles II) and declared war on him and his associates. In the same year his forces were defeated, and he was himself killed, at the battle of Airds Moss in Ayrshire.

In the winter of 1688–89 his followers, the Society People or Cameronians, rabbled the Curates of the South-West. *A Minister* is a Curate, distinguished by his gown from the cloaked presbyterian clergy.

112–13. *I'l indeavour ... putt on*: Will claims that if he is to impersonate a presbyterian minister successfully, he must turn himself into a complete fool.

116. *plyabl*: 'ready to yield, docile' (*OED*, s.v. **Pliable 2**). To maintain superiority in his relationship with Frank, Will somewhat exaggerates the readiness of the ladies.

117. *restless*: 'unable to rest'.

118. *yeards*: after this, B and C, followed by the printed texts, insert *after prayers she walks there*.

118. Stage direction: The action hitherto has taken place on the inner stage, representing Lady Murray's yeards. Will and Frank move through the proscenium arch towards the outer stage, representing the street, the South Back of Canongate, now Holyrood Road. There two groups of hatted individuals appear, one entering right, the other left.

with hatts: clergymen wore hats. Prosperous laymen were bewigged; the less prosperous went bare-headed or wore caps. Most university teachers were clergymen.

120–49. *What Grave ... chifest qualitie*: this is the first of two dumb shows, in which people of a thematically important class pass across the stage to the accompaniment of Will's commentary and Frank's bewilderment. For the second and longer, see below, 4.4. The first group consists of beneficed presbyterian clergymen, probably including members of the Comitie, the second of teachers, Regents, in the recently purged Tounis College.

120. *No*: 'know'.

122. *foolishness of preaching*: ironic: see 1 Corinthians 1. 21: 'it pleased God by the foolishness of preaching to save them that believe'.

123. *in a literall sense*: Paul used the term 'foolishness' allegorically (see above, 80–81n), intending that it should be taken in the opposite sense. Will insists that in terms of presbyterian praying and preaching the face value is more appropriate. Cf. above, 87–9 and n.

124. *Pindarick*: reference to the style of the Greek poet Pindar (518–438 BC), whose language is often characterized by deliberate discontinuities of syntax and logic. In Britain the Pindaric ode was a popular literary form from the time of Abraham Cowley (1618–67).

125–6. *Ave Maria ... Lord's Prayer*: in Catholic devotions, the Lord's Prayer is usually followed by the *Ave Maria* ('Hail Mary'). The episcopalian Pitcairne is having a little dig at Roman Catholicism, of which he disapproved (MacQueen and MacQueen 2009: 31).

128. **giddines**: inserted in MS, not obviously in Pitcairne's hand; *God* deleted, but retained in B, C and the printed texts.

128. *dictats ... preface it*: presbyterian sermons claimed to be based on direct inspiration rather than thought or design.

129–30. *grasce ... gifts*: the concepts are linked in Pauline, and therefore Calvinistic, theology. Justification is by grace (Romans 3. 24); so too are gifts (Romans 12. 46–8; cf. 1 Corinthians 12. 4–11).

131. *throng about them*: 'abundant among them'. Scots *throng, thrang*, is etymologically the same as English *throng*, 'large number of people, crowd', but came to be used adjectivally.

131–2. *talents to ansr for*: a reference to the Parable of the Talents (Matthew 25. 14–30), in which the lord demands an account of the talents (monetary units, each equivalent to 3000 shekels) which, during his absence, he has entrusted to servants. Will interprets the talents as intellectual abilities, 'carnall and humane learneing' (104), often decried by presbyterian preachers, and, equally often, he suggests, lacking in them. Such preachers correspond to the servant entrusted with a single talent, which he buried in the earth, because he feared his lord. On returning, the lord condemned him to be bound and cast into outer darkness, where 'there shall be weeping and gnashing of teeth'.

132–3. *cry doune ... learneing*: cf. previous note; also Salathiel's words (below, 3.3, 10–11): 'Quhat hath Carnal reasone or humane learneing to doe with Christ's Spouse?'

135. *Christ's vyneyeard*: the Church; cf. Matthew 21. 33–41, the Parable of the Householder who let out his vineyard to husbandmen with unfortunate results.

is butt ill tenent-sted: 'has bad tenants'; *tenent-sted* means 'occupied by tenant-farmers'.

136. *as we say of our lands*: Frank and Will are both lairds, landowners with estates let out to tenant-farmers.

137. *tenents*: B and C, followed by the printed texts, read *tennendrie*, 'tenantry'.

my little interest: 'my little estate'; cf. MacFarlane, *Geographical Collections* (*SHS* II. 11, quoted in *SND*): 'On that same syde farder downe the water stands the house of Drummochrin which is but a small Interest, but a most lovely thing.' This sense of the word does not appear in *DOST*, but is the development of an earlier usage, 'the fact of having a right or claim to the possession or use of something; cf. e.g., Hope, *Major Practicks* II, 193: 'The superior persewing his wassall to sie his haulding is not oblidged to show his interess or titile.' Hope's collection was formed during his lifetime (1573–1646) but was finally published only in 1737. This last usage is also found south of the border; see *OED*, s.v. **Interest 1a.**

138. *lay*: 'untilled'.

139. *homlie*: 'homely', i.e. in their sermons and prayers; cf. above, 2.2, 47–8 and n.

139. *Master*: Christ.

140. *Convention*: 'gathering (usually formal)'.

140–59. *a Convention ... chifest qualitie*: the focus of the attack shifts, to become the Tounis College specifically, with implicit extensions to other Scottish, and British, universities; cf. above, pp. xx–xxiii; below, 3.3, 7–24; 5.1, 12–139.

141. *divided into two Classes*: as students are divided into classes, but also referring ironically to the classifications, the categories, of Aristotelian and scholastic logic, still much favoured in some University circles; see below, 3.3, 7–12. Will is parodying the speech of an old-fashioned University Regent.

143–4. *primum Cognitum*: scholastic Latin, 'the first object of knowledge'; see *Stanford Encyclopedia of Philosophy*, online edition, 'Influence of Arabic and Islamic Philosophy on the Latin West' 6.2: 'It was due to Avicenna that the *primum cognitum* ... became a central topic of medieval Latin metaphysics. The question of the *primum cognitum* was variously answered. For Guibert of Touyrnai, Bonaventure and Henry of Ghent, God is the *primum cognitum*, for Thomas Aquinas and Duns Scotus being (*ens*), for Berthold of Moosburg the good.' Will is deriding the university teaching of his time; cf. especially below, 3.3, 7–22.

144. *Heterogeniall*: 'of completely different character', 'diverse'.

148. *fourth*: after this B and C, followed by the printed texts, read *and if it could be, would believe a fifth*.

loss my place: 'lose my post'; *loss* is Scots for *lose*.

oath: the Oath of Allegiance (above, 1.1, 68n). If he had not sworn, he would have been 'purged' from his University post.

150. *doune goes the oaths*: the oaths are swallowed with no regard to their meaning.

Claikns: not in *DOST*, but probably pl. vbl. noun of **Clek, Cleck(e**, used transitively of birds, 'to hatch (young) from eggs' (*DOST*), with the meaning 'hatchings, young fowls'. In *SND* **Cleckin, Clecking** has the sense 'A brood, litter, especially of cats, rabbits or mice; in some districts, however, exclusively of fowls', the latter sense illustrated by a quotation from Scott's *The Monastery*, c. 4: 'I wish there wasna sic a bird as a goose in the wide warld, forby the clecking that we hae at the burn-side.' For *Claikns*, B, C and the printed texts read *chicks, chickens* or *tender chicks*.

The ample meal following Sunday 'exercise' became the subject of adverse episcopalian comment; cf. the address to his minister by Arthur Johnston, in *Apologia Piscatoris*, 185–8:

> Si mihi luce sacra labor interdicitur omnis,
> Cur tibi sacrata luce culina calet?
> Cur teris ore dapes, et dentem dente fatigas?
> Cur sinis ancillam caedere cortis aves? (Geddes 1892: 154)

> (If my work is altogether forbidden on the holy day, why is your kitchen hot during the sacred hours? Why do you grind a feast in your mouth and weary tooth with tooth? Why do you let your maid slaughter the barnyard fowls?)

152. *bretheren had agreed better*: reference to Psalm 133. 1: 'Behold how good and how pleasant it is for brethren to dwell together in unity', sung (in the metrical version) to conclude sittings of the General Assembly.

After *bretheren* B and C, followed by the printed texts, read *of Iniquity*.

155. *scoller*: 'pupil'.

156. *plott*: third appearance of the word.

157. *tell*: 'disclose', 'reveal'.

158. *Ingenuity*: 'honourableness', 'high-mindedness'; Latin *ingenuitas*, 'the condition of a gentleman, good birth'.

160–209. *Ho-ho-ho-ho etc ... Ho-ho-ho-ho*: the dialogue between Huffie and Whigridne is omitted in the 1722 print, but occurs in B, C and the later prints.

161. *tymely*: 'early'.

162. *beastly eguipage*: his dogs.

eguipage: 'equipment', 'apparatus of war'. Whigridne is joking.

163. *A hunting*: Lady Murray's yeards make a strange site for Huffie's expedition. He may be on his way from the Castle to Holyrood Park and Hunter's Bog. There may also be a reminiscence of his exploit in using his whip on the lady Mortonhall when she reproved him for hunting in her park; see above, **Drammatis Personæ**, 7n.

divertisement: 'entertainment, amusement' (French *divertissement*). B and C, followed by the later printed texts, have the more usual *diversion*.

163–4. *toyl and fatigue of business*: ironic; see above, 1.3, 2.1.

166. *weighty affairs of the nation*: Whigridne was President of the parliament; see above, **Drammatis Personæ**, 5n; his primary object was 'the furtherance of old Resolutioner policies' (Ferguson 1968, 1).

172. *brass*: 'brace', 'a pair', in particular, 'a pair of hunting-dogs'; cf., e.g., Shakespeare, *3 Henry VI*, 2.5, 129–30: 'Edward and Richard, like a brace of greyhounds/ Having the fearful flying hare in sight'.

173. *weall-pointed*: 'well-directed'. 'Pointed' suggests 'pointer', the hunting-dog, trained to indicate 'the presence and position of game by standing rigidly looking towards it' (*OED*, s.v. **Point**, *v*. **11**). In *OED* the earliest instance of this sense of the verb is some fifty years later; it occurs in W. Somerville, *Field-Sports, a Poem* (London, 1742), 257, but without any suggestion that the usage is new. As a dog's name it occurs in Matthew Prior's poem, written in 1716, *Alma: or the Progress of the Mind*, 1, 319: 'The Sport and Race no more He minds:/ Neglected Tray and Pointer lye;/ And Covies unmolested fly' (Prior 1721).

It is perhaps worth mentioning that Pitcairne and Prior were friends.

173. *lybells*: 'legal indictments', here also with strong overtones of 'a leaflet or pamphlet ... assailing or defaming the character of a person' (*DOST*, **Libel(l 4 and 5)**). In hunting terms, the *lybells* are Whigridne's dogs. Cf. also below, 4.2, 89, *Universall lybell*.

173–4. *wolvs out of Christ's vyneyeards*: a figure perhaps derived from Matthew 7. 15–16: 'Beware of false prophets, which come to you in sheep's clothing, but inwardly they are ravening wolves. Ye shall know them by their fruits. Do men gather grapes of thorns, or figs of thistles?' See also above, pp. lxx–lxxi.

174. *ane old tyk for them*: proverbial (Wilson 1970: 194, under **Dog at it, To be [old]**).

174. *tyk*: tyke, 'an ill-bred dog, a mongrel, a cur' (*DOST*, s.v. **Tyk(e)**; the word is generally pejorative; cf., e.g., the cadger's remark on the apparently dead fox lying in the highway: 'I trou ye haue bene tussillit with sum tyk,/ That garris you ly sa still withoutin steir' (Henryson, *Morall Fabillis*, 'The Fox, the Wolf, and the Cadger', 2065–6) (Fox 1981: 79).

175. *rune doune*: i.e. as dogs run down a hunted beast.

hope: 'expect'.

178. *othrgate*: 'otherwise'.

worrie: 'kill by biting or shaking'.

179. *matines*: 'mastiffs' or 'large watch-dogs' (Fr. *mâtin* from OFr. *mastin*; cf. *mastiff*). The word was applied abusively to persons = 'brute, cur'; see *DOST*, s.v. **Matine, Matt-, Matheyne**, where, in both examples quoted, the word refers to humans. The primary reference in older forms directly derived from OFr. *mastin*, **Mastin** and **Mastis**, is to dogs, sometimes hunting-dogs: 'Gif ... the mastis be nocht in bande, he that aw that mastice sal be ... fully in the forfait to the king' (Forest Laws, *APS* 1, 326/2). Here the primary reference is to dogs, but, as the dogs are metaphorical extensions of Whigridne, the secondary meaning, applied to him, is at least subliminally present.

The earliest example of the word in *OED* is from Oliver Goldsmith's *History of the Earth and Animated Nature* (London, 1776), referring to an experiment by the French naturalist Buffon (1707–88). Goldsmith's information was derived from an early volume of Buffon's vast *Histoire Naturelle* (44 vols., 1749–1804); probably he borrowed the word directly from this.

180. *interdict*: vb. from noun *interdict*, 'in Scots law a remedy roughly comparable to English *injunction*. Its main use is to stop ... the continuance or repetition of some right vested in the pursuer' (Walker 1980: 629). King William is about to abolish the hunting (persecuting) rights of Whigridne and his associates.

forest: a legal term, 'woodland district, usually belonging to the king, set apart for hunting wild beasts and game etc.' (*OED*, s.v. **Forest 2**). King William, metaphorically, is proposing to enact new laws of the forest (Scotland), which will prohibit the hunting of Curates; see below, the closing words of 3.3, the Moderator's opening and concluding words in 4.2, coupled with the remarks of Turbulent at the end, and the latter part of 5.3.

180–81. **they tacking the formula**: insert in Pitcairne's hand; presumably to replace *they behaving as becoms*. Not in B, C or the later printed texts.

181. *formula*: 'A set form of words in which something ... is prescribed by authority or custom to be used on some ceremonial occasion' (*OED*, s.v. **Formula 1**). 'King William in January last (1691) desired them, by his letter to the General Assembly, to re-admit into the Exercise of the Ministry, so many of the Episcopal Presbyters as should be willing to submit to and comply with a Formula which his Majesty sent to them, and appointed to be the Terms of Communion betwixt the Parties' (Curate 1692: 28).

182. *my father*: George Melville, 4th lord and 1st earl of Melville (1636–

1707), Secretary for Scotland 1689–91, Commissioner to the General Assembly, 1690; see below, 4.4, 73–101.

my brother: Alexander Melville, styled Lord Raith, eldest son of George Melville above. He was Treasurer-depute. He predeceased his father, leaving Huffie to succeed to the earldom.

184–90. *Let them ... the Indies*: This brief appearance of Visioner and Novell serves to recall the theme, introduced in 1.3 and further elaborated in 3.3, of the plantation of the recently purged churches with new ministers.

The stage direction indicates that the pair cross the inner stage, representing Lady Murray's yeards, while Whigridne and Huffie have moved to the outer stage, representing the South Back of Canongate.

186. *fill them againe with frish men*: i.e. 'appoint new presbyterian ministers'.

them: 'the purged churches'.

187. *butt speack disorderlie*: obscure; *butt* is probably a contracted form of *behuvit*, '[it] becomes, befits [you]'; cf. such later Scots forms as *bude, buid, beet, bit* (*SND*, s.v. **Bude**); 'It befits you [as an Episcopalian] to speak in an out-of-order way.' For *butt* B, C and the later printed texts read *but*; for *disorderlie*, *discreetly*, thus reversing the meaning of the words.

188. *losed*: 'lost'; cf. above, 148n.

190. *monsters*: cf. 1.1, 17, etc.

191–2. *If I whip ... temple of the Lord*: cf. Huffie's reference to 'scurges of the Lord', above, 1.3, 16.

192. *lett my right hand forgett its cuneing*: cf. Psalm 137. 5: 'If I forget thee, O Jerusalem, let my right hand forget its cunning.'

194. *Counsell*: the Privy Council, of which both Whigridne (Crawford) and Huffie (Leven) were members.

195. *the fellow*: i.e. a Curate.

complyd: i.e. signed the Allegiance and Assurance and prayed for William and Mary.

197. *ordine Alphabetico*: Latin, 'in alphabetic order'.

198. *Curat*: the case before the Privy Council is that of an episcopalian clergyman. Whigridne intends to offer false evidence, recorded apparently in his pocket book, evidence which will be corroborated by Huffie and Garless.

199. *beaddall*: 'church-officer', in close attendance on the minister.

201. *people of God*: i.e. militant Covenanters.

Bothwell Bridge: site of the battle, 22 June 1679, in which the Covenanters were routed by government forces.

203. *Storie*: i.e. the whole charge is a fiction.

207. *Comittie*: the Commission for Visitations on the South Side of Tay.

207. *Minthouse*: the Edinburgh Mint, in South Gray's Close, adjoining the Cowgate.

Lord Garless: The original reading in A was *Lord Acrless*, a reading preserved in B, C and the later printed texts. Pitcairne has overwritten *Ac-* with *Ga*. Lord Garless is presumably James Stewart (d. 1746), styled Lord Garlies, later 5th earl of Galloway and 5th Baron Garlies and a member of the Privy Council.

208. *confederat*: 'ally', 'fellow-conspirator'.

209. Stage-direction, *tranie*: 'train', 'followers' (i.e. the dogs).

Act 3, Scene 2

The setting is the same as that in 1.2.

Solomon's clumsily unsuccessful attempt at Laura's seduction at once corresponds, and stands in contrast, to Will's less clumsy, but equally unsuccessful, attempt in 3.1. to seduce Violetta. Notably contrasting is 4.1, 21–95, Frank's courtship of Laura.

It is hinted throughout the play, although never made explicit, that the Old Ladie intends to marry off Violetta and Laura to Covenant and Solomon. Solomon may partly be motivated by the belief that this is so.

1–2. *stubborn, obstinat Nice*: Laura is stubborn and obstinate because she persistently holds to the episcopalian tradition of the three-fold ministry, bishops, priests and deacons in descending order of authority. Presbyterians held by parity, 'Equality among the members, or among the ministers, of a church' (*OED*, s.v. **Parity 2**).

2–3. *Union & Comunion ... members*: note the ambiguity of the Old Ladie's words, understood by her as referring only to the Church, but containing a *double entendre* of which she is herself unconscious, although Solomon is not.

5–6. *twixt Ministers ... 2 lay Elders*: Solomon accepts only the more limited version of parity.

7. *first postur in tyme of exercise*: for 'exercise' see above 1.2, 9n.

In A *first postur* is left unexplained. In B, C and the printed texts, however, the reading is *fittest posture*. An explanatory dialogue follows:

Old Lady. But as to the fittest posture in time of Exercise?
Solomon. Indeed I can never get her convinced, but that standing is be far the most convenient.
Old Lady. But remains she still obstinate as to her perseverance?

Presbyterians avoided kneeling during church services. Laura, it is clear, persisted in the episcopalian practice.

7. *posture*: 'position', 'attitude'.

exercise (together with *standing* in B as quoted): *double entendre*; see above 1.2, 10–19n.

8–9. *falne member*: *double* (or rather *triple*) *entendre*. Solomon refers, first, to Laura's tendency to kneel during the service; second, to 'fallen' humanity; third, to his own sexual member.

10. *experience*: i.e. the treatment he proposes to himself for Laura.

10. *inbearing*: 'capable of producing a vivid impression on the mind; impressive; persuasive' (*DOST*). Something of the later sense, recorded in *OED* and *SND*, 'officious, anxious to ingratiate oneself, obsequious, toadying' is perhaps also present. *SND* adds 'often also implying interfering meddlesomness, forward to the point of rudeness, pushing, intruding'. This is certainly relevant to Solomon's behaviour.

10. Stage Direction, *Exit Old Ladie*: not in MSS or printed editions, but certainly implied by the subsequent action and Solomon's final reflections, below, 61–2.

12. *hope*: 'expect with desire' (*OED*, s.v. **Hope 3**).

12. Stage direction: so in A; *retires*, it should be noted, is not the same as *withdraws* or *exit*. Laura is allowed no more than attempt to leave. The 1722 print adds *He catcheth hold on her*.

14. *Pray stay a little*: the Maid attempts to interpose.

dressing herself: the assumed time is still early morning.

15. *present*: B and C, followed by the printed texts, have the slightly better reading *instant*, 'pressing, insistent'.

in season & out of Season: 'at all times, without regard to what is considered opportune' (*OED*, s.v. **Season 7**). *In season* and *Out of season* are terms also used of game, meaning 'at/ not at/ the time for hunting, catching etc.' Solomon is hunting Laura, whether the season is, or is not, appropriate. The metaphor of hunting runs through the play. *In season* also means 'in heat', a state characteristic of Solomon.

17. *prick haist*: primarily 'haste caused by a goad or spur', from the verb *prick*, 'spur or urge a horse on' (*OED*, s.v. **Prick 11**); cf. *Sir Ferumbras* (EETS, 1879), 6308: 'Richard prykede forþ an haste,/ As harde as he may þraste'; Spenser, *Faerie Queene*, 1.1, 1: 'A Gentle Knight was pricking on the plaine.' A possible secondary sense is 'haste caused by the penis, by the sexual urge'; *prick* in this sense is on record from the sixteenth century. The context suits both meanings.

17. Something like the following direction should be inferred: *Solomon thrusts the Maid aside, probably with some violence; she exits in distress.*

17. *Solomon*: after this, B and C, followed by the printed texts, have [*aside*.

I'm resolved ... for once: the prints mark this as an aside.

impudent: 'shameless'.

19–20. *these two fair breasts ... paritie in Church members*: an extreme example of the *homelie expressione* cultivated by presbyterian ministers; see above, 2.2, 47–8n. It has also a relevance to Song of Solomon 8. 8, quoted above, 2.2, 68n. Solomon might claim to be following the Old Ladie's request that he should convince Laura of the necessity for parity in the Church, but he is also taking the opportunity of handling her breasts, revealed as they are by her state of partial undress.

21. *insult or tirranize*: as Presbyterians held that bishops did over the inferior clergy.

22. *live in brotherlie unity*: cf. Psalm 133. 1: 'Behold, how good and how pleasant it is for brethren to dwell together in unity'; cf. also above, 3.1, 23 and n.

24. *misticall (bodie)*: in Pauline terms, the Church; cf., e.g., Colossians 1. 18: 'And he [Christ] is the head of the body, the church.' The phrase 'mystical body' became a theological commonplace.

26–7. *your Church Government*: i.e. Presbyterianism, with its doctrine of clerical parity. Laura holds to the episcopalian system.

B and C, followed by the printed texts, read *Kirk government*. It is perhaps more likely that in hostile conversation with a presbyterian minister Laura would use the English *Church* rather than Scots *Kirk*.

28–9. *Antichristian name of parson*: cf. above, 3.1, 63n. Solomon is hostile, partly because, in his time, the word *parson* had English and epis-copalian associations, partly because the term had long been in use during the pre-Reformation Catholic period in Scotland (in *DOST* the earliest example of the word in the sense 'holder of a parochial benefice, in full possession of its rights and dues' is dated ?1073). During the seventeenth century, moreover, in England as well as Scotland, the term had tended to become derogatory; cf. the remark made by Gilbert Rule's old opponent (above, **Drammatis Personæ**, 9n), Edward Stillingfleet (1635–99), bishop of Worcester (quoted in *OED*, s.v. **Parson 1**): 'A Vicar cannot appoint a Vicar, but a Parson may. And altho that Name among some may be used as a Term of Reproach, yet in former Ages *Personatus* and *Dignitas* were the same thing.' Something of this derogatory sense persisted in eighteenth-century English usage; cf., e.g., the characters of Fielding's Parson Adams and Sterne's Parson Yorick. Laura deliberately exploits these overtones.

29. *But this leads me*: an example of the illogical, inspirational transitions characteristic of presbyterian discourse at this time.

31. *protestant Woman*: Solomon implies that Catholic women are shameless. He also ignores the fact that he has interrupted Laura while she is dressing.

33. *strowting out*: 'swelling', sticking out', from **Strout, Strut(t,** *v.* **9** (*DOST*). 'His belly began to strout, and was like to crack for fulness' (Sir Thomas Urquhart, *Rabelais* 1. xxi). B and C, followed by the printed texts, read *strutting*.

35. *Men ... endure it*: ironic.

mettall: 'mettle', 'the "stuff" of a person or persons, what he "is made of" or is worth' (*DOST*, s.v. **Met(t)al(l, Met(t)ale, Met(t)el(l 4** *fig*. **a**).

37. *handle ... so closlie*: cf. above, 3.1, 24 and n.

39. *the pulpitt*: i.e. the vagina.

41. *have not*: B reads *ha'nt*.

41. *allow*: B and C, followed by the later printed texts, read *atone*.

42. *retirement*: 'a place or abode characterized by seclusion or privacy; a retreat' (*OED*, s.v. **Retirement 4**). Here 'retiring room', 'dressing room', 'bedroom'.

46. *fear*: 'fair', 'beautiful'.

parish: 'perish'.

47. *Sanctuarie*: i.e. Heaven, regarded as the sky; cf. Psalm 102. 19: 'For he hath looked down from the height of his sanctuary; from heaven did the Lord behold the earth.'

48–9. *I'le cure ... the sprit*: another fine example of 'allegory' (above, 3.1, 101–103n).

49. *bed of roses*: the phrase appears to have been coined by Marlowe in his lyric 'The passionate Shepheard to his loue': 'And I will make thee beds of roses' (Tucker Brooke 1954: 550, 9). It is, of course, inappropriate for a presbyterian clergyman attempting the conversion of an Episcopalian – even less appropriate if an actual bed is visible.

49–50. *perfumed with Lillies*: not in B, C or the printed texts.

50–51. *O, the hight ... active Love!*: parody of Ephesians 3. 17–19: 'that ye, being rooted and grounded in love, may be able to comprehend with all saints what is the breadth, and length, and depth, and height; and to know the love of Christ, which passeth knowledge'.

active: 'practical', i.e. 'physical'.

52. *Hold, Sir, fforbear!*: Solomon clasps Laura and attempts to kiss her. She thrusts him away.

54. *Foch*: 'faugh', an expression of disgust; cf. Jonson, *Cynthia's Revels* 3.2, 11: 'Fough, he smells all lamp-oil.'

sent: 'scent' (vb.); 'exhale an odour, smell' (*OED*, s.v. **Scent 3**).

strangelie: 'strongly'. B and C, followed by the printed texts, read *strong*.

54. *saik*: 'sack', 'a general name for a class of white wines formerly imported from Spain and the Canaries' (*OED*, s.v. **Sack**, *sb.*³ 1).

57. *wry mouth*: cf. above, 3.1, 27n.

58. *monkie face*: the phrase is first on record in Florio's Italian dictionary (1598, mentioned above, 3.1, 71n.). Not in *DOST*. There is a rather puzzling reference, '*monkey-faces*, mimulus (Bnff., Abd. 1963)', in *SND*, s.v. **Monkey 1** (2). *Mimulus* is late Latin for 'little mime'. 'Monkey-face' was used as a taunt, particularly by girls, when the editor was at primary school in a Glasgow suburb during the 1930s.

59. *trade*: Laura dismisses any idea that Solomon has a calling or profession.

After *trade*, B and C, followed by the printed texts, insert 'and make you appear'.

mortified: 'dead to sin or the world; having the appetites and passions in subjection; ascetic' (*OED*, s.v. **Mortified 1**).

sant: 'saint'. For Paul the word signifies 'Christian'; see, e.g., Philippians 4. 21: 'Salute every saint in Christ Jesus.' It was applied to themselves by the Covenanters and other Puritans. By others, often, as here, used ironically.

63. *hes my thoumb under her belt*: 'has me tied to her apron-strings, has me under complete control'. Proverbial; see *ODEP*, 820, where both examples quoted are Scottish.

64. *I wish ... also*: Solomon adapts the proverb to his frustrated desires.

Act 3, Scene 3

The setting is as in 1.3 and 2.3, and represents the interior of the West Kirk, St Cuthbert's. Solomon is seated separately.

In the stage direction Lord Whigridne is called Mʳ Whigridne, perhaps to illustrate presbyterian parity, but more probably by a slip on the part of the transcriber.

The scene is primarily concerned with 'planting', the filling of pulpits made vacant by the purge of episcopalian clergy. Salathiel, however, introduces another important theme by way of an account of the method of teaching used in the Tounis College (and indeed British universities generally) to train future ministers, a method which indicates the hostility of the presbyterian church to the new mathematics and natural philosophy (physics). Salathiel is primarily concerned with putting forward his own pupils for the many pulpits now vacant. His words, however, give a peculiarly Scottish slant on a major aspect of European intellectual history at the time, the scholarly and scientific struggle between Ancients and Moderns, which marked the earlier stages of the Enlightenment. Presbyterians like Salathiel, who cling to scholastic logic, are on the side of the Ancients, the ultimate losers, despite their temporary ascendancy in Scotland. Will, Frank and Novell, like Pitcairne and his collaborators, are Moderns.

The Committee are more interested in the proposal to accept men who had once aspired to the episcopal ministry, but are now prepared to repent of their former 'sins'.

1. *By his providence*: for the phrase, cf. 1.3, 90 and n.

den: 'done, finished (with)'. This past participial form of the verb *dae*, 'do', does not appear in *DOST*; in *SND deen, dene*, are given, for the most part with a N or NE provenance; cf. the ballad 'Lord Ingram and Chief Wyet' (Childe 1885, 66B; Skene MS [taken down in the North of Scotland 1802–3], p. 16): 'There is a brotch on a breast-bane,/ An roses on ane's sheen;/ Gin ye kend what war under that,/ Your love wad soon be deen.'

For other northern features in the Moderator's language, cf. above, 1.3, 27 and n.

2–4. *den ... planting*: the Moderator indicates that the 'purge' of episcopalian clergymen is now complete, leaving the Committee only the task of filling the vacancies thus created.

4. *in the beginning*: echo of Genesis 1. 1: 'In the beginning God created the heaven and the earth.' The Moderator hubristically thinks that his Committee has, in effect, brought about a new Creation.

5. *predestinat*: 'foreordained by divine decree' (*DOST*). Here, however, the past participle passive is used as if it were the present active, 'foreordaining by divine decree'; *for that* indicates that Salathiel is referring to the new order which the Committee has brought about. Predestination is, of course, a central doctrine of Calvinist theology.

5–6. *Nam Reges ... orbos*: as it stands, the phrase is nonsense, indicating the poor quality of Salathiel's (Gilbert Rule's) Latin. There is no real need to attempt emendation; nevertheless, one might suggest 'Nam Regi in exemplo totus compositur orbis [terrarum]' (for the entire world is fashioned as a (warning) example to the king). The phrase would then have an application both to the ousted King James and to the usurping King William. The latter had little sympathy with the work either of Committee or General Assembly; see below, 5.3, 104–119.

7–26. *I must ... sicker of them*: second satirical account of the University system; see above, 3.1, 140–59.

7. *our Colledge*: the Tounis College, Edinburgh University, of which Gilbert Rule had become Principal on the expulsion of the episcopalian Alexander Monro (d. 1698). He is urging the suitability of Edinburgh graduates to fill the church vacancies.

8. *M^r M – sie*: Andrew Massie, Regent in the Tounis College, who, before and after the Revolution, presided over the students' graduating *theses philosophicæ* (in 1683, 1687 and 1695; see Aldis 1970: nos. 2435, 2725, 3571). Pitcairne perhaps refers to him in a Latin epigram, 'Ad Walterum Dennistonum Ludi Magistrum Mussilburgensem' (MacQueen and MacQueen 2009: 180).

9. *dispatch*: here, probably, 'conclude or settle a business; get through, have done (with)' (*OED*, s.v. **Dispatch 10**). The reference is to the effectual concluding of disputes with theological opponents by the use of scholastic logic. Salathiel seems to be praising scholastic rather than the Ramean logic favoured by many Protestant universities elsewhere (Baker 1952: 98–110); see too above, pp. xxi–xviii.

Cattigorietuaclie: for 'categorical' or perhaps its synonym, 'categorematical' – in either case, an ignorant mispronunciation of the kind supposedly characteristic of Gilbert Rule. To 'dispute categorically' is to dispute by categories, 'a term given to certain general classes of terms, things or notions; the use being very different with different authors' (*OED*, s.v. **Category 1**); cf. Jeremy Taylor, *Real Presence and Spiritual of Christ in the Blessed Sacrament Proved against the Doctrine of Transubstantiation* (London, 1654), xi, § 14: 'Can there possibly be two categorematical, that is possible, substantial infinites?' The basic Aristotelian categories were (1) Substance or being, (2) Quantity, (3) Quality, (4) Relation, (5) Place, (6) Time, (7) Posture, (8) Having or possession, (9) Action, (10) Passion.

Sincategormatice: i.e. 'syncategorematic', from *syncategorem*, a term used in logic to indicate 'a word which cannot be used by itself as a term, but only in conjunction with another word or words; e.g. a sign of quantity (as *all*, *some*, *no*) or an adverb, preposition or conjunction' (*OED*).

Both terms were used in medieval and early modern logic; see, e.g., Broadie 1983: 33–5, 64–8. They belong to the language of the Schoolmen, despised by the humanists and scientists, the practitioners of *humane Reasoneings* (17–18). Milton's denunciation of the English universities shows that it was not only in Edinburgh that this kind of teaching was customary: he talks of 'honest and ingenuous natures coming to the universities to store themselves with good and solid learning and there unfortunately fed with nothing else but the scragged and thorny lectures of monkish and miserable sophistry, were sent home again with such a scholastic burr in their throats as hath stopped and hindered all true and generous philosophy from entering' (*Reason of Church Government* 2. 'Conclusion'; Hughes 1957: 686). Such training, Milton thought, led to an acceptance of prelacy and the Divine Right of Kings. Salathiel obviously did not agree.

Milton's own use of scholastic language while he was an undergraduate at Christ's College, Cambridge, may be seen in the early '*Anno Ætatis XIX. At a Vacation Exercise in the College*', where 'Ens is represented as Father

151

of the Predicaments, his ten sons, whereof the eldest stood for Substance and his canons.' Ens then addresses Substance in a series of witty couplets. 'The next Quantity and Quality spake in prose; then Relation was called by his name' (Hughes 1957: 30–32).

10. *vane philosophie & Mathematicks*: hendiadys; the primary reference is to the natural philosophy of the sixteenth and seventeenth century, first exemplified by the work of Galileo Galilei (1564–1642) and Johann Kepler (1571–1630), then by that of René Descartes (1596–1650; cf. below, 17 and n.) and Isaac Newton (1642–1727); see above, pp. xxii–xxv.

Implicit also may be a reference to Thomas Hobbes (1588–1679), a geometer as well as a philosopher, whose *Leviathan* had appeared in 1651, to the *Ethica ordine geometrico demonstrata* of Baruch Spinoza (1632–77), published in the year of his death, and to John Locke (1632–1704), not a mathematician, but a philosopher who distrusted scholastic logic, was influenced by Descartes, and admired Newton. His *Essay Concerning Human Understanding*, the first edition of which bears the date 1690, appeared, in fact, at the end of 1689.

Salathiel's failure to mention Newton, who was much in the world's eye at this time, is probably intended to demonstrate his own ignorance.

Theological hostility to mathematics turned on the claim that it offered a way to truth entirely independent of the Bible. Such hostility was equally evinced by churchmen of different denominations and in different countries. Descartes, for instance, found himself in trouble, not only in catholic France, but also in calvinist Holland.

See Baker 1952: 303–23.

12. *contraire to reasone*: Many cherished doctrines of the Christian Church, regardless of denomination, were called in question by Moderns like Newton, Locke and Pitcairne; cf., e.g., the heading in Locke, *Essay* 4.18.5: 'Revelation cannot be admitted against the clear Evidence of Reason'.

13–14. *Quhat hath ... Spouse?*: Salathiel echoes the views of the most extreme protestant sectarians (Baker 1952: 103–108).

14. *Christ's Spouse*: the Church; here in particular the presbyterian Church of Scotland.

17. *Colledge*: B reads *Universitie*.

18–19. *perjured themsels ... good doings*: cf. above, 3.1, 143–50 and n.

19–20. *on man*: David Gregory (1661–1708), professor of mathematics in the Tounis College and probable co-author of *The Phanaticks*; see above, pp. xliii–xlviii.

19. *far a' that*: 'for all that', 'despite everything'.

man: 'maun', 'must'.

give: 'provided that'.

20. *Niper-lyke*: 'neighbourly', i.e. 'fellow-members of a community'.

Lad's: 'Lord's', i.e. 'God's'; cf. *Gad* for *God*.

fountaines: 'sources', i.e. schools and colleges.

22. *Cart's*: Descartes'; see above, 10n.

Descartes is originally 'a habitation-name, with fused preposition de, from places in the parishes of Rochecorbon and Sanzay in Indre-et-Loire called *Les Cartes*'. Salathiel thinks of it as derived from the name of an estate, *Cart*, and in Scots fashion calls the supposed landowner by the name of his estate.

23–4. *supreame & unaccomptable*: central tenet of the doctrine of the Divine Right of Kings, 'the conception of a sovereign raised above all laws with power to abrogate them, who alone can give binding force to enactments and invest custom with legal sanctions' (Figgis 1922: 233); cf. Romans 13. 1–7; 1 Peter 2. 13.

25–6. *That's ... planting*: the Moderator fails to see the point of Salathiel's college talk and is anxious to proceed to the main business of the meeting.

25. *That's a' true*: 'that's all true'.

26. be *sicker of them*: B and C, followed by the printed texts, omit the phrase here, but inserts it after *if we cold* (23).

sicker: 'sure'.

28. *Malignant*: 'episcopalian'.

expectants: candidates for the ministry who have not yet received a licence to preach.

29. *bulls of Bashan*: from Psalm 22. 12: 'Many bulls have compassed me: strong bulls of Bashan have beset me round.'

therfor: what follows typifies the inspirational logic of presbyterian discourse.

31. *Bull-beating*: 'bull-baiting'.

32–4. *Now ther ar ... all God's messins*: cf. Curate 1692: 127, quoting 'one Mr. Robert Gourly': 'There are God's Dogs, and the Devil's Dogs.'

33. *Mastivs*: 'mastiffs'.

34. *messins*: 'small pet dogs'; cf. Dunbar's poem (aimed at James Dog or Doig, Keeper of the Queen's Wardrobe): 'He is ower mekle to be your messan./ Madam, I red you, get a less an./ His gang garris all your chalmeris schog./ Madam, ye heff a dangerous dog.' (Bawcutt 1998: 72, 21–4) The image of presbyterian clergymen as God's little pet dogs is as homely and incongruous as Dunbar's. Cf. too Laura's reference to her pet dog (above, 3.2, 52–3).

35. *able divins*: cf. Solomon's earlier speech, above, 1.3, 62 and n.

Spouse: the Church.

36. *in season and out of Seasone*: cf. above, 3.2, 15 and n.; a catch-phrase, characteristic of Solomon.

38. *28 years*: from Restoration (1660) to Revolution (1688); cf. above, 1.3, 69.

39–40. *naturall ... grace*: *naturall*, 'belonging to the world of nature' is opposed to *supernatural*, 'heavenly'; if the supernatural gift, *grace*, were to be added to the natural gifts of some Malignants, it should be possible to admit them to the presbyterian order.

41. *bryd's bed*: i.e. the Church. As always, Solomon's imagery is strongly sexual.

43. *indued with*: 'invested with', 'endued with'.

44. *share*: B, *geare*. C and the printed texts read *grace*.

45. *Mʳ Turncoat*: a former episcopalian expectant, now eager to join the presbyterian Establishment.

51. *tents of sin*: cf. Psalm 120. 5: 'Woe is me ... that I dwell in the tents of Kedar.' Kedar was a nomadic tribe, descended from Ishmael and some-times regarded as Midianite. By definition, therefore, they were a sinful people.

publicklie: i.e. by attending episcopalian services.

51–2. *committed ... whore*: an amalgam of Old and New Testament phra-seology; cf., e.g., Numbers 25. 1: 'the people began to commit whoredom with the daughters of Moab'; 2 Chronicles 29. 16: 'And the priests ... brought out all the uncleanness that they found in the temple of the Lord'; Romans 1. 24: 'Wherefore God also gave them up to uncleanness.'

whore: here 'episcopalian church order'. The image derives from Reve-lation 17. 1–2: 'Come hither, I will shew unto thee the judgment of the great whore that sitteth upon many waters: with whom the kings of the earth have committed fornication, and the inhabitants of the earth have been made drunk with the wine of her fornication.' Protestants at the Reformation regarded this prophecy as referring to the Roman Catholic church; Calvin-ists extended it to include any denomination which permitted episcopacy.

53. *My Lord*: Turncoat inadvertently addresses the Moderator as if he were a bishop. Cf. above, 1.1, 151–3; 1.3, 81.

54–5. *I never ... adulterie*: Turncoat betrays his upbringing by failing to understand the Moderator's scriptural metaphors.

repenting stool: the stool of repentance, 'a public and eminent seat erected towards the lower end of the church about two yards from the ground either about some pillar or in some conspicuous place. The seat is capable of accommodating six or eight persons' (*DOST*, s.v. **Stul(e, Stole, Stuil(l 2**, quoting an extract from P. Hume Brown, *Early Travellers in Scot-land* [Edinburgh, 1891], 144). On this, those found guilty of transgression (for the most part fornicators) were exposed to public humiliation during church services on one or more Sundays. Cf. the opening of 2.2 above.

55. *consequentlie*: Turncoat's logic is questionable.

56–7. *out of ... Speack*: cf. Matthew 12. 34: 'out of the abundance of the heart the mouth speaketh'.

58–9. *language of the beast*: cf. Revelation 13. 1, 5: 'And I stood upon the sand of the sea, and saw a beast rise up out of the sea ... And there was given unto him a mouth speaking great things and blasphemies.' The reference is to the plain language of episcopalian discourse as opposed to the biblical metaphorics of the Presbyterians, *the leed* [language] *of the Sancts*.

doesno know the leed of the Sancts: for this B and C, followed by the printed texts, substitute the more English *do not understand the language of the Sanctuary*. The original scribe has taken *Sancts* (Saints) as an abbreviation of *Sanctuary*.

60–63. *Mr Covenant provd ... a bed &c*: cf. above, 1.3, 58–9; the text has not been identified and may never have existed. Kirkton in his *History of the Church of Scotland 1660–1679* (Stewart 1992: 74–7) laments the re-establishment of the episcopate, but introduces no such figure.

61. *14 Black birds*: there were two archbishops and twelve bishops in Scotland, the archbishops of St Andrews and Glasgow, the bishops of Aberdeen, Argyll, Brechin, Caithness, Dunblane, Dunkeld, Edinburgh, Galloway, the Isles, Moray, Orkney and Ross.

62. *text of Revelatne*: Revelation 2. 22: 'Behold, I will cast her into a bed, and them that commit adultery with her into great tribulation, except they repent of their deeds.' The reference is to the church of Thyatira in Asia Minor, which had permitted the activities of 'that woman Jezebel, which calleth herself a prophetess' (2. 20). It is difficult to see any connection between this and episcopal arrangements in Scotland.

68. *Turk ... papist*: Turks and Jews were not Christians. It is a sign of the times that Turncoat regards Roman Catholics as even further from Christianity. Pitcairne had little time for Roman Catholicism, but nevertheless intends us to see the irony.

69. *a good prisbiterian in my heart*: a similar argument was put forward by the fornicatrix, above, 2.2, 7–11 and n.

74. *reprobated*: 'rejected', 'condemned by arbitrary divine fiat'. The term was much used by Calvinist theologians; 'Calvin attributed great importance to predestination in both its forms – election and reprobation' (Wendel 1965: 264). Divine reprobation, however, is properly restricted to human beings. Turncoat's eagerness to adopt a Calvinistic mode of speech makes him wrongly apply the term to an order.

76–7. *he says ... in the world*: Whigridne deliberately misunderstands.

78. *tack order*: 'take measures, steps' – more a paronomasia than a threat.

80–1. *Confession of Faith* : see above, 2.3, 73n; pp. xix–xxi.

83. *Spirituallie*: B and C, followed by the printed texts, read *supernatu-rally*.

84. *Nae more, my Lord Moderator*: Ruling Elder inadvertently addresses the Moderator as if he were a bishop. B and C, followed by the later printed texts, read *See yet* and omits *my Lord*.

86 *Whole Duty of Man*: see above, **Prologue**, 22n.

87. *Covenant*: B and C, followed by the printed texts, are probably right to give the following words to Salathiel.

88. *Biblia, Biblie*: Covenant/Salathiel gives the nominative and genitive singular of the word in the very late Latin feminine singular form. He shows no awareness of earlier Latin usage or the Greek plural original.

90. *Moderator*: B and C, followed by the printed texts, omit; the words which follow become a continuation of Salathiel's speech.

without qualifications or restrictions: B and C, followed by the printed texts, read *without qualifications, restrictions and reservations*. For *and* the printed texts read *or*.

91. *Not only materialiter but formaliter*: i.e. in form (*formaliter*) and substance (*materialiter*), a distinction more intended to sound impressive than to be relevant. Stylistically, it may be intended as a parody of the words in the Oath of Allegiance (above, 1.1, 49n): 'as well *de jure*, this is of right king and queen, as *de facto*, that is, in the possession and exercise of the government'.

94. *Universall redemption*: as put forward, e.g. in 1 John 2. 1–2: 'And if any man sin, we have an advocate with the Father, Jesus Christ the right-eous: And he is the propitiation for our sins: and not for ours only, but also for the sins of the whole world.' This doctrine makes no appearance in any of the 33 articles of the Confession of Faith.

reprobation: nothing in the Old or the New Testament supports the Calvinistic doctrine of reprobation, i.e. predestination to damnation. Even in Romans 1. 28, 'And even as they did not like to retain God in their knowledge, God gave them over to a reprobate mind', abandonment by God is the consequence rather than the cause of human behaviour.

96. *twe*: 'twae', 'two'.

97. *long gift of prayer*: the (supposedly supernatural) gift of extempore interminable public prayer.

101–2. *Gray, Guthrie ... Rutherford*: three 'saints' of the Covenant. The eldest, Samuel Rutherford (c. 1600–61), became minister of Anwoth in Kirkcudbrightshire in 1636, but as an extreme Presbyterian was in the same year exiled to episcopalian Aberdeen, where he engaged in contro-versy with the 'Aberdeen doctors' (below, 4.4, 184n.). He was restored to Anwoth in 1638 and in 1639 became professor of divinity, later Principal, in St Mary's College, St Andrews. In 1643 he was one of the Scottish commissioners at the Westminster Assembly. In 1644 he published in London his most influential work, *Lex Rex, a Dispute for the Just Prerogative of King and People*, copies of which at the Restoration were burnt by the common hangman in Edinburgh and St Andrews. He also wrote *The Divine Right of Church Government and Excommunication* (1646; above 2.3, 105n) and an attack on religious toleration, *A Free Disputation against Pretended Liberty of Conscience* (1648). On the return of Charles II, he was charged with high treason, but died before standing trial.

He exchanged letters with people of importance across Scotland, letters collected and posthumously published (1664) in the Netherlands under the title *Joshua Redivivus, or, Mr Rutherford's Letters, divided into two parts*; a second edition (Edinburgh, 1671) and many others followed, right up to the present day. Cf. below, 5.2, 45 and n. For samples see Curate 1692: 98–108, and, more sympathetically, Jack 1971: 173–81; Reid 1982: 44–52.

James Guthrie (1612–61) was originally an Episcopalian, but became a Presbyterian under Rutherford's influence. By 1648 he had become the leader of the Remonstrants (later Protesters), the radical wing of the presbyterian party. In 1650 he forced the excommunication of John Middleton (c. 1608–74), episcopalian commander of royalist forces in the Highlands. Middleton was forced to do public penance in sackcloth in St Mary's Kirk, Dundee. He never forgave Presbyterians generally, or Guthrie in particular. Since 1649 Guthrie's charge had been in Stirling; he was now expelled, but along with two other ministers formed a separate 'protesting' presbytery of Stirling. At the Restoration Middleton, now an earl, became King's Commissioner to the Parliament and saw to it that Guthrie was arraigned for high treason. He made a brilliant defence, but was found guilty and hanged in the Grassmarket on 1 June 1661.

Guthrie's main published works were *The Causes of the Lord's Wrath against Scotland* (Edinburgh, 1653) and *Protesters No Subverters* (Edinburgh, 1658).

Andrew Gray (1633–56), when still a very young man (1653), was appointed minister of the Outer High Kirk, Glasgow (part of a subdivided Glasgow Cathedral). He was a charismatic preacher, but died of plague three years later. His sermons were published posthumously. The best known is *The Mystery of Faith Opened Up* (Glasgow, 1659). These sermons retain some attraction to the present day. Gray's *Works*, first collected in a single volume in 1762, were reprinted as recently as 1992 (*The Works of the Reverend and Pious Andrew Gray formerly Minister of the Gospel in Glasgow* [Ligonier, Pa., 1992]).

103. *bennieson*: 'blessing'. The usual phrase is 'the blessing of God'; there is irony in the use of the word 'Covenant'.

106–7. *rich nobles ... wark of the Lord*: cf. the complaint, above, 1.3, 2–6.

106. *gentils*: 'men of good birth and breeding', 'the gentry'.

108. *lend us a fist*: B and C, followed by the later printed texts, read *lend God a lift*. For *lift* the 1722 printed text reads *list*.

110. *As the Lord livs*: a frequent Old Testament oath; cf., e.g., 1 Samuel 14. 39: 'For as the Lord liveth, which saveth Israel, though it be in Jonathan my son, he shall surely die.'

111–12. *not many nobles ... or wise*: a reminiscence of 1 Corinthians 1. 26: 'For you see your calling, brethren, how that not many wise men after the flesh, not many mighty, not many noble, are called.'

112–13. *And think that ... true kirk*: dramatic irony. The audience understands the words in a sense opposite to that intended by the speaker.

115. *ill reports*: cf. below, 4.2, 131–3 and n.; 5.3, 5, 104–18.

115–16. *we'l do ... undon*: Moderatorial tautology.

Act 4, Scene 1

The stage setting is like that of 3.1, save that the back shutters reveal an image of the main building of Heriot's Hospital.

Heriot's yeards: cf. above, 3.1, 101n; see too Stevens 1859: 78–9: 'The Heriot gardens encompassing the Hospital, consisted of several inclosures kept in a very tasteful manner. They were long celebrated as a fashionable promenade. No expense was spared to make this place of public resort at once beautiful and really useful. In their "injunctions" to the gardener on the 30th September 1661, the Governors inserted this clause, – "That the easter yard, on the south part thereof, be planted with all sort of *phisical, medicinal*, and other *herbs*, such as the country can afford, conform to the fullest catalogue that can be had, that such who intend to *study herbs* may have full access there, they not wronging or molesting the samen; and that in the remanent of that yaird, which is called the wilderness or maze, the walks be kept clean." This may justly be regarded as the first Botanic Garden in Scotland.' A quotation from Pennant is appended as a footnote: 'The gardens were formerly the resort of the gay; and there the Scotch poets often laid, in their comedies, the scenes of intrigue' (Pennant 1774: 56). Clearly enough Pennant refers to the present scene; 'often' is an exaggeration.

For *Enter Laura and Violetta in a walke*, the 1722 printed text reads *Enter Laura in a Walk, Sola*. Violetta's remarks in lines 4–6 are omitted, while Laura's (1–3, 7–11) are combined into a monologue. This probably represents an earlier version of the text, another trace of which is the singular *Exit*, rather than the plural *Exeunt*, in the stage-direction after line 11.

Stage Direction, *Enter Laura and Violetta*: Despite her earlier words

(3.1, 100–103) Violetta has taken pains to arrange a meeting between Laura and Frank. She tactfully disappears once her object is achieved.

1. *your servand*: i.e. 'the person whom *you* described as *my* servand (i.e. one who professes his service to a woman as a lover or paramour', *DOST*, s.v. **Servand(e 9)**. Laura is irritated by the apparent failure of Violetta's scheme (3.1, 100–103) to bring Frank and her together in Heriot's yeards.

B and C, followed by the printed texts, simplify by adding, after *servand*, *said his friend used to walk here*.

1–2. *to walk ... toun fops*: above, 3.1, 105.

3. *dull*: 'slow of understanding'. Laura's impatience makes her blame Will as well as Frank.

6. *sotts*: 'fools', 'idiots'.

8–10. *cane speak sense ... good manners*: Laura balances Frank's good sense and manners against the overblown language and lack of manners among young Presbyterians.

8. *doe his Courtesie rycht*: 'behave like a gentleman'.

10. *sett forms*: the pattern of worship set out in the *Prayer Book*.

10–11. *nothing know ... of ther duty ... to ther soveragne*: as exemplified by the recent revolt against King James.

15. *fellwo*: 'fellow'.

16. *feared*: 'frightened', 'terrified'. B and C, followed by the printed texts, have the more English *as would fright*.

Necromancer: one who obtains knowledge of the future by conjuring up the reluctant spirits of the dead. Perhaps a reminiscence of the Witch of Endor (1 Samuel 28. 7–25) and an echo of the continuing witch-phobia of the later seventeenth century.

17. *master*: supposedly Christ, but with a strong suggestion that his master is, in fact, the Devil.

18. *With ane Emphasis*: 'emphatically'.

18. *K of ffrance*: Louis XIV, to Presbyterians and Whigs a bloody tyrant, to Jacobites an ally and supporter.

bloodie: B, C and the printed texts omit.

21. *nou for gravitie*: Laura recollects that in Heriot's yeards she should be meditating after prayer (3.1, 100–103). During the remainder of this scene her words and actions are more or less governed by this idea. She presents herself as a devout young Presbyterian.

22–23. *I'le think ... laugh*: the epitome of Scottish Calvinism; cf. the Old Ladie's remark, below, 5.2, 78–9.

24–5. *Madam ... walk*: Frank makes his approach to Laura in a fashion which contrasts markedly with that of Will to Violetta in 3.1. Nevertheless, his behaviour still breaches the normal code of polite manners.

27. *hazarting my owne Reputatne*: a young woman should not be seen walking with a young man in a public place.

27–8. *ruine ... you may hav*: if Frank were seen walking with a young woman to whom he had not been formally introduced, it might spoil any claim he had to respectability.

title: B and C, followed by the later printed texts, read *little*.

30. *walk by*: 'walk past', 'deliberately ignore'.

31. *lyk a merchant*: like a member of the commercial class, not a gentleman.

Exchange: 'a building in which the merchants of a town assemble for the transaction of business' (*OED*, s.v. **Exchange 10**). During Pitcairne's lifetime, and for some time after, such a building did not exist in Edinburgh; the Royal Exchange in the High Street was built 1753–61, and was soon taken over by the corporation to become the present City Chambers. Frank, the traveller, is thinking in terms of London or some continental bourse.

31–2. *some places wher I hav bene*: Frank plays on his experiences as a traveller.

33–6. *If it be ... confuse you*: Laura plays hard-to-get, while assuring Frank that she has no intention of making a fool of him.

34. *all in toune*: so B; C and the printed texts read *all the street whores in [the] town*.

36. *nobody sees to confuse you*: i.e. no witnesses are present to cause you embarrassment. Laura pretends that she is leaving Frank.

37. *escape not so*: Frank restrains Laura, but politely. Contrast Solomon's behaviour in 3.2, 28–31.

38–9. *to heir on ... yesterday*: i.e. the sermon preached by Solomon (not in text) before he absolved the fornicatrix, above, 2.2. Frank is unaware of the dramatic irony, that his words will also cause Laura to recall Solomon's behaviour under the pretext of instructing her in the doctrine of parity.

39. *cruelly*: B and C, followed by the printed texts, read *unmercifully*.

peice: B and C, followed by the later printed texts, read *parcell*.

41. *it's Charitie ... in Love*: cf. Song of Solomon 2. 5: 'Stay me with flagons, comfort me with apples: for I am sick of love.' Frank does not yet dare to name the object of his love. Laura understands his real objective, but makes a pretence of not doing so.

42. *it will out*: i.e. the fact that she too is in love.

42–4. *On conditione ... pray for you*: Laura, in her assumed character, offers to pray for Frank's success in love – but only if he leaves her alone.

45–7. *If you be ... I'm sur*: Frank plays along with Laura, while at the same time flattering her, and hinting that she is well acquainted with his inamorata.

45. *my intercessor*: i.e. 'the person who prays for me'.

48–9. *Mack ... can for you*: Laura is prepared to be an intermediary with her supposed friend, provided that too much is not asked of her.

50. *you'r the fair on*: i.e. 'you're the woman I love'. Frank blurts out the truth.

51. *good things*: i.e. that she is young, rich, handsome etc.; above, 44.

52. *truely*: B, C and the printed texts omit.

52. *still belived them so*: B and C, followed by the printed texts, read *I still believed them of myself.*

53. *flatterer*: Laura insinuates that Frank is flattering her to gain his own ends.

54. *no declared rivall*: Frank ignores the implications of 'flatterer', but deduces from 'first' that no one else has presented himself as a suitor for Laura.

55. *gett you on*: 'get you one', i.e. 'get a rival for yourself'.

57. *er I cane love ... be at that*: Laura admits that she might love Frank.

60. *disclame*: 'lay no claim to'; Frank asserts that all merit appertains to the lady, none to himself, the stance of the traditional courtly lover.

61. *Charity waxeth cold*: proverbial, *ODEP*, 115, based on Matthew 24. 12: 'And because iniquity shall abound, the love of many shall wax cold.'

62. *Libertie to serve*: 'Libertie' here means 'permission', but there is also verbal play on the opposition of 'liberty' and 'serve'; cf. in the *Prayer Book* 'Collect for Peace' the paradoxical 'whose service is perfect freedom'. The paradox forms part of the language of courtly love; cf., e.g., the elaborate version in *Kingis Quair*, 1276–8: 'cum to largesse from thraldom and peyne,/ And by the mene of luffis ordinance,/ That has so mony in his goldin cheyne' (McDiarmid 1973, 114).

63. *Exept*: 'expect'. Laura's response is cynical. During her subsequent series of testing questions, she purports to be an ardent Presbyterian and ends with the imposition of a task to be performed by her lover, a task on which Violetta and she have already agreed and which she knows will be extremely uncomfortable for Frank.

65. *earnest*: 'pledge' (the kiss which Laura refuses).

67. *swap*: 'strike' (a bargain).

68. *day*: B and C, followed by the printed texts, reads *Sunday*.

71. *evry Sunday in the week*: i.e. every day in the week would be a Sunday; cf. the proverbial Month of Sundays.

72. *plasme*: 'psalm' (with metathesis of *s* and *l*; the form is probably, however, simply the result of scribal error). The reference is to the Metrical Version, used by Presbyterians. B and C, followed by the printed texts, read *psalm.*

74–5. *first of Revelatne to the end of the Genesis*: Genesis is the first book of the Bible, Revelation the last; Frank shows his ignorance of the Scriptures by turning them on end.

76. *ane ill Divine*: Laura comments on Frank's mistake. She is justified by his later performance, when disguised as a Presbyterian preacher (5.2).

78. *I*: B and C, followed by the printed texts, read *you*.

81. *doe my duty*: i.e. 'bear sons and daughters'. Laura's response is tantalisingly ambiguous; she would do her duty only if she were allowed to behave in other respects as a Presbyterian matron. The audience knows that this last is not her intention.

82. *glad*: B and C, followed by the printed texts, read *good*.

familie exercise: 'family worship' (but note the *double entendre*).

84. *plott*: 'plan'. Note the recurrence of the word; see above 2.2, 51 and n.

86–7. *my sister ... Camrad*: above 3.1, 87–96.

99. *ordined*: 'appointed', 'assigned'.

100. Stage direction: after *Exit*, B, followed by the printed texts, adds *muttering his Grace*. C and the later printed texts add the beginning of an actual grace, *O God of all power and glory, who hast created us at this time –*

Act 4, Scene 2

The setting is again the West Kirk. Fourth meeting of the Comitie. Committee members everywhere will recognize the accuracy of the portrayal.

1–2. *Bretheren ... wark*: see above, 1.3, 89n.

2. *God's providence*: B and C, followed by the printed texts, insert *special* between *God's* and *providence*. The phrase special providence means 'a particular act of direct divine intervention' (*OED*, s.v. **Providence 5**). If the reading is accepted, as it probably should be, it reflects hubris on the part of the Moderator.

4–5. *Court ... God*: see above, 1.3, 2–6.

7. *act about plantations*: Act XV of the 1690 General Assembly, dated 13 November 1690. The Assembly, however, passed no acts resembling the ones quoted below, 9–15 and 50–8. These are satiric inventions.

7–8. *for that*: B and C, followed by the printed texts, insert *is*.

8. *madle with*: 'deal with' (but probably with some suggestion of the more modern, pejorative sense of 'meddle').

9. **Moderator & the**: inserted in Pitcairne's hand and a different ink. B, C and the printed texts follow.

11–12. *groath ... preaching of the same*: the internal contradiction is not noted by any member of the Committee.

14. *diligent search ... Randie beggers*: a deliberate *non-sequitur* to the self-contradictory preamble of the act as given.

After *Randie beggers*, B, C and the printed texts insert *and Sabbath breakers*.

vagabonds: 'persons of no fixed abode'.

Randie: 'riotous', 'aggressive'. Over the centuries Scottish parliaments (but not the General Assembly) passed a number of acts against randy beggars.

16. *The Clerk ... reads*: Turbulent is the only member to see anything odd in the act read to the Committee. He points out the fact with characteristic abruptness.

After his interruption, B and C, followed by the printed texts, insert a remark by the Moderator: *Is not this the act about Plantations you are reading, Clerk – I mean the act of the Assemblie.*

19. *Don't disturb the Comittee*: the Moderator fails to see the point and attempts to silence him.

20. *delated*: 'denounced', 'reported'.

21. *Contumatious*: 'contumacious', 'stubbornly resistant to authority'. The word also refers to contempt of court (in modern terms). Contumacy rendered the contumacious person subject to whatever penalties the court might impose. (I am grateful to Professor Hector MacQueen, for this, and some later, legal information.)

22. *ordins*: 'orders'. Note the assumption that the Church can issue orders to the civil magistrates.

notice: 'keep a check on'.

22. *ay and whill*: 'always until' (Scots legal phraseology).

23. *Extractum ... Spalding*: notary public's certification of authenticity (quite unnecessary here).

24–5. *I say ... plantations*: despite the Moderator, Turbulent persists.

34. *What if we doe, Sir?*: i.e. regard Prelates and Curates as vagabonds etc.

hazard: 'risk'. B and C, followed by the printed texts, read *harm*.

35. *vott*: the Moderator inclines to the democratic method of decision, whether or not it is an appropriate way of resolving the question in hand.

37. *the Comittee*: B and C, followed by the printed texts, read *the determination of the Committee.*

40. *hes rid*: 'has read'.

41. *rid our feet out of*: 'free us from, relieve us of'.

44. *glingentibus non dabitur*: another instance of Salathiel's poor Latinity; he is groping for the word *contingentibus* (contingent (affairs), contingencies) in his attempt to quote a scholastic tag, irrelevant to the matter in hand, *de futuris contingentibus non dabitur determinata veritas* (definite truth about future contingencies will be unobtainable). B and C, followed by the later printed texts, read *contingentibus non datur*, with the present tense of the verb. In the 1722 printed text the Latin is even more garbled than in A: *defecturis con ingentibus non datur determinata veritas*.

47–8. *you ar ... this trouble*: the Moderator is angry, mainly because Turbulent has all along been right.

48–9. *ryt ... & not wrong*: another Moderatorial tautology.

50–58. *The generall ... Apostats*: see above, 6n. The nearest approach to this supposed act of the 1690 Assembly is the 'Instruction to the Commission for Visitations on the South and North Sides of Tay' (Session XV, November 13, *post meridiem*), the tone of which is studiously moderate; see, e.g., § 7, 'That they be very cautious of receiving information against the late Conformists, and that they proceed in the matter of censure very deliberately, so as none may have just cause to complain of their rigidity, yet so as to admit [i.e. allow] no means of information [i.e. no second-hand information], and that they shall not proceed to censure, but upon relevant libels and sufficient probation'. For Pitcairne and his associates such language merely provided a cover for the actual behaviour of the Committee. Their version reveals what they saw as the Assembly's true purpose.

54–5. *Arminianism ... Nestorianism*: Arminianism is the theological system developed by the Dutch theologian Jakob Hermandszoon (1560–1609), according to which Divine sovereignty is compatible with a real freewill in men, that Jesus Christ died for all men, and that doctrines of predestination are unbiblical. By Calvinists it was regarded as heretical; Episcopalians in particular they regarded as tainted with this heresy. Earlier heresies tended to become lumped together indiscriminately with Arminianism – Arianism, which denied the true divinity of Christ, Pelagianism, which emphasized human free-will, and Nestorianism, which held that there were two separate Persons, one divine, the other human, in the incarnate Christ. Episcopalian doctrine, as set out in the Thirty-Nine Articles, is opposed to all these 'heresies'.

58. *Apostats*: 'apostates', those who abjure or forsake their religious faith. No Committee for Receiving Apostates existed.

61–6. *3 things ... consideratione*: Salathiel proposes to solve the problem by the use of scholastic distinctions. The Moderator prefers to rely on the aristocratic statesmanship of Lord Whigridne.

65–6. *now in hand ... consideratione*: Moderatorial tautology.

67–80. *Such is the sence ... error of prelacy*: A wandering, irrelevant speech by Whigridne, beginning with a modesty topos, all too well justified; cf. above, 1.3, 102 and n.

70–80. *Communion terms ... error of prelacy*: terms under which Episcopalians might be allowed to continue their ministry in the presbyterian church. Whigridne, however, mistakenly believes that the subject under discussion is the Eucharist, Holy Communion, and proceeds to a general discussion of that subject. Cf. below, **Preface**, pp. 224–5.

71–2. *last first ... of the last*: parody of Matthew 19. 30: 'But many that are first shall be last; and the last shall be first'; cf. Matthew 20. 16, also Mark 10. 31, Luke 13. 30.

75. *Prisbyterians from both*: Presbyterians sit to receive Communion, Protestants (Episcopalians) kneel, Roman Catholics stand.

80. *error of prelacy*: i.e. Episcopalians admitted people to Communion more readily than Presbyterians did.

81–2. *Will your ... understand you*: despite himself, the Moderator is baffled by Whigridne's remarks; cf. above, 1.3, 85–6.

83–5. *Though I ... fortificatne*: Solomon puts in his oar, partly, at least, to further Wordie's position as an able, gifted man; cf. above, 1.3, 70–2 and n. 75.

87. *exquisitive*: 'searching, penetrative'.

88. *depositne*: 'deposition', 'the action of deposing or putting down from a position of dignity or authority' (*OED*); cf. John Ayliffe, *Parergon juris canonici Anglicani* (London, 1726), 206: 'the word Deposition properly signifies a solemn depriving of a Man of his Clerical Orders by the way of a Sentence'.

A different usage appears below, 136 and n. Word-play may well be involved.

88–9. *libella Universalis ... Universall lybell*: cf. below, **Preface**, p 227.

A libel is a summons to appear before a particular court on a particular charge at a particular time. 'Ane libel is ane petitioun maid in writ be the persewar [plaintiff], contenand the naims of the Judge, of the persewar, and of the defendar [defendant], the thing that is clamit, and the cause quhairfoir the samin is clamit and askit' (Balfour 1963, 313).

What Turbulent proposes, however, is not a summons addressed to a named person or persons, but a universal or general summons, naming no person, but indicating only the class of person summonsed – in this particular case, clergymen of the episcopalian persuasion. Such a procedure was illegal: 'Ane libel beand sa general that na conclusioun or sentence may be gevin speciallie thairupon, is inept and irrelevant; because *omnis sententia debet esse certa*. And na special sentence may be gevin upon ane general libel [i.e. no particular individual may be called to account on an unspecific summons]' (Balfour 1963: 317).

The position may be illustrated by an extract from *The Sheriff Court Book of Fife* (Dickinson 1928: 16), quoted in *DOST*, s.v. **Libel(l 4**: 'Tharfor the said decret of forfaltour is vncert ... and promulgate vpoune ane vnecerte, inept & generale libell.'

The authorities quoted establish the rule primarily in civil law, but it applied equally in ecclesiastical cases. Most of the procedural rules and terminology referred to originated in Romano-canonical law long before the Reformation. The literature is pretty clear that these procedural rules continued into the post-Reformation Kirk, just as they had long before the Reformation seeped into the secular courts. In the seventeenth century people could not conceive any other way of thinking or talking about such things (note from H. L. MacQueen).

89–90. *two days compeirance ... same day*: *compeirance* is 'appearance as a formal act, especially in a court of justice' (*DOST*); *two days compeirance* means 'two days notice to compear at a particular court', an impossibly short period for the majority of ministers *on this syde and the othr syd of Tay*. The sitting of the court, moreover, was to last for no more than the morning and afternoon of a single day. Failure to compear entailed the forfeiture by the defendant of whatever lay under dispute, in this case, the living which he held.

For *days*, B reads *Dyets of*.

93–4. *To what ... fear*: cf. Curate: 132: 'Once in the Monthly Fast-day ... I heard him [Mr Kirkton (Covenant)] discourse to this Purpose ... I shall shew you five lost Labours, three Opportunities, three Fears, three Lamentations, three Prophesies, and a word about poor Scotland.'

96. *act prohibiting all ansring of Lybells*: i.e. contrary to natural justice, the defendant would not be allowed to mount any defence.

97. *falts as weall tto be done as done*: 'not only past offences, but others hypothetically to be committed in the future'. Thus, where no proof exists that a Curate has already offended, it will still be possible to condemn him for acts he will, in the judgement of the court, commit in the future; see below, 5.3, 50–3. Again, the proposal is contrary to all natural justice, and even, as Orthodox remarks, blasphemous.

97–9. *first question ... kirk*: whatever course is to be followed, the Curates are to be expelled.

99. *plant the kirk*: i.e. 'put in a new minister with full presbyterian credentials'.

100–101. *nethr in this syde nor the othr sid of Tay*: Covenant means episcopalian clergymen in the Highlands and Islands. Ruling Elder's comment, which follows, demonstrates the extent of a Presbyterian's mastery of mathematics.

104–5. *difficultie ... printed*: libels were normally handwritten. Covenant is concerned at the sheer number required, if all episcopalian clergy were to be served with a summons.

105–6 *indirect dealling ... owne cause*: Precisely! See below, 119n, *declinators*.

108. *last day*: i.e. the Day of Judgement; Matthew 24. 31–46; Revelation 20. 11–15.

108–10. *Did Josua ... befor hand*: i.e. during the conquest of the Promised Land by the Israelites under Joshua, the successor of Moses; see the biblical book of Joshua, *passim*.

109. *apperance*: B and C, followed by the later printed texts, read *Compearance*.

110–12. *Did Christ ... be the lug*: a specimen of 'homely, coarse, and ridiculous Expressions, very unsuitable to the Gravity, and Solemnity, that becomes Divinity' (Curate 1692: 23). Turbulent treats the clearance of the Temple as if it had occurred at a country fair.

See Matthew 21. 12–13; Mark 11. 15; Luke 19. 45–6.

111–12. *tack ... be the lug*: 'take by the ear', i.e. 'deal individually with'.
huckster: 'pedlar', 'hawker'.
wyff: 'woman'.

113. *Strange*: 'strong', 'powerful'. The Committee finds the biblical precedents particularly telling.

114. *what say you, my Lord?*: as usual, the Moderator defers to Whigridne.

115–24. *ffirst, to Conclud ... work of the Lord*: Whigridne's words bear no relation to the question at issue but wander into a disquisition on the structure of government in the Kirk, thereafter introducing an obscure reference to the weather and gardening. Note too the unconscious oxymoron in *ffirst, to Conclud*.

121. *wather*: 'weather'; B and C, followed by the printed texts, add *in the winter time*.

125. *Wher ar ... ar gon, Sir*: probably addressed to Covenant. The Moderator is much impressed by Whigridne's oracular utterances.
I fear: 'I'm afraid'. The Moderator has noted Covenant's *fear* and remarks, ironically, that he thinks Whigridne has banished it. B and C, followed by the printed texts, read the less pointed *I trow*.

127. *But still ... proposalls*: Covenant is not wholly convinced. He wishes more discussion of his proposals.

128–9. *A Comittee ... fears*: for Turbulent committees are the answer to all problems.

132. *privat Baptisme and Comunion*: two episcopalian practices condemned by Presbyterians, who held that all such ceremonies should be performed publicly during a church service. The relevance of this interjection to the matter under discussion is not clear.

134. *Multitud*: B and C, followed by the printed texts, reads *Tumult*.

134–9. *Lett us pray ... on gate*: cf. above, 1.3, 38n, etc.

139. *on gate*: '(on) one (and the same) way', 'of one mind'. B, C and the printed texts read *we go all one Gate*.

140–2. *I heir ... belive it*: the 1722 print lacks this passage.

140. *to be dissolved*: see below, 5.3, 5–6 etc.

142. *do not belive it*: as often, the Moderator is wrong.

144. *home stroack*: 'a blow that strikes home', 'a telling, mortal stroke' (against the Curates).The idiom is English rather than Scots; there is no parallel in *DOST* or *SND*. *OED*, however, gives two examples, both from a religious (Puritan) context: 'You hit me home' (Foxe 1837–41, VII, 281); 'God when he striketh, smiteth home' (Day 1586, 1, 137).

145. *Comitties*: more committees!

declinators: 'a formal plea or exception declining to admit the jurisdiction of a particular judge or court' (*DOST*); cf. above, 105–6 and n.

146. *depositions*: 'the testimonies given by a witness in court' (*DOST*). See above, 88n.

seekness: 'sickness'. For spiritual sickness, see above, 1.3, 55; 2.3, 144 and n.

acts of transportabilitie: cf. above, 2.3, 58 and n.

Act 4, Scene 3

The Abbagate: the gatehouse at the entrance to the Abbey of Holyrood and the palace of Holyroodhouse. The form is anglicised from the earlier *Abbey yett* (Chambers 1847: 247). The proscenium arch represents the gate itself; the shutters to the side represent the approach to the main buildings, the abbey and palace, painted on the back shutters. Huffie and his entourage enter stage left, the direction of Holyrood Park.

This scene is missing from the 1722 print, but present in all other sources.

shouldiers: 'soldiers'.

2–3. *disaffected ... Church and State*: i.e. he accuses him, on wholly inadequate grounds, of being an Episcopalian (Church) and a Jacobite (State).

3. *Guard*: the City Guard; see above, **Drammatis Personæ**, 26n; 2.1, 8n.

4. Stage direction: Soldier and Huntsman exeunt stage right in the direction of the Guardhouse.

8. Stage direction: Soldier and dogs exit by way of the proscenium arch in the direction of Holyroodhouse.

9. *Collonell's dogs*: presumably dogs belonging to the officer commanding Edinburgh Castle garrison.

13. *two myls within the toune*: 'within two miles of the town' (see above,

p. 35) where Huffie himself had been hunting and had invited Whigridne to join him; above, 3.1, 127ff.

16. Stage direction: Soldier returns from the direction of the palace.

17. *dog*: B and C, followed by the later printed texts, read *the little dog*.

17–18. *thorow the prison window*: B and C, followed by the later printed texts, omit *thorow* and *prison*.

18. *gate*: B and C, followed by the later printed texts, have the more probable reading *grate*, 'one of the spars between the bars of a grating' (*OED*, s.v. **Grate 8**; not in *DOST*). The reference is to the bars outside a cell window.

20. *Shuitt*: 'shoot'.

21. *littering*: 'idling', 'dawdling' (loitering).

Act 4, Scene 4

Parliament Close is the square between St Giles' and the former Parliament buildings. The shutters represent the Close, perhaps with part of St Giles' visible, and the entry to the Laigh Parliament. Will and Frank enter outer stage right, and pause to watch the crowd, and in particular the Privy Councillors arriving stage left for the meeting mentioned above, 3.1, 193. The scene is mainly occupied by the sketches (in effect, political cartoons) of individual Councillors provided by Will for the benefit of Frank, just returned from abroad.

1–4. *I cannot ... for her*: the idealistic Frank revolts at the scheme imposed on him by Laura, above, 4.1, 86–91.

2. *almost loss*: B has the better reading *almost as good loss*.
loss: 'lose'.

3. *double-necked Clock*: above, 3.1, 88n.
Covenant: above, pp. xvi–xvii; 1.3, 44n, 85n.
Confession of Faith : above, pp .xvii–xviii; 2.3, 72n.

5. *It must be ... young Lady*: the more pragmatic Will keeps a closer eye on the profit to be gained. The reference is to the 'fortunes' inherited by Violetta and Laura, characteristically a matter of much importance for Will.
2000 lb.: B reads *Twenty Thousand pounds*.

5–6. *the end's pleasant ... rough and odd*: variant of the proverbial 'The end crowns all (or, the work)' (*ODEP*, 220).

8. *looks weall*: 'has a brave, gallant appearance'; *look* is used in the sense 'has the appearance of being, seems to the sight' (*OED*, s.v. **Look 9**).

9–34. *Indeed ... historie*: a satiric portrait of Huffie, the earl of Leven; cf. above, **Drammatis Personæ**, 7n. Huffie agreed with Whigridne that he would attend the meeting of the Privy Council, above, 3.1, 193–209.

10. *big*: 'enterprising', 'important'.

12. *and he will* –: B and C, followed by the printed texts, insert the following words, assigned to Frank: *And what will he? Perhaps something of no great import.*

13. *saws*: 'proverbs', 'maxims', 'wise sayings', often used ironically; cf. Shakespeare, *As You Like It*, 2.7, 156: '[the Justice] Full of wise saws and modern instances'.

14. *interest*: 'the relation of being objectively concerned in something, by having a right or title to, a claim upon, or a share in' (*OED*, s.v. **Interest** 1). Compare and contrast above, 3.1, 137 and n.

16. *no party ... fixx him*: i.e. he could not maintain a consistent loyalty to any party.

22. *stat Hector*: obscure. If *stat* = 'stated', the phrase may mean 'a (self-) avowed Hector'. If *stat* = 'Estate', the estate of the nobility in parliament, 'the Thrie Estaitis', the meaning may be 'a person who plays the part of Hector in his Estate', with Hector, as in the *Iliad*, sole protector of his people. Note that the name Hector had by this time acquired the connotations of the *miles gloriosus*, the boastful but cowardly military bully, a stock comic character; cf. the verb 'hector' and the participle 'hectoring'. Cf. too the characterization of Huffie in relation to that of Thraso in Terence's *Eunuch*; above, p. liii.

23. *strouting*: 'blustering'.

branking: 'bearing oneself extravagantly', 'showing off'. B and C, followed by the printed texts, have the more English *bawling*.

25. *blazon*: 'coat of arms'.

26. *compounded in*: 'made up from'.

27. *his Lady's Whigrie*: above, **Drammatis Personæ**, 7n.

Whigrie: 'Whiggery', 'extreme presbyterian practices'.

29. *the thing*: B and C, followed by the later printed texts, read *the only thing*. The 1722 printed text has *the one thing*.

32–3. *underselled Judas*: Judas sold Christ for thirty pieces of silver (Matthew 26. 15).

34. *blazing*: 'boasting' (with overtones of *blazon*). B reads *blazoning*.

41–58: *Befor his Cuntry ... best securitie*: a hostile portrait of Robert Kerr (1636–1703), 4th earl (later 1st marquess) of Lothian, son of the cultivated, luke-warm Covenanter and half-hearted royalist, the 3rd earl, William Kerr (c. 1605–75). Robert Kerr inherited many of his father's characteristics. Both were probably influenced by the eirenic Englishman, Robert Leighton (1612–84), for twenty years minister of their home parish, Newbattle, Midlothian, then, 1661–71, bishop of Dunblane, thereafter briefly archbishop of Glasgow, a post from which he resigned in 1674. The younger Kerr was educated abroad, at Calvinist Leiden and Catholic Saumur, Angers and Paris, where his curriculum must have included law. He had some military experience before his succession to the title in 1671. In 1681 he signed the English Test Act, thus acknowledging himself an adherent of the Church of England. In 1686 he was briefly a Privy Councillor under James VII, but was soon dismissed. He supported the 1688 Revolution and in May 1689 regained his position on the Privy Council. In August of that year he became Justice-General, with supreme jurisdiction in criminal cases, a position which he retained until his death. He was appointed High Commissioner to the 1692 General Assembly, charged with implementing King William's recommendation that episcopalian ministers should be admitted to the Church, provided they accepted the Confession of Faith and accepted the authority of the presbyterian church courts. When the Assembly failed to implement those recommendations, Kerr dissolved it. He was blamed for the fiasco and spent much time thereafter in improvements to his house, Newbattle Abbey, and in playing his favourite stringed instruments. His health was not good. In 1701 he received the title of marquess. In 1702 he became a Commissioner for union with England. In February 1703 he died 'from a diseased gall bladder and the effects of *whooring and the clap* [gonorrhea]'; see article in *OxfDNB*.

42–4. *pleasant sort ... Bells letters*: grounds for most of this description will be found in the note immediately preceding.

43. *fineness*: 'showiness'.

44. *Bells letters*: '*belles lettres*', 'elegant or polite literature'. The first example of the phrase quoted in *OED* is from Steele's *Tatler*, 230 (1710): 'The Traders in History and Politicks, and the Belles Lettres'. The present example is a little earlier.

44–6. *such a damned figur ... Gentleman of Hell*: i.e. Kerr must owe his position to diabolic intervention.

45. *since he wes Clad in silk and Ermine*: i.e. 'since he became a judge'.

48. *fox*: B and C, followed by the later printed texts, read *fop*. The 1722 printed text absurdly reads *Son*.

long pedant speech: i.e. *The Earl of Lothian Justice general of the Kingdom of Scotland, his Discourse to the Lords of Justiciary at the Opening of the Court at Edinburgh January the 27th. 1690* (Edinburgh, 1690). The speech is not particularly long (two printed pages), nor particularly pedantic.

49. *against his predicessors*: Kerr's immediate predecessors as Justice-General – George Livingston, 3rd earl of Linlithgow (1684–9), James Drummond, 4th earl of Perth (1682–4) and William Douglas, 3rd earl of Queensberry (1680–2) – had rigorously imposed the law on Covenanters. Kerr does not mention them by name, but the implications of his discourse are clear.

50. *shelvs & splitting*: the third paragraph of the speech (p. 1) reads: 'I

171

desire not to look back, or make any Reflections upon the by past Miscarriages; I wish they were so buried in Oblivion, that there were no Remembrance nor Vestige, but in so far, as to be a Beacon to make us hold off from making Ship-wrack upon the same Rocks: I pray God save us from yet undiscovered Shelves.'

50. *shelvs*: 'reefs'.

splitting: 'shipwreck' (as when a ship *splits* on a reef).

50–1. *adding the graine ... equitie*: the final paragraph of the speech (p. 2) opens thus: 'And if (for my part) I should be so Happy, as but to add one grain weight to the Scale of Equity, I should esteem it the greatest Advantage.'

50. *graine weights*: the grain is the smallest unit of weight in the avoirdupois and other systems of measurement, equivalent to 0.0648 gram.

51–2. *seen abroad by that speech*: elliptic; 'seen (a copy of) that speech (when I was) abroad'.

53–8. *He'il tell you ... best securitie*: I have found no external confirmation of Will's assertions, which stand in marked contrast to the general tenor of Kerr's speech, where the focus is on 'the Divine Precept, of doing to another what we would have done to ourselves' (cf. Luke 6. 31).

Curiously, in the 1722 print, this speech is given to Frank.

56. *panall*: 'prisoner at the bar', 'defendant' (Scots legal term).

60. *Thomas of Mamsbury's State of Nature*: The reference is to Thomas Hobbes' *Leviathan* (1651) 1.13: 'In such condition, there is no place for Industry; because the fruit thereof is uncertain: and consequentlie no Culture of the Earth, no Navigation, nor use of the commodities that may be imported by Sea; no commodious Building; no Instruments of moving, and removing such things as require much force; no Knowledge of the face of the Earth; no account of Time; no Arts; no Letters; no Society; and which is worst of all, continuall feare, and danger of violent death; And the life of man, solitary, poore, nasty, brutish, and short.'

Hobbes (1588–1679) was born in Malmesbury, Wiltshire.

63. *Scarlett*: the usual Scots parliamentary robes were scarlet. By wearing a plainer garb, Whigridne demonstrates his extreme Presbyterianism.

my old phanatick inquisitor: i.e. Whigridne, the earl of Crawford; see above, 1.1, 15–40. Note the suggestion that he is the presbyterian equivalent of the Spanish Grand Inquisitor.

64. *mouths gon to the othr side*: i.e. his mood has changed. During his interview with Frank he was surly and suspicious; as he arrives for the Privy Council meeting he is in the best of tempers; cf. above, 3.1, 172–81.

For *othr*, B and C, followed by the printed texts, read *one*.

66. *worldlie wisdome*: usually regarded as the opposite of sanctity.

67. *dyed*: 'coloured (red)'.

dyed a Callender: Whigridne is a major presbyterian 'Saint'. In the church calendar, major saints have the day of their festivals marked in red – 'red-letter days'.

69. *his pocket*: i.e. the pocket-book in which Whigridne claims to keep a systematic, alphabetical list of Episcopalians, with notes of their offences; see above, 3.1, 195.

71–3. *His mouth ... meaneing*: as has been shown by many of Whigridne's remarks to the Committee, he has great difficulty in expressing himself lucidly.

73. *Staffe*: his staff of office as President of the Parliament.

Supporter: B and C, followed by the printed texts, read *pillar*.

75. *provost*: 'chief local magistrate and administrative official in a burgh, a town with a royal or baronial charter' (royal burgh or burgh of barony). Some were very small.

76. *20s. of common good*: the common good was 'the burgh fund consisting of profits of burgh lands, fees paid on admission of burgesses etc.' (Donaldson and Morpeth 1977: 44). A burgh with a common good of twenty shillings, one pound Scots, was extremely small.

77. *lay Elder*: cf. above, 1.3, 66; **Drammatis Personæ**, 15n.

77. *snail's horn*: horns are 'the tentacles of gastropods, especially of the snail and slug' (*OED*, s.v. **Horn 6**), extremely sensitive and vulnerable because tipped with the creature's eyes. As a consequence, snails are extremely averse to putting them in possible contact with anything else. In effect, they are cowards. Compare a passage from Pitcairne's exact contemporary, the episcopalian divine John Sage (1652–1711), later first non-diocesan bishop in Scotland, writing against Gilbert Rule (Mr Salathiel of the play): 'What human patience can be hardy enough for entering the lists with pure barking and whining? With original dullness? Who can think of arming himself against the horns of a snail?' (Preface to *The Fundamental Charter of Presbytery, as it hath been lately established in the Kingdom of Scotland, examin'd and disprov'd* [London, 1695], quoted in Reid 1982: 11).

79. *mack duity planie*: obscure; perhaps a mistranscription of *mack divinitie plainie* (make divinity complain or lament). B and C, followed by the printed texts, read *make Duty plain*, which, in context, lacks point.

81. *beloved*: Will is parodying the style of address in a presbyterian sermon.

83. *forfalting*: 'forfeiting' (his lands and rents).

83–4. *next revolutne*: i.e. the restoration of James VII.

86. *shittine monster*: portrait of the effective head of Scots government, the Secretary and King's Commissioner, George Melville (1636–1707), 4th Lord Melville and 1st earl of Melville, Huffie's father. Melville was 'low, thin, with a great Head, a long Chin, and little Eyes' (Macky, *Memoirs of*

the Secret Services, 203, quoted in *OxfDNB*, s.v. **Melville, George**, fourth
Lord Melville and first earl of Melville), which explains the description of
him here as a misshapen monster. He had been an adherent of Charles II's
illegitimate son, the protestant James Scott, duke of Monmouth, executed
for his rebellion against James VII and II in 1685. Before this, Melville
had already come under suspicion in connection with the Rye House plot
(1683) which aimed to make Monmouth rather than James successor to the
throne. Melville fled to the Netherlands, only returning after William and
Mary had been proclaimed. In May 1689 he became sole Secretary of State
for Scotland. In January 1690 he was appointed High Commissioner to the
Parliament and on 10 March first attended the Privy Council. In June of
that year he presided over legislation re-establishing presbyterian church
government.

86. *shittine*: 'defiled with excrement'.

87. *looks*: MS *looks looks*; dittography.

Coatch: 'coach'. As befits his office, Melville arrives in some state.

88. *some underclark second *man second**: the asterisks mark an addition to the MS in Pitcairne's hand. In context, the phrase indicates a very
minor official, deputy to a deputy to an assistant clerk, afraid of losing his
job.

B and C, followed by the printed texts, read *underclerk second man*.

89. *burden of informatne*: i.e. he is laden with official documents.

90. *spane*: 'span' (as unit of measurement), referring to Melville's dimin-
utive stature.

91. *bodie politique*: cf. 1.1, 88 and n. By his use of the phrase Pitcairne
makes an ironic identification of Melville with Hobbes' *Leviathan* (1651),
'called a Common-Wealth or State ... an Artificiall Man; though of greater
stature and strength than the Naturall, for whose protection and defence it
was intended' (Hobbes, *Leviathan*, 'The Introduction'). Will's subsequent
words (69–77) describe the Scottish Leviathan in some detail.

92. *confoundedly*: 'confusedly' (reflecting the confusion in the body
politick).

92. *excressents ... kirk*: the excrescents are the legs, which should give
support and stability to the entire body. Melville's shaky legs represent what
Will regards as the equally shaky underpinning of the state by the presbyterian church.

94–6. *on his breast ... hereticos*: the Scottish Leviathan carries his policy
documents in bags, one, presumably the most cherished, at his breast and
two on his back. According to Will, the first contains the Covenant (probably the National Covenant of 1638), one of the others the Westminster
Confession of Faith (1643), the other probably Calvin's *Defensio ortho-
doxae fidei de sacra Trinitate, contra prodigiosos errores Michaelis Serueti*

Hispani (Geneva, 1554), a tract 'which defended the ancient Augustinian principle of repressing heresy by the secular sword' (Wendel 1965: 98), and which was directed against Michael Servetus (1511–53), burned at the stake in Geneva for his anti-trinitarian heresy. Will changes the title of the tract to make clear the present implications for such heresies, in Calvinist eyes, as Episcopalianism.

96. *jure gladii Coercendos esse hereticos*: 'heretics are to be repressed by the law of the sword'.

100. *begets monsters*: the earl had eight sons; see too next note.

104–6. *familie ... rulers & governours*: Melville himself was Secretary, his eldest son Alexander was Treasurer Depute and his third son David (Huffie) Keeper of Edinburgh Castle. All were members of the Privy Council.

112. *Catterpillars*: cf. Shakespeare, *Richard II*, 2.3, 164–5: 'Bushy, Bagot, and their complices,/ The caterpillars of the commonwealth', the figure perhaps derived from the title of Stephen Gosson's *The School of Abuse, Conteining a plesaunt inuectiue against Poets, Pipers, Plaiers, Iesters and such like Caterpillers of the Commonwelth* (London, 1579).

112–13. *old wry-necked fellow*: James Dalrymple (1619–95), 1st Viscount Stair. Early in his career he became a regent in Glasgow University, responsible originally for Greek and dialectic, but later undertaking supervision of students through the entire curriculum and also the publication of their graduating *theses philosphicae*. Throughout his life he remained a scholar and philosopher. He also had some military experience. As a lawyer, admitted advocate in 1648, he was self-taught. During the Cromwellian interlude he served as a legal commissioner, but retained favour after the Restoration, becoming Lord President and a member of the Privy Council in 1671. In 1681 the first edition of his epoch-making *Institutions of the Law of Scotland* was published in Edinburgh. In the same year he refused to take the Test oath, resigned as Lord President, and fled to the Netherlands. He returned with William, was re-appointed Lord President in 1690 and granted the title Viscount Stair.

By his opponents, and with some cause, Stair was regarded as a master schemer for his own, and his family's advancement. 'From the beginning of the revolution, if not before, Sir James Dalrymple and his eldest son were planning the re-establishment and expansion of the family interest' (Riley 1979: 16).

wry-necked: Stair had a 'twisted neck concealed behind his full-bottomed wig' (*OxfDNB*, s.v. **Dalrymple, James**).

115. *against natur*: because run by such unnatural monsters as Dalrymple and Melville.

116. *true-blew*: 'ultra-presbyterian'.

175

118. *philologie*: 'liberal education' (in Latin and Greek).

118. *fool in print*: Will intends a reference to Dalrymple's *Institutes* (perhaps because he had a preference for the rival *Institutes of the Laws of Scotland* [Edinburgh, 1684] by the royalist and Jacobite Sir George Mackenzie of Rosehaugh [1636–91]) and probably also to his huge *Physiologia Nova Experimentalis in qua, generales notiones Aristotelis, Epicuri, & Cartesii supplentur: errores deteguntur & emendantur: atque claræ distinctæ & speciales causæ præcipuorum experimentorum, aliorumque phænomenωn naturalium, aperiuntur* (Leiden, 1686). The Newtonians Pitcairne and Gregorie, speaking through Will, may well have particularly disapproved of this last, a treatise on physics. Will may also have had in mind the anonymous tracts on political and religious affairs attributed to Dalrymple. These include *An Apologie for presbyterie, for removing prejudices. By a well-wisher to the true Gospel ministry* (Edinburgh, 1689), *A Political Conference between Aulicus, a Courtier; Damas, a countryman; and Civicus, a Citizen; clearing the original of civil government, the powers and duties of soveraigns and subjects, etc.* (London, 1689) and *A farther Vindication of the Present Government of the Church of Scotland (established in a Presbyterian Parity), from some mistakes about its nature and native consequences, occasioned by the Apologie published for Presbyterie in the year 1689 and by what hath since ensued in this Church and Kingdom* (Edinburgh, 1691).

120. *generatione*: Stair had five sons, four of whom had already become lawyers and politicians of some note.

The eldest, John (1648–1707), had been (1688–9) Lord Justice Clerk and was now Lord Advocate; from 1691 he was joint Secretary, at first with Melville, later with James Johnston. His part in the planning of the Glencoe massacre (1692) led in 1695 to his dismissal as Secretary, but he continued in parliament as one of the two representatives of the royal burgh of Stranraer, Wigtownshire. He became 1st earl of Stair in 1703.

James (1650–1719), was one of the principal clerks of the Court of Session, but is better remembered as an antiquary. In 1697 he was created a baronet as Sir James Dalrymple of Kelloch.

Hew (1652–1737) was one of the two parliamentary representatives of the royal burgh of New Galloway, Kirkcudbrightshire. In 1695 he became Dean of the Faculty of Advocates. In 1698 he succeeded his father as Lord President after a vacancy. He was made a baronet as Sir Hew Dalrymple of North Berwick and took the legal title Lord North Berwick

Thomas (1663–1725) became First Physician to the King in Scotland.

David (c. 1665–1721) was admitted to the Faculty of Advocates in 1688. By 1698 he was one of the two parliamentary representatives of the royal burgh of Culross, Fife. In 1700 he acted successfully for the defence when

Pitcairne was arraigned for suspected Jacobite correspondence. A year later he was made a baronet as Sir David Dalrymple of Hailes. In 1703 he became joint Solicitor General. He was Lord Advocate 1709–11 and 1714–20, Dean of the Faculty of Advocates 1712–21.

The series of Latin poems composed by Pitcairne on Viscount Stair and his family (MacQueen and MacQueen 2009: 184–7) reveals an attitude notably different from the one expressed here.

122. *westerne brood*: the original Stair estate was in Ayrshire. Stair himself acquired extensive properties in Wigtownshire.

old Sir Harries: 'absolute devils'.

123. *pettship*: the same as *petery*, 'the occupation or characteristic activity of a "peat", an advocate who is the favourite or protégé of a particular judge' (*DOST*, s.v. **Pet(e, Peat, Pait** n³). Here the particular judge is the Lord President, Viscount Stair, and the advocates to whom he grants favours are his sons.

125. *suum cuique*: Latin, 'to each his own', a reference to one of the principles which Stair regarded as the foundation of law, 'Honeste vivere, alterum non laedere, suum cuique tribuere' (Stair 1981: 74, 'to live honourably, not to harm another, to give each his own', quoting Justinian and the *Digest*). Jacobites commonly applied the phrase *suum cuique* particularly to the exiled King James, a usage obviously unpleasing to the Dalrymples, whence the qualification *at least in on caice*.

126. *hangd yet*: after this, C and the later printed editions insert the following:

Frank: These are gentlemen of the long robe too; they are your new Lords of Session, I'll warrant you.

Will. Ay, they are new judges all over, and novices too; many of them neither know nor care for the old laws and constitutions of this kingdom; and for the new ones, they make any thing of them they please. They are the strangest mix'd multitude that ever was seen; some of them are Presbyterians, some Episcopals, and most of them have no religion at all.

Frank. But they must profess to be Presbyterians.

Will. Yes, that they do, and would profess any thing for their interests. Lying, cheating, and rebellion, are hereditary to many of them, and fall as naturally to their share, as the name they bear, or their father's estate. Some of their names make a greater figure in the registers of the kirk, than in the records of the state; for public adulteries are now become the mark of a true reformer; and they who invade other men's properties are thought the only fit men to secure ours. – Sees thou that dark gloomy ey'd fellow with the wooden leg? He may be called crooked justice indeed, for his mind is as deformed as his body; he's a true emblem of the whole bench. In short, Sir, that judicature, which was so famous for justice and literature when you

177

went abroad, is now patch'd up of a pack of country lairds, and old sense-less, greedy, covetous clerks, with two or three pick'd advocates, who are purely led by their interest and honour: many of them have not the knowl-edge to administrate justice, and they have all of them taken the assurance, and sworn against it.

The *fellow with the wooden leg* is Sir David Hume or Home of Crossrig (1643–1707), who became a lord of session in 1689, a lord of justiciary in 1690. He lost his leg in 1681, the result of an accident. See *OxfDNB*.

The phrase *famous for justice and literature* is an oblique reference to the achievements of the former Lord President, Sir George Lockhart (c. 1630–89) and the former Lord Advocate, Sir George Mackenzie (1636–91) of Rosehaugh. Pitcairne celebrated the two in Latin epitaphs (MacQueen and MacQueen 2009: 68–75, 305–8, 311–13).

127. *Caball*: an oblique reference equating the group described to the earlier unpopular group of Charles II's ministers – Clifford, Ashley, Buck-ingham, Arlington and Lauderdale – who favoured the alliance with Louis XIV, which led to the disastrous Second Dutch War of 1672–4. The Cabal remained in power from 1667 to 1673.

128–32. *Yes ... good old cause*: a difficult passage. It would appear that this group, unlike the earlier Cabal, was not really concerned with political power, but only with their own immediate physical satisfaction, always with the qualification that the source of their pleasures must be protestant. They are *zealous reformers*, unwilling to have any flirtation with Catholicism. This is Pitcairne's dismissive portrayal of the faction which, from 1689 to 1692, John Hay (1626–97), 2nd earl, later 1st marquess of Tweeddale, attempted, rather ineffectually, to foster from the distance of London, partly in his own interests, partly in defence of Episcopalians, partly against Melville, still more against Stair's eldest son, Sir John Dalrymple. An administrative reshuffle brought Tweeddale the Chancellorship in 1692.

130. *singing*: B and C, followed by the printed texts, read *sighing*. The reading in A is perhaps affected by *singer*, later in the same line.

prisbiterian sweet singer: a slighting reference to the Sweet Singers of Borrowstounness (Bo'ness, West Lothian), also known as Gibbites, followers of Muckle John Gibb (d. 1720?), a Cameronian shipmaster, who had absorbed Anabaptist ideas in Holland. In 1680 twenty-six of his women followers, many married, together with three men, took to the Pentland Hills, south-west of Edinburgh, where they spent much of their time singing the metrical versions of Psalms 74, 79, 80, 83 and 117, all, save the last, laments over the destruction of Jerusalem and appeals to God for its resto-ration. Psalm 117 is brief, two verses appealing to the nations to praise the Lord 'for his merciful kindness is great toward us: and the truth of the Lord endureth for ever'. The group received the ironic name Sweet Singers.

Afterwards they retreated to the wild country between Lothian and Tweeddale, where all received Old Testament names, Gibb himself becoming King Solomon, a name with obvious sexual implications, also exploited elsewhere in the play. In May 1681 they were arrested and imprisoned. Many of the women were quickly released. Gibb himself eventually attracted the rather amused attention of the Royal Commissioner to the Scottish Parliament, the duke of York (later James VII) and in August he too was released. His delusions became wilder and in 1684 he was re-arrested and sentenced to transportation. He probably remained in New York colony for the rest of his life, gaining a reputation for spiritual power among the local Native Americans.

132. *good old cause*: usually Protestantism, in particular Presbyterianism; here self-interest and indulgence.

132–6. *one of them ... human reason*: John Hay (1645–1713) Master of Yester, later (1697) succeeding his father as 2nd marquess of Tweeddale. He was the ineffective custodian of his father's interests in Scotland. Lockhart describes him thus: 'The Marquis of Tweedale never obtained any other character than that he was a well-meaning, but simple, man. And I have the charity to believe he was forced against his will, by his friends and these he trusted (who made a meer tool of him), to enter into many of the bad measures he pursued. So I may safely say he was the least ill-meaning man of his party, either through inclination or capacity' (Szechi 1995: 66). Will is less charitable.

Despite his infirmities, Hay held many important offices. In particular he was a Privy Councillor before and after the Revolution.

137. *plott*: another instance of the word; see above, 2.2, 51 and n.

137. *Chamberlin' wife*: steward's wife. There may be a reference to some contemporary scandal, but, if so, I have failed to identify it.

141–84. *That's a pack ... Case of Alledgiance*: extended description of the Club, 'an association formed by the opposition to the ministers of William of Orange' (Donaldson and Morpeth 1977: 42). It met at Penston's tavern in the High Street, where it planned action to disrupt Melville's administration. A number of disparate interests were combined. 'Chagrin gave leadership and direction to the dissidents ... Montgomerie [Sir James Montgomerie (d. 1694) of Skelmorlie, Ayrshire] was ambitious for power rather than the spoils of office, and this distinguished him from his contemporaries, most of whom could be life-rented if not bought and sold ... Skelmorlie had hoped to be secretary and would settle for nothing less. Argyll [Archibald Campbell (1658–1703), 10th earl and 1st duke of Argyll], too, was offended at being passed over and made common cause with Montgomerie. More honest but less acute and influential pillars of the club ... were Sir Patrick Hume of Polwarth [1641–1724], Fletcher of Saltoun [1653–1716] and Forbes of

Culloden [c. 1644–1704]. Many of the military officers were also smitten by politics of the factious, opportunistic type. In addition some Jacobites like James Ogilvie [1663–1730; in 1701 created earl of Seafield] acted with the club, partly to protect themselves from attack and partly to keep matters unresolved as long as possible in the well-founded belief that this might be of service to King James' (Ferguson 1968: 7–8). Also associated with the Club were such men as William Johnston (1664–1721), 4th earl, later (1701) 1st marquess, of Annandale, and William Ross (c. 1656–1738), 12th baron Ross.

141. *Jacobitish Williamits*: the Club included among its members some who had held office under King James and were now eager for the same privilege under King William. They included William Douglas (1637–95), 1st duke of Queensberry, and Sir George Mackenzie of Tarbat (1630–1714), 1st Viscount Tarbat, later (1703) 1st earl of Cromartie. They form the group now 'rewarding the favors done the(m) be K.J. on ... K.W.' (113–14). On the other hand, some Williamite members – Annandale, for instance, and Ross – were prepared to accept the restoration of James, provided it entailed the transfer of power from Melville and his associates to themselves.

144. *the(m)*: MS *the*.

duty full sone: William became James' son-in-law by his marriage in 1677 to Mary, James' daughter by his first wife, Anne Hyde; above, 1.1, 144n. He was also, incidentally, James' nephew; his mother, James' sister, was Mary Stuart (1631–60), daughter of Charles I and wife of William II, prince of Orange.

144–5. *lawll successor*: *lawll* probably = **Lel(e, Leil(l**, 'legally valid, legal' (*DOST*); cf. Gilbert Hay, *Buke of the Law of Armys* 4. cix, ad fin: 'Bot trewly, as to the successioun that the pape has maid with the consent of the Quene Jownelle, I traist it be bathe lele and lauffull.' It is difficult to account for the spelling *lawll*; there may be a conflation with **Lawfull**, used by Hay as a synonym.

The phrase is used ironically.

145. *They ... restor K.J.*: a reference to the conspirators who took part in Montgomerie of Skelmorlie's plot: 'In the winter of 1689 Montgomerie had concocted a fantastic scheme whereby presbyterians and Jacobites were to work together for the restoration of James VII, who was supposedly to countenance a system of presbyterian church government ... the plot was detected, and the main men involved tumbled over themselves to make abject, but disingenuous, confessions. The fullest relation was made by Annandale in London in the summer of 1690; that of lord Ross was less trustworthy, while Montgomerie, who had also gone to London in an attempt to win favourable terms, lost his nerve and went into hiding'

(Ferguson 1968: 18; for more detail see P. A. Hopkins, 'Sir James Mont-gomerie of Skelmorlie' in Cruikshanks and Corp: 1995, 39–60).

plott: another instance of the word.

146. *misticall letter*: not certainly identified, but perhaps part of the content of the 'black box' sent by King James to Skelmorlie; see Riley 1979: 40–41.

148. *to the king*: in place of this, B and C, followed by the printed texts, read *escape and all this suffering for the King*.

149–50. *Duks ... Lords*: i.e. probably, the duke of Queensberry, the marquess of Atholl, the earls of Annandale, Arran and Linlithgow, Viscount Tarbet and the 12ᵗʰ Baron Ross.

151. *these with papers in on of ther hands*: probably the delegation sent to London in 1689 with the offer of the crown to William and Mary, if they accepted the proposals set out by the convention of that year, in particular the Claim of Right, the Scottish counterpart of the English Declaration of Right, stating that James had forfeited the throne, and offering it to William and Mary. The Claim included a clause in which prelacy was condemned as 'a great and insupportable grievance and trouble to this Nation'. All three members of the delegation – the earl of Argyll for the Lords, Sir James Montgomerie for the barons and Sir John Dalrymple for the burgesses – were committed presbyterians.

156. *plott & reveall*: another probable reference to Montgomerie's plot, from which Argyll and Dalrymple seem in fact to have remained aloof.

Note yet another recurrence of the word *plott*.

157. *placate*: to publish by a placard 'a sheet of paper written or printed on one side, suitable for public display' (*DOST*, s.v. **Placard, Placat(t)**).

159. *modells*: 'patterns', hence 'plans', 'plots', 'notions' (usage not recorded in *DOST*, *SND* or *OED*).

159. *Merks*: *merk* is a money of account, two-thirds of a pound Scots or 13s. 4d. By the late seventeenth century the pound Scots was roughly equivalent to an English shilling. 1000 merks, which had once seemed a fortune, had thus, by the time of the play, become an impressive-sounding, but relatively small sum; cf. the lament for the old Scots money in Galt's *The Last of the Lairds*: 'It was a black day for Scotland that saw the Union signed, for on that day the pound sterling came in among our natural coin, and, like Moses' rod, swallow't up at ae gawpe, plack, bodle, mark, and bawbie, by which monie a blithe ranting roaring rental of langsyne has dwynet and dwinlet into the hungry residue of a wadset' (Gordon 1976: 9).

163. *politicks*: 'statesmen', 'politicians' (*DOST*, s.v. **Politik B. 1**). B reads *Politicos*, the 1722 printed text *Politicans*, the later printed texts *Politicians*.

165–71. *A Calfe ... to gett on*: probably a derisive reference to Archibald

Campbell, 10ᵗʰ earl (from 1701 1ˢᵗ duke) of Argyll. During the 1680s he
lived in London in great poverty. As a result of his father's refusal in 1681 to
give unqualified assent to the Test Act, the Argyll estates had been forfeited.
In 1685, when his father led a rebellion against James VII and II and was
executed, young Campbell threw himself on the royal mercy, turned temporary Catholic, and offered to serve against his father, thus obtaining a small
pension from the king. In 1688 Sir James Montgomerie brought him over
to the Netherlands, whence he returned to London with King William, and
afterwards to Edinburgh. His return is metaphorically described as 'a declaratione that he hath not a pocks' – i.e. the he is not a Catholic or a supporter
of King James.

He became one of the delegates who offered William and Mary the
Scottish crown. He became a member of the Club, opposed to Melville's
government, but did not really become prominent as a politician until the
later 1690s. His private life was dissolute. In 1696 he and his wife of almost
twenty years separated. His death resulted from stab wounds gained in a
brawl in a brothel.

166. *north Quintra*: 'north country', i.e. 'Highland'.

166. *feil*: 'fool' (NE dialect form).

172. *disbanded*: B reads the less satisfactory *discontented*.

173. *ther old Master*: King James.

ar now mocked: i.e. the regiments have been disbanded.

new on: 'new one', i.e. King William.

174. *on ... deil's Coyn*: not identified.

176–8. *young ... rebellion*: a reference to the savage purgation of King's
College, Aberdeen, in 1690. I have not identified the *spark of 22*, but he was
clearly a soldier, a dragoon, entrusted with the 'purgation' of the university,
'dragooning' it into allegiance to King William ('rebellion') and ultra-Pres-
byterianism ('Whigrie').

178–81. *Collnell ... as himselfe*: not identified.

179. *in buff*: 'in the buff', 'naked'.

179. *Killickrangie*: see above, p. 115; 2.1, 26n, 32.

183. *new doctors*: not identified.

183. *old ones*: the Aberdeen doctors, a scholarly group of professors and
ministers, the best known of whom are John Forbes of Corse (1593–1648),
professor of divinity in King's College, and Robert Baron (c. 1596–1639),
professor of divinity in Marischal College, both in Aberdeen. They were
active in a pamphlet war against the National Covenant (1638), opposing
Samuel Rutherford during his exile in Aberdeen (above 3.3, 101–2n).
Forbes also opposed the Solemn League and Covenant (1643) and as a
consequence went into exile in Holland. His great work, *Instructiones*

historico-theologicae de doctrina Christiana, was published in Amsterdam (1645). He was able to return to Scotland in 1646, but died not long after.

184. *Sharlock, Case of Alledgiance*: William Sherlock (1639/40–1707) was a Church of England clergyman, who wrote against both Dissenters and Catholics. Initially, at the Revolution, he declined to take the oath of allegiance to William and Mary, but soon thought better of it, writing in his own defence 'The Case of the Allegiance due to Sovereign Powers stated and Resolved according to Scripture and Reason, and the principles of the Church of England. With a more particular respect to the oath lately enjoyned, of allegiance to their present Majesties, K. William and Q. Mary', dated London 1691, but actually published in late 1690.

187. *dennertym*: dinner-time, i.e. probably 12 noon. The time was perhaps indicated off-stage by chiming a bell, representing St Giles' bell or that of the Tron-kirk, so much disliked by Robert Fergusson (McDiarmid 1956: 97–9); cf. above, 1.2, 67 and n. This is the time at which Violetta has arranged (above, 3.1, 75) that Will and Frank are to call on the Old Ladie.

188–9. *bespeack the Curate*: i.e. make arrangements for their marriages to Violetta and Laura.

190. *Cloaths are ready*: i.e. garments for their disguise as presbyterian clergymen.

Act 5, Scene 1

The Cross was in the High Street, about one third of the way from St Giles' to the Nether Bow Port. It was 'a handsome octagonal building ... surmounted by a pillar bearing the Scottish unicorn' and was 'the great centre of gossip ... The principal coffee-houses and booksellers' shops were close to this spot. The chief merchants, the leading official persons, the men of learning and talents, the laird, the noble, the clergyman, were constantly clustering hereabouts during certain hours of the day. It was the very centre and cynosure of the old city' (Chambers 1847: 168). The building was probably painted on the back shutters for this scene, with representations of other buildings on the side shutters.

As 'the great centre of gossip', the Cross is the natural place for Novell and Visioner to meet and ply their trade. Their gossip soon turns to the use of classical Latinity and to mathematics, the latter already the subject of a brief discussion in 3.3, 1–19. Both, however, are relevant to the Scottish church and universities in the late seventeenth century and therefore thematically to the play; see above, p. lx.

1. *Good morrow*: the greeting indicates that the assumed time is still morning. The action is to be regarded as more or less simultaneous with that of the preceding scene.

1–2. *quhat is all on*: 'which is much the same'.

3–4. *late battle ... Dauphin takne*: a typical piece of news-mongering; cf. above 1.1, 241–4; Jonson, *Staple of News*:

> They give out here, the grand signior
> Is certainly turn'd Christian; and to clear
> The controversy 'twixt the pope and him,
> Which is the Antichrist, he means to visit
> The church at Amsterdam this very summer
> And quit all marks of the beast.   (3.1, 269–74)

The grand signior is the Moslem sultan of Turkey; Holland was a strenuously protestant place; the Pope, as often in protestant propaganda, is equated with the Antichrist mentioned in 1 and 2 John.

The source of Visioner's story is presumably a *Gazette*; cf. above, 1.1, 215–40; for the sometimes fantastic unreliability of these publications, cf. *Tarugo's Wiles* 3, pp. 24–7 (Sydserff 1668).

2. *late battle*: after the capture of Mons (8 April 1691) the only battle of note was Leuze (20 September 1691), won by the French.

Dauphin: Louis de France (1661–1711), only son of Louis XIV and Maria Theresa. He commanded forces, not in Flanders, but on the middle Rhine.

3–4. *to all intents and purposes*: proverbial (Wilson 1970, 405).

5–6. *Cuius Contrarium est Verum*: Latin: 'the opposite of which is true'. There may be a reference to a song, popular in England at least during the seventeenth century and sometimes given a political slant, the refrain of which ran 'Oh, the cleane contrary way'.

7–8. *Dauphin ... bred protestant*: i.e. he is to become Salathiel's pupil at Edinburgh University, the Tounis College. As the Dauphin at this time was thirty years old, the news should have sounded improbable, even to Visioner. Perhaps he has confused the Dauphin with his eldest son, Louis (1682–1712), duc de Bourgogne, who himself briefly became Dauphin after the death of his father. Louis XIV was eventually (1719) succeeded by his great-grandson, Louis XV (1710–74).

8, 14. *Mr*: 'Magister', 'Master'; i.e. schoolmaster, tutor.

10. *present tyrant*: Louis XIV.

12–46. *learned his Latine ... sounds weall*: the discussion turns primarily on Salathiel's poor Latinity. Visioner's remarks illustrate the general decline of humanistic studies among the Presbyterians, a decline which became precipitous after the 'purging' of the Scottish universities. Humanistic studies turned first and foremost on the refinements of a classical Latin style, exemplified by the works of such earlier Scots as Hector Boece,

George Buchanan, John Barclay, Arthur Johnston, and by Pitcairne's own Latin poems and his prose *Dissertatio de Legibus Historiæ Naturalis* and *Epistola Archimedis ad Regem Gelonem*.

14. *under ane ill Mr for that*: B and C, followed by the later printed texts, read *on an ill road for it*; the 1722 printed text *in an ill case for it.*

15. *Prisciane*: Priscianus (early sixth century AD), Latin grammarian, author of *Institutiones Grammaticae*, which, together with the *Ars Major* and *Minor* of Donatus (fourth century AD) long served as the basic authority on Latin grammar and usage.

16. *true Latine*: i.e. classical Latin, the language of Cicero and Virgil, regarded as a model by renaissance humanists and their successors.

18. *ane oratne*: 'one of the speeches said in the college this winter' (below, **Preface**, p. 225).

21–2. *Roman Latine*: i.e. *true Latine*. Visioner misunderstands the term.

24–5. *Roman popish Latine*: scholastic Latin, the Latin of the Roman Catholic church services. After *Latine*, B and C, followed by the printed texts, read *the language of the Beast. I have that Charitie for Mr Salathiel: you might as soon Induce him to hear Mass as to speak Roman popish Latine*; cf. below, 28–9.

28. After *worse!*, B and C, followed by the printed texts, insert *that's Pagan Latine.*

29. *presbyterian Latin*: i.e. Latin like that used by Gilbert Rule in 'his Latin speeches, or rather his Scotch speeches ending in Latin terminations' (below, **Preface**, p. 226); dog-Latin; for a specimen see below, 34–5.

assemblie: the General Assembly of the Church of Scotland.

30. **the language of the whore**: inserted in Pitcairne's hand.

whore: the Roman Catholic church, believed by many Protestants to have been prefigured by the biblical 'great whore that sitteth upon many waters' (Revelation 17. 1).

34–5. *Si aliquis ... guiltus Idolatrie*: supposedly 'If any man will worship a false god, or the true God, as has not been prescribed [or 'as is not in Scripture'?], that man is guilty of idolatry.' *Aliquis*, however, means 'someone', not 'any'; *virus* therefore is unnecessary and, of course, the correct form of the word is *vir*. *Colebit* does not mean 'worship', but 'cherish, care for, protect, be the guardian of'; *fasum* for *falsum* is influenced by Scots *fause*. The phrase *falsum deum* suggests 'deceptive, deceitful divinity' rather than 'false god'; in context *ut non scryptum est*, literally 'as it has not been written', is meaningless. In B, C and the printed texts, the reading *prescriptum* for *scryptum* does not improve matters. The second *virus* is unnecessary as well as incorrect. *Guiltus* is not Latin but English/ Scots 'guilty' with a Latin nominal suffix. *Idolatrie* (*Idolatriae*) is a late borrowing from Greek, found only in Church Latin.

The **Preface** (below, p. 225) states that the sentence occurred in 'a public lecture', apparently given in winter 1690/91 and that it became notorious. No MS or printed exemplar of the lecture appears to have survived.

36–8. *Ye may ... popistic Latin**: inserted in Pitcairne's hand; see above, 24–5n.

40–41. *Biblia ... supernaturalibus*: 'construed' by Visioner, below, 42–6. In Church Latin, as in the Greek from which the word is borrowed, *biblia* is neuter pl., 'books', referring to the individual 'books' which make up the Bible; *biblia*, fem. sg., as here, is only found in very late texts. *Apprehendere*, in the sense 'grasp with the mind, understand' is first found in a late medical author, the African Caelius Aurelianus (fifth century AD). The combination of *apprehendere*, used in this sense, with *potest* is doubly barbarous. Neither *mediis* ([by] means), nor *supernaturalibus* (supernatural) is classical Latin; *supernaturalis* appears to be a coinage by St Thomas Aquinas (c. 1225–74).

45. **with -bus & -orum**: inserted in Pitcairne's hand; not in B, C or the later printed texts. The 1722 print has *bus* and *oribus*. *-bus* is the termination of the dative and ablative pl. in Latin nouns of the 3rd, 4th and 5th declensions and adjectives of the 3rd declension; *-orum* is the ending of the genitive pl. in nouns of the 2nd, 3rd, 4th and 5th declensions, adjectives of the 2nd and 3rd declensions. In prose and verse both endings were often used to assist rhythm and balance.

49. *freight*: 'panic', 'terror'. The effect is stronger than that of modern 'fright'; cf. Shakespeare, *Othello*, 2.3, 232–4:

> Myself the crying fellow did pursue,
> Lest by his clamour, as it so fell out,
> The town might fall in fright.

late persecutne: the so-called Killing Time, the years 1681–85 when the prosecution of the Covenanters reached its height. Gilbert Rule was not then in Scotland.

50–1. *devill's Cichen fyre*: *Cichen* is 'kitchen'. For a related use of the metaphor, cf. in Henryson's *Preiching of the Swallow*:

> The bodie to the wormis keitching go,
> The saull to fyre, to euerlestand pane.
> Quhat help is than this calf, thir gudis vane,
> Quhen thow art put in Luceferis bag,
> And brocht to hell, and hangit be the crag? (Fox 1981, 75, 1932–6)

The body goes to the grave, the worms' kitchen; the soul, like a dead game-bird, is put in Lucifer's bag, then hung in his kitchen until it is ripe for eating.

bougle: 'bogle', 'ghost', 'phantom'.

53–4. *Cora, Dathan & Abiram*: Korah, Dathan and Abiran, who rebelled against Moses and Aaron in the wilderness 'and the earth opened her mouth and swallowed them up' (Numbers 16. 32).

57. *media vox*: 'middle voice', the 'voice' of the Greek verb, intermediate between active and passive, which 'generally signifies that the subject performs an action *upon himself* or *for his own benefit*' (Goodwin 1894: 90). Visioner has already (18) credited Salathiel with knowledge of Greek; it would appear that he adorned his lectures with the minutiae of Greek grammar.

57. *sinecategormatice*: see above, 3.3, 9 and n.

61–63. *Spoyled much ... you know quhat*: an early instance of this unsavoury trope. Rule was a prolific author.

62. ***paper***: inserted in Pitcairne's hand.

65–6. *against some ... renoune*: Rule's books are mainly controversial; e.g. *A Modest Answer to Dr Stillingfleet's Irenicum, by a learned Pen* (London, 1680), in response to *Irenicum. A weapon-salve for the churches wounds. Or the Divine Right of particular forms of church-government* (London, 1661), by Edward Stillingfleet (1635–99), bishop of Worcester, or his *Vindication of the Church of Scotland* (Edinburgh, 1691) and his *Second Vindication* (Edinburgh, 1691), directed against *The case of the present afflicted clergy in Scotland* by John Sage (1652–1711), *Historical Relation of the late General Assembly, held at Edinburgh from Octob. 16. to Nov. 13. in the year 1690* (London, 1691), by John Cockburn (1652–1729), and *A Memorial for His Highness the Prince of Orange* (London, 1691), by Sir George Mackenzie of Tarbat ((1630–1714). His opponents were all Scots and Episcopalians; for Sage, see above, 4.4, 77n.

70–118. *Government ... puppies*: the actions of Salathiel as Principal of the College are judged, by Novell at least, in terms of Hobbes' analysis of government (*Leviathan* (1651), c. 19, 'Of the severall kinds of Commonwealth by Institution ...', and c. 29, 'Of those things that Weaken, or tend to the DISSOLUTION of a Common-wealth').

70. *no Government at all*: i.e. it is not a monarchy; Salathiel's word in the College is not law. Nor does the student-body, the people, have the final say; it is not a democracy. Nor is it an aristocracy. The consequences are necessarily fatal; 'For whereas the stile of the antient Roman Commonwealth, was, The Senate, and People of Rome: neither Senate, nor People pretended to the whole power; which first caused the seditions, of Tiberius Gracchus, Caius Gracchus, Lucius Saturninus, and others; and afterwards the warres between the Senate and the People, under Marius and Sylla; and again under Pompey and Caesar, to the Extinction of their Democraty' (*Leviathan*, 1651, c. 29, p. 171).

73. *People, say on!*: 'People, forsooth!'; literally, 'People, speak out!'

187

(*DOST*, s.v. **Say, Sa** v. **11**). This particular idiom is not recorded. Perhaps rather 'People, let someone say.'

Malguided: (not in *OED* or *DOST*) 'ill-guided', 'misguided', probably with overtones of *malignant* in the next line.

rambling: 'unsettled'.

74. **Yo**: inserted in Pitcairne's hand.

malignant: 'episcopalian'.

Masters: Regents and professors, the teaching staff of the College.

75. **warp**: (correction, in Pitcairne's hand, of MS *wranp*), 'a perversion or perverse inclination of the mind' (*OED*, s.v. **Warp 8**). The present example is considerably earlier than any quoted in *OED*.

76. *fools' scollars*: 'pupils of foolish malignant Masters'.

changed: 'expelled', 'purged'.

80. *Conventione*: meeting of the Scottish Three Estates held with less formality than a parliament; it had no judicial but only legislative and tax-imposing powers. In 1689 a convention rather than a parliament declared that James had abdicated and acknowledged William and Mary as monarchs.

84. *huft and hist*: 'huffed and hissed'. B has *me* as object, C and the printed texts *us*. The student body came from predominantly episcopalian families.

huft: this usage is not recorded in *DOST* or *OED*; *SND* has '**Huff**, *v.*, *n. int.* **III** *int.* "Of a sudden flying movement: puff!"<|>', quoting a single example, a verse by Hew Ainslie (d. 1878), first published in 1892, 'Whan, huff! aff she's flying,/ Flaff, like a flee', with which cf. the Wolf's words in 'The Tale of the Three Little Pigs', 'I'll huff and I'll puff, and I'll blow your house down.'

85–6. *the old Masters*: the episcopalian former regents and professors.

be the Authoritie: 'by the authority (vested in them)'. B and C, followed by the printed texts, read *their* for *the*.

93. *Primar*: 'Principal'.

Philosophie: inserted in Pitcairne's hand. The text is perhaps intended to read 'more logick, Mathematicks and Philosophie'. B and C, followed by the printed texts, read *no more Mathematicks and Philosophie than their Regents*.

Under Philosophy Pitcairne included such studies as he and his friend Robert Lindsay (c. 1652–1675/6) pursued in the College under the regency of Sir William Paterson: 'Plato and some bits of Dr Henrie More, Ficinus' (MacQueen and MacQueen 2009: 302). He refers particularly to the *Phaedrus* of Plato, the *Commentary* on that dialogue (Florence, 1496) by the Neoplatonist, Marsilio Ficino (1433–99), and the treatise by the Cambridge Platonist Henry More (1614–87), *The Immortality of the Soul, so farre forth as it is demonstrable from the Knowledge of Nature and the Light of Reason*

(London, 1659; above, pp. xxxii–xxxiii). Also included under the term is Natural Philosophy, Physics, closely related to Mathematics, as is illustrated by the title of Newton's great work, *Philosophiae Naturalis Principia Mathematica* (The Mathematical Foundations of Natural Philosophy) (London, 1687).

94. *Metaphisicall jargone*: arguments using such terms of abstract logic as *categorematical* and *syncategorematic*, scholastic logic; see above, 57; 3.3, 9n. After *jargone*, B and C, followed by the later printed texts, add *and little of that too*.

107, 108, 109. *Balls, Ball, Boulis*: not certainly identified, but possibly Robert Boyle (1627–91), author of *The Sceptical Chymist* (1661), who favoured experiment as the best way to arrive at truth and distrusted scholastic logic. Against the latter he wrote, among much else, *The Origins of Forms and Qualities* (London, 1666). He also wrote 'a long series of diffuse, but lucid, religious treatises, in which he sought to vindicate the harmony between the new scientific methods and the Christian faith' (*ODCC*, s.n.). The best known of these is *The Christian Virtuoso* (London, 1661), where *Virtuoso* is more or less the seventeenth-century equivalent of the modern scientist. Implicit in his work is the belief that there are other sources of truth than Holy Scripture, something which, of itself, was enough to turn more extreme Presbyterians against him. Still worse was his declared opposition to religious persecution. His main spiritual adviser was Bishop Stillingfleet, whose doctrines Gilbert Rule publicly opposed (above, 65–6n). Generally, Boyle's work is based on principles almost wholly antagonistic to those of Rule.

108. *strenuis strenua opposita*: Latin; 'strength opposed to strength'. Apparently ironical.

109. *poor Boulis*: Boyle had been in bad health before his death on the last day of 1691.

110. *enervatus*: Latin; 'castrated'.

112. *damed*: 'dammed', i.e. 'restrained'.

113. *Insolence ... frequentlie*: Novell is playing on the etymology of the word 'insolence', Latin *insolentia*, 'unusualness'.

115–16. *like the dissolveing ... Conventicles*: the conventicles (illegal Covenanting religious services held in the open air, usually in remote places) were often broken up by a party of dragoons.

118. *Tod*: 'fox'.

120. *extravagant*: 'wandering beyond the permitted boundaries'.

Mathematicall Atheists: mathematical truths do not depend on biblical authority and as a consequence mathematicians found themselves liable to charges of atheism. Mathematics, moreover, and astronomy were closely linked. The system developed by Kepler, Galileo and Descartes, together with its apparent corollary, presented by the mathematician Thomas Digges (c. 1546–95) and the magus Giordano Bruno (1548–1600), the plurality of worlds and infinitude of space, tended to deprive 'human life and terrestrial history of the unique importance which the medieval scheme of things had attributed to them ... The theory of the plurality of inhabited worlds tended to raise difficulties, not merely about minor details of the history included in the Christian belief, but about its central dogmas' (Lovejoy 1936: 108). The equation of mathematician and atheist became almost a commonplace. God was the ground of the system put forward in mathematical terms by Baruch Spinoza (1632–77): 'So it came to pass that they [the theologians of the Middle Ages and Renaissance] stated with the greatest certainty that the judgments of God far surpassed human comprehension: and this was the only cause that truth might have lain hidden from the human race through all eternity, had not mathematics, which deals not in the final causes, but the essence and properties of things, offered to men another standard of truth' (Spinoza 1979: 32), a standard which for him turned on the concept of God. Yet for more than a century after his death Spinoza was styled an atheist. Even David Hume calls him 'that famous atheist' (Hume 1960: 241). So far as Hume himself was concerned, the words were, no doubt, ironic, but reflected the view of most of his contemporaries.

This passage reopens the debate on the place of mathematics in education and society; cf. above, 3.3, 10n, 19–20n.

121. *all ar Atheists Except Mathematicians*: i.e. only mathematicians, with whom Novell would probably have classed the scientists of the Royal Society, can appreciate the nature of God. Mathematical truths are absolute and are observed most spectacularly in the material creation. To use a phrase coined two-and-a-half centuries later, 'The universe appears to have been designed by a pure mathematician' (Jeans 1931: 132), with which cf., e.g., a passage from *The Christian Virtuoso* (mentioned above, 107, 108, 109n): 'The consideration of the vastness, beauty, and regular motions of the heavenly bodies; the excellent structure of animals and plants; besides a multitude of other phænomena of nature, and the subserviency of most of these to man; may justly induce him, as a rational creature, to conclude, that this vast, beautiful, orderly, and (in a word) many ways admirable system of things, that we call the world, was framed by an author supremely powerful, wise, and good can scarce be denied by an intelligent and unprejudiced observer' (Boyle 1744: 5. 42). Note the emphasis on 'regular motions', 'structure', 'orderly'. Lovejoy (Lovejoy 1936: 99–143) long ago noted the continuity of this line of thought with the classical and medieval principle of plenitude. For an earlier Scottish parallel, cf. the prologue to Henryson's *Preiching of the Swallow*, 1650–1712 (Fox 1981: 65–7).

123–5. *I'm told ... no God*: Visioner believes that the first and second propositions in Euclid are the theorems which he quotes. Neither proposition is in fact a theorem; both are problems, 'To describe an equilateral triangle on a given finite straight line' and 'From a given point to draw a straight line equal to a given straight line'. Visioner obviously knows nothing of Euclid.

124–5. *the world is eternall*: i.e. the universe has no beginning and no end, a heresy based on Aristotle as interpreted by the Arabic philosopher Averroes (1126–98) and put forward at Paris by Siger of Brabant (c. 1225–c. 1282). It was refuted by St Thomas Aquinas (c. 1225–74); see, e.g., *Summa Theologica*, Question 46, Article 1 (Pegis 1945: 447–52).

125. *ther is no God*: if the world is eternal, God, as Creator and final Judge, is an unnecessary hypothesis.

126. *Compact with the devill*: the implication is that mathematicians, like witches, must have sold their souls to the devil, a belief common enough in the seventeenth century.

130. *lyk an old horse ... brack out in anothr*: probably proverbial, but I have found no parallels. B and C, followed by the later printed texts, read *his follie is Like a sore in an old horse*. The 1722 printed text has the more elaborate *his Folly is like the old Man's sore Horse's Back*.

133. *German randy beggar*: not identified.

135–9. *My reasin is ... prophessor of Theologie*: Visioner proposes to continue the campaign against mathematics, specifically by moving the present incumbent of the Chair, David Gregory (above, pp. xxxiv–xlv; 3.3, 19–20 and n.), from the chair of mathematics to the position of extraordinary (i.e. personal) professor of theology, where he would have no chance of teaching the nefarious art. Gregory is in league with the devil (above, 126 and n.), so must be treated with circumspection.

139–68. *Ther coms Huffy ... the lyk againe*: passage omitted in the 1722 printed text.

146. *50,000 men in arms*: by the time of the War of the Grand Alliance the size of regular forces had greatly increased. The comte de Guibert (1743–90) noted that 'instead of small armies charged with grand operations we [now] find grand armies charged with small operations' (Guibert 1770).

156–7. *Collonell's dogs*: above, 4.3, 9.

156–7. *you*: Huffie? Visioner?

Clap: 'gonorrhea'.

159–60. *He advanced ... baggage boys*: the appointment of Huffie as Keeper of Edinburgh Castle (Commander-in-Chief) is attributed to the relative success of his regiment at Killiecrankie (above, **Drammatis Personæ,** 7n), a success ridiculed as no more than murdering a dozen or two army-followers, women and baggage boys.

162. *dogs of the Government*: see above, 4.3; the dogs are dogs of the

Government because they belonged to the Colonel in charge of the Castle garrison.

167. *brunt for a witch*: in Scotland the burning of witches continued until 1727; it was something of a commonplace throughout the seventeenth century. The motif is recurrent in the play.

Act 5, Scene 2

The setting is the same as in 1.2, but initially the proscenium shutters are closed, hiding the inner stage. The front stage represents the Old Ladie's 'hall', the landing in front of her door, approached by steps from the auditorium, steps representing the stairs of the Edinburgh 'land' in which she lives. It is to be understood that an ousted Curate lives 'next door', on a lower floor, perhaps in the basement.

The action in this scene has something of the nature of farce. Frank makes blunder after blunder, but eventually redeems himself by his dispatch of Huffie, and so is given the last word.

1. *Metamorphosis*: 'transformation', here with a particular reference to the Latin epic, the *Metamorphoses*, in which Ovid (43 BC – AD 7) 'attempts no less a task than the linking together into one artistically harmonious whole all the stories of classical mythology' (Goold 1977: xi). These stories generally involved some process of more-or-less miraculous transformation – hence the title.

2. *Jupiter ... toun bull*: Will refers to *Metamorphoses* 2, 833–75; 8, 120. Jupiter seduced the Sidonian girl, Europa, by appearing to her as a gentle white bull. When she attempted to ride on his back, he carried her to the sea and swam with her to Crete, where presumably, although this is not stated, he ravished her. She became the mother of Minos, first king of Crete.

In Ovid the bull is a beautiful, peaceful animal: 'nullae in fronte minae, nec formidabile lumen:/ pacem vultus habet' (857–8) (his brow and eye would inspire no fear, and his whole expression was peaceful). Will's words are reductive; he brings down the status of the animal to that of a town-bull, maintained as a common stud for a township's cattle. He reveals something of his own nature by the choice of figure.

3. *a matter*: 'one matter' (i.e. no matter).

6. *puerfull*: ('powerful') 'efficient'.

6. *Jupiter ... shower*: Danae conceived Perseus when Jupiter, under the form of a miraculous golden shower, visited her in prison. Ovid thrice refers briefly to the story (*Metamorphoses* 4, 610–11; 6, 113; 11, 117). Frank's image is more romantic than Will's.

The references make it fairly clear that both Will and Frank regard children as the main purpose of marriage. They belong to the landed gentry for whom legitimate inheritance is a priority.

8. *meane*: 'mien'.

11. *Antichrist, the Whore of Babylon*: above, 5.1, 3–4n; 30n. For *Babylon* B reads *Babel*.

12. *Government*: the covenanting Presbyterians are against any secular government.

12. *solve the Caices of Conscience*: cf. below, 99. Devout Presbyterians tended to have crises of conscience; cf., e.g, the alternative title to the *Therapeutica sacra, seu, De curandis casibus conscientiae* (Edinburgh, 1656) of David Dickson (1583?–1663; see below, 43n), *Sacred healing, or, Concerning the cure for cases of conscience*. Dickson was expert in such matters: 'Upon the Sabbath evenings many persons under soul-distress used to resort to his house after sermon, when usually he spent an hour or two in answering their cases, and directing and comforting those who were cast down. In all this he had an extraordinary talent; indeed he had the tongue of the learned, and knew how to speak a word in season to the weary soul. In a large hall, which was in his own house, there would sometimes have been scores of serious Christians waiting for him after he came from church' (Howie 1902: 292). Cf., too, the full title of *Bessie of Lanerk* (below, 35n).

13. *devour pigeon pyes ... boulles of Sack*: cf. above, 3.1, 150 and 150n; below, 52, 109–10.

B has *Capons and* before *pigeon pyes*.

14. *bisheheave*: scribal error for *misbehave*, i.e. 'play the role poorly'.

15. *acted our parts*: 'had a rehearsal'.

16. *Theatre*: the Old Ladie's lodgings.

17–25. *Then ... of Jerusalem*: Will parodies the style of a presbyterian sermon. He is working himself into the part he has to play.

17. *sincere*: a favourite word among presbyterian divines.

18. *Sparkish*: cf. above, 3.1, 53n. Here however the English associations of the word predominate; cf. also below, 184n.

18. *mean*: 'mien'; cf. above, 8.

beloved: another favourite word among presbyterian divines.

19. *ffrench fashions & phrases*: 'fashionable physical and verbal mannerisms'. The France of Louis XIV tended to be regarded elsewhere as the home at once of elegance and moral decadence.

20. *Corrupt inclinatns*: 'corrupt' by reason of Man's Fall in the Garden of Eden, Original Sin. The corrupt inclination to speak sense marks the beginning of the Enlightenment, exemplified by such thinkers as Hobbes, Locke and the natural scientists.

21. *sillabe*: 'syllable'.

brieffe, or semi-breiffe: 'breve, or semibreve', the former a 'double whole-note. Formerly the short note of music, but as the longer notes have fallen into disuse and shorter ones have been introduced, it has become the longest (twice the length of the semibreve or whole-note)' (Kennedy 1980: 94). Frank is to linger over the pronunciation of every syllable.

23. *period*: 'complex sentence in periodic style'.

24. *lye*: cf. above, 1.2, 51–2 and n.; below 271n.

Incessantly: inserted in Pitcairne's hand; present in B, C and the printed texts.

sweir: 'swear', 'blaspheme'; cf. below, 104 and n.

25. *seidge of Jerusalem*: the future emperor Titus brought the four-year siege of Jerusalem (AD 66–70) to a successful (from his point of view) end. The famine during the siege is vividly described by Josephus in his *Bellum Judaicum* (Thackeray *et.al.* 1926–65).

26. Stage direction: the proscenium shutters open slightly to allow Rachel to look out, then, as she calls to her mother, slide apart revealing the Old Ladie's apartment.

30. *Nices invited to denner*: cf. above, 3.1, 94–6.

30. *bravest*: i.e. they are young and handsome. For the most part, her mother's acquaintances are 'antediluvians', ministers, that is to say, who were expelled from their charges immediately after the 1660 Restoration and only restored after the 1688 Revolution.

31. *Grace ... familie*: appropriate opening words for a minister; cf. Luke 10. 5 (Christ's instructions to the Seventy): 'And into whatsoever house ye enter, first say, Peace be to this house.' 'Grace, mercy and peace' is a Pauline formula of personal greeting; see, e.g., 1 Timothy 1. 2: 'Unto Timothy, my own son in the faith: Grace, mercy, and peace, from God our Father and Jesus Christ our Lord.' Also present in the words, however, is an element of dramatic irony. The grace, mercy and peace intended by Will correspond not at all with the Old Ladie's understanding of the words.

32. *Mr's*: 'Master's', i.e. 'Christ's'.

33. *We owne no masters*: Frank's first blunder. He fails to grasp the Old Ladie's meaning and speaks, not in his assumed part, but as a free citizen and landowner. Fortunately the Old Ladie misunderstands his response to her words.

B reads *owe* for *owne*.

34. *Master of masters*: Christ.

34–5. *How could ... ask for me*: the Old Ladie is a little offended that the two ministers have called on *my Lady Conventikl* (3.1, 97) before coming to her.

35–6. *I have fedd ... tribulatne*: i.e. she has sheltered covenanting ministers during the Killing Times, 1681–85.

37. *press*: 'cupboard'.

Closett: small room off the larger one represented by the inner stage; see above, 1.2, initial stage direction.

37–8. *Mr Covenant and Mr Solomon*: for the close relationship between these two and the Old Ladie see also above, 2.2, 78–80; below, 150, 169. As already noted, they are possible suitors for Violetta and Laura.

39. *your two Neices*: As Will realizes, Frank's main concern leads him into a second blunder. The Old Ladie's brief response is mainly dismissive, but perhaps hints at the beginning of vague suspicions concerning the two strange clergymen.

40. *Thou'l Spoyle*: B reads *certainly* before *Spoyle*.

43–7. *rare Collection ... Invisible World*: the Old Ladie is proud of her library and thinks it will impress visiting ministers. Frank, in particular, knows nothing of the contents.

43. *Dickson's Sermons*: David Dickson has already been mentioned (above, 12n). He was a Glasgow graduate, who in 1618 became minister of Irvine in Ayrshire. He was closely associated with the National Covenant of 1638, and engaged in a polemical war with the Aberdeen Doctors (above 4.4, 144n). In 1640 he became professor of divinity in Glasgow and in 1650 was translated to the corresponding Edinburgh chair, at the same time becoming minister of the second charge in St Giles'. At the Restoration he refused to take the Oath of Supremacy and was ejected from chair and church, dying in 1662.

Among his many writings, the most popular were his expositions of biblical texts in the form of sermons, *A Short Explanation of the Epistle of St Paul to the Hebrews* (Aberdeen, 1635), *A Brief Exposition of the Euangel of Jesus Christ, according to Matthew* (Edinburgh, 1647) and *A Brief Explication of the Psalms* (3 vols., London, 1652–54). It is to these that the Old Ladie refers.

44. *11 Pynts ... Breeches*: not identified. The comic title may be an invention.

Pynts: 'points'. 'Point' is used in the sense 'A tagged lace or cord, of twisted yarn, silk or leather, for attaching the hose to the doublet' (*OED*, s.v. **Point II 5**).

44–5. *Ther's Bessie ... Letters*: B omits.

44–5. *Bessie of Lanerk*: probably *Conflict in conscience of a dear Christian: named Bessie Clarksone in the parish of Lanerk, which she lay vnder three yeare & anhalf* (Edinburgh, 1632), by William Livingstone (1576 – c. 1640). I have not discovered anything further about the author.

45. *Saml. Rutherford's Letters*: see above, 3.3, 101–2n. As there noted, the *Letters* enjoyed a long popularity; their style is pilloried in Curate 1692: 98–108.

By her use of Rutherford's Christian name, the Old Ladie probably indicates that he had been an acquaintance of hers.

45. *Good news from Heavn*: probably *The Godly Mans Gain and the Wicked Mans Woe; or, good news from heaven for the righteous* (London, 1665), a sermon on Isaiah 3. 10–11: 'Say ye to the righteous, that it shall be well with him ... Woe unto the wicked! It shall be ill with him.' I have not discovered anything about the author, Matthew Killiray, except that he was probably a Church of England clergyman and held the degree of BD.

46. *Satans Invisible World*: George Sinclair (?d. 1696), *Satans Invisible World Discovered: or, A choice Collection of Relations anent Devils, Spirits, Witches and Apparitions* (Edinburgh, 1685).

Sinclair was a St Andrews graduate. In 1655 he became professor of philosophy at Glasgow University. He declined to submit to episcopacy and was deprived in 1667. In 1688 he was recalled to the University, where in 1692 he became professor of mathematics and experimental philosophy. Most of his writings have an obvious relation to science: *Tyrocinia mathematica* (Glasgow, 1661), *Ars nova et magna gravitatis et levitatis* (Rotterdam, 1669), *Hydrostaticks* (Edinburgh, 1672), *Natural Philosophy improven by new experiments* (Edinburgh, 1683), *Principles of astronomy and navigation* (Edinburgh, 1688). From the MS notes taken by students of David Dickson's lectures on the Confession of Faith he made a translation, *Truth's Victory over Error* (Edinburgh, 1684).

At a first glance, *Satans Invisible World* stands completely apart from Sinclair's other works. It is intended, however, as a scientific demonstration of the existence of the malignant supernatural, and, incidentally, a justification of witch trials and condemnations. Disbelief in this aspect of the supernatural was regarded by most people as heresy, although in the latter years of the seventeenth century it was becoming common among the intelligentsia. The heresy was supposed to have begun with the New Testament Sadducees and is consequently described as Sadduceism. *Satans Invisible World* is intended as a refutation, following the tradition of *An Antidote against Atheisme* (London, 1653), by the Cambridge Platonist Henry More (1614–87) and the better known *Philosophic Endeavour towards the Defense of the being of Witches and Apparitions* (London, 1666) of Joseph Glanvill (1636–80), re-issued as *Some Philosophical considerations touching the being of witches and Witchcraft* (London, 1667), then as *A blow at modern Sadducism* (London, 1668) and finally re-edited posthumously by Henry More as *Saducismus Triumphatus* (London, 1681).

Another Scottish work with kindred intentions, but much less emphasis on witchcraft, is *The Secret Commonwealth of Fauns, Elves and Faeries* by the Gaelic-speaking clergyman, Robert Kirk (1641?–1692); for details see the edition by Stewart Sanderson (Folklore Society: Cambridge, 1976).

46–7. *What think you ... World*: B omits. This, in effect, is a leading question; the Old Ladie is anxious to discover whether Frank in particular holds sound views on Sadduceism.

48. *Indeed ... I heard*: Frank's third blunder; he has never heard of *Satans Invisible World*.

50–1. *Everie thing ... all that*: Will rescues Frank.

51. *all that*: the meaningless phrase is twice (below, 70–71, 124) repeated; it may indicate that at these points the actor was encouraged to extemporize.

52. *Botle of Sack*: cf. above, 13 and n.

53–74. *it's a sade world ... meditatne*: cf. above, 1.1, 55 and n. The Old Ladie's virtuoso *speaking of the tyms*, perhaps partly inspired by the *Botle of Sack* which has been circulating, is brought to a conclusion only by the entry of her nieces at line 74. Note her characteristic abundance of compound adjectives – *Minister-Mocking, parents-disobeying, reformatne-overturning* etc. She reveals her hypocrisy by her treatment of the poor man at the door (49–50), an Episcopalian, probably a Curate, who has been 'rabbled' by the mob in Ayrshire or Galloway (above, 1.1, 104 and n.) and reduced to beggary. Will does his best to keep up with her, but eventually (53) confesses himself vanquished. Frank's performance is miserable.

The Old Ladie is probably making a further test of the two ministers' credentials. A genuine minister would have had no difficulty with endless elaborations on the subject.

This passage varies considerably in the MS and printed texts. The variants may have been introduced by actors who regarded this part of the text as a good opportunity for improvisation.

56. *praying-Sensorious*: for *praying* B has the better reading *prying*.

57. *Gospel-renouncing*: for *renouncing* B reads *overturning*.

wordlie Wor[l]d; **Minister-mocking, filthie, Sabbath-breaking**: inserted in Pitcairne's hand. Lacking in B, but present, with some variation, in other texts.

58–9. *A Malignant ... parents-disobeying World*: lacking in B, which reads *a murdering, whoring, lying, coveting world. In a word, 'tis an uncharitable wardly warld.*

58. *Minister-mocking*: dramatic irony; the Old Ladie is talking to someone who is himself mocking a minister.

59. *parents-disobeying*: more dramatic irony; the Old Ladie is about to learn that her daughter, and the nieces to whom she stands *in loco parentis*, have all disobeyed her.

61. *west cuntrie rabble*: see above, 1.1, 253n.

62–3. *Beat him doune stairs*: the Old Ladie realizes from the Maid's words that the beggar is an Episcopalian, probably a Curate. She reacts accordingly, in an unchristian fashion.

63–5. *beggarlie ... reformatne-overturning world*: The Old Ladie's mind is still running on the poor man and his beliefs.

64. *guadie*: gaudy. B reads *giddie*.

68. *Mes John*: the disguised Frank; see above, 1.2, 1n. He has roused the Old Ladie's suspicions by his uncharacteristic behaviour in taking no part in the dialogue.

A mistakenly reads *Mes James*, i.e. Wordie. B and C, followed by the later printed texts, correctly read *Mes John*.

69–71. *It's ane abominable ... And all that*: Frank's fourth blunder. See also above 51n.

74. Stage direction, *Enter ... laughing*: Violetta and Laura are enjoying the plight of their suitors. They annoy both Will and the Old Ladie.

78. *Countenance*: B and C, followed by the printed texts, add *ye impertinent Jad*.

78–9. *Ye 'l laugh in hell yet*: semi-proverbial; cf. above, 4.1, 22–3.

81. *revered*: B, C and the later printed texts correctly read *reverend*.

82. *infuse*: *double-entendre*; compare, e.g., Bellenden, 'The Proheme apon the Cosmographe' (Tod Ritchie 1928: 9–20), 129–30: 'So is ane man consave/ Of seid infuse in membris genitive.'

85. [offers to lead Laura] *... best we cane*: Frank's fifth blunder.

86. *Nay stay, Sir*: the Old Ladie has some suspicion of Frank's intentions and introduces a new test.

87. *speak a word*: 'preach', 'lecture on a scriptural text'.

ordinarie: 'a regular reading from the Bible as observance within a household' (*DOST*, s.v. **Ordinary 3**). 'My ordinary this morning was from the 9th verse of this 5th chapter to the end' (Pringle 1847, 459). This usage is entirely Scots.

Walter Pringle of Greenknow (1625–67) was a Covenanter of some note (see *OxfDNB*). The Old Ladie's use of the word, and her practice, emphasizes that she belongs to the same tradition.

88. *Revelatione ... ten horns*: see Revelation 17. 3, 7–17.

89. *Bible*: B and C, followed by the printed texts, read *Great Bible*, i.e. 'family Bible'.

Psalme book: the metrical Psalter of Francis Rouse (1579–1659) was published in 1643 in London and commended by the Westminster Assembly (1643–53). A much revised form was adopted for use in Scotland by the 1650 General Assembly and has remained ever since in use by the Church of Scotland.

91. *premunire*: Latin *praemunire*, 'to protect, secure', in English law 'the name of a royal writ designed to protect the royal rights of jurisdiction' (Walker 1980: 975) and intended particularly to protect the interests of the king against encroachments by the Church or other foreign power.

Best-known among several Statutes of Praemunire is that enacted in 1392/3, during the reign of Richard II (1362–1400). In 1529 Cardinal Wolsey was tried under it. The Royal Marriage Act (1772) was the last act to subject anyone to the severe penalties involved.

From this primary reference developed the meaning found here, 'a situation or condition likened (gravely or humorously) to that of one who has received a *praemunire*; a difficulty, scrape, fix, predicament' (*OED*, s.v. **Praemunire 3**). Some trace of the original reference persists in Frank's use of the term; by donning the garb of a presbyterian clergyman he thinks he has set himself, as a churchman, against the secular monarchy, whether that of James VII or William II.

92. *louse*: 'loosed', 'set free'.

92–3. *try the lyke experiment*: Frank unconsciously uses the language of the new experimental science.

95. *Not, Madam*: B has *Not I, Madam*.

99. *caice of conscience*: see above, 12n.

100–3. *horns ... relating to 't*: double-entendre throughout. The surface-meaning is that Frank is an authority on the meaning of 'horns' in Revelation and that he has a work on the subject in the press. 'Horns', however, are the traditional symbol of cuckoldry. Will insinuates that Frank is an expert on this latter subject and indeed, at this very moment, is pursuing an affair with a married woman. One meaning of *press* (82) is 'a cupboard into which a bed could be folded', or simply 'a bed (of this kind)' (*DOST*, s.v. **Press 1b**). The insinuation is particularly intended for Laura's ears. She reacts later (below, 145–6). Small wonder that Frank swears in his vexation.

104. *God damn thee*: Frank's sixth blunder. His oath upsets the Old Ladie; cf. above, 24.

105–7. *heird a Curate swear when he came up the stairs*: Will again comes to Frank's rescue. The Old Ladie is prepared to believe anything bad about episcopalian clergy. The Curate, who is to marry Will and Frank to Violetta and Laura, lives in a lower flat on the same stairway as the Old Ladie. Will is shamelessly content to slander him and so maintain his own pretences.

109. *keep back denner*: cf. Laura's remark, below, 130–1.

113. *Who made man?*: probably an imperfect recollection of a Catechism. The first question in the Scottish Shorter Catechism is 'What is man's chief end?'

114. *a dead lift*: '(like) a raising of the dead'. For a different use of *lift*, see above, 1.3, 20–24n.

114. *pinching occasne*: 'critical juncture'.

116. *exercise standing*: cf. above, 1.2, 12, 12–25n.

118–19. *The Gentleman ... this tyme*: Violetta unsuccessfully tries to

rescue Frank. Incidentally, she also betrays her knowledge of his real identity by using the simple term 'Gentleman' without any qualification such as
'Reverend'. This helps to increase the Old Ladie's annoyance.

121. Stage direction: *throws up*: see above, 2.2, 21n.

accordinglie: 'suitably', 'properly'. B and C, followed by the later
printed texts, have *ackwerdly*, 'backhandedly', which perhaps fits the situation better. Frank is not accustomed to handling a family Bible.

122–4. *Ten horns ... and all that*: Frank in desperation extemporizes
ignorantly, but in a way which, for the moment, impresses the Old Ladie.

123. *old translatne*: probably the Calvinistic, and long popular, Geneva
version of the Bible (1560), as opposed to the Authorized or King James
version (1611). The latter was known as the 'new translation' even late in
the seventeenth century (McGrath 2001: 289). Frank knows that the Geneva
Bible exists, but has no knowledge of its contents, which do not include
more then twentie heads and fourty 4 horns.

126. *Now I pitie him*: Laura's heart is at last softened.

too: inserted in Pitcairne's hand; present in B, C and later printed
editions.

128–9. *womone ... apron string*: proverbial (Wilson 1970: 908).

131. *rathr fast ... lectur*: cf. above, 109.

131. *loss*: 'lose'.

138. *S'. Peter's keys*: Matthew 16. 19: 'And I will give unto thee the keys
of the kingdom of heaven', Christ's words to Peter, on which the Popes, as
Peter's successors, based their claim to final authority in the Church, a claim
which was anathema to Protestants.

138. *his day*: 29 June. If Laura is accurate, the action of the play supposedly takes place on 28 and 29 June 1691.

Pitcairne tended to observe, or at least to be aware of, Saints' days; see
MacQueen and MacQueen 2009: poems 108, 114–16 (pp. 252, 260–1).

140. *O Abominable! ... day*: the suggestion that a Saint's day should be
observed is shocking to the presbyterian Old Ladie. Presbyterians do not
observe Saints' days. Laura knew the effect any mention of one would have.

After *day* B and C add *here*. The printed editions follow.

141. *Would St Peter ... the dead*: Acts 9. 36–41, the raising of Tabitha
(Dorcas) by Peter. Violetta knows her Scriptures but displays her knowledge
with some cynicism.

144–5. *no Lectur heir this day*: Laura's stratagem has succeeded.

147–8. *S' Matthew's ... S' John's too*: Frank again shows his ignorance.
St Matthew's day is 21 September, St Andrew's 30 November, St John's 27
December.

149. *brunt at a staik*: another reference to witchcraft and the punishment
associated with it..

150–1. *match ... or no*: Solomon refers to his attempted 'conversion' of Laura (and also, by implication, Violetta). The acceptance of Presbyterianism is figuratively regarded as a marriage to the Lord and (again by implication) to the receipt of Solomon's particular attentions.

154. *on her*: B and C, followed by the printed texts, have the better reading, *on thir side*.

155. *bans*: the word probably implies that public prayers had been offered for the conversion of Violetta and Laura.

158. *contract*: the proposal for spiritual marriage.

158. *putt too*: 'set in place', i.e. 'put on the finger' (*DOST*, s.v. **Put 51a**).

159. *Imagination*: 'something merely imaginary', 'a fantasy'. Solomon has in mind his own failure with Laura.

160–4. *All meer stories ... carnall*: Frank still misunderstands. Will sets him right.

160. *meer stories*: B and C, followed by the printed texts, read *mysteries*. The word in A may well result from a misreading.

161. *He'l have aneugh a doe*: vernacular Scots, 'He'll hae aneuch adae'. The phrase is ironic. Frank is recollecting aspects of his own somewhat troubled experiences regarding Laura.

161. *a doe*: B and C, followed by the printed texts, read *to do*.

162–4. *Dull ... carnall*: B and C, followed by the later printed texts, include the direction [*aside to Frank*] for this passage.

163–4. *The sens ... carnall*: i.e. Solomon's meaning is allegorical, not literal.

164. *carnall*: 'fleshly', i.e. 'literal'. The choice of word, however, shows that Will knows something of Solomon's usual behaviour.

165. *Frank*: B adds [*aside*].

165–5. *thrid heavns*: the reference is to Paul's words in 2 Corinthians 12. 2–4: 'I knew a man in Christ above fourteen years ago (whether in the body, I cannot tell; or whether out of the body, I cannot tell: God knoweth;) such a one caught up to the third heaven. And I knew such a man (whether in the body, or out of the body, I cannot tell: God knoweth;) How that he was caught up into paradise, and heard unspeakable words, which it is not lawful for a man to utter.' Frank shows an unexpected knowledge of one passage of Scripture.

167. *hold my tongue*: Frank has learned his lesson.

167. B and C, followed by the printed texts, insert the stage-direction [*Enter Covenant.*

168. *part of your denner*: initially, at least, Covenant's language is more pragmatic than Solomon's.

169. *ship be come*: proverbial (Wilson 1970: 723, 'Ship comes home, When my'). The date of the earliest example quoted by Wilson is 1851.

170. *Who deil ... that*: Frank fails to grasp the proverb. He assumes that there must be a biblical reference.

171. *Noah's ark*: Genesis 6. 13–8, 19.

S' Paul's ship: Acts 27. 1–44.

172–4. *If she ... and familie*: dramatic irony. The comforts are the marriages of her daughter and nieces, a matter of satisfaction for the young women, not the Old Ladie.

174. Stage direction: Solomon and Covenant wish to talk with the Old Ladie about Rachel's pregnancy and do not want the two strangers to overhear. They usher her into the same small room (*Closett*) in which they had themselves been sheltered during the Killing Time.

putt: B and C, followed by the later printed texts, read *pull*.

179. *Pray a word about horns*: i.e. 'deliver a lecture/sermon on horns'. A mocking playfulness on the part of Laura, which also, in view of Will's earlier remarks (100–101) is probably mingled with a little anxiety, even jealousy.

180. *No tyme*: Will realizes that their opportunities are limited and is anxious for haste.

to be fooled: 'to play the fool', 'for fooling'. I have found no exact parallel for this usage. Nearest is Wycherley, *The Plain-Dealer* (1677), 4.1, 11–12: 'Have a care, Sir, my heart is too much in earnest to be fooled with' (Weales 1966: 464).

181. *Cloacks*: the voluminous cloaks of presbyterian ministers (above, 1.1, 12), under which Violetta and Laura conceal themselves.

184. *reverend Sparks*: in effect an oxymoron; cf. and contrast 3.1, 53 and n.

185. *discretely*: Scots usage; 'Discreet: not rude, not doing anything inconsistent with delicacy towards a female' (Jamieson).

honestly: 'honourably'. B reads *tenderlie*, C and the later printed texts *reverently*.

186–7. *mumbld o'r the matrimonie*: 'performed the marriage ceremony'.

mumbld: the word shows a certain lack of sympathy for religious rites as performed by the clergy; cf. Lindsay, *The Tragedie of the late Cardinal Beaton*, 381–5:

> nor yit of clatterraris,
> That in the kirk can nother sing nor saye,
> Thocht thay be clokit vp in clerkis arraye,
> Lyke doytit Doctoris new cum out of Athenis,
> And mummyll ouer ane pair of maglit matenis. (Hamer 1931: 141)

matrimonie: 'marriage ceremony', as in 'sacrament of matrimony';

cf., e.g., Dunbar, *Tretis of the Twa Mariit Wemen and the Wedo*, 152–3: 'Sen man ferst with matrimony yow menskit in kirk,/ How haif ye farne?' (Bawcutt 1998: 45). This sense of the word is perhaps commoner in Scots than in English.

188–207. *lead on ... farr to goe*: the 1722 text lacks this passage.

188. *Instantlie*: 'closely'. B reads *stoutly*, 'bravely, courageously'.

188. Stage direction: the group pass from the inner stage to the proscenium, towards the steps from proscenium to auditorium, as Huffie ascends. At the top, he jostles Frank, ignoring, or despising his clerical garb.

toward the Curat's: B and C, followed by the later printed texts, read *towards the stairs*.

191. *I forgive you*: Frank maintains his clerical role.

192. *O God*: B and C, followed by the later printed texts, read *'Sblude*. *breeding*: 'manners'.

192. Stage direction: when he drops his cloak, Frank is revealed in his usual non-clerical garb.

193. *Scollar*: 'pupil', with reference to Huffie's threat to teach him breeding.

195. Stage direction; *wrong sid upmost*: 'inside out'.

197. *Ladys*: above, **Drammatis Personæ**, 7n.

Boatmen, hyrers, dogs: above, 2.1; 4.3.

201. *Laques*: 'lackies'. B reads *Tykes*.

about or: B reads *at our*.

or: 'our'.

202. *mattle*: 'mettle'.

206–7. *on qualitie of ane presbiterian Minister*: i.e. they are all turncoats; cf. above, 1.1, 73–4n. The primary reference is to the clergymen (the majority) who had accepted the Indulgencies offered by Charles II and James VII (1669, 1672, 1687), then in 1688 turned, not only against James, but also against any kind of religious toleration.

207. Stage direction: Violetta, Laura, Will and Frank exeunt by way of the steps to the auditorium. Old Ladie, Solomon and Covenant enter from the closet onto the inner stage.

208. *them ... they*: i.e. Will and Frank disguised as Mr Samuel and Mr John. The Old Ladie has expressed her doubts about the two supposed clergymen.

209. *work in the vyneyeard*: Matthew 20. 1–16.

210. *work ... few*: Matthew 9. 37; Luke 10. 2.

211. **Mr John, Mr Samuel**: Pitcairne's hand, inserted in A; present in B, C and the printed texts.

213. *whom'd*: 'whom would'.

216. *Covenant*: 'marriage vows'. The word, however, is deliberately ambiguous and apparently acceptable in the eyes of the Old Ladie.

Mrs: pl. of *Mr*, i.e. Mr Samuel and Mr John.

217. *will be back shortlie*: B and C, followed by the later printed texts, read *they'd both be instantly back again*.

219. *Love*: 'like'; I have found no exact parallel to this particular usage, but cf., e.g., Alexander Scott 'Ane Ballat maid to the Derisioun and Scorne of wantoun Wemen', 57–61:

> Sum luvis, new cum to toun,
>> With jeigis to mak thame joly;
> Sum luvis dance vp and doun,
>> To meiss thair malancholy;
>>> Sum luvis lang trollie lolly.   (Cranstoun 1896: 21)

220. *what wes ... James?*: the Old Ladie's concern about the two bogus clergymen has prevented her from fully understanding the news brought by Solomon and Covenant.

220. *Mes James*: Wordie.

222. *foul play*: 'sexual intercourse'.

223. *marriag ... evne*: proverbial (not in Wilson 1995).

224. *dominie*: 'clergyman' rather than the more usual 'schoolmaster'. This sense is evidenced in England from the second half of the seventeenth century, perhaps influenced by Dutch usage (*OED*, s.v. **Domine 2**). Not in *DOST*. In *SND* the earliest example quoted is the anonymous 'Ministers make poor testaments;/ No Dominies for me Lady', dated c. 1700.

The Old Ladie is the widow of one of the landed gentry and is horrified that her daughter should marry out of her class.

227. *What hear*: after *hear* B and C, followed by the later printed texts, insert *I*.

deboshed: 'debauched', 'seduced'.

227–8. *family abused*: see above, 224n.

229. *Hist!*: 'Hush!' (B *Whisht!*). Solomon attempts to comfort the Old Ladie.

230. *weall-gifted*: cf. Violetta, above, 3.1, 54–6: 'the good gift of prayer (quhich perhaps he will putt in exercise 2 hours on his bridall night quhen I would wish he were looking after some othr thing)' and, more particularly, Solomon, above 3.3, 95–7: 'A rar gifted brother this! He looks not to have the twe Corner Stones, the twe Cardinall graces, the good gift of preaching & lectureing together and the long gift of prayer.' In Solomon's opinion, Wordie has both, fairly obviously without the drawback specified by Violetta.

232. *evit*: 'avoid'; Latin *evitare*. *OED*, s.v. **Evite** remarks: 'in 18ᵗʰ–19ᵗʰ

c. almost peculiar to Scotch writers'. The latest English example offered is from Quarles, *Emblems* (1635).

234–7. *It's but a Ceremony ... all ther liffe*: Presbyterians were opposed to all forms of ceremony.

238. B and C, followed by the printed texts, insert a line: '*Rachel*: Mother, You forgive me? Do you not?'

241. *I'm sure your good sone*: 'for sure, I'm your son-in-law'.

245 *read*: B reads *heard*.

248. *weal inclined*: 'well-disposed'. There is, however, a *double-entendre* in the word *inclined*; cf., e.g., Henryson, *Testament of Cresseid*, 558–9: 'My mynd in fleschelie foull affectioun/ Was inclynit to lustis lecherous' (Fox 1981: 129); *King Hart*, 15–16: 'He wes inclynit cleinlie to remane,/ And woun vnder the wyng of Wantownness' (Bawcutt 2003, 141); Scott, 'A Luvaris Complaint', 29–32:

> Quha suld my dullit spreitis raiss,
> Sen for no lufe my lady gaiss?
> Bot and gud scheruice my^t hir maiss,
>   Scho suld inclyne. (Cranstoun 1896: 47)

249. *constant hearer of Sermons*: dramatic irony; cf. 1.2, 1–29 and nn. After *Sermons*, B and C, followed by the printed texts, add: *and Lectures. I never miss her from any*.

252–3. *wher ar the two ministers?*: the Old Ladie does not recognize that Will and Frank are the two ministers.

254. *cheated*: Violetta ironically pretends that she and Laura have been misled into marriage by the disguise adopted by the two young men. This is the reverse of the truth. The disguise was her own idea.

256. *Consent*: the Old Ladie is the legal guardian of the two girls.

259. Stage direction; *Snaick off*: 'sneak off', but with overtones of *snake*, 'serpent'. They realize that their hopes of marriage have disappeared.

263. *hynous*: 'heinous'.

266–86. *That's no great matter ... I'faith*: Laura attempts to revenge herself on the Old Ladie, and more particularly Rachel, for their earlier treatment of her.

267. *gaind by your seing us*: i.e. they owe their husbands to the effects of the Old Ladie's supervision.

268. *insupportable burthen*: oblique reference to her pregnancy.

268. *not*: B reads *none*.

273. *wordie*: 'worthy'.

273. B and C, followed by the printed texts, insert: '*Rachel*: Yes, half a year ago'. In an attempt to preserve her reputation, Rachel deliberately lies; cf. above, 24; 1.2, 51–2.

275. *betrothed*: not quite the same as 'married'.

with her mother's consent: B and C, followed by the later printed texts, read *with her own and her mother's consent*. Rather than tell a direct lie, Wordie equivocates.

279. *bucksome*: 'pliant'.

280–1. *sweet daughter ... gentleman*: expansion of the proverbial 'Like Lord, like chaplain' (Wilson 1970: 485). For *sweet daughter* B and C, followed by the printed texts, read *sweet young daughter*.

287–8. *But come ... work of the day*: Violetta sees no point in reopening old wounds.

Let's mynd: B reads *Let us in and mynd*.

289. *And the work of the nyht too*: Frank has the last word.

Stage direction: A reads *and Wordie & Rachel*; B and C, followed by the later printed texts, read *Wordie and Rachael*.

Act 5, Scene 3.

The setting is as in 1.3.

1–4. *Bretheren ... therof*: in B the Moderator gives his introduction in words which differ slightly from the text in A, *Wee are again Reassembled about his own wark. I hope ye will not wearie; 'tis all one Interest to make a clean house and ye will be on the wings of the prayers of the flowere of the Godly of Scotland*. This comes close to the texts of C and the printed editions and may represent auctorial revision. Note in particular the characteristic Moderatorial tautology in *again Reassembled*.

1. *assembled*: for the use of the word, cf. below, 189 and n.

2–3. *mack a Cleane house*: 'make a clean sweep'. The Committee has already dealt with Mr Shittle and Mr Turncoat, each representing a section of the Episcopalians. The Moderator knows how he intends to finalize the business (by dealing with Mr Orthodox, representing the remainder), but each member of the Committee in attendance has his own ideas.

4–6. *My Lord Whigridne ... affairs*: in 3.1, 194 Whigridne says that he will go to the Committee directly from his encounter with Huffie. Later in the day he must attend a meeting of the Privy Council. In 4.4, 61 ff he is seen arriving at the parliament, presumably to attend the meeting of the Privy Council, which has been brought forward to consider the letter sent by King William (below, 120–33). It is for this reason that he cannot attend the Committee.

4. *excuse*: 'apologies'.

9. *I think ... 6th part of them*: Turbulent's comment is just and his proposal sensible, but he is at once put down.

12. *west quintra beleever*: i.e. an extremist, a layman, from Ayrshire or Galloway.

13. *sheen leir*: 'soon learn' (NE dialect).

14. *baptiz and marry*: B and C, followed by the printed texts, read *gi'* [give] *the Communion, baptize and marrie*. Lay administration of the sacraments, particularly Communion, would shock an episcopalian audience.

15. *tak a word of*: ?'dispute with', 'take action against'. Colloquially, the pl., *words*, sometimes means 'contentious or violent talk between persons, altercation' (*OED*, s.v. **Word 5**); the sg. here seems to have much the same meaning. There are parallels in later Scots; 'Often did he ask me to "speak a wird" to his refractory laddie' (1892, *SND*, s.v. **Word 1.1**, viii); I have myself heard the threatening 'I'll hae a word wi' him.'

16. *drest*: 'brought to a satisfactory state'.

our owne: i.e. the episcopal church in Scotland.

gaylie: = *geylie*, 'pretty well'. An early example; cf. *SND*, s.v. **Geylies 2** (i): 'Bra'ly, finely, Geily at least' (J. Kelly, *Complete Collection of Scottish Proverbs* [1721], 400). In *DOST* the closest parallel quoted is G. Stuart, *A Joco-Serious Discourse between a Northumberland Gentleman and his Tenant a Scotchman* (London, 1686), 'Epistle Dedicatory': 'Any of your enemies (of which ... yo've had a gay convenient number)'. Note too the colloquial Scots phrase of agreement, 'Geylie that'.

Semantically, Scots *gey* and *geylie* are extensions of meaning from Scots and English *gay* and *gaily*. Figuratively, the gaily dressed English whore is to be transformed into her *gaylie drest* Scottish equivalent.

17–18. *of old ... malignants*: a reference to the purgation of royalists and Episcopalians from the Scottish army of Charles II before the engagement with Cromwell and the English parliamentary army at Dunbar, 3 September 1650. The officers, in particular, had tended to adhere to the doctrine of regal Divine Right. In order to gain Church and government support for his cause, Charles II had been obliged to subscribe to the Solemn League and Covenant. As a consequence, the Scottish army was 'altogether governed by the Committee of Estates and Kirk, and they took especial care in their levies not to admit any Malignants or Engagers, placing in command, for most part, Ministers' Sons, Clerks and other sanctified creatures, who hardly ever saw or heard of any sword but that of the spirit' (Sir Edward Walker, *Historical Discourses* [London, 1705], 162, quoted in Carlyle, *Oliver Cromwell's Letters and Speeches* [London, 1845], III, 15–16). Salathiel fails to appreciate the irony of his comment; at Dunbar the purged army suffered a humiliating defeat.

19. *purg K Wm's armie*: an impossible aim, as the Moderator later (20) points out.

20–1. *seing ... good cause*: i.e. to defeat Louis XIV.

207

21–2. *nam ubi ... proportionalia*: Latin: 'for where the end is most brief, there the means [to that end] ought to be proportionate'. For *brevissimus* B and C, followed by the printed texts, read the barbarous *bonissimus* (for *optimus*, 'best'), a reading which corresponds better than that in A with the general level of Salathiel's Latinity; *brevissimus* may well represent a misreading, or a correction, on the part of the A scribe.

23. *Outts*: 'Hoots!', an interjection 'expressing annoyance, disgust, incredulity or remonstrance, or in dismissal of an opinion expressed by someone else' (*SND*). Not in *DOST*. Cf. above, 1.3, 28n.

Greek: the Moderator again demonstrates his ignorance.

24–5. *putt ... reach*: proverbial (Wilson 1970: 780, 'Stretch your arm (Put your hand) no further than your sleeve will reach'); cf. above, 16n.

25. *fittest*: B reads *safest*. Either reading emphasizes cowardice on the part of the Moderator.

27. *who have not mynd to defend themselvs*: B and C, followed by the later printed texts, read *who have not many to defend them*. The 1722 prints read *who are both forsaken by God and Man*.

28. *signe*: B and C, followed by the later printed texts, read *tocken*. The 1722 prints read *mark*.

tocken may indicate a reminiscence of 2 Thessalonians 1. 4–5: 'So that we ourselves glory in you in the churches of God for your patience and faith in all your persecutions and tribulations that ye endure: Which is a manifest token of the righteous judgment of God, that ye may be counted worthy of the kingdom of God, for which ye also suffer.'

29. *28 years*: 1660–88; cf. above, 1.3, 52 and n.; 3.3, 31 and n.

31. *We did thrive under our persecutne*: cf. Curate 1692: 34: 'one Reason of their malicious and crabbed Nature may be, that they never suffered Affliction; for after they abdicated their Churches in 1662, they began everywhere in their Sermons to cant about the Persecution of the Godly, and to magnify their own Sufferings; by this Means they were pampr'd instead of being persecuted; some of the Godly Sisters supplying them with plentiful Gratuities to their Families, and Money to their Purses; they really lived better than ever they did before, by their Stipends'. To support this, he adduces the evidence of Alexander Shields (?1646–1700), author of the voluminous *A Hind Let Loose* (n.p., 1687), whom he describes as 'one of their honestest and best Writers': 'Though in the Wilderness of Prelatick, Erastian, and Antichristian Usurpations, we did not meet with Miracles, yet truly we have experienced Wonders of the Lord's Care and Kindness, and for all the Harrassings and Persecutions, &c. the poor Wilderness Wanderers have look'd as Meat-like and Cloath-like as others that sat at Ease in their Houses, and drank their Wine and their strong Drink.' I have not found the source of the quotation; so far as I can see, it is not *A Hind Let Loose*.

32. *evidently*: B and C, followed by the later prints, read *obviously*. The 1722 prints lack either word.

32. *wicked*: B and C, followed by the later prints, read *the wicked*. The 1722 prints agree with A.

33–4. *east side of Tay*: this area, extended to Aberdeenshire and the Moray coast, was the heartland of Scottish Episcopalianism.

35–7. *They say ... affrayd of him*: Covenant shows some slight inclination to sympathize with Orthodox, although the phrase *good enough at his owne trad* (his own *trade*) shows that he thinks of him, not as a minister, but as someone pursuing a different, even a rival, occupation. The Moderator is quick to point out the danger of leaving such men in charge of parishes.

40. *Arminiasme or Arrianisme*: see above, 4.2, 54–5 and n.

41. *dry moralitie*: see above, **Prologue**, 22n and the other references there cited. The more extreme Presbyterians were, in effect, antinomians, holding that justification resulted only from election, the arbitrary divine choice of a particular human being for salvation. The doctrine lies at the heart, for instance, of James Hogg's *Private Memoirs and Confessions of a Justified Sinner*; see below 159n. Cf. too Curate 1692: 3: 'They call peace, Love, Charity, and Justice, but dry Morality only'; *ibid.* 23: 'Morality with them is but old, out-dated, heathenish Vertue, and therefore such a book as the *Whole Duty of Man* is look'd upon with wodeful Contempt by them: Frazer of Brae [*Turbulent*], one of the greatest among them, professes downright, that there is no Gospel, nor any Relish of it, in that Book, and that *Aristotle's Ethicks* have as much true Divinity as that Book hath. And *John Vetch* of *Woodstruther* says, That that Book is too much upon Moral Duty. A certain Lady of their Stamp, getting it once into her Hands, and hearing that it was a moral Book done by an Episcopal Divine, she made a Burnt-Offering of it, out of her great Zeal against Episcopacy and Morality.'

For *The Whole Duty of Man* see above, **Prologue**, 22n.

Presbyterian condemnation of dry moralitie continued through the eighteenth century, often becoming the object of satire; cf., e.g., Burns in 'The Holy Fair', 118–35:

> But hark! the tent has chang'd its voice;
> 　　There's peace and rest nae langer;
> For a' the real judges rise,
> 　　They canna sit for anger.
> [Smith] opens out his cauld harangues
> 　　On practice and on morals;
> An' aff the godly pour in thrangs,
> 　　To gie the jars an' barrels
> 　　　　　　A lift that day.
>
> What signifies his barren shine
> 　　Of moral pow'rs an' reason;

> His English style, an' gestures fine,
>> Are a' clean out o' season.
> Like SOCRATES or ANTONINE,
>> Or some auld pagan heathen,
> The moral man he does define,
>> But ne'er a word o' faith in
>>> That's right that day.   (Kinsley 1968: I, 133)

The reaction of the Committee to the mere words resembles that of 'a' the real judges' to Smith's sermon.

42–3. *Huge ... doctrins*: B reads *Soul-Killing Error, huge Error, Soul-Killing Doctrine.*

43–4. *Cutt ... ground*: the 1722 editions read *cut down the charming Gourd. Gourd* (French *gourd*, 'benumbed, stiff') is an adjective, used here as a noun, and sometimes applied to Episcopacy: 'that old gourd wicked oak' (R. Baillie, *Ladensium autokatakrisis. The Cantaburians self-conviction* [Edinburgh, 1640], I, 287 [see *DOST*, s.v.]; the work is an attack on the high-church doctrines of Archbishop Laud). If this represents the original words of Pitcairne and his associates, they may have confused the word with the noun *gourd*, as found, e.g., in Jonah 4. 6–11. *Charming* is 'enchanting, bewitching' in a pejorative sense. The A text may be a deliberate alteration.

46. *fenced*: 'opened' (Scots legal term).

46–7. *in Christ's owne name ... no appeall*: the court, that is, the Committee, usurps the powers of Christ at the Last Judgement; hence the Moderator's assertion that there is to be no appeal against its decision.

47–8. *We designe to be moderate ... tack your kirk*: in his letter read to the General Assembly on 17 October 1690, King William remarked: 'Moderation is what religion enjoins, neighbouring churches expect from you, and we recommend to you' (*GA Acts* 1843, article II). On 18 October the Assembly replied: 'We assure your Majesty, as in the presence of God and in expectation of his dreadful appearance, that we shall study that moderation which your Majesty recommends, as being convinced that it is the duty which religion enjoins and neighbouring churches do most justly expect from us; desiring in all things to approve ourselves unto God as the true disciples of Jesus Christ, who, though most zealous against all corruptions in his church, was most gentle towards the persons of men' (*ibid.*). The Moderator hypocritically keeps to the requirements of the final relative clause by offering no violence to the person of Mr Orthodox, zealously proposing to do no more than rob him of his church. The comment of Mr Orthodox (42–3) has thus some considerable justification.

49. *falts as weall to be done as done*: cf. above, 4.2, 74–82. Covenant's amendment (together with Turbulent's proposal of *ane universall lybell*) has already been put into effect.

The words are accidentally omitted in the 1722 texts. Orthodox in his reply refers to them.

53. *living*: B mistakenly reads *Liberty*.

55. *universall lybell*: cf. above, 4.2, 88–9 and n.

57. *Law of natur and nations*: cf. Walker 1981: 75: 'This is the law of nature, known naturally, either immediately, like unto those instincts which are in the other creatures, whereby they know what is necessary for their preservation'; *ibid.* 77: 'Besides this natural, necessary, and perpetual law, God hath also given to men voluntary and positive laws'; *ibid.* 79: 'the law common to many nations is that which is commonly called *the law of nations*'.

61. *concerned ovir*: B and C, followed by the printed texts, read *to answer*.

63–89. *Wheras ... and destroyed*: this is the *Universall lybell*, proposed by Turbulent above, 4.2, 75. In A the name and parish of the accused are left blank; in B the name is given in the generalized form *A.B.*, the parish as *M*. The wording of the *lybell* is a satirical invention by Pitcairne but not without some justification; cf. below, **Preface**, p. 227: 'The most part of the articles of the *Libella universalis* was made use of by him [Turbulent, Mr Fraser of Brae] to thrust out the Episcopal clergy of Fyfe. *Mr Johnston* of *Burntisland*, and *Mr Johnston* of *Saline*, were both suspended by him for being ordained by a bishop, and recommending *The whole duty of man*; and many more, for these, and the rest of the ridiculous articles in that universal libel; (for I assure you that was their exact way of libelling). The Episcopal ministers could not have the liberty to see or hear the witnesses depose against them; and particularly, when *Mr Bowes*, minister at *Abbotshall*, quoted an act of parliament to this purpose, *Mr Fraser* told him roundly, that he was not to be governed by the acts of parliament, but by the spirit of God.'

With the long list of charges, compare and contrast the even longer series of Acts of Parliament which mark the climax of Lindsay's *Ane Satyre of the Thrie Estaitis* (3793–3951). Lindsay's document is the theatrical high in the optimistic adumbration of reform; in *The Phanaticks* this is the corresponding nadir.

66–7. *for they ar ... diminish from them*: an apparent *non-sequitur*. The underlying reference, however, is to the three-fold order of bishops, priests and deacons, for which the Presbyterians claimed there is no scriptural warrant.

68. *stinted*: 'fixed'; 'in the controversies of the 17th c. frequently applied to set liturgical forms as opposed to "free" prayer' (*OED*).

68–70. *Lord's Prayer ... his liftyme*: cf. below, **Preface**, p. 227: 'This hero [Turbulent] made a speech against the Lord's prayer, not long ago, in his own church at *Culross*, going through all the articles of it, proving that we should not say it. *1ˢᵗ* (says he) *We cannot say, Our Father which art in heaven, except we know we were predestinated; for I'm sure the devil's a father to many of you.* He goes on, *If you were going to bed at night, it were nonsense to say, Give us this day our daily bread. The,n* (continues he) *if I were owing any of you 1000 merks, none of you would forgive me; so no more can you say, Forgive us our debts as we forgive our debtors.* So after this fashion he refuted the saying of the Lord's prayer.' Cf. too Curate 1692: 13–14: 'They have quite banished the use of the Lord's Prayer ... The smoothest Reason that they alledge for their forbearing it, is, That the Use thereof is inconvenient ... I doubt not but that many have heard long e're now of a Conference betwixt my Lord B- and a ruling Elder in the North. In short, it is this: Five Presbyterian Preachers last Year, [1691] appointed themselves Judges, to purge two or three Dioceses in the North. They took to assist, or to accompany them, some whom they call Ruling-Elders, one of whom entreated my Lord *B-* to further with his Help the happy and blessed Reformation, particularly by giving in Complaints against igno-rant, scandalous, and erroneous Ministers, that the Church of God might be replenished with the Faithful: Truly then *(saith my Lord)* there is one whom I can prove to be very Atheistical, Ignorant, and Scandalous. At which the ruling Elder began to prick up his Ears; *And pray you, Sir,* (says he) *Who is the Man? Indeed* (says my Lord) *I will be free with you, it is Mr. James Urquhart, one of your own Preachers, who is come with you now to sit as a Judge upon others; and by Witnesses of unquestionable Honesty I can make it appear that he said, if ever Christ was drunk upon Earth, it was when he made the Lord's Prayer. And I appeal to your self, who are a Ruling-Elder, whether or not this be Blasphemy? Some other Things of scandalous Nature I can prove against him. O but* (says he) *we are not come here to judge our Brethren, our business is with the Curates.'*

Mr James Urquhart was a member of the Commission for Visitations on the North Side of Tay (*GA Acts* 1843, 1690, article XVII).

72–3. *The Whol Duty of Man*: see above, **Prologue**, 22n.

75. *Catechiseing*: 'giving instructions in the Catechism', that is to say, 'an instruction to be learned of every person before he be brought to be confirmed by the Bishop' (*Book of Common Prayer*). Included are the Apos-tles' Creed and (only in the Scottish form) the Gloria, together with the Ten Commandments and the Lord's Prayer.

76. *lectureing*: i.e. 'expounding the Scriptures'.

77. *administrats*: B and C, followed by the later printed texts, read *administers*.

privatlie: this was forbidden in the presbyterian church. Episcopalians permitted it, but it was always regarded with some reservation.

212

charmeing: putting a spell or charm (on someone); cf. above, 35n.

78. *since the blessed Revolutione*: since 1688/9. B and C, followed by the printed texts, use this phrase to introduce article 8.

With *blessed Revolutione* contrast below, 149–92.

80. *concurrance*: B reads *Countenance*. The printed texts and C agree with A.

80. *the K.*: B and C, followed by the printed texts, read *the destroying of the K.*

85. *wer re-established*: B and C, followed by the printed texts, read *should be brought back again.*

88. *deprived and*: B and C, followed by the printed texts, read *deprived, deposed and.*

90–1. *positively ... not done*: the Moderator reverses the order of the General Confession for Mattins in *The Book of Common Prayer*: 'We have left undone those things which we ought to have done; And we have done those things which we ought not to have done.'

95. *infamous*: 'of evil fame or repute' (*DOST*).

100. *lend*: 'loan'.

101. *stipend*: 'salary'; 'in Scotland practically confined to the payment received by a clergyman' (*OED*).

101. Stage direction: *On knock at the door*: cf. the knocking at the gate in *Macbeth*, 2.2 and 3.

102. *rape*: 'rap'.

112. *God's work*: B reads *God's own work.*

112. *then*: B and C, followed by the printed texts, read *e'en in the next place.*

113. *better obey God than man*: Acts 5. 29: 'We ought to obey God rather than man.' Not in B, C or the printed texts.

114. *first*: not in B, C or the printed texts.

120–35. *Gentlemen ... W.R.*: William resented the actions of the Commission, but sent no such letter. For the actual sequence of events see Riley 1979: 63–5.

122. *driving*: 'moving with force or speed, rushing, dashing' (*DOST*); the phrase *driving so furiously* is probably an echo of 2 Kings 9. 20: 'the driving is like the driving of Jehu the son of Nimshi; for he driveth furiously'. B reads *driving on*, but is not followed by C or the printed texts.

126. *jus divinianus*: probably a scribal mistranscription of the reading preserved in B, *Ius divinums* (the final -s indicating the vernacular plural). The reference is to the supposed Divine Rights of the presbyterian church; cf. the title of Samuel Rutherford's book, *The Divine Right of Church-Government and Excommunication*, mentioned above, 2.3, 105n. Also intended is a cross-reference to the doctrine of the Divine Right of Kings.

213

127. *who hes*: B and C, followed by the printed texts, have the more English reading *which hath*.

130. *We command you*: B retains the Scots form of the verb, *We commands you*.

to dissolve: B, but not C or the printed texts, reads *to be dissolved*.

133. *W.R.*: William *Rex*, King William. Not in B.

135. *broad seall*: i.e. the Great Seal. 'The Great Seal is affixed to proclamations, writs, letters patent, and documents giving power to sign and ratify treaties' (Walker 1980: 536). Salathiel implies that God, as King, has thus confirmed the authority of the Committee by the issue of letters patent in the form of the Old and New Testaments.

136–7. *The Ks right ... privative*: Salathiel means that, in terms of God's letters patent, the king has no power to dissolve the Committee, his power being *accumulative*, 'characterised by accumulation', rather than *objectively privative*, 'having the quality of depriving in relation to its object (i.e. the Committee)' – a fairly meaningless scholastic distinction.

137–8. *no be affraid ... doe to us*: cf. Psalm 56. 11: 'I will not be afraid what man can do unto me.'

138. Stage direction: for *all the Comittie cry 'yes'* B and C, followed by the printed texts, read *The Committee Crys out 'And not to be afraid what man can do.'*

140. *for*: B reads *or else*. The 1722 prints read *or*, C and the later prints *else*.

141. *draw*: B and C, followed by the printed texts, have the more modern form, *drag*.

144. *young man yet & he hes*: B and C, followed by the printed texts, read *King* for *man*. In the presence of the Captain, the Moderator restrains his language, putting the blame on the king's counsellors rather than the king himself.

145. *double*: B and C, followed by the printed texts, correctly read *double verse*, i.e. eight lines in common metre. The reading in A probably results from a copyist's mistake.

148. *a day-long a word*: so B. C and the printed texts have variants on *a Word a Day long*. After *word* B and C, followed by the printed texts, read *Els I'll interrupt you. Therefore*.

149–50. *We have brought our hogs to a bra mercate*: proverbial (Wilson 1970: 376). Note the change in the Moderator's tone, emphasized by the later *perfidious usurper*, etc.

bra: 'braw', 'fine, splendid'.

151–2. *wicked limb ... devill*: not in B, C or the printed texts.

151–2. *compact with the devill*: note the suggestion that the churchmen's support of William is in fact a pact with Satan, like that supposedly made by witches and warlocks.

152. *dethroned ... father & Uncle*: B and C, followed by the printed texts, read *dispossest his old honest Father of the Crown*.

William was the son of James' sister, Mary, who married William II, prince of Orange. His wife was Mary, James' elder daughter by his first wife, Anne Hyde.

153. *curst*: not in B, C or the printed texts.

156. *against all deadlie*: 'against all mortals'. The phrase is common in Scots legal usage (*DOST* s.v. **Ded(e)ly, Deidly b.**).

155–8. *He promised ... may come o't*: the Moderator's sentiments resemble those of the old covenanting woman Elizabeth Maclure in Scott's *Old Mortality*: 'And anes it was thought something might be made by bringing back the auld family as a new bargain and a new bottom ... and sae, though ae part of our people were free to join wi' the present model and levied an armed regiment under the Yearl of Angus, yet our honest friend [Balfour of Burleigh] and others of purity and doctrine and freedom of conscience were determined to hear the breath o' the Jacobites before they took part again them' (Mack 1993: 331).

James, titular earl of Angus, later 2nd marquess of Douglas (c. 1646–1700), raised a regiment, later known as the Cameronians or Scottish Rifles, from among the extreme Covenanters, particularly of Lanarkshire, to resist the Jacobite army after Killiecrankie. On 21 August 1689 they successfully held Dunkeld, Perthshire, against a much superior Jacobite force and thus saved the Lowlands from invasion and the situation in Scotland for King William. Many of their fellows (like Mrs Maclure) disapproved even to the extent of considering negotiations for the return of King James. The Moderator now concurs, although previously he and his clerical brethren had lent their support by a proclamation displayed at the Cross and harbour of Leith, from which the Cameronian regiment had embarked on their way by sea to Perth or Dundee, from which they marched to Dunkeld.

The proverbial 'We sud no doe ill that good may come o't' (Wilson 1970: 562) sums up the Moderator's regret. They are now being punished for the evil they did by supporting the usurper in the hope that he would forward ends regarded by them as good.

The reference to Leith and Angus' regiment is missing from B, C and the printed texts.

159. *Conscientia Hollandia*: Latin: 'a Dutch conscience'.

160. *atheisme*: the primary reference is probably to the rather limited Dutch toleration of the Jewish philosopher Baruch Spinoza (1632–77), who remained in Holland despite the fact that in 1656 he had been excommunicated from the Amsterdam synagogue for 'atheism'. His mathematically expressed concept of God as immanent rather than transcendent was regarded by most of his contemporaries as atheistic.

161. *in Irland ... us*: B and C, followed by the printed texts, read *In Scotland Presbyterie, In Ireland Popery.*

poprie: the first civil article of the Treaty of Limerick (3 October 1691) declared that 'the Catholics of Ireland in general were to enjoy such privileges "as they enjoyed under Charles II and as were consistent with the laws of Ireland". Ginkle [William's commander in Ireland] pledged his word that their Majesties would endeavour to reduce the number of attainders and procure further securities for the Irish Catholics from Parliament' (Curtis 1964: 273). The clause, like most of the treaty, was soon violated.

161–2. *Infer ergo*: Latin: 'Conclude therefore'. B reads *in fine*, 'in the end'. C and the printed texts omit, or substitute *infero ergo*, 'I conclude therefore'.

162. *Si aliquis ... est*: Latin: 'If any man is guilty of idolatry, that man is'; cf. above, 5.1, 34–5 and n. B has *aliquus* (impossible Latin for anyone but Salathiel) for *aliquis* and *Idolatrie* for *Idolrie*. The text varies in C and the printed editions, but most lose point by repeating the text in 5.1, 34–5.

163–5. *He pretends ... Spaine etc.*: a reference to the mixture of religious beliefs among the constituent members of the Grand Alliance during the Nine Years War.

165–6. *if the house ... about it*: proverbial (Wilson 1970: 259); cf. Swift, *A Complete Collection of Genteel and Ingenious Conversation ... in Three Dialogues* (London, 1738), Dialogue II: 'You are come to a sad dirty house; I am sorry for it, but we have had our hands in mortar.' The text refers to the negotiations during the building of the 'house', the Grand Alliance.

167–8. *That tyrant ... his owne*: cf. above, 1.1, 68 and n.

169–71. *ther's a man ... goes frie*: reference obscure. The corresponding passage in the **Preface** (below, p. 227) names the first man as 'the E. of H-' (presumably the Earl of Home), the second as 'the E. of S'. This looks like a reference to John Dalrymple (1648–1707), son of the 1st Viscount Stair, widely regarded as a villain (see above, 4.4, 120n), but he became an earl only in 1703.

171. *frie*: B and C, followed by the printed texts, continue *up and down the Streets.*

172. *his Ambition's hellish Hypocarit*: for *his*, B and C, followed by the printed texts, read *K. Will:*

Hypocarit: 'hypocrisy'. Probably sg. of the plural form *hypocreeties*, on record on the nineteenth century with the meaning 'hypocrisies' (*SND*). Not in *DOST* or *OED*.

173. *Jeroboam*: first king of the ten tribes making up the northern kingdom of Israel, which separated from Judah and Benjamin (1 Kings 12.

17–14, 20). He reigned 924–03 BC. His chief offence was to set up two golden calves, one at Dan, one at Bethel, saying 'Behold thy gods, O Israel, which brought thee up out of the land of Egypt.'

173. *Ahab*: seventh king of Israel (1 Kings 16. 29–22, 40). He reigned 873–51 BC and, under the influence of his wife, the Sidonian Jezebel, 'did more to provoke the Lord God of Israel to anger than all the kings of Israel that were before him' (*ibid.*, 16. 33).

his Q.: Mary II, daughter of James VII and II.

174. *painted Jezebell*: 2 Kings 9. 30.

After *painted* B and C, followed by the printed texts, insert *whore*.

174–5. *the dogs ... yet*: 1 Kings 21. 23; 2 Kings 9. 36; 10. 30–37.

For *her blood* B and C, followed by the printed texts, read *both their bloods*. For the fate of Ahab see 1 Kings 21. 19; 22. 38.

175. *Nebigodnazer*: i.e. Nebuchadnezzar, king of Babylon.

176. *to eat ... with beasts*: Daniel 4. 32–3.

the unnaturall ... he brings: B and C, followed by the printed texts, read *they are more Unnaturall than any Brute*.

theu: sg. of *thewis*, 'personal qualities or characteristics; customs, habits, behaviour' (*DOST*; no example of the sg. is given). In OE and early ME, sg. *þeaw* is not uncommon, but later the form virtually disappears; see *OED*, s.v. **Thew**.

177. *All kings ar tyrants*: this is an extreme statement. In general, Presbyterians were more moderate, holding with George Buchanan that only the rule of a tyrannical monarch justified rebellion or assassination.

177–8. *Church never thrives ... on ther bloods*: a reversal of the dictum of Tertullian (c. 160 – c. 220): 'As often as we are mown down by you, the more we grow in numbers; the blood of Christians is the seed' ('semen est sanguis Christianorum; Apologeticum' 50, 13); traditionally 'the blood of martyrs is the seed of the Church'. There is probably also a satirical side-reference to the episcopalian cult of the executed Charles I, 'Charles, King and Martyr' (Farmer 1987: 455).

178–9. *Now togethr ... did agane. It*: B and C, followed by the printed texts, read *100 pounds for one of their heads again. O! that*. In A the Moderator prays for the return of one of the commissioners who sentenced Charles I to death; in B and C he asks for the head either of William or his queen. Cf. below, **Preface**, p. 225: 'Mr Kennedy ... would take off a tyrant's head (for so he names all Kings) with as great pleasure as he, just now possesses a curate's living.'

181. *proved 3 year agoe*: presumably in *A Rational Defence of Non-Conformity* (London, 1689).

182–3. *is on ... Confederatione*: B and C, followed by the printed texts, read *will not break off*.

Confederatione: the Grand Alliance against Louis XIV.

184–5. *the kings ... Christ*: Revelation 19. 19: 'And I saw the beast, and the kings of the earth, and their armies, gathered together to make war against him who sat on the horse [Christ], and against his army.'

185. *Laws*: B and C, followed by the printed texts, read *Cause*. The reading in A is almost certainly the better; the laws of Christ are implicitly contrasted with the laws of earthly kings. Turbulent is prepared to defy the latter for the sake of the former.

185–6. *then ... verse*: B and C, followed by the printed texts, read *therefore follow the advice*.

186–7. *Lett us ... from us*: Psalm 2. 3: 'Let us break their bands asunder, and cast away their cords from us.'

B and C, followed by the printed texts, read *Lett us brack their bonds and cut their cords asunder &c.*

187–8. *Oaths ... Assurance*: see above, 1.1, 49 and n.

188. *bretheren in the west cuntrie*: see above, 1.1, 204n; 5.2, 49n.

189–92. *and lett ... potentats of earth*: B, C and the printed texts omit.

189. *our Assemblie*: 'our next meeting' – not a reference to a General Assembly; cf. above, 1 and n.

190. *in Glasgow*: to avoid the attentions of the Edinburgh City Guard and to be more under the wing of *our bretheren in the west cuntrie*.

193. *overtur*: 'proposal'.

We'il all follow it: B and C, followed by the printed texts, read *We'll follow your advyce*.

194. *Pack you of*: 'Clear off!'

rebells: not in B. C and the printed texts read *ye Villains*.

197. *Your Moderator ... wound o't*: Professor McGavin suggests that this refers to an attempt to pick off the king's seal from the document; the seal would leave a red 'wound' mark of dried wax on the paper. B and C, followed by the printed texts, omit.

200. *verse*: stanza 3 of Psalm 109 in the Metrical Version appointed for use in the Church of Scotland. James Hogg made use of this and the two succeeding stanzas in *The Private Memoirs and Confessions of a Justified Sinner* (Hogg 1983: 32), 'verses', as he called them, 'which it is a pity should ever have been admitted into a Christian psalmody'. The singing of the psalm marks a turning point in the life of the Justified Sinner; he takes it as proof 'that his father and brother were cast-away reprobates, aliens from the church and the true faith, and cursed in time and eternity' – a conclusion which leads him to the murder of his brother and the death of his father. The Committee similarly (and with similar implications) condemn King William to perdition.

B includes the first two lines of stanza 4, 'Few be his dayes and in his

Room/ His Charge an other take'; 'an other' is glossed as 'K. Ja:' and in line 4 of stanza 3 'Satan' is glossed 'i. K. Lewis' (Louis XIV).

C and the printed editions include a distorted version of the entire stanza 4, but have no glosses.

It was usual to end meetings by singing a psalm. The 1690 General Assembly, like its successors, ended with the very different Psalm 133:

> Behold, how good a thing it is,
> and how becoming well,
> Together such as brethren are
> in unity to dwell!

Epilogue

1. *Circumstance*: 'the collective details of a matter' (*DOST*, s.v. **Circumstance 2**).

1, 4. *plott*: see above, 2.2, 51n. So far, at least, as it deals with the clergy, *The Phanaticks* lacks a well-rounded conclusion. The **Epilogue** defends the authors' apparent failure to provide one. The action simply corresponds to the way in which the fanatics behave. Verbally, the defence turns on two of the multiple significances of the word *plot*, 'the plan or scheme of any literary creation' and 'conspiracy' (*OED*, s.v. **Plot, 6, 7**). The use of the word in the play has already been emphasized; see above, 2.2, 51 and n.

Thomas Otway (1652–85) was another dramatist who exploited the word. *Venice Preserved, or, A Plot Discover'd* (1682: Gosse 1932: 241) is a play written from a Tory viewpoint against the background of the Popish Plot and the Exclusion crisis, the latter both directed against the duke of York, the future James VII and II. The 'Prologue' opens thus:

> In these distracted times, when each man dreads
> The bloody stratagems of busy heads;
> When we have feared three years we know not what,
> Till witnesses began to die o' th' rot,
> What made our poet meddle with a plot?
> Was't that he fancied, for the very sake
> And name of plot, his trifling play might take?
> For there's not in't one inch-board evidence,
> But 'tis, he says, to reason plain and sense,
> And that he thinks a plausible defence.
> Were Truth by Sense and Reason to be tried,
> Sure all our swearers might be laid aside;
> No, of such tools our author has no need,
> To make his plot, or make his play succeed. (1–14)

For Pitcairne and his fellow-authors, the Glorious Revolution was a more successful version of earlier political plots, but the later 'conspirators' seemed even less rational than Titus Oates and his dupes. Pitcairne and his friends use the same defence as Otway; they use their commonsense and speak truth.

2. *Our authors*: in A the phrase is written twice (dittography). This is the only occasion in A on which the plural, *authors*, appears, but cf. above, **Prologue**, 31–2n; below, 10, *our author* (followed in the next line by the pl. pronoun *we*); Appendix I, p. 231.

out of meer design: 'deliberately'.

3. *the phanaticks ... represent*: a probable indication of the title of the play; see Introduction, above, p. xiii.

4. *intent*: 'purpose'; *no fixt plott nor regular intent* refers primarily to the Committee's sudden reversal of loyalties in 5.3, but includes their earlier jangling among themselves. It also has a more extended application to the vacillations in general Whig policy.

5. *throu thick & thine*: proverbial (Wilson 1970: 810).

6. *always*: B, followed by the printed texts, reads *lumbled* ('jumbled'), perhaps a deliberate alteration by Pitcairne.

7. *interest*: 'advantage'.

drivs ... furiouslie: cf. above, 5.3, 96. The Presbyterians are compared to the regicide Jehu, 'for he driveth furiously' (2 Kings 9. 20). Jehu (845–817 BC) was anointed tenth king of Israel before killing his predecessor, Ahab. There is an implied parallel with King William.

8. *ruls ... policie*: cf. Hobbes 1973: 93: 'the Rules, whereby every man may know, what Goods he may enjoy, and what Actions he may doe, without being molested by any of his fellow Subjects'.

policie: 'established system of law and order'; cf. 'The true church ... in her ... presbyteries, sessions, policie, disciplines' (National Covenant 1638, quoted in *DOST*, s.v. **Policie 2**).

9. *freinds they*: B, followed by the printed texts, reads *freedome may*. If the reading in A does not represent a textual corruption, *freinds* is used ironically of the Presbyterians.

10, 11. *truth ... truth*: cf. above, 1, 4n.

12. *honest Torries*: the phrase hints at the existence of 'dishonest' Tories, of which there were quite a few.

king: James VII and II.

13. *stab*: B, followed by the 1722 print, has the better reading *stobb*, 'a thrust with a pointed weapon, a stab' (*DOST*). The reference is to political assassination. The authors may have had in mind the murder on 31 March 1689 of the head of the Scottish judiciary, the Lord President Sir George Lockhart (c. 1630–89), by John Chiesley of Dalry. Pitcairne obviously thought that this had political and religious implications (MacQueen and MacQueen 2009: 70).

14–15. *westerne ... State*: Pitcairne puts the behaviour of the State, the Scottish parliament, in 1689 and subsequently, on the same level as that of the *westerne mob*, who had 'rabbled' the Curates.

16. *abdiceate*: see above, **Prologue**, 14n.

20. *prase*: probably 'phrase' rather than 'praise'. B, followed by the printed texts, reads *phrase*.

mistresss: pl., 'mistresses'.

22. *decorum*: the neo-classical dramatic principle of making words correspond to the rank and position of the speaker.

23. *Jack*: cf. **Prologue**, 9 and n.

never: B, C and the printed texts read *ne'er*, a pronunciation demanded by the rhyme with *prayer*.

25. *vougue*: 'vogue'. The earliest examples of this word are all from Scots sources; see *OED* and *DOST*.

27–8: *Let ... any more*: epilogue and play conclude on an appropriately Jacobite note.

Appendix I

The Preface

In MS C the **Preface**, which follows, appears after the **Prologue** and **Dramatis Personae**. It is the first item in the 1752 and subsequent printed editions. Almost certainly it is the work of Archibald Pitcairne. It is in accordance with his literary habit; he wrote explanatory 'Keys' to many of his Latin poems (MacQueen and MacQueen 2009: 44–5). This is a more extended example of the same practice and is a document of some historical and critical importance. The text is that of MS C.

Preface

A Play in our nation, where witt so seldom appears, will be gazed upon by some, who doe not understand the nature of the thing, and laughed at by others who think witt and Ingenuity like fine Perriwigs and fashionable Cloths must be fetched from fforraigne places to serve their Caprice or please their humour. I have seen 5 some pieces of witt in our own Countrie which If they had come from ffrance or England would have been Esteemed the highest dashes of some Excellent pen; yet they lay here unregarded and neglected by the most part of our Intelligent men. This sufficiently argues, that we generally have a disgust of our own and a too 10 great fondness for things which come from abroad. The English have a fare different Humour from this. They admire nor applaud anything But what growes in their soil and is produced in their own airs. I think they are too Indulgent and partiall to themselves, and we are too severe and sharp to one another. Both Extreams 15 should be shuned, and therefore I intreat my Countrymen in their Censuring and judging this work, they would only Consider the play and not Regard the persons that write it. In defence of this essay, we must Ingadge two parties, the Fanaticks and Critticks. The fanaticks wil call us Aeithists as they term those who oppose 20 them in the least punctilio. This is all the answer we Cane expect from them, for they are blest with stupidity and even satyre proof, soe they jogg on securly and persues their own interests with outt careing what the world knowes or says of them. Wee will take

some more pains to please the Criticques and will give them ane   25
Ingenious account of the whole matter. Wee accknowledge ther
is not in our play the same Embellishment of art, politeness of
Language or Regularity of plot, which is offerred in some of the
late English Comedies. The people we live among are narrow
and stingy and we are not sharpened with the Converse which   30
other places allow. Besides it is our first Essay, which Merits
some excuse, and the truth of the matters of fact may make also
some attonment for our faults. We have not had time to give our
Inventions scope, But only to Rouse up and Energie our memory;
we have rather played the pairt of a trew Historian than of ane   35
Exact comedian. The most pairt of the stories here Related were
said by one or other of the prysbeterian parties. We have sometime
put those tales in the mouth of others then those who said them,
but that very seldom. Nor could we bring on the stage all the
members of the generall Assemblie for that would have spoyled   40
the decorum of the play. But I hope the judicious and Impartiale
Reader shall safely decerne; that we have attributed nothing to any
but what is suitable and agreable to his Caracter.

That the E of Cr– (who is under the name of my Lord
Wiggriden) did severall times Mistake the meaning of the Ass.   45
Is as certain as any thing cane be for when the brethren were
speaking about the terms of Comunion with the Episcopall partie,
He took it for the sacrament of the Lords Supper and soe made a
Redicolous speach to that effect. The brethren who had no honour
to his Carrecter told him Roughly that he knew not what he was   50
saying: for they think ill manners as essentiale to Religione as
want of sense. That he called the whole crowd of people dispersed
through the Assemblie-house a board (as he called the Counsill-
table) Is knowen by every body who frequented their meetings.
That we make him take plantations of Gairdines for plantations   55
of Kirks is naturall enugh for a man who understands nothing
but Gairdenrie and frequently uses to mistake. He always mixeth
together bitts of Nehemia and pieces of Arcadia, as we may
see in the printed Speach before the parliment which I beleeve
is the strangest medley ever wes seen. That he sought moneths   60
to advise and fitt himself for beeing a member of the assemblie
when it was to sitt but one is Clear from the Historicall account
of the Gen-Ass. The matters of fact in it none yet had the brow
to deney. For all his pretences to Religion, yet to obligde one
friend or Complement one, whom he's affraid on: He'l doe things   65

both against his Conscience and his reason. For soe he latly told the Viscount of Tarb: he had done in Subscriving ane act for his pensione. His malice and Injustice to the Episcopall Clergie ev'n to those who comply'd to the Civill Goverment; Is well knowen in this kingdome, and that his sense is as litle as his estate, which   70
is none att alle, No man who hath any sense doubts on't.

The Mod. Mr H. K. hath matter eneugh to doe his bussiness on, and is not oblidged much to borrow his Expressions from his canting Bretheren, every body who had the honour to see him in the Chair must confess that he begane his speaches with   75
a By his providence we are met here in this place We are again reassembled and Ile tell you possitivly what it is, and Negativly what it is not, and such happy stumble as this into pure nonsense. He was so violent a firie that he was Excomunnicated long agoe by the prysbyterians them selves as a fire brand sent from Hell   80
to inflam Christs kirk here on earth, It's knowen that he prayed in the assemblie to drowne the noise and silence the bable of the brethren He uses his own words in all the prayers Except this on He desires Grace from God If he would Expect Glory which indeed is borrowed from one Mean a brother of his, who preaches   85
just now att Dalkieth. The Curats must fall a victim to his fury, for none of them tho' they fully Comply cane keep their Livings while he poseses his Chair, Tho the Nobility and Gentry yea King and Queen, should Request it, Kings as well as Curats if they be not Covenanted (for soe they frase it) must be deposed yea killed   90
to if they be not for the good cause. They say the Mod. Is witty (and his own partie calls him packie). The only Instance of this which I know is that he made a better bargain then Judas for Iudas sold our Saviour for thirty pieces of silver But Mr Ke– got ane hundered pieces of gold for his pairt in selling K-C the I. poor,   95
sillie, fickle Iudas repented and flang back the money again. Butt wise stedfast Mr Ke– keeps well what he got and thrists for more and would take a tyrants head (for so he names all kings) with as great pleasure as he just now poseses a Curats Leaving.

When we Represent Mr Gilbert Rule (who is under the name   100
of Mr Salathiel Littlesense) Wee don't confine ourselves closely to his discourses in the Gen. Ass. But we take in some of his speeches said in the Colledge this winter. That famous saying of his in a publick Lecture: *Si aliqus virus* etc. Is so knowen through the town that he is Nicknamed Doctor Guiltus from   105
that very thing. If I should tell his manadgment in the College

this winter and his Latine Speeches or rather his Scots speeches
ending in Latin terminations, with a thousand other follies and
Villanies, It would make a pleasant eneugh Comedie by itself,
and Sufficiently expose the whole Prysbyterians who have picked   110
him out of their whole partie to fill such a Considerable place
and to succeed so Excellent a man as the Learned Dr Monro.
Ignorance, which is a fitter parent of Impudence than Devotione,
made this fellow attacque the learned Dr Stilling-fleet, with
ane impertinent scrible on ane impertinent subject to witt the   115
Iure divino-ship of presbytrie, which few men of witt Sense or
Ingenuity ever pretended to mentain. I am Confident If I should
Rake the Dunghill of his Crimes and folly Declare his Ignorance
and Knavry to the world, none would read his writings who read
his life, in short his, Carrecter is always to be Nibling att speeches   120
often speaking nonsense and still wrong Latine.

It were ane unpardonable fault if the worthy Mr Kr– did not
bear a considerable pairt in our play, he who hath the trew meen,
Gesture, actions, and Speaches of a Comedian, when he hath
once got into the pulpit; the people of the town use to flock about   125
him as they use to doe about a stage player. He'll tell yow from
any text of five Lost Labours, 3 opportunities 3 Lamentattions
3 woes 3 prophecies 3 doubts, 3 fears, 2 proposalls, & a word
about Scotland and ane other about a Dog and so he's done. Then,
when he's to fall upon Controversie drawing up and down his   130
breeches, he'll tell you he must take a word of a whore (for soe
he names the Church of Rome) so that leads him to speak about
the Virgine Mary, whom he says hir husband Joseph felt the first
night he beded with hir, and found hir with Child, he Immediatly
concluded she was a whore, as I would have done my self (says   135
he) and was goeing to putt hir away, for who could have been
Jealous of the Holy Ghost.

He's as comicale in giveing the Comunion, for latly at Cramand
he clapt a bitt of breid in his nixt nighbours hand, and said, Saint
eat this and your breads broken, then he took the cup and desired   140
them all to drink heartilie for they were all very welcome; we
must give you Some account of his way of praying, He'l pray that
God would bring back our banished King then he will make a long
stop, and soe will suprize the audience and tell god not to mistake
him: For it's not K Ja. But King Jesus who hath been banashed   145
these 28 years. Then quhen he prays for people troubled in spirit,
he'l tell its a wholesome disease; and wish that many moer were

soe, because he was once bound himself. He justly bears the name
of plain dealer, for he opposed the whole ass. Often and stumbled
into many sad truths, he said their fool praying was Hipocritical,   150
and the were seeking their own Intrests. And in a Sermone latly
preached he fairly arraigned the Goverment and said the E. of H–
who's trew to his god and his King in his own fashion he's Clapt
up in prisone, But the E. of S who's trew to none of them, he's att
present freedome. I think (says he) our Goverment Shall Never be   155
right. His Sermons are comedies without plots, they are the Chat
of the Taverns and Coffee-houses. The divertisment of the Young
people in town. In Short he's more famous for those Notes of
Sermons then the other is for his Latine, when he takes a freak in
his head, he's for moderation, nor out of any frndness he has for   160
the Episcopalle Clergy But out of ane Humour of Singularity, a
Spirit of Contradiction, and oftentimes for want of thinking; for
he who Speaks without thinking cannot be very Consequentiale
to himself, but fall Into a great many absurdities.

Mr Fr– Br. deserveth the name of Turbulent very well for he's   165
as huffing, insolent crossgrained a fellow as ever lived – his whole
trade when he was Young was to debeauch Ladys waiting wemen,
But now when he's graver he talks obscenly and Shewes a thing
not to be named to the maid, as he did to a great many wimen
Latly at the Cross of Duneferling. Now for wimen he takes wine   170
and drinks as great a Quantity of hard sack, as Curats doe of Ale;
his pairty calls the fumes of the Liquor the operations of the spirit
of God, and his fury and madness they term trew Zealousness. The
most part of the Articles of the Lybella Universalis was made use
of by him to thirst out the Episcopall Clergy of ffyfe. Mr Johnson   175
of Bunisland and Mr Johnsone in Saline were both suspended
by him for beeing ordeaned by a Bishop and Recomending the
whole duty of man, And many more for those and the rest of the
Redicolous articels of that universall Lybell (for I assure you that
was the Exact way of Lybelling) The Episcopall Ministers could   180
not have the Liberty to see or hear the witnesses depose against
them And Parlary when Mr Bows minister of Abbotshall quotted
ane act of parliment to this purpose Mr Fr. Told him Roundly that
he was not to be governed by the acts of parl[iment] but by the
Spirit of god; This Hero made a Speach against the Lords prayer   185
not long ago in his own Church att Culross, goeing throughout
the articels of it proveing that we should not say it,/1st/ says he
we cannot say our father which art etc. Except we know we are

227

Predestinatt, For I am sure (said He) the Devill is a father to many
of you. he goes on, if you were goeing to bed att night, it were 190
Nonsense to say Give us this day our daily bread, Then Continues
he if I were owing any of you a 1000 Mks none of you would
forgive me; Soe no more cane you say forgive us our debts as we
forgive our debtors Soe after this fashion he refused the saying
of the Lords prayer But ane other Presbyterian minister in the 195
north was much franker and said if ever Christ was Drunk in his
life; It was when he made this prayer. In short we have made Mr
ffr– speak nothing but what he actually said ether in the Gen.
Ass. In his sermons, or in the Presbytrie of Cullross of which he
is moderator. 200

Mr Da.– W– is called Mr Solomon Cherrietrees for that famous
action of his In getting with Child the Lady Cherrietrees in that
instant time, when the souldiers were searching the house to Carry
him away to suffer the Just punishment of a Rebell and a traitour.
We ingeniously Confess that all the speeches said by Mr Solomon 205
were not actuale said by Mr Da.– But I think all that was Sayed
is agreable eneugh to his Carrecter, who is so famous for Love-
intrigues who preaches so oft out of the Canticles and talks so
much in his Sermons of Beds of Roses and Damms of Love. Tho
he be pretty old yet Nature is not so Decayed in him as in the 210
other. He carries about with him, the old man in the Literale sense,
he's a compleat Tartuffe; and under the marks of pietie he acts his
Lacivious tricks. Not a year ago he sent for a woungh wench and
told her that She was with Child. She answered she was not with
Child then he said he ought to see if it was so, Soe he handled 215
hir breasts and Bellie very Roughly, and after this he sat down
and prayed a long while with hir. The Maid Gives this account
hir selff. Modestie would not allow hir to Say more. But we May
Easily Guess the rest out.

I shall not mention the Extraordinarie avarice and Covetousness 220
of the Presbyterian Ministers, which is more peculiar to them then
to any sett of men in the world. Neither Shall I tell you they
Devour Widows houses, chouse old Sillie weomen, ruin good
families, and by their Sneaking and Cheating get good Estates to
them Selves, even in the times of Persocutione (as they call them) 225
ffor I don't pretend to give ane exact account or History of the
Lives and actions of these Presbyterian Hero's that would swell
the preface to a Bigg Volume But I only relate some matters of
fact without which our play cannot be well understood Since these

are the Chief Champions for the good old Cause and God-Like 230
Saints of the Covenant, who by their own parties are esteemed
by fare the best and most learned, the most Eminent for gifts and
graces; It will be no Difficulty to make a judgment of the rest of
them.

That pairt that Mr Shittle bears in this play is a Carractor of the 235
whole complying Episcopall ministers. I shall name Mr De– who
made ane adress to the Comissione of the Kirk, telling them that he
and his bretheren had fully Complyed with the Civill Goverment
and would as frankly comply with their kirk Goverment and
desired to act as prysbyters in the Church. The adress was refused 240
and it was Resolved that none who served under Episcopacy and
had taken the test should be admitted to the Kirk. ffor say they if
we Should admitt these men who have Changed their principalls
and broken their oaths we could not be Secure of them. Tho' we
had them under a thousand tyes, Yet they should be readie to 245
Join with prelacie if it should please the prevailing partie to Set
it up again. Then we being the Smaaler pairt (say they) should be
thrast out again. The reasone is sufficiently good for these who
are only led by intrest. The speiches made by Mr Turncoat are
the very words which were spoken by Some Young men who had 250
their education under Episcopacie. I could name Some of them
Bu they are So Sillie and mean spirited fellowes that I think it
not wirth my times to trouble my Reader or myself in takeing a
particular Notice of them. The Love Scenes Contean the trew way
of the Presbyterian wooing. The Scenes betwixt the new mongers 255
Conteans the trew and genuine Language of the Biggots of both
parties, and the Scene about the Carracters needs no Commentary
since they are just and Exact.

Haveing briefly related the Matters of fact of which our play is
made up I Shall in a few words answer the objections which Shall 260
be made up against the manner of writing it. First then perhaps
the Criticques perhaps will Say that our play is made up of two
plots. The one of Love and the other about the Gen. Ass. Suppose
this were trew, we might defend our Selves by Example of some
of the ancients and Moderns too, of noe Small note who have 265
done this. But we are not oblidged to seek Shelter under authority
ffor reasone will sufficiently defend us. Our Intire and uniform
plot is to represent the villanies and follies of the presbyterians in
their publickt meetings and private transactions of their life; and

how have succeeded in both, we leave it to the judgment of the 270
Ingenious Reader.

Secondly It may be said that the Scene about my Lord Huffie
hath no connection with the plot and that is Lordship makes a
meor Parenthesis in our play. I answer that he does so in the State,
and Dashes so through thick and thin that its hard to get him keept 275
out of any thing. Besides, all the matters of fact said about him are
very trew and He's a great Hero in the Reformation And I doe not
see but this Scene agrees also well with the principall plot, as the
Reconcilment of Thais and Phaedra in Terences Eunuch with the
marriadge of Chairea and Chremes's sister, which is principally 280
intended by the Poet Yet it is thought Regular eneugh by all the
Judicious Criticks.

The third objectione is made by the grave and Serious men,
who don't quarell the Regularity of the plot but are Startled att
some Expressions. They say we make the Canticels a pimp to 285
Lust and that our Lovers fetch their Complements and make their
assignations out of that book which is formalie to Burlesque the
Scripture.

These Gentlemen's Zeall hath by fare got the better of their
reasone if they would Consider the ancients behaviour in this 290
matter they would soon have Cooler thoughts. Juvenall in his
Satyrs paints the vices of the age in Uglie Broad terms, Just as they
were acted out of a meer designe to Lash men from their follies,
and fright men from their vices by the Uglie Representations
of them. Even the Scripture it self brings in the fool saying in 295
his heart there is noe god. and Absalom consulting and acting
Treasone against his father and King, Yet for all that the Penmen
are naither to be accused of Aitheism nor Treasone. Why may not
we also bring in Hipocrites with Religion in their Mouths acting
the greatest Villanies that was ever heard on. 300

Fourthlie It may be objected, That for all our pretences to
truth and sincerity of matters of fact yet we talk att Random in
the last Scene Where we make the Presbyterian Ministers Speak
Basly and maliciously of all Kings, Tell the Captain of the Guard,
that they had a Comissione under the broad seal of Heaven, and 305
so refuse to rise till they were Compelled by force, and then to
run away in Confusione cursing their Enemies. This is Easily
answered If we Consider that the general assemblie always used
to Condradett and thwart the state, as is clear by severall of their
actts, but particulary by one which bears the name of Ane act and 310

declaration of the Gen. Assemblie against the act of parliament and Committee of Estates.

It may Likeways be Considered that the presbyterians are Enemies to Monarchy, for this is the third time that Presbyterians have been Established in Scotland and Still upon the death and 315 banishment of some of their lawfull Soveraigns. Also It Cannot be deneyed, but the present Presbyterian Ministers have alse much fury and alse litle wit, as in the time of Cromwell when the sate without ane order from the state and acted Independentlie on it, till Colnell Coterall was Sent with a Regiment to Raise 320 them. They told him they had a Comission to sit and presented the Bible to him, he desired them to read it, The brethren were a Litle puzeled att that, when the Colnell Threatned to Drag them thence; Soe they were forced to Rise and never mett till this time. The Chorus is as pertinent as anything cane be, Since they are a 325 set of men who nevar forgive ane Injury, and in stead of praying for conversion they power down Curses for the Confusion of their Enemies.

Our designe in this Essay is fully to Represent the Vilanie and follie of the phanaticks soe when they are in Sober mood They 330 may Seriously reflect on them and Repent for what is past and make ane mends for the future if it be possible. Or else that the Civill Goverment may be awakened and Rouzed to ridd us of the Impertinencie and Tyrrannie of this Gang, who Inguriously treat all good and learned men and are enemies to Humane Society itself. 335 This play was begune Just after the King of ffrance took Monse, as is clearly intimated in the first Scene, But by Reasone of some Gentlemans goeing to the Country who was Concerned in itt it Lay Dormant four Moneths then it was sett about again, and was very soon Compleatted. We Confess it was hastilie hudled together, 340 ffor we were not fourthnight about the haill work by Reasone of a Multitude of bussiness the Authors were Intangled in. I hope this will also draw a favourable Censure from the Ingenious reader. It was the Imployment of our Idle hours and we were Sufficiently pleased and Diverted by it, In Short Reader If thow take halfe 345 alse much plesure in reading it as we did in wryting it Thow will naithor think thy money nor paine ill bestowed.

Notes

1. *witt*: 'That part of speech or writing which consists in the apt association of thought and expression, calculated to surprise and delight by
its unexpectedness' (*OED*, s.v. **Wit 8**). 'True wit is Nature to advantage
dress'd,/ What oft was thought, but ne'er so well express'd' (Pope, *Essay
on Criticism*, 297–8). Wit in the play is to be found in the presentation of
Presbyterianism under many aspects, all immediately recognizable.

4. *Perriwigs*: 'large wigs of the kind worn by men of fashion and position in the seventeenth and eighteenth centuries'.

8. *dashes*: 'strokes', 'touches'; 'a hasty stroke of the pen' (*OED*, s.v.
Dash sb. **6**), but the usage here differs slightly.

17. *censuring*: 'giving an opinion upon' (with the suggestion that the
opinion is unfavourable).

18. *not Regard the persons that write it*: i.e. leave out of account the fact
that the authors are Episcopalians and Jacobites.

26. *Ingenious*: 'ingenuous', i.e. 'simple', 'straightforward'.

27. *politeness*: 'polish'.

29. *late English Comedies*: Pitcairne probably had principally in mind
comedies by such authors as Cowley and Crowne; see above, Introduction.

34. *Energie*: 'energise', 'operate' (Greek ἐνεργεῖν). Apparently a hapax.
Not in *OED* or *DOST*.

36. *Exact*: 'highly skilled', 'accomplished', 'refined'.
comedian: 'writer of comedies'.

41. *decorum*: 'unity', 'harmony'.

44. *E of Cr–*: earl of Crawford; see above, **Drammatis Personæ**, 5n.

46–9. *when the brethren ... effect*: cf. above, 4.2, 59–67.

57. *Gairdenrie*: 'horticulture'. Apparently a hapax. Not in *DOST* or
OED.

58. *Nehemia*: the book Nehemiah in the Old Testament.
Arcadia: Sir Philip Sidney's famous romance, *The Countesse of
Pembrokes Arcadia* (1590).

59. *printed Speach*: i.e. *The speech of William, Earl of Crawford, president to the Parliament of Scotland, the twenty second day of April, 1690*
(Edinburgh, 1690).

63. *brow*: 'face', 'impudence'.

67. *Viscount of Tarb*: Sir George Mackenzie of Tarbat (1630–1714), in
1685 created Viscount Tarbat and in 1703 earl of Cromartie.

72. *Mod.*: 'Moderator'.
Mr H. K.: Mr Hugh Kennedy; see **Drammatis Personæ**, 13n.

79. *firie*: 'firebrand', 'incendiary'. Apparently a hapax. Not in *DOST* or
OED.

85. *Mean*: not identified.

84. *Dalkieth*: Dalkeith, Midlothian, to the south-east of Edinburgh.

92. *packie*: 'pawky'; 'shrewd, astute, sagacious, sharp' (*SND*). 'We call one Pawky, who is witty, sly or cunning in his words or actions, especially the first, but without any harm or bad designs' (Ruddiman, s.v. **Paukis** in 'A Glossary, or Alphabetical Explanation of the hard and difficule words in *Gavin Douglas*'s Translation of Virgil's Æneis' in Ruddiman 1710), quoted in *SND*; cf. among many possible illustrations, the character of the Provost of Gudetown, James Pawkie, in John Galt's *The Provost* (Edinburgh, 1822).

95. *K-C*: King Charles [I].

100. *Mr Gilbert Rule*: see **Drammatis Personæ**, 9n.

104. *si aliqus virus*: see above, 5.1, 34–5n.

112, 114. *Dr Monro ... Dr Stillingfleet*: see above, **Drammatis Personæ**, 9n.

116. *Iure-divino-ship*: see above, 5.3, 126n.

122. *Mr Kr–*: Mr James Kirkton; see above, **Drammatis Personæ**, 10n.

127. *five Lost labours ... done*: cf. above, 4.2, 93–100.

127. *Lost Labours*: possibly a side-reference to Shakespeare's *Love's Labours Lost*?

138. *Cramand*: Cramond, Midlothian, near Edinburgh, at the junction of the river Almond with the Firth of Forth.

146–7. *people troubled ... wholesome disease*: cf. above, 2.3, 116–17.

149. *plain dealer*: probably a reference to Wycherley's comedy, *The Plain Dealer* (1677).

150. *fool praying*: cf. 1.3, 39.

152–5. *the E. of H– ... be right*: cf. above, 5.3, 169–71. The E. of H– is almost certainly the Jacobite, Charles Home, 6th earl of Home (d. 1706). Less certain is the identification of the *E. of S*. The unpopular John Dalrymple, 1st earl of Stair (1648–1707), would seem a likely candidate, but he remained a viscount until his earldom was created in 1703.

157. *divertisment*: entertainment; cf. Pepys, *Diary*, 7 January 1667: 'To the Duke's house, and saw "Macbeth", which though I saw it lately yet appears a most excellent play in all respects, but especially in divertisement, though it be a deep tragedy; which is a strange perfection in a tragedy, it being most proper here, and suitable.'

163. *Consequentiale*: 'characterised by logical sequence or consistency' (*OED*, s.v. **Consequential 4**).

165. *Mr Fr– Br*: James Fraser of Brae; see **Drammatis Personæ**, 8n.

170. *Duneferling*: Dunfermline, Fife.

174. *Lybella Universalis*: see above, 4.2, 75 and n.

175. *thirst*: 'thrust'.

176. *Bunisland*: Burntisland, on the Fife coast of the Firth of Forth.

Saline: Fife, midway between Dunfermline and Dollar.

178. *the whole duty of man*: see above, **Prologue**, 22n.

179. *Redicolous articels*: see above, 5.3, 63–89.

182. *Abbotshall*: i.e. Linktown, now part of Kirkcaldy, on the Fife coast of the Firth of Forth.

183–5. *Told him ... spirit of God*: cf. 5.3, 98–9.

185–97. *Speach ... this prayer*: cf. 5.3, 68–9 and n.

186. *Culross*: burgh in West Fife, on the Firth of Forth; the parish church was originally the chapel of Culross Abbey, founded 1217.

189. *Predestinatt*: 'predestined to salvation'; cf. Romans 8. 29: 'For whom he did foreknow, he also did predestinate to be conformed to the image of his Son, that he might be the firstborn among many brethren.'

195. *ane other Presbyterian minister*: Mr James Urquhart; see above, 5.3, 68–9n.

201. *Mr Da.– W–*: Mr David Williamson; for him and his exploit at Cherrytrees see above, **Drammatis Personæ**, 12n.

208. *Canticles*: the biblical Song of Solomon.

209. *Beds of Roses and Damms of Love*: cf., e.g., above, 3.2, 45–51.

Damms: pools; cf. Song of Solomon 7. 4: 'thine eyes like the fish pools in Heshbon'.

209–11. *Tho he be ... the other*: cf. above, 3.2, 40–2.

211. *the other*: Mr Fraser of Brae; cf. above, 165.

211. *the old man*: cf. Ephesians 4. 22, 24: 'That ye put off concerning the former conversation the old man, which is corrupt according to the deceitful lusts ... and that ye put on the new man, which after God is created in righteousness and true holiness'.

212. *Tartuffe*: a reference to Molière's dark comedy *Le Tartuffe* (1664), which provoked outrage on its first performance. The principal character, Tartuffe, is a religious hypocrite, who swindles his way into control of the credulous Orgon's estate and in Act 3, scene 3 (a scene which bears some resemblance to 3.2 of *The Phanaticks*), also attempts the seduction of Elmire, Orgon's wife.

213. *woungh*: mistranscription of *young*(*h*).

215–16. *handled ... roughly*: cf. above, 3.2.

233. *chouse*: meaning uncertain; possibly a mistranscription of *cozen* (cousin etc.), 'beguile, cheat'.

224–5. *get good Estates ... Persecutione*: cf. above, 5.3, 31.

236. *Mr De–*: not identified.

2257. *Scene about the Carracters*: i.e. above, 4.4, where the politicians are described as they arrive at Parliament House.

279–80. *Reconcilment ... Chremes's sister*: a reference to Terence's Latin comedy *Eunuchus* (161 BC); see above, pp. lii–liii.

283–300. *The third objectione ... ever heard on*: the argument here is relevant to Solomon's attempted seduction of Laura (above, 3.2). Solomon certainly belongs among the 'Hipocrites with Religion in their Mouths' (274). It is Will, however, not Solomon, who makes the most effective use of the Canticles (above, 2.2). The supposed parallel with Juvenal and the Scriptures is, at best, inexact.

291. *Juvenall*: the Roman satirist Decimus Junius Juvenalis (c. 65 – c. 140).

Pitcairne in his sometimes tortuous way, may have associated Song of Solomon with a passage in Juvenal which culminates in the famous line, 'cantabit vacuus coram latrone viator' (X, 22, 'the empty-handed traveller will sing in the presence of the robber'). Canticles bears an obvious relationship to *cantabit*. In one of his Latin poems (MacQueen and MacQueen 2009: Poem 95, p. 238) Pitcairne used another line from this Satire, 'quanto delphinis ballaena Britannica maior' (X, 14, 'by the same measure as the British whale is said to be bigger than dolphins') in an intertextuality which is equally oblique.

295–6. *Scripture ... noe god*: Psalms 14. 1; 53. 1: 'The fool hath said in his heart: There is no God.' The reference implies that Will and Solomon, are both fools.

296–7: *Absalom ... King*: see 2 Samuel 15. 1 ... 18. 33. Also present is a fairly obvious reference to Dryden's *Absalom and Achitophel* (1681–82) and to the events of 1688, when William of Orange overthrew his father-in-law, King James.

303–7. *Presbyterian Ministers ... their Enemies*: see above, 5.3, 135–96.

310–12. *Ane act ... Committee of Estates*: the reference is to an act passed in the 18th session of the 1648 General Assembly: 'Act and Declaration against the Act of Parliament and Committee of Estates, ordained to be subscribed the 10th and 12th of June, and against all new Oathes or Bands in the common Cause, imposed without consent of the Church'.

314. *third time*: in 1592 parliament first authorized a presbyterian polity. 'James [VI] seems to have determined to rely on the ministers until he had broken the threat of Roman catholicism' (Donaldson 1965: 193). Episcopal government was restored by the General Assembly of 1610. The General Assembly of 1638 deposed the bishops for a second time, but they were restored by the Act Rescissory of 1661. Pitcairne associates the initial establishment with the execution of Queen Mary in 1587, the second with the fate of Charles I in the Civil War, his execution in 1649, and the subsequent exile of his sons.

318–24. *time of Cromwell ... till this time*: see Dow 1999: 103–4.

324. *till this time*: no General Assembly met from 1648 until 1690.

327–8. *power down Curses*: cf. 5.3, 149–83.

331–5. *Repent ... Humane Society itself*: the authors' intention is like that of Juvenal, above, 268–70. If they fail, they invoke the full rigour of the law to amend matters.

336. *Just after ... Monse*: i.e. soon after 28 March (n.s.), 1691; see above, 1.1, 23–5 and n.

337–9. *some Gentleman*: probably David Gregorie who 'travelled to England in the summer of 1691' to seek support for his candidature for the Savilian chair of astronomy in Oxford, to which he was appointed in December 1691 (Guerrini in *OxfDNB*).

339. *four Moneths ... Compleatted*: i.e. the approximate date of completion was August 1691.

342. *Authors*: Pitcairne, Gregorie and Stott; see Introduction.

347. *money*: this suggests at least the hope of a printed edition considerably earlier than that of 1652.

Appendix II

De Archibaldo Pitcarnio Elogia
(Judicial Record about Archibald Pitcairne)

Apart from his contribution, whatever it may have been, to *The Phanaticks*, this poem appears to be the only piece by Bertram Stott to have survived. The text is taken from *Selecta Poemata* (Pitcairne 1727), pp. 84–7.

The metre of the poem is the closed Ovidian elegiac couplet. There are a number of Ovidian reminiscences; some too of Virgil and Horace. For the most part, the mythological references are to stories found in Ovid's *Metamorphoses*. The Stephenson of line 53 is Pitcairne's father-in-law, Sir Archibald Stephenson (1630–1710), a distinguished physician, apparently a friend, or at least disciple, of William Harvey, and close friend of a Hume (Home), probably Charles Home, 6th earl of Home (d. 1706). If the identification holds, the poem belongs to the last year of Stott's life. Pitcairne refers to his death in a letter dated 20 September 1707 (Johnston 1979: 48).

The final reference to Pitcairne as moderate in his cups stands in complete, but believable, contrast to the tales of him as a drunkard, put about, for the most part, by presbyterian opponents.

.De Archibaldo Pitcarnio Elogia.
Ad A. Pitcarnium, Bertrami Stoti Angli Epistola.

Pitcarni, duplici quem munere ditat Apollo,
    Quem Musæ & Medicæ detinet æquus amor,
Si natura tibi rerum cognoscere causas,
    Sique Mathematices solvere dura dedit;
Dic mihi (namque potes) cur Bacchi tanta potestas?   5
    Et cur mortales in sua fata ruunt?
Cur ego cui primâ risit Venus alma juventâ,
    Ingratus placidæ desero castra Deæ?
Pocula Circæo capio cur tincta veneno,
    Imperium agnoscens , sæve Lyæe, tuum?   10
Natura assiduo nutat stupefacta labore,

Et malè lethiferum sustinet ægra Deum.
Forma viri languet nullã medicabilis arte,
   Insanumque fugit non reditura salus.
Mens etiam tanquam Lethæis obruta lymphis   15
   Deficit, & nimio torpet inepta mero.
Bacche vale, meliora peto: me rursus alumnum
   Jactat Amor, rursus me Venus æqua vocat.
Vilior haud memorem fecit quid turba Deorum,
   Nec repetam raptus, Mars, vel Apollo, tuos.   20
Ipse Deûm genitor, qui fulmine concutit orbem,
   Submittit Cyprio fulmen inerme Deo.
Hoc probat in Danaën qui decidit aureus imber,
   Nymphaque cœlesti per mare vecta bove.
Cum Ledam petîit falsi sub imagine cygni,   25
   Lascivus mediis arsit adulter aquis.
Juppiter exemplo quod vindicat, & jubet idem,
   Me bene dignus amor, si Jove dignus erat.
Uror, & O utinam sociales sentiat ignes,
   Pulchra Parismonio juncta puella toro.   30
Talis Latmæo formosa cacumine Phœbe,
   Obscuri thalamos Endymionis adit.
Talis in Ausonio Venus est spectata theatro,
   Anchisa, amplexus dum petit illa tuos.
Et nisi me fallat divinæ gratia formæ   35
   Nec placuit Phœbe, nec Venus ipsa magis.

Plus meditor xxxxxx

Sed frustra, nam me, vultu suadente, Lyæus
   Admonet his verbis, & jubet esse suum:
'Jurgia quid jactas? An nos prohibemus amorem?
   Perdomuit Paphius nos quoque sæpe puer.   40
Quem meminisse juvat, cum me Minoia nympha
   Accepit thalamis ambitiosa novis!
Lætior accepit nunquam vel Juno Tonantem,
   Nec Sappho amplexu te meliore fovet.
Confiteare, novam quoties tibi commodo flammam,   45
   Hãc flammã accensus fortius urit amor.
Nec mihi displiceat si tempus carmine fallas;
   Carminibus semper Bacchus amicus erat.
An non se tollit Venusinus in æthera Cygnus?

Dum Phœbi laudes measque canit.   50
Quid male-sane times? Per me mens libera curis
    Emicat, atque salus vix peritura viget.
Nonne Stephensoni plaudit mihi blanda senectus?
    Nonne capit grato pocula mixta mero?
Nonne sedet vivax socialiter inter amicos?   55
    Dum Phœbo dignas spargit ubique sales.
O utinam terras iterum Medea revisat,
    Jucundum & renovet læta juventa senem!
Hoc prohibet fatum: per quem vixêre tot ægri,
    (Sed serus) Stygias ipse videbit aquas.   60
Harvæi socius campos lucosque pererret,
    Atque Humii potior sit comes ille sui.
Cum tamen Elysii, perfecto temporis orbe,
    Ætherias tandem fas sit adire domos,
Nectare diffusus mecum super astra recumbet,   65
    Et dabitur Baccho liberiore frui.
Ergo redi, modico juvet indulgere Lyæo:
    Pitcarni exemplum sic imitere tui.
Ille venit nostras, sed non periturus, ad aras,
    Nec nimio fuerit victima vana foco.   70
Ille litet Genio, non insipiente palato,
    Facundo calices dum bibit ore meos:
Arrident Phœbus, Musæ, suavesque lepores;
    Dulcè poëta bibit, dulcè poëta canit.'

Judicial Record about Archibald Pitcairne
The Letter of Bertram Stott Englishman, to A. Pitcairne

Pitcairne, whom Apollo enriches with a double gift, who loves Muses and Medicine alike, if nature has given you the power to understand her laws and to solve mathematical difficulties, tell me (for you can do so), why Bacchus has such power and why mortals rush on their own fate? Why do I, on whom nurturing Venus smiled in my early youth, ungratefully desert the citadel of the gentle goddess? Why do I accept the cups tincted with Circean venom, acknowledging your empire, savage Lyaeus? Nature staggers, stupefied by her ceaseless labour, and in her weakness scarcely stands up to the death-dealing God. The body weakens, beyond the power of any medicine, and health flees the sick man, never to return. As if overwhelmed by the waters of Lethe, the mind too fails and grows stupidly sluggish from excessive drink.

Bacchus, farewell! I look to improve. Cupid once more boasts me his disciple, once again benign Venus calls me. Let me banish from memory the deeds of the inferior Gods, nor recall the rapes committed by you, Mars, or you, Apollo. The very father of the Gods, who batters the world with his thunderbolts, tamely submits his bolts to the Cyprian God. The proof is that he descended on Danae in a golden shower, and the nymph borne across the sea by a celestial bull. When he sought Leda under the guise of a swan, the adulterer's licentiousness flamed in the midst of the waters. Jupiter justifies by example and orders the same [for us]. Love befits me well if it befitted Jove. I am aflame, and O that a lovely girl united with me on a Parismonian couch should sense a fellow fire! So beautiful Phoebe on the top of Latmos approached the bed of humble Endymion. So, in the Ausonian theatre, Venus was seen as she seeks your embraces, Anchises. And, if I'm not mistaken, neither Phoebe nor Venus herself received more pleasure from the grace of a divine form.

I intend more. xxxxxx

But all in vain, for Lyaeus with persuasive countenance admonishes me in these words and orders me to be his man.

'Why quarrel with me? Do I forbid love? The Paphian boy has often conquered me too. How pleasant it is to remember the moment when the Minoan girl embraced a new lover in accepting me! Juno was never happier to receive the Thunderer, nor did Sappho ever enfold you with a better embrace. Confess, how often do I bestow on you a new flame? Kindled by that flame, love burns the hotter. Nor does it displease me if you cheat time with a song – Bacchus was always a friend to songs. Does not the Venusinan swan raise himself to the skies, while he sings Phoebus' praises and mine? What are you afraid of, madman? By me your wit is freed from worries and springs out and you flourish in almost perpetual health. Surely Stephenson's bland old age confirms my words? Doesn't he take cups mixed with the wine that pleases him? Doesn't he sit socially with his friends, full of life, scattering abroad his witticisms, worthy of Phoebus? Would that Medea could revisit earth again and that joyous youth might renew the merry old man! Fate forbids, and the man who has saved the lives of so many sick people will himself see (but late!) the waters of Styx. May he wander through the plains and groves [of Elysium] in the company of Harvey and may he be the preferred companion of his own Hume! When at last in the completed course of time, it is fated that he comes to the ethereal homes, gladdened by nectar, he will recline with me above the stars and the enjoyment of a less restricted Bacchus will be granted him.

Return, therefore. Indulge, please, in a moderate Lyaeus and thus follow the example of your friend, Pitcairne. He comes to our altars, but not to be sacrificed, nor will he have been the futile victim of too much fire. He makes sacrifice to my divinity with the palate of a connoisseur as he quaffs my cups with eloquent lips. Phoebus, the Muses and the delightful Graces smile their approval. Sweetly the poet drinks, sweetly the poet sings.'

Index